CASE STUDIES FOR ORGANIZATIONAL COMMUNICATION

Understanding Communication Processes

Joann Keyton
University of Kansas

Pamela Shockley-Zalabak
University of Colorado, Colorado Springs

Roxbury Publishing Company
Los Angeles, California

Note to Instructors: A comprehensive Instructor's Manual is available on request.

Library of Congress Cataloging-in-Publication Data

Case studies for organizational communication: understanding communication processes / [editors] Joann Keyton, Pamela Shockley-Zalabak.

p. cm.

ISBN 1-931719-12-8

1. Communication in organizations—Case studies. I. Keyton, Joann. II. Shockley-Zalabak, Pamela.

HD30.3CS367 2004

302.3'5—dc21 2003043192

CIP

CASE STUDIES FOR ORGANIZATIONAL COMMUNICATION: UNDERSTANDING COMMUNICATION PROCESSES

Publisher: Claude Teweles
Managing Editor: Dawn VanDercreek
Production Editor: Jim Ballinger
Production Assistant: Joshua Levine
Copy Editor: Pauline Piekarz
Cover Design: Marnie Kenney
Proofreader: Scott Oney
Typography: SDS Design info@sds-design.com

Printed on acid-free paper in the United States of America. This book meets the standards of recycling of the Environmental Protection Agency.

ISBN 1-931719-12-8

ROXBURY PUBLISHING COMPANY
P.O. Box 491044
Los Angeles, California 90049-9044
Voice: (310) 473-3312 • Fax: (310) 473-4490
Email: roxbury@roxbury.net
Website: www.roxbury.net

Contents

Section 1: Organizational Culture

Section 2: Virtual Communication in Organizations

Section 3: Teamwork and Group Processes

Section 4: Decision Making and Problem Solving

Section 5: The Individual and the Organization

Section 6: Diversity in Organizational Communication

Acknowledgments

We wish to thank the following colleagues for their insightful reviews of our book: Janie Harden Fritz (Duquesne University), Dennis Gouran (Pennsylvania State University), Teresa Harrison (Rensselaer Polytechnic Institute), Rosanne Hartman (State University of New York, Geneseo), Sandra L. Herndon (Ithaca College), Michele Jackson (University of Colorado at Boulder), Krishna P. Kandath (University of New Mexico), Michael Kramer (University of Missouri), John Llewellyn (Wake Forest University), Marie Mater (Houston Baptist University), Peter Monge (University of Southern California), Tracy Russo (University of Kansas), Craig R. Scott (University of Texas at Austin), Timothy Sellnow (North Dakota State University), Christina Stage (Arizona State University), William Todd-Mancillas (California State University, Chico), Robert Ulmer (University of Arkansas at Little Rock), and Heather L. Walter (University of Akron). ✦

Teacher Introduction

The Case Study Method as a Pedagogical Technique

Case methods have been employed at least since the 1920s to encourage reflection, integration of theory and practice, and problem solving. They have been widely used because they illustrate the nonlinear, complex, and context-specific reality of organizations (Kitano & Landry, 2001). Well-developed cases can offer insight into organizational practices, procedures, and processes that are not otherwise available for classroom use. Case studies allow students the opportunities to analyze critical incidents, translate their knowledge into practical applications, and develop strategies for their own organizational communication practice.

Literally all of the undergraduate organizational communication textbooks now include cases as an in-text pedagogical technique. The cases here support and extend the use of cases in teaching organizational communication as they are longer and more complex. As a result, the cases will provide you with a richer set of assignment options. There you will find:

1. A one-paragraph case overview (including type of organization, key actors and issues in the case).
2. A one-sentence learning objective that identifies the central communication problem in the case.
3. A list of keywords and their glossary definitions.
4. A series of questions for written essays and potential/probable answers.
5. A series of discussion questions.

6. Other teaching ideas including assignment alternatives, audio-visual materials, and websites that support the case.
7. Short paragraphs describing any conceptual analysis that could aid in understanding and teaching the case.
8. Bibliography of resources for the instructor.
9. Bibliography of resources for students.
10. Epilogue of the case (if appropriate).

Discussion of cases can foster students' reasoning, enhance development of theoretical and practical knowledge, and increase awareness of personal beliefs and values (Lundeberg, 1999). We believe this happens most effectively when students are encouraged to develop multiple alternatives as case solutions. Critical learning occurs when students analyze each solution, compare and contrast multiple solutions, and then choose one believed to be most effective at improving communication or sustaining effective communication.

We believe cases are most effectively used when there is both independent and interdependent learning. Not only should students be assigned to independently analyze the case and make recommendations, students should also learn to listen and respond to other students' ideas about the case. Cases can augment or extend content presented in class or in the text you use.

Because cases are complex and realistic depictions of organizational communication, the same case can be approached from a number of perspectives. Consider assigning different groups of students to take the roles of different characters, or to make recommendations based on competing theories or perspectives.

We believe that instructors should be actively involved in the case analysis process. Here are some methods for using cases to create interdependencies with your students:

1. Let students generate questions about the case for you to answer in class.
2. Help students generate criteria for deciding if the recommendation or alternative chosen will be effective.
3. Cases can be used to improve critical thinking skills. Ask students: What's the evidence for your claim? What are your assumptions? Biases? Emotional responses?
4. At the end of case discussion, give closure by summarizing:

- What was learned?
- What communication skills would students need to implement recommendations?
- To what other contexts would recommendations apply?

There are a variety of methods for using cases as a pedagogical technique. Here are some of our favorites:

1. To enhance the communicative aspect of the case, ask that students practice effective communication in their case discussions. You could assign students to practice a particular communication skill (i.e., a specific listening or speaking strategy) during their discussions with one another.
2. Cases can be used as the basis for oral presentations. Assign two students or two groups to debate alternative recommendations and then take questions from other students.
3. Assign students to write a one-page position paper describing the overarching communication problem that needs to be addressed in the next 3 to 4 hours. Next 24 hours? Next week?
4. Use the case as stimulus for a test. Given the case beforehand, the exam can be a test of the degree to which students understand and apply communication principles and concepts.
5. As a group assignment, each group is responsible for delivering the following as written or oral presentation:
    - A statement that defines/describes the communication decision, dilemma, or problem.
    - A procedural statement for addressing or solving the problem.
    - A list of resources (physical, monetary, human resources) needed for implementation of the proposed solution to the problem.
    - A timetable for implementation.
    - A statement of expected benefits or expected impact of the proposed solution.

6. Assign students to one role in the case and have them develop a communication plan for themselves, their team, or their organization.
7. Assign students to develop a training program to respond to the communication problem or challenge in the case.
8. Use the case as a stimulus for students to design an organizational communication assessment.
9. Based on the organization presented in the case, assign students to develop a selection or recruitment interview for one or more of the jobs described in the case.
10. Usc the case as a basis for developing a team meeting procedure.
11. Using the key character as the stimulus, assign students the project of designing a leadership development program (e.g., training, coaching, counseling, mentoring).
12. Use the case as a basis for developing a code of ethics for the organization or a profession.
13. Use the case as a basis for developing a public relations or external communication plan.

References

Kitano, M. K., & Landry, H. (2001, June). Instructional cases: Learning from the dilemmas of practicing teachers. *Roeper Review, 23,* 206–218.

Lundeberg, M. A. (1999). Discovering teaching and learning through cases. In M. A. Lundeberg, B. B. Levin, & H. L. Harrington (Eds.), *Who learns what from cases and how? The research base for teaching and learning with cases* (pp. 3–23). Mahwah, NJ: Lawrence Erlbaum. ✦

Using Cases to Learn About Organizational Communication

Nearly everyone who works can tell at least one story about his or her work experiences. Funny, disgusting, sad, motivating, amazing—some stories are about the mundane day-to-day events at work; other stories are about pivotal events, or turning points, in a person's work life. The cases in this book are stories, or narratives, about the work experiences of individuals and teams in a variety of organizational settings. As you learn about organizational communication, you can use cases to (a) broaden your perspective on what it means to work, (b) gain an understanding of work settings or occupations with which you are unfamiliar, and (c) develop greater understanding of the ways in which communication is central to getting work done. Cases are also useful as a guide to identifying and developing your competences to determine actions appropriate for a variety of work situations.

What Are Cases?

Cases are examples or illustrations of organizational problems or challenges. A case gives information about the organization—its people and its performance. By itself, a case is a good story. A case becomes a learning experience when we apply the theories we study in an effort to determine the best solutions for resolving the issues presented in the case. The case study approach to organizational communication provides an opportunity to blend theory, analysis, and practice in our efforts to better understand how communication processes create and shape organizational events. Case studies provide rich opportunities to apply theory to organizational practice. They bridge the gap between reading about organizations and theory and knowing what to do in actual organizational situations. They also expand our analytical and critical capabilities as we examine dynamic and complex events for their impact on organizational behavior. And they help us develop strategies and approaches for application to real organizational problems or challenges. The primary purpose of the case study approach is to develop our abilities.

Cases are presented in story or narrative form with enough detail so you can use your knowledge and analytical skills to develop and test alternatives for satisfying the problem presented in the case. The cases presented here reflect real communication situations and problems, and were developed based on real organizational experiences. Although the cases are authentic with respect to the portrayal of communication in organizations, authors were required (in most cases) to fictionalize some aspects of the communication, individuals, and organizations described to maintain the anonymity of the individuals and the organizations.

The purpose of a case is to focus on social actors in an organizational context to examine the role of communication. You will not find this focus limiting. To the contrary, you will find that each case describes the messiness associated with organizational communication practices. For example, if the case is predominantly about an organization's culture, you will find that threads of the case also pertain to leadership and team behavior. A case about an organization's use of technology will also reveal issues about intercultural communication issues, politeness norms, and respect. A case about individual decision making will also reveal aspects of strategic planning and customer service. As such, cases reflect the nonlinear, complex, and embedded practices of organizational communication. Your role as a student is to examine each case for patterns and anomalies of communication practices.

Using cases, you will have the opportunity to

- View communication in its organizational context, with all of its complexity and messiness.

- Be drawn into what really happens rather than be told what should happen.
- Understand the effects of history as well as watch history unfold.
- Identify problems that participants may not recognize.
- Discover communication exemplars as well as inefficiencies or ineffective practices.

Using Cases in the Study of Organizational Communication

Although not wholly generalizable, the situations described in the cases can provide you with a realistic preview of how communication actually is practiced in organizations. The cases can also provide you with a preview of the communication situations and dilemmas you will likely encounter in the workforce. Each case concludes with a communication problem, dilemma, situation, or question that needs resolution. Thus, the cases will test your analytical reflection, theoretical analysis, problem analysis, generation of alternative solutions, and solution selection abilities.

Throughout the collection of cases, you will find that some of the case characters communicate effectively, whereas others display communication problems. Some of the communication issues are verbal, whereas others reflect communication issues that surface in the use of nonverbal, electronic, and written channels. The cases explore formal and informal organizational communication at all levels—individual, supervisor to subordinate, team, and organizational. Some cases focus on communication within an organization, whereas other cases include situations in which employees communicate with constituencies outside the organization.

The cases provide rich descriptions of different types and sizes of organizations—for profit and nonprofit, service and manufacturing, public and private, family-owned business and large conglomerate. In addition to these rich organizational descriptions, the cases present characters in a variety of occupations and jobs—colleagues and coworkers, supervisors and subordinates, employees, volunteers, and all levels of management.

After reading each case, you should be able to make recommendations about the communication problem or challenge described in the case. We encourage you to develop multiple alternatives and then to test those alternatives based on theories and perspectives of organizational communication you are studying. What would each theory or perspective suggest as a solution? How could you combine or integrate solutions? How would your proposed solution differ if you took the point of view of another character in the case?

The Case Study Method

The case study method is based on a systematic search of the case for the complex processes, events, or factors that have contributed to the presented problems, issues, or circumstances. Case analysis requires that we develop an understanding of a variety of reach-based theories, propositions, and positions, which can then be used to explain the behaviors exhibited in a particular case. These theories, propositions, and positions are also used to support the types of decisions and actions we propose as case solutions. In other words, case study analysis can be both explanatory and prescriptive. Analysis aims to provide theory-based explanations of events as opposed to anecdotal or conventional wisdom explanations. (In many cases, of course, theory-based and conventional wisdom explanations are the same.) Prescriptions are recommended courses of action based on an examination of options and theory-based reasoning for recommended decisions.

How to Read a Case

Although there are many ways to use case studies to enhance your learning of organizational communication, we recommend that you take the following steps when a case is assigned. First, read the case, paying particular attention to how the key characters communicate and the nature of the relationships key characters have with one another. What are the salient issues and problems of this case? What are the symptoms of the communication problem? What is the root cause of the communication problem? And do not forget to identify what elements of communication were effective. Summarize what happens in the case in one paragraph, describing the key characters and the key events. As you write the summary, consider the time frame and the setting of the communication described. Developing a one-paragraph summary will help you as you complete the assignment given by your instructor.

With the case read and summarized, reflect back on the case to identify the character in the case most like and the character least like you. Acknowledging the perspective from which you read the case will help you challenge and test solutions that you eventually develop. Second, develop a list of questions you have about the case. A good place to start developing questions is to ask what the case reveals that is interesting and unique. Third, develop a list of statements about the case that you can defend. Be sure to note which information in the case you could use as data in the defense of your conclusions. Fourth, what organizational communication theories, perspectives, or research support your conclusions? Which theories, perspectives, and research challenge what is presented in the case? With these steps complete, you are ready to identify appropriate strategies for solving problems illuminated by the case.

A Practice Case

The case that follows was written about the experiences of two individuals who have traveled the same path you are taking. Marcus and Yasmin have recently completed their B.A. degrees in communication at a public university; both are in their first professional full-time jobs. Marcus and Yasmin are good friends. Throughout their college careers, their friendship solidified as they attended a number of classes together and both participated in their university's student government association.

Making the transition from student to employee, Marcus and Yasmin promised one another that they would stay in touch after graduation. Shortly after taking their first jobs, both realized how difficult it was to maintain their social time together while they were employed full-time in a job they viewed as a career. The case allows you to eavesdrop on Marcus and Yasmin as they reflect on their job-hunting experiences and relay some of the lessons they learned as first-year employees.

The case notations illustrate key points in the case, identify points at which the interaction reveals the characters' descriptions and analyses of how communication is practiced and performed in their organizations, and illuminate instances in which characters' interaction presents communication challenges or opportunities of which not even the characters may be aware. As suggested above, an example case analysis follows that includes a summary providing a contextual description and time line of the case, as well as a description of the key characters and their communication styles and relationships, the salient issues and problems of the case, symptoms and root causes of the communication problem described by the characters, and effective elements of communication. The example analysis also includes a list of questions about the case, a list of statements about the case, and a list of organizational communication theories, perspectives, or research that could be used to analyze the case. Finally, the example analysis provides a list of strategies for solving problems illuminated by the case. ✦

Example Case

Just Part of the Crop

Joann Keyton

"Sisters. Uhhh," she said with mocking disgust. "Once a big sis, always a big sis."

"What are you complaining about now?" Marcus* asks Yasmin as he searches the menu for dinner. It had been almost a year since Yasmin and Marcus had graduated from college. Although they saw each other frequently at friends' parties and weddings, they hadn't had time to have the type of soul-searching conversations they enjoyed while in school.

Description about Yasmin and Marcus' relational history

"My sister and her friends graduate this spring and they're always asking me how to look for a job . . . what do I think about this and that company . . . how much am I making . . . it just goes on and on," Yasmin explains. "I realize they haven't had much job experience. But every time I go home they launch into this barrage of questions."

Description about the primary communication problem presented in the case: Yasmin's younger sister (and her friends) wants advice about looking for a job after graduation. Yasmin and Marcus reflect on their experiences in developing résumés, answering job ads, and going on interviews.

"Well," Marcus replies, "don't you remember what it was like when we interviewed for our first jobs?"

"Sure, and I'm sympathetic and helpful to a degree. But at some point, they just have to develop their résumé, answer some ads, and go on some interviews. It's just not a perfect—or a pretty—process." Yasmin stops the conversation to peruse the menu. Finding what she wants to order, she snaps it shut. "So, what are you going to order?"

"Could you just make up your mind without surveying me?" Marcus asks with a laugh. "Sometimes you take the data collection thing too far. This is dinner, not a human resources survey."

The waitperson arrives and asks for their order. Both Yasmin and Marcus start to talk at once, and then realize they are ordering the same thing. They laugh at themselves, like only good friends can.

Additional description about Yasmin and Marcus' relational history, and their college and work histories.

It's been like this for a long time. Yasmin and Marcus met each other when they were the only two freshmen senators to their university's student government association (SGA). Although both had been very involved in organizations at their high schools, the university's SGA required a different level of involvement . . . the decisions the senators made influenced university governance. In their four years representing the School of Communication, Yasmin and Marcus worked to end plus/minus grading, persuaded the provost to change the final exam schedule to accommodate both full- and part-time students more effectively, raised considerable funds to support a developmentally disabled person who lived near campus, and created a separate student organization to manage the SGA's entertainment programming.

Not only were Yasmin and Marcus effective student leaders, they also worked part-time in the university's recruiting office. Yasmin enjoyed going on recruiting trips to regional high schools, whereas Marcus was particularly effective in helping to develop the office's written materials and in collecting survey data from students and parents who visited the university's campus.

Both were majors in the School of Communication. Yasmin majored in organizational communication and Marcus majored in interpersonal communication, so their part-time positions were good fits with the careers they hoped to pursue.

Waiting for their dinner to arrive, Marcus restarts the conversation. "Don't you remember what it was like for us when we were looking for our first jobs? We had some pretty strange ideas about what it meant to work. We really thought we were the cream of the crop." He paused. "Turns out, we were just *part* of the crop."

Notice how Marcus has shifted the conversation to reflections about what it means to work.

"Yeah," muses Yasmin. "I thought that at five o'clock, that would be it. I could go home and I wouldn't have anything to do once I got home. I

Here Yasmin identifies three initial shocks: (a) believing she would have more free time, (b) believing that doing your job well was all that was needed, and (c) the stress of being in one place for 9 hours.

was going to have so much more free time than I had when I was in school because when you got home, work was over." Pausing to take a drink, Yasmin continues sarcastically. "Right. Just like if you went in and did your job well you'd be recognized. You know . . . I truly thought it was what you did and not who you knew. Oh, and the other thing . . . do you remember how long 8 to 5 really was your first week on the job? I was so exhausted. I didn't realize how short an attention span I had until I had to sit in one space from 8 to 5. I thought I was going to die."

Here Marcus contributes his initial shock: believing that his work group would replicate his cohesive group at the university.

Marcus responds, "Yeah, I remember thinking that once I was employed I'd be a member of a cohesive work group—like we were in SGA—and all of us in the work group would go out for five o'clock happy hours and stuff. I don't know . . . it was some type of a 'real-working-adult' fantasy I had."

The waitperson interrupted their conversation to deliver their salads. They stopped for a moment to enjoy the beginning of their meal, but within a few minutes Yasmin started once again to reflect on their first *real* jobs.

Yasmin recognizes that the information her sister is asking for is the same information she was seeking during her job hunt.

"I don't know why I'm so annoyed with my sister and her friends for asking about my salary," Yasmin admits. "Now that I think about it, I did the same thing she's doing. I had no idea what a decent salary was when I was looking for a job. And I was scared that I wouldn't make enough to do all the adult things I dreamed of . . . you know . . . getting my own apartment, buying a new, not a used, car . . . oh, and buying new corporate suits. When I asked my friends and family about salaries, everybody told me all these horror stories about how I'd start out at 21 or even lower. So when they offered me $27,500, I remember thinking that I was really rolling in it."

"Until you found out how much is taken out for social security, income taxes, and medical insurance," Marcus interjects.

"Yes, now I truly understand what my parents were talking about. Before I got my first paycheck I didn't really comprehend their criticism that they make X amount of dollars, but they don't see it. And my mom was always complaining that the government was wasting her money. But the most painful part was paying for parking. It's expensive to park downtown," Yasmin emphasizes.

Here Yasmin and Marcus talk about discovering the difference between gross and net pay.

"Yeah, that's one of the benefits of working out east at the office park. I don't pay for parking. Of course," Marcus says jokingly, "it's a lot easier for me to get lost. All those buildings look alike. I swear it took me the entire first week to figure out which way to walk out of the circular garage to find the right tower to enter."

Notice how Marcus uses this same topic to introduce another new-employee discomfort: finding one's way around in an unfamiliar environment.

Marcus continues, "What really got me was when my medical insurance kicked in. I didn't even go to

Marcus picks up the issue of paying for benefits and intertwines it with recognition that he did not realize how basic benefits were paid for by both the company and the employee, and how it was his job to help other employees understand basic issues he had difficulty accepting.

the doctor these last 12 months, but I guarantee you I feel like I paid a doctor's salary in my insurance premiums." Pausing for a moment to butter a dinner roll doesn't dampen his complaint. "I hadn't paid for insurance before. I had no idea how much it cost. And this is how naive I really was . . . I was hired to work in human resources and I had no idea how benefits and stuff work. I guess, on some level, I thought that the company paid for everything, all the benefits. I didn't realize there was a premium. Looking at my paycheck, I thought, 'What does this deduction mean?' Here they were training me to interview potential new employees and I didn't have a clue about how benefits really worked."

Notice how Yasmin returns the conversation to the discrepancy between gross and net salary.

Yasmin takes over the conversation. "What was hard for me was not knowing how to calculate the taxes so I knew what I'd be actually taking home. So when they made me the salary offer, I really felt like I was kind of gambling. I did remember from one of my business classes that we were told to calculate our take home as 70% to allow for taxes and insurance. But one of my friends told me it would be more like a 20% deduction. Guess which one I believed?"

Information about Yasmin and Marcus' current employers. Ridley, their friend, is introduced. Notice how a pattern or style of conversation is developing between

The conversation continues until their dinners arrive. They talk some about their jobs—hers at Sentry-Shield and his at Omega Plus—and some about the people they went to school with. Even though they haven't seen one another for several months, not since Ridley's going-away party, Yasmin and Marcus' conversation retains its typical character—they weave in and out of topics easily, somehow managing to always return to anything left unfinished.

Yasmin and Marcus. They appear to be comfortable weaving in and out of topics, underscoring their comfort and familiarity with one another.

"Well," asks Marcus, "what *is* your sister going to do?"

Marcus returns to the problem of the case: Yasmin's younger sister (and her friends) wants advice about looking for a job after graduation.

"She doesn't know. She's more concerned that she's going to have trouble selling her communication degree."

"Is it in org com, like yours?"

"Yes, she's following in her sister's footsteps." She pauses. "Should I be proud, annoyed . . . or should I caution her?"

"You mean about how to defend her communication degree when she's interviewing for a job?" Marcus asks.

Here the conversation turns the viability of a communication degree and the need to explain to potential employers the benefit of a communication degree.

"Right, it was amazing to me. I was so proud of my communication degree because I had a high GPA and I could see the relevance of communication in everything I did. I just expected that others would too. But that first job interview really was an eye-opener."

"Right," agrees Marcus. "I can remember after my first interview thinking, 'That interviewer doesn't clearly understand the value of communication.' And he was a recruiter no less. I remember coming home dejected thinking that they're not going to pay me much because I had to explain to the interviewer what I

Marcus ties his thread of the conversation back to his reflections on convincing his parents that a communication degree was the right degree choice.

learned in my communication classes. But, hey, I had to explain to my parents what I was doing in communication," Marcus adds with a grin. "But after that first job interview, I had to do a lot of rationalizing . . . you know . . . did I do the right thing getting a com degree? I'm really glad I had that experience before I interviewed with Omega Plus."

Yasmin quickly says, "Isn't that post-decisional regret? We studied that in our decision-making class. Remember Professor Walters? He was sooooo good. We should go back and see if he's going to retire soon. Doesn't he have a cabin in the woods in Montana?"

"Montana, yes. Good, yes. But so stingy with the As," Marcus replies.

They finish their dinners and order coffee and dessert; their conversation continues.

Once again, Marcus brings the conversation back to the problem of the case.

"You never did tell me what your sister was going to do."

"Right," says Yasmin. "I have told her a few things."

"For instance?"

"Well, I did finally tell her the story about the whole application process . . . remember, you're the only one I ever confessed that to. I was too ashamed to tell anyone else."

"Yes, your secret's safe with me," Marcus said in a hushed tone. "What exactly did you tell her?"

"You know, how they called me in for the interview and I didn't even remember turning in an application to them. When I got to the interview, the interviewer said she was impressed with my cover letter and everything, and I didn't even remember that I had applied. I was sending in so many applications—five a week. That was my goal. On Friday, I had to make sure that I had put five résumés in the mail.

Yasmin confesses her ambiguity in her initial interactions with her current employer.

Yasmin describes her job-seeking strategy.

"And you know, I always thought that I would work for someplace really fabulous, a big-name retail organization, or some huge financial institution. I never imagined working for a company that I had never heard of before. When I saw their ad, it was blind . . . you know the kind, describes the job and gives you a post office box to respond to. The job sounded interesting, so I thought, 'I'll just send in a résumé. I've got to get five out.' I was working on pure quantity . . . hoping to increase my odds that one would pick me out of all the people applying. And so I'm waiting to hear from all these fabulous companies that I had applied to. And I get this call from the recruiter. When I answered the phone I know I said 'Who?' like an idiot. And she said 'SentryShield.' And I was like 'Great. Sure. Yeah. I'll come in for an interview.'

Yasmin discloses her ignorance in identifying potential employers by limiting her job search to companies she knew about.

Yasmin describes the problems inherent in answering a blind ad (company name is concealed, a general post office box is the only address).

"I was immediately on the Internet, looking up SentryShield. I wanted to have some idea of what they did. I was amazed to find that it was the parent company for eight other national companies. Who

Yasmin describes searching for information on the company prior to the job interview. Her attempts at organizational anticipatory socialization help her avoid entry shock and decide if there is a good match between her and the potential employer's organizational culture.

would have guessed that they're one of the top three home security companies and that their national headquarters was here? How could I not know that . . . I've lived here all my life!"

"So you told her all that? Your sister, I mean," asks Marcus.

This interaction indicates Yasmin's faith and trust in Marcus. She tells her sister the story, but describes the experience as happening to Marcus, not to her.

"Well, kind of. I told her most of it. But I changed the name of the company."

"Why?" Marcus asks suspiciously.

"Because I also told her it was you," as Yasmin points her finger at Marcus.

"Me?!"

To deflect further conversation about this use of their friendship, Yasmin turns the conversation to Ridley, a mutual friend.

"What are best friends for? Speaking of friends," Yasmin continues, "I saw Ridley last week. He was in town visiting his parents," as she tries to change the subject. "Remember when we were getting ready to graduate . . . anybody he met, he'd pimp that résumé. 'Oh, hey. Can I get you a copy of my résumé?' 'Hey, do you know Bob Jones? I'd love to get a copy of my résumé in his hands.' "

Notice how both Yasmin and Marcus dismiss Ridley's job-seeking strategy of zealously using personal networks to extend his job search.

"He *is* my friend . . . but I did hate doing anything with him while he was looking for a job. He was pimping the résumé the whole time. And I was like, well, I don't want to pimp myself to these people."

Yasmin tests her analysis of Ridley's strategy by comparing it to job-seeking advice

Yasmin asks, "Remember Dr. Ferguson's interviewing class? I asked her if it was cocky to put my SGA activities and achievements on my résumé. She said that we needed to brag on ourselves. I can hear her saying, 'If you don't, no one else will.' I guess I have a hard time with shameless self-promotion."

given by one of their professors.

"No, that's what Ridley did. There is a difference between shameless self-promotion and being proud of your accomplishments."

Marcus confirms Yasmin's evaluation of Ridley's strategy.

"I couldn't figure out where to draw the line," Yasmin replied, shaking her head.

They smiled, remembering their friend Ridley and their professor, Dr. Ferguson. They did have a great time in school. It was too bad they couldn't coordinate their schedules to see each other more often.

Marcus chimes back in, "So, are you going to tell your sister to read the parachute book?"

Marcus, once again, returns the conversation to the case's initial problem: what Yasmin should tell her sister about searching for her first job.

"You mean *What Color Is My Parachute?* I gave her my copy. She'll probably copy my answers!"

Changing the subject, Marcus asks, "So what is it really like at SentryShield?"

Marcus' question to Yasmin creates a significant but related shift in their conversation.

"Not much different than when I started a year ago. Let me tell you what happened today." Yasmin starts to laugh. "I do have to make some recommendations about first-day orientation. You won't believe what happened to this new employee.

Yasmin introduces this organizational story with the acknowledgment that she was not responsible for the new hire's uncertainty or stress, and that she would fix this apparent problem in her organization.

"It was her first day. She came in really early . . . guess she wanted to impress us. And all of our outside doors were locked . . . you know, for security reasons. She finally found her way in. I think she just followed someone in when they slid their ID badge through the security checkpoint. I was there early too—but hard at work already. I didn't hear anyone and all of a sudden, 'Yasmin, it's me, Judy! It's my first day. How do I get to my desk?' I said, 'Aren't you supposed to be meeting Beth?' That's my boss—her boss, too. She said, 'Yes, she told me to meet her at her office. I don't know where her office is.' She looked really embarrassed. I promised not to tell Beth. So I took her to get an ID badge and then showed her to Beth's office. But Beth wasn't in yet. So I stood there with her for a while. Finally Jim, our vice president, came in, looked directly at Judy, and asked, 'Are you the temp?' Judy piped up, 'No, I'm hoping I'm going to be permanent' before I could introduce her as the new HR assistant.

Yasmin continues with this story. Notice how Yasmin uses Judy's first-day experiences to frame her first-day at the organization.

"Beth's phone rang, so I picked it up. It was Beth. She asked, 'Is Judy up there? Tell her to come down to the first floor, we've got orientation set up for her across the street. And I'm late.' Beth is always late. So I got to whisk Judy off to orientation. The last thing Judy said to me was, 'You know, it was like my mom dropping me off at kindergarten.' I should have told her that it was exactly like that my first day on the job. We simply must do a better job on an employee's first day.

Yasmin concludes the story about Judy by returning to the ambiguity and uncertainty theme evident

"Later that afternoon I saw Judy wandering around the eighth floor, where our offices are. She was almost in tears. When I walked up to her she said, 'I don't quite know how to get back to my desk. All the cubicles look the same. You turn a corner, and it's just cubes.' Poor kid."

throughout their conversation.

"I know how she must have felt," Marcus said empathically. "My first day was overwhelming too. The first day it's meet-and-greet this person, then meet-and-greet the next person. Each one giving me the spiel on what he or she does and what the department does. I had no idea that Omega Plus was such a complex place. I'm just listening to all this stuff flying around me. I have no context for making it make sense. And by ten o'clock, I was just like . . . whoo! You know, overwhelmed. I spent my whole first day meeting people. It was insane."

Taking his turn, Marcus discloses his confusion and anxiety in meeting so many people and obtaining so much information on his first day on the job.

Yasmin agrees. "It's amazing how draining that is. My first day . . . I felt like I had been through sorority rush again, you know, where your face just cramps because you've been smiling all day at everyone. I was trying really hard to appear interested in everything everyone said. And I thought, ohmygosh . . . all I want to do is go home and go to sleep!"

Yasmin acknowledges Marcus' disclosure by comparing the first day at a new job to sorority rush.

"But the freakiest part," Marcus chimes back in, "was when everyone knew my name—'cause I was the new guy—and I didn't know their names . . . hey, I had a hard time keeping their names and positions straight! I know now that they were just trying to make me feel wel-

Marcus points out the dialectical tension in first-day introductions.

come, but it just freaks you out a little bit."

Notice here that Yasmin identifies a solution to this type of newcomer's anxiety.

"I've made it a practice . . . when somebody new comes we say 'Hello, my name is Yasmin. I work in communication, and I know you won't remember my name next time you see me, but I'll make sure to say hi to you and I'll tell you who I am again. So don't freak out about asking me.' The funny part? They always remember my name because I'm the one they didn't have to remember."

Their conversation quiets down, the way conversation can between good friends.

Now Yasmin returns to the central problem of the case: what to tell her sister about searching for her first job after college.

"So, what would you tell my sister? What advice would you give her?" Yasmin inquires.

Marcus sums up his advice for Yasmin's sister by stating the theme of their conversation.

"Oh, that's simple. You've got to have tolerance for ambiguity those first few days."

Notice how addressing Yasmin's problem of providing job-seeking advice for her sister provided these two friends with the opportunity to disclose and vent about their job-seeking experiences and the stress of being a new employee.

"Hmmm, that's good. I think I'll tell her to find that one person she can ask questions of and then make that person this deal: Let me drive you insane asking you questions and I promise you in one month I will not ask you another question. We will have a day when I ask you no questions."

"Now that is confidence," Marcus quips.

"Well, it worked."

"Really?"

"Sure. On July 14th I asked no questions." Pausing for humorous effect, Yasmin is also testing Marcus's faith in her. And then she continues, "Now July 15th, I had like a thousand questions. But I asked no questions on the 14th."

"Are you going to tell your sister that?"

"Sure I am. Any other suggestions, wise guy?" ✦

It should be obvious by now that Yasmin is a problem-solving–oriented person. She provides one final solution to help new employees overcome new job jitters.

*This case has been developed based on real organization(s) and real organizational experiences. Names, facts, and situations have been changed to protect the privacy of individuals and organizations.

Example Case Analysis

The following presents a case summary and contextual description, a timeline, key characters and information about their communication styles and relationship, salient issues raised in the case, symptoms and root cause, and effective elements of communication.

Marcus and Yasmin have recently completed their B.A. degrees in communication; both are in their first professional full-time jobs. Throughout their college careers, Marcus and Yasmin developed and solidified their friendship as they participated together in their university's student government association, and by being classmates in a number of classes. Now, one year later, Marcus and Yasmin meet for dinner. Yasmin complains to Marcus about her younger sister, who is pestering Yasmin for information about conducting a job search. The conversation between Marcus and Yasmin alternates between reflecting on their own job-hunting experiences and identifying helpful advice for Yasmin's sister.

As friends, Marcus and Yasmin have a comfortable conversation style allowing them to weave in and out of topics. They are comfortable joking with one another and with disclosing some of their anxieties about looking for a job and being organizational newcomers. Yasmin seems more problem-oriented than Marcus; however, Marcus seems better at keeping their conversation on track.

During the process of identifying job-seeking advice for Yasmin's sister, Marcus and Yasmin disclose and vent about their job-seeking experiences and the stress associated with being new employees. Overall, their revelations describe the uncertainty and ambiguity they encountered during the job-seeking and newcomer stages, as well as solutions they devised to confront these challenges. Their stress or anxiety would be the symptom for the root problem of being first-time job seekers and not recognizing the differences they would encounter between school and work environments. They faced uncertainty in the following ways: answering blind ads in the job-seeking stage, having difficulty distinguishing between positive and shameless self-promotion in the job-seeking stage, acknowledging the need to sell their degree, having unrealistic job expectations, and not realizing the difference between gross and net salary. Indirectly, Yasmin and Marcus revealed the anxiety and ambiguity associated with being the new employee.

Both Yasmin and Marcus were effective storytellers. The ease of their conversation was apparent, as dropped threads of conversation were easily retrieved.

Questions About the Case

1. How do blind ads work? Wouldn't a person have some idea about what company placed the ad by the job description given?
2. Both Marcus and Yasmin were portrayed as successful and involved students. Why didn't their school-based experiences provide more guidance as they entered the job market?
3. What are effective strategies for searching for a first job?
4. What communication strategies should I use for increasing my personal and professional networks while looking for a job?
5. In the job interviewing, selection, and hiring processes, when is it appropriate to ask about benefits and other issues that will affect my paycheck?
6. How should I reply when employers ask about my degree in communication?
7. How can I be well prepared for the first day of a new job?
8. When I am employed, what communication strategies can I use to ensure that new employees have good first-day experiences?
9. Is there any way to practice, or be prepared for, the ambiguity I will face on my first day at a new job?
10. What advice would I give Yasmin's sister?

Statements About the Case

1. Marcus and Yasmin are good friends. Conversation between them is comfortable and relaxed; they trust one another with disclosure.
2. Marcus is skilled at bringing the conversation back to Yasmin's original question.

3. Despite their success at school, Yasmin and Marcus both encountered ambiguity and difficult communication situations as organizational newcomers.
4. Yasmin and Marcus had difficulty adjusting from being in a school environment to being in an office environment.
5. It appears that Yasmin developed solutions for problems she encountered as an organizational newcomer, hoping to relieve the communication stress and ambiguity of other newcomers to her organization.

Theories, Perspectives, or Research That Could Be Used to Analyze the Case

1. Uncertainty reduction.
2. Organizational assimilation.
3. Organizational anticipatory socialization.
4. Realistic job preview.
5. Selection interview.
6. Organizational entry.
7. Employee orientation.

List of Strategies for Solving Problems Illuminated by the Case

1. When searching for a job, keep a list of letters and applications sent, as well as copies of job ads.
2. Prior to a selection interview, research the organization (search the Web and business press, and ask friends and relatives about the organization).
3. Before a selection interview, develop answers to probable questions that could be difficult to answer (e.g., "Tell me more about your degree in communication.").
4. During a selection interview, ask the interviewer to describe a typical day for someone in the position for which you're interviewing.

5. Talk to friends and relatives who have recently made the shift from being a student to being an employee. Ask for their advice on making this transition and on being an organizational newcomer.
6. When entering a new organization, expect some level of uncertainty and ambiguity. Ask questions and observe others to reduce the uncertainty and stress of being a new employee. Each day try to learn three new things about the organization's culture that will help you effectively communicate on your job.
7. Each day on a new job, learn and use the names of two people in your work unit.
8. After you've been on the job awhile, plan to help newcomers (informally or formally) through the transition. ✦

Section 1

Organizational Culture

Briefing Paper

Organizational Culture

Organizations often have long histories and established ways of accomplishing their goals. Taken with other formal and informal organizational processes, how an organization organizes itself, makes decisions, and values leadership help us identify and describe its culture. In essence, a culture is reflected by how an organization does things and how its employees talk about how they do things. Organizational culture is the unique sense of place that an organization generates through its communication processes. Organizational culture reflects the shared realities and shared practices in the organization and how these realities create and shape organizational events. Organizational culture is the unique symbolic ground that becomes the self-definition or self-image of the organization.

With culture as a metaphor for organizational communication, we can explore how organizations and their employees use language, symbols, jargon, and specialized vocabulary. We can examine behaviors exhibited in the rituals and rites of organizational life, as well as identify the general standards or values of the organization as described in stories, legends, and reminiscences. There is a danger, however, in oversimplifying culture as a single set of commonly held values, beliefs, actions, practices, rules, and dialogues mutually supported by all organizational members. In reality, organizations commonly reflect subcultural consensus and even lack of consensus about values, beliefs, actions, practices, rules, and dialogues. Thus, embedded in this notion of culture as a metaphor for organizational communication is a view of organizations as dynamic, continually changing, and meaning-producing bodies.

The basic assumption of the cultural approach to organizations is that organizations exist as the communicative constructions of members as they go about their everyday organizational lives. A culture is something that an organization is, rather than something an organization has. Meanings may not be based on the *objective* reality of a situation, but on what people believe is true. These shared meanings are expressed through symbolic forms (such as stories, myths, rituals, newsletters, and so on), and they allow people in a given context to develop distinct ways of perceiving, interpreting, and explaining events. Communication is the means by which culture is enacted. An organization's culture is composed of the assumptions, values, expectations, and everyday performances of members as they interact with one another, share experiences, create understandings, and forge their organizational realities. Thus, culture is exhibited in organizational artifacts, espoused values, and underlying assumptions.

Artifacts are everything that one sees, hears, and feels when one encounters an organization, from employee picnics to annual reports, from how cubicles are decorated to official titles on a company's organizational chart. Any visible organizational structure or process can be an artifact. Whereas artifacts are easy to identify, it is more difficult to identify the organizational values—the strategies, goals, and philosophies of the people in this group—that give meaning to these artifacts. Indeed, it is quite difficult to reconstruct from artifacts alone what those things mean in any given group. All values start from the influence of individuals who prevail, but what prevails can have status only from the point of view of members of the group. Values that are shared inevitably become transformed into nondiscussable assumptions supported by articulate sets of beliefs, norms, and operational rules of behavior. These assumptions can become so taken for granted that there is little variation in the cultural unit. Although that may seem positive, strong consensus to an assumption will often be countered by other interpretations.

To what degree is organizational culture shared among an organization's employees? In some organizations, meanings of artifacts, values, and assumptions are widely shared to the point that a strong, consensual culture exists. Some writers have differentiated between strong cultures and weak cultures. In strong cultures, everyone seems to similarly understand the processes of communicating and shares the same emphasis on goals and values. Although it might at first seem that an organization would want a strong, rather than a weak, culture, strong cultures are not necessarily advantageous for an organization. Strong cultures often have dysfunctional elements embedded within them. For example, organizations with strong cultures often have difficulty innovating and coping with change.

More contemporary views of organizational culture allow for a more complex view of organizational culture, with the possibility of division within an organization's culture. Indeed, most cultures have a great deal of diversity, ambiguity, and tension built into them. Rather than being integrated, as a strong consensual culture would be, some organizational cultures consist of conflicting subcultures. When this happens, ambiguity is present to a greater degree and cultural differentiation or fragmentation occurs. Why would this happen? People act on cultural assumptions, but they do so imperfectly, constantly interpreting their own particular version of the organizational reality they perceive. This creates tension between sets of cultural norms. Organizational cultures that are fragmented with high degrees of ambiguity evidenced or are composed of multiple subcultures with tension across them are more complicated. Because these types of cultures are more complex and tend to possess more tension and ambiguity, it would be easy to conclude that strong, consensual, and integrated cultures are preferable. In fact, several writers on organizational functioning have suggested that through engendering strong cultures, organizations enhance their successes. However, other writers have commented on the positives *and* negatives of strong cultures.

Regardless of the degree of cultural consensus, communication among organizational members provides a way for them to share or contest their organizational experiences and realities. In this dynamic view of culture as communication, organizational realities are constantly subject to change as organizational members react to new information and circumstances.

Suggested Readings

Deal, T. E., & Kennedy, A. A. (1982). *Corporate culture: The rites and rituals of corporate life.* Reading, MA: Addison Wesley.

Eisenberg, E. M., Murphy, A., & Andrews, L. (1998). Openness and decision making in the search of a university provost. *Communication Monographs, 65*, 1–24.

Eisenberg, E., & Riley, P. (1988). Organizational symbols and sense-making. In G. M. Goldhaber & G. A. Barnett (Eds.), *Handbook of organizational communication* (pp. 131–150). Norwood, NH: Ablex.

Eisenberg, E. M., & Riley, P. (2001). Organizational culture. In F. Jablin & L. Putnam (Eds.), *The new handbook of organizational communication* (pp. 291–322). Thousand Oaks, CA: Sage.

Jones, M. O. (1996). *Studying organizational symbolism: What, how, why?* Thousand Oaks, CA: Sage.

Martin, J. (1992). *Cultures in organizations: Three perspectives.* New York: Oxford University Press.

Martin, J. (2002). *Organizational culture: Mapping the terrain.* Thousand Oaks, CA: Sage.

Morgan, G. (1997). Creating social reality: Organizations as cultures. In G. Morgan, *Images of organizations* (pp. 119–152). Thousand Oaks, CA: Sage.

Putnam, L. L., Phillips, N., & Chapman, P. (1996). Metaphors of communication and organization. In S. R. Clegg, C. Hardy, & W. R. Nord (Eds.), *Handbook of organizational studies* (pp. 375–408). Thousand Oaks, CA: Sage.

Putnam, L. L., & Sorensen, R. L. (1982). Equivocal messages in organizations. *Human Communication Research, 8,* 114–132.

Schein, E. (1992). *Organizational culture and leadership* (2nd ed.). San Francisco: Jossey-Bass.

Schein, E. H. (1996). Culture: The missing concept in organization studies. *Administrative Science Quarterly, 41,* 229–240.

Shockley-Zalabak, P., & Morley, D. D. (1994). Creating a culture: A longitudinal examination of the influence of management and employee values on communication rule stability and emergence. *Human Communication Research, 20,* 334–355. ✦

Chapter 1

Contemplating My First Year

Joy L. Hart

Looking back on accepting the job offer, I felt like I was on top of the world. My interview at Networked Nation* went so well, and I was thrilled to be starting out with such a prestigious firm. I even remember joking with my mom that I had nowhere to go but down! Little did I know about the upcoming day-to-day realities of my new workplace.

In part, I was thrilled because I'd be building on my communication degree, but I'd also be developing new skills, which would make me even more marketable—both internally and externally. And I'd start with a job title, Information Liaison, that just sounded important! At 23, I was Casey Long, Information Liaison. I wasn't sure what the future would hold, but I could easily see myself staying at Networked Nation, or NetNat as we call it, for many years—maybe even until retirement. It really seemed like that good a place. And I knew that if I ever decided to leave, this position and the skills I'd build would look great on my résumé.

In my first interview, I met with Delia Davis. She easily impressed me. She was probably in her mid-30s, and already she was heading a major division, Analysis. Plus, she was friendly, energetic, smart, funny, and highly committed to NetNat. And if I got the position, she'd be my division head. I knew immediately that I'd like working for Delia. At the second interview, Delia introduced me to Matt MacIntosh, her vice president. Matt seemed nice enough too, although a bit distracted. At the time, I thought that maybe he was just busy and might have been concentrating on other upcoming tasks. He did compliment me on several of my accomplishments, proving, at least, that he'd read my résumé.

Two days later Delia called to say that both she and Matt rated me as their top applicant and offered me the position. I was truly thrilled and couldn't wait to start work. I just knew I would like working in a professional environment and having access to so many experts across various fields.

I guess it's kind of laughable to me now, but then somehow I really believed that I knew what working at NetNat would be like. Some of my jobs during school, things I knew about various organizations, and my impressions of Delia and Matt just crystallized in my head, so that I actually felt confident that I already knew what sort of work environment NetNat would be. Clearly, I was more than a little naive. I pictured a professional context with experts working together, sharing information, and achieving common goals. I imagined us working as one big team, and I looked forward to being a member of the team.

Day One

I don't remember being at all scared or apprehensive that first day. I was excited about starting and fairly confident that I'd fit in and do well. I was a bit awed by the sheer amount of work produced by the various divisions of NetNat, and I was looking forward to meeting people and seeing how the whole place functioned.

Maybe the first few minutes should have been a clue. I'm a pretty friendly person, and so even though I hadn't really met anyone there, except Delia and Matt, I said things like "Hello," "Good morning," and "How are you?" to people in the hallways and on the elevator. I remember thinking that people were reserved, but at that point, I just thought that they were trying to figure out who I was or something.

When I got to our offices, Delia greeted me and stressed how pleased she was that I was joining her staff in the Analysis Division. She was friendly, just like I'd remembered, and all seemed to be going well. Next, Delia showed me to my office, walked me around, and introduced me to the 10 other division members, and made sure that I had everything I needed. Then she gave me directions to the Human

Resources (HR) office, so I could complete the rest of the required introductory paperwork.

There I introduced myself to Marcus, the HR staff member who enrolled new employees. He made a weird comment. He said something like, "We'll get your paperwork filled out, and then someone here will eventually get around to processing it." The last part of his comment seemed unprofessional to me, but I thought that maybe he was tired or just having a bad day, though he seemed pretty disinterested and bored by the whole process of meeting me and setting up my paperwork. I try not to make snap negative judgments, but I recall thinking that if this was Marcus' usual behavior, I wouldn't want him in HR in my company.

After the HR setup, I went back to my office and started getting the place organized. That's when Derek Serendi, one of my colleagues in the division, whose office was two doors down, poked his head in and asked, "So, Casey, how did the HR check-in go?" When I said something like, "The paperwork's all complete, so I guess that I'm official now," Derek chuckled. He then added, "Well, let's hope so, but HR is famous for its messes, so I wouldn't count on that just yet." And then he turned and left without any more explanation.

Derek's comment made me reflect back on my interaction with Marcus. Perhaps he wasn't just having a bad day or operating with low energy—maybe his behavior indicated problems with his work, or even problems with the whole division, as Derek had indicated. I made a mental note to check back with HR in about a week to make sure that my setup materials for payroll, health insurance, and retirement had been processed.

At lunch, I took my food to the picnic tables scattered across NetNat's lawn. It was a lovely day, and small groups of employees were seated at various tables. When I didn't see anyone I knew, I took a seat alone at one of the tables. As I ate, I could hear parts of the conversation of the three people at the adjacent table. They were making fun of Delia, calling her "uptight," "a taskmaster," and a "goodie-two-shoes." Some projects were being discussed, but I couldn't hear the specifics. Then the same group turned to gossiping about Matt. Some of the gossip was related to work ("He's in trouble on that Seattle project," "James doesn't like him"), but other aspects were strictly personal ("problems at home," "He's deeply in debt").

Pretty soon, Samuel asked if he could join me. Although I'd met him just that morning, I was so relieved and pleased to have someone be friendly. And frankly, I was happy to have someone distract me from the gossip. Samuel was an analyst with our division, so in trying to make conversation I asked him a little about his job and how long he'd been there. He'd been with NetNat for five years, "longer," he said, "than most people last." Samuel said that he liked working with Delia, and I said that I was impressed with her in the interview. I asked him what working with Delia on a daily basis was like.

Samuel stressed, "Delia has standards, but other divisional heads around here don't. She's good to work for and treats us well, but most managers here are just playing a game until they can find something better." And I remember him saying, "We do important work, directly tied to NetNat's goals, and Delia is proud of that. But staff elsewhere aren't as interested in being successful. They aren't as important to the organization." Stressing that I should "just wait and see," Samuel added, "We've got a really good group—by far the best at NetNat. Most of the other units employ pretty worthless folks really. I hate to say it, but a lot of them are just losers. They're lost, they don't do their work, and they're jealous of us. Delia's hired the best people—smart, kind, and good workers—and people elsewhere resent her successes and ours."

Returning to work, I thought a lot about this conversation with Samuel. I appreciated his willingness to share his viewpoints, and based on what he'd said, I was even happier to be in Delia's division. But something about his overall attitude bothered me. I wondered, "Wasn't it possible to say at least one good thing about another unit or individual at NetNat? And how has NetNat had so much success and gotten so much recognition if the overall staff is generally so bad?"

The afternoon of my first day passed quickly and quietly. I got my office completely organized, and I was ready to begin NetNat tasks.

Week One

My first day previewed my first week. People in the lobby and hallways didn't speak to me or to each other. Maybe I should have noticed this behavior during my job interview, but I guess I was a little nervous then, and, in reality, I really wasn't in the hallways very long.

When I spoke first, people replied but were brief and brusque. At breaks and lunch, people either seemed to talk with one or two members of their own division or to sit alone. During lunch, I continued to overhear groups bash other divisions and organizational leaders but praise their own division. Whether the group was from a production division, such as Research, Analysis, or Printing, or a support division, like Technology, Accounting, or Human Resources, they praised themselves and questioned or condemned others. Comments like "If the technology folks could keep the systems up, then we could meet our deadlines without so much stress. Of course, it's too much to hope that they'd know what they're doing" were frequent. Beyond questioning work output or quality, employees disparaged different divisions by picking on the division head ("With a manager like that, what can you expect!") or key division members ("Robin can slack off because she's Bill's pet").

During my first week at NetNat, most members of my division told me negative things about the staff and work climate in other divisions. I overheard many people gossip about other divisions, organizational leaders, and a number of staff across all areas. People seemed friendly enough to others within their division, but no one seemed to like or trust anyone else. There was little interaction across divisional boundaries. However, there was considerable coordination across projects, mostly handled by division heads, so I guessed that this was one way that gossip started. The interlinking projects, plus the quarterly organizational status reports, let others see who was meeting goals—and who fell short.

Month One

By the time I had been employed at NetNat for four weeks, I realized reality just wasn't going to live up to my initial expectations. What I came to realize was that what I experienced that first week was the reality!

In the midst of this, I was looking forward to the first monthly staff meeting. It seemed like a good opportunity to meet people across the whole organization. Plus, I wanted to hear the CEO talk about the various projects at NetNat and see how people responded to him.

According to Derek, one ritual of these monthly meetings was the free coffee, bagels, and fruit put out for staff half an hour before the meeting time. I noticed this half hour marked on the agenda as "Coffee and Conversation," with an encouraging note to be sure to attend this part of the monthly staff meeting. I thought, "Perhaps NetNat is just more formal than other places I've worked or maybe the gossip and dislike gets in the way of meeting people." But I also thought that functions like this one encouraged getting to know others and could help in meeting people across divisional lines.

I went to the coffee session just as it was scheduled to begin. But I was one of only a few people there. Though I rarely have difficulty starting conversations with anyone, the conversations I attempted with the three other people just fizzled. A few more people came in, took coffee and food, and then left. It was nearly time for the meeting to begin, and I realized that I'd seen maybe only 15 out of a staff of more than 100 persons.

By the time the meeting started, only 30 people were there. People on the agenda gave their reports and the CEO spoke briefly, but no one else made comments or asked questions when invited. Near the meeting's end, each division head was asked to introduce new staff members working in their units, while the new staff stood so that "everyone could get familiar with them." I thought that this gesture was a nice one to welcome newcomers, but really no one welcomed me individually after the meeting.

In the days following the meeting, I half expected that when I saw someone from the meeting, they might say hello. They didn't. When I tried to initiate conversation, they smiled, maybe said a couple of words, let their eyes shift downward, and walked on.

It was also during this first month that I started hearing more stories about life at NetNat. Delia told me about arriving at a restaurant for a meeting with potential new clients. She found another division manager already seated at the table; rather than introduce Delia to the potential clients, he chose to ignore her—and continued to do so for the entire evening.

Samuel told me about the holiday parties given by NetNat. Along the lines of a traditional gift exchange, staff members were asked to bring a small gift suitable for another member of the organization. The previous year members of our division, Analysis, all focused their gifts on improving the skills of lazy workers. For example, they gave others calendars, memo pads to write down tasks, and plaques to overcome defeat. Although the analysts seemed to think that these gifts were very funny, members of other divisions were offended.

A similar story was told about one of the Halloween events. Each year staff members were encouraged to dress up in costume, with prizes offered for the top three costumes. One year Beth, from

Accounting, decided to come as a *sloppy worker.* Despite the usual professional dress atmosphere of NetNat, she wore wrinkled blue jeans, a T-shirt with stains, and old tennis shoes. Her usually neat hair was disheveled, and she had written the words "Sloppy Worker" across the back of her T-shirt. Workers in other units were offended—they took Beth's costume selection as a criticism of their own work, assuming that she was saying that they were all sloppy.

I wondered why a place like this one—where across divisions people don't really talk or seem to respect each other—would even have holiday parties. Derek said that "these things are just always scheduled." So I wondered if maybe they linked back to a happier time in NetNat's history or if maybe, like the Coffee and Conversation time slot, they were management's attempts, however feeble, to encourage positive interaction.

I heard lots of other stories, too—stories of people being rude to each other, stories of arguments, stories of dislike and resentment, and stories with negative information about people's personal lives. Interestingly, within our division, my coworkers also told stories of their own and divisional successes, funny events, and some aspects of their personal lives. But information passed along about employees outside the division all seemed to be negative. And even when it seemed that a person didn't have enough information to really know what someone else's intent was, still the interpretations were almost always negative. And the storyteller always seemed sure that his or her interpretation of events was the correct one.

I got to know members of my own division fairly well, and I liked all of them. They took pride in their work and in the accomplishments of the unit. And they were easy to work with, except for their negative attitudes about employees in other divisions. Even then, I had reservations about completely accepting these evaluations, and I questioned how every one of the hundred plus employees, except those in this one unit, could be bad.

During my third week, Chip, who was in my division and whose office was next door to mine, resigned. He said he'd located a similar position closer to his spouse's family. Then in week four, Dale, another colleague whom I really liked a lot, submitted his letter of resignation. He had accepted a more lucrative offer elsewhere. When I asked Samuel if the organization was going to do anything to try to keep these two excellent employees, he replied, "Oh, no, you just get used to losing people around here. Gosh, our turnover rate runs nearly 40% a year."

It was a memorable month. I liked my colleagues, but despite my efforts, I'd hardly met anyone working in other areas. I'd heard my unit celebrate its successes, past and present. But I'd heard nothing good about other units or the people within them. And I'd heard about lots of negative behaviors. It seemed easy to see why people didn't want to spend time with those working in other areas.

Year One

In key ways, my first day, first week, and first month previewed my first year at NetNat. In fact, they rather accurately predicted divisional lines and associated behaviors. It seemed that everyone knew just what to do—snidely degrade others, downplay others' work and contributions, and build allegiances only inside their own division. There was a strong organizational culture, with highly shared values. But these values were to protect one's own division, to resist coordination with other divisions when possible, and to dislike those in other units.

Over the course of the year, I did get to know a handful of people working in other units. This happened largely because, due to my background in market analysis, I was briefly loaned out to the Research Division. The bulk of my time was still allocated to my usual responsibilities, but 25% of it was devoted to working on two market analysis projects. Leon, the division head of Research, was professional and treated me quite well. He was different from Delia, but he worked well with members of his unit. Although he seemed somewhat disorganized and *spacey,* I saw enough good things about him to quell the rumors I'd heard about him being nasty, impatient, and irritable. In fact, Leon seemed rather likable and funny to me.

It was also during this period that I got to know Avie and Belle, two long-term employees. While they were both heavily negative regarding most areas of NetNat, they provided me with lots of details on the organization's history, however biased these details might have been. It was from them that I learned about Trevor, a former CEO who played favorites with division heads. According to Avie and Belle, division heads worked against each other to secure favor with Trevor. Jealousy and tension developed and worsened as employees within the units worked to support their manager so that their division would be elevated. There were other such stories and many speculations, and I wondered what NetNat's culture had been like prior to Trevor being at the helm and about the degree to which his unfairness shaped the current organizational culture.

Leon liked my work a lot, and he kept kidding me about "keeping me." I didn't really think that he was serious, and this just seemed like a way for him to pass along a compliment. So I was a little surprised when, on a Friday, Leon pitched the idea of my coming to work full-time for his division. I was hugely complimented, and I told Leon so. But I also said that I liked my regular unit and wanted to return to work there. I added that, because I'd liked the projects in Research and the people there, if Leon wanted to talk to Delia about continuing to use me on some projects, that was fine with me.

When I got to work on the following Monday, my coworkers were in an uproar. Delia had mentioned the conversation with Leon to others in the unit, and they'd labeled it "stealing." In fact, they kept saying things like they couldn't believe "that Leon would try to steal Casey away from us, especially after we'd been so kind as to loan her out for a bit." But, of course, they concluded that "In some ways, it was only natural, as we do have the best people in this division." And further, they said, "Delia saved the day by talking about all of our projects and priorities and how Casey was instrumental to them. She'd never let Leon control us."

Although I was pleased that Delia saw me as instrumental, I wished that she'd talked with me about how I'd like to spend my work time. I felt that I'd put the division and Delia first in my answer to Leon. I guess that I just really wanted Delia to put more emphasis on my wishes in this situation. And even more important, I'd been in another division and seen firsthand the good people and good work there, so I knew how arbitrary the divisional perspectives were. Also, by this time, I knew how deeply ingrained these views were and how difficult it would be to change them.

Maybe the thing that bothered me the most was that it seemed that little was being done toward positive change. Division heads were as much caught up in the rumor mill as regular employees. This culture had been in place for a long time, and the top leaders, who frequently traveled on business, seemed oblivious to the need for change. Further, despite working with good people in two divisions, I was beginning to realize that the more one heard about life at NetNat, the more stressed one became. Before, I'd always thought that close working relationships reduced stress, but in this environment I could see that being close with others meant hearing lots of negative information. This, and the expectation that I would participate in such conversations, increased my stress. I started thinking about how such stress might influence employees in the long run. Maybe employees at NetNat rumored to be lazy were really just burned out from having to deal with so much negativity and work-related stress.

I'm usually a pretty quick study and can fit in and adapt in lots of situations. To some extent, this was true at NetNat—I worked successfully enough in two divisions. But I didn't feel all that successful overall. Sure, I was getting my tasks done and getting some degree of praise for them, but I didn't feel like I was making a real difference in this environment. And I didn't really know how a workplace culture like NetNat could change and what role I might play in that process. In large part, these factors influenced my thinking on likely leaving NetNat in the near future.

Shortly after my one-year anniversary, NetNat's CEO stepped down to pursue other business interests. Elizabeth Tinker, a well-liked and well-respected executive in a similar organization, was recruited to head NetNat. It was rumored that Elizabeth was a "people person," who placed strong emphasis on cooperation, coordination, and teamwork.

As I contemplated this first year, I asked myself if I should look for employment elsewhere. And I wondered what the new CEO might do to improve life at NetNat. ✦

*This case has been developed based on real organization(s) and real organizational experiences. Names, facts, and situations have been changed to protect the privacy of individuals and organizations.

Chapter 2

Change, Coalitions, and Coping

JOY L. HART, SHIRLEY WILLIHNGANZ, AND GREG B. LEICHTY

As Maria* rounded the corner, Randy saw Andrew flash three fingers at her. But Randy had no idea what this gesture meant. He felt like a stranger in his own company. Randy had started Sports Gadgets with his wife, Nancy, 15 years earlier, and he couldn't believe that it could come to this—and never so fast.

When Maria saw Andrew flash the three fingers at her, she instantly knew exactly what it meant: "Don't let the pigs get you to roll in the mud with them." Maria and Andrew were part of a group of managers who had had difficulty coping with all of the changes over the past year, and they felt as alienated at Gadgets as Randy did. In part to poke fun at situations, but mostly as a measure of sheer support, Maria, Andrew, and some of the other managers had developed a list of ten supportive phrases, each with a corresponding number, so that they could easily flash them at each other with hand signals or jot them quickly on papers in meetings. Seeing Andrew flash the number three did seem supportive, but it also seemed sad, as it reinforced to Maria how much of a bunker mentality they had developed.

As she rounded the corner and saw Andrew's *sign language,* Maria glanced guiltily at Randy. She wondered if her workplace would stay this way or if it was possible to go forward—or back—to a place where people liked and trusted each other. She asked herself, "How did we get here?" Although Maria had her support group of like-minded managers, she felt alienated by upper management, the other managers, and what she saw as problematic methods of making decisions and conducting business.

Randy, too, felt alienated, but for different reasons. The company he had built had changed. Some of the changes were welcome ones, but others were unsettling. He saw divisiveness increasing in the ranks and insulated groups like Maria and Andrew's forming. And although he didn't exactly understand all that was going on, like the flashing of hand signals, he did understand that this wasn't the Gadgets Way—or at least not the way of the old Gadgets.

Changes at Gadgets

The Early Days

Gadgets had been a proud company with a committed workforce. Randy and Nancy, a young couple who liked to play around with making useful objects and who valued the freedom of working for themselves, had started it on a shoestring budget in their garage. They had tried more traditional lines of work, but by 25 years of age, they knew that they were looking for something different. They began by focusing on something they loved—bicycles.

Randy and Nancy developed products for their own bikes and ones they thought that bicycle enthusiasts everywhere would enjoy. At first, they manufactured various types of holders (e.g., drink holders, money holders, key holders), and then they expanded into other bicycle products (e.g., reflective wear). Eventually, Gadgets produced gear for other sports and outdoor activities, such as swimming, tennis, camping, and motorcycles. Where others failed in small business, they had thrived; they had the drive, and enough energy, charisma, intelligence, and what some might call raw luck (but others would label insight and positioning) to succeed.

When they first began to expand their garage operation from two persons to six employees, they chose people who shared their values about work. Gadgets sought out individuals like Sean (still with the company) who made few distinctions between work and play, and who built strong friendships, deep with commitment and steeped with caring, with the members of the organization. Through this commitment and caring, the group came to regard each other as family.

And their bonds were tightly forged—they celebrated each other's successes, mourned each other's losses. During the busy periods, they'd all pitch in and work long hours each day and extra on the weekends. During slow times, they'd take longer breaks, play sports or cards for part of the day, or brainstorm together about how to get business back on track. Like a family, in hard times everyone pulled together, and layoffs weren't even considered. And as in many families, every holiday was a festive occasion, with parties, special foods and events, and gifts. Work was regarded as fun. Even after years on the job, Sean commented, "People ask why I work so much. But really what I do isn't work. I come here to have fun. Sure, I get work done while I'm here, but I come here because I enjoy it."

Continued Expansion

It seemed that the founders of Sports Gadgets were blessed with more than their share of success. They made money, their employees worked hard and were happy, and they were doing work that they loved. As time went by, this synergy, and solid leadership from the two founders, led Gadgets down a path of continued expansion and success. Gadgets added employees, moving from 6 to 20 and ultimately to more than a hundred. It left the garage behind and occupied a new manufacturing facility. By its fifteenth year of operation, it had increased its annual sales to more than $7 million.

The Gadgets Way

Although Gadgets had some ups, such as securing financial backing and creating market niches, and downs, including difficulty meeting delivery schedules and occasional declines in sales, during its early years in operation the philosophy had been consistent. Everyone was valued, and everyone worked together. Managers, and even the owners, spent time on the shop floor. Managers didn't sit in offices; they managed by walking around. (Or, as Nancy often did, they skated through the plant on roller skates, narrowly missing equipment and people, the objects of good-natured ribbing.) Often, managers and the owners stopped by to talk to employees, sometimes about how jobs were going, sometimes about how they or their children were doing. In busy phases, both managers and owners would roll up their sleeves and join in the work of the shop floor. And as both the owners and managers had made their rise through the business, they knew most of the tasks very well. Employees commented on how nice it was to have their bosses participating in this work, too. It symbolized that people at the top knew the basics; like the elders in a good family, they had experience and they were available to share it with the rest of the family.

Despite the tensions and growth pains common in any family, Gadgets retained its unique perspective on how organizational work should be done. All did their work and all participated. All shared of themselves. The owners and managers were available. People routinely talked about their personal lives and personal concerns, as well as work-related issues. Many members of the same extended families were hired at the company. The owners dispersed advice and often bailed people out of trouble. Stories abounded of the owners loaning money to workers for car repairs, medical bills, and even jail bond. Several workers talked about feeling better after seeking advice from Randy or Nancy.

Historically, Gadgets had been a freewheeling environment. People brainstormed, shared opinions, and relied on Randy and Nancy's intuitive judgment. Some workers called this "seat of the pants" decision making, but they liked the casual, freewheeling style and face-to-face contact. Some said decisions were made in hallways and on the shop floor, and they liked these factors too. In his own words, Randy was a "benevolent dictator." "I want these to be good jobs for people," he said. "When you talk to people you have to listen to them. You've got to feel like you are one of them and they are one of you. The only way you're going to survive is if there aren't lines between labor and management. We're all on the same team. We're family."

To the Next Level

The business had been flourishing and, after some 15 years in operation, was well established. However, the owners, Randy and Nancy, believed that to move to the next level of success, the company needed to make a transition and expand into other sectors of the market. To do this, they felt that the company needed more professional management to replace their seat of the pants, entrepreneurial style, and so they decided to retire. Retirement meant moving out of the day-to-day operation of the business, but they planned to continue to chair the governing board and retain the majority of company stocks. As Randy noted, "We'd taken it as far as we thought we could. It was time to bring more balance, discipline, and long-term planning into the company to supplement its existing strengths."

So far, they had trained workers and cultivated them for managerial positions. They knew the strengths of this approach—managers fully understood and followed the Gadgets Way. However, because most of the managers had worked their entire careers at Gadgets, they had little knowledge of nor experience with other ways of doing things. Likewise, although employees had received job-related training at Gadgets, some had not completed high school and few had pursued any education beyond high school. Workers promoted from within knew the Gadgets Way and how to operate within that system, but not another.

But now Randy and Nancy believed that continued growth and market expansion would best be achieved by financial and managerial expertise, even beyond their own. They sought professional managers, with college degrees and diverse experience. They assumed that their replacements would share their views on training and cultivating employees and that long-term employees would share their knowledge of production and Gadgets methods with these newcomers—thus, Gadgets would benefit from the influx of new ideas mixing with the established and proven methods of success.

When announcing their retirement and upcoming move across the country, they also welcomed the new CEO, Benny, a seasoned professional recruited from the outside for his business accomplishments and in particular his *numbers* background. Benny had training in accounting and finance and was delighted to have the opportunity to lead Gadgets into its next phase of success—targeted as annual revenues exceeding $20 million within the next five years.

Cultural Warfare

Workers were sad to see Randy and Nancy go, but they knew that they would stay in touch. They also knew that things would be different without the founders and with Benny, but they had no idea how different. Despite whatever changes, they mostly expected life at Gadgets to go on much as it always had.

Behind the closed door of his new office, Benny congratulated himself on his new position heading Gadgets and the opportunities it offered. In his mind, he was clear about what the owners wanted him to do: "Expand the company, institute professional management practices to make production more efficient, and increase profits." Based on years of experience, he thought that he knew just how to do it. His vision extended into the future, but he also recognized some practices at Gadgets that were going to obstruct his plans for the company. "Clearly, there are things that need to change," Benny said aloud to himself. "The Gadgets ship needs a lot of tightening up to expand on its previous successes." Coming from his accounting background, Benny wanted to instill the discipline of using hard numbers when making decisions.

In contrast with the philosophies of the company founders, Benny believed that workers worked, managers managed. Rather than relying on intuition or a "feel" for what was needed, he wanted data, "hard data," he called them, "numbers to indicate directions to take." Managers and workers at Gadgets weren't used to operating this way, so often they didn't provide Benny with what he considered "appropriate numbers." In the words of one manager, "You can't talk to the guy. Anything you want to do, he wants it in a memo, with numbers. It takes so long we can't get anything else done."

What Benny perceived as worker and manager unwillingness and ineptitude at providing data frustrated him. Angry, he stressed to himself, "They don't have the most basic procedures set up here. Every time we need to make a decision or something needs to be done, we have to start from scratch because there's no record of what's been done in the past, no description of how things are usually done, and no facts to guide any deliberation. We don't deliver products on time because of this lack of efficiency, and that hurts our ability to bid on big contracts. Nobody knows what their jobs are because everybody does everything—most of the managers spend their time wandering around chatting with people and never get anything done."

Benny found many of the routine practices at Gadgets to be unprofessional and unproductive. For example, he was highly irritated with Gloria, Gadgets' long-term human resources manager. She was highly popular with workers, and many of them leaned on her for social support. With Randy and Nancy gone, Gloria had assumed many of the supporting, nurturing behaviors that workers had come to expect. But, in Benny's view, she didn't act like a member of the management team. Rather, in his assessment, she spent her time listening to the problems and complaints of workers and spent too little time on her core job functions, such as overseeing the annual performance appraisals, keeping attendance records, and maintaining files of job applicants. In a move that surprised workers across the plant, Benny fired Gloria.

Some speculated that Benny was trying to pass off his own problems on other managers. There was further speculation that Gloria was just the first of many people that Benny planned to fire. Gloria's firing was threatening to people who had already spent a long time with the company. If Gloria could be discarded after so many years of faithful service, then no one was safe. Years of good service suddenly didn't seem to count for much. The familiar routines of the company were disappearing and there wasn't anything positive to replace them so far as long-term members of the company were concerned.

Although Gloria's refusal to comply with the new regime and Benny's subsequent decision to fire her were extreme examples of the changed environment, even managers who tried to adopt Benny's ways didn't fully understand them. For example, Sean asserted that "Benny just collects data. He wants numbers, then more numbers, and then additional information. But he gets mired, and then he can't act. At least we used to fly high, even if sometimes we went in the wrong direction. Now, we're like an ostrich with its head in the sand."

While Sean, a long-term employee in marketing, tried to adapt to the new methods, other managers developed a bunker mentality. They were afraid of displeasing Benny and of losing their jobs, like Gloria, but they resented and resisted the new system. Maria and her cohorts described the organization as "sick," "destructive," and "in chaos." They felt isolated and abandoned, adrift with no close family other than their self-selected unit. And they felt threatened enough to need nearly constant support from each other, which of course required more time to talk and less time to do their jobs.

Benny may have envisioned a calm, ordered, and professional environment, but his vision was seen as sterile, detached, and impersonal. Indeed, Benny came to be an icon of a cold, detached, and impersonal rationality. He talked to managers and other employees about tasks and when he wanted something done, but made no efforts to get to know them or to discuss non-work-related topics. He was repeatedly referred to as the "numbers guy" or someone who always "wanted everything in writing." Numerous employees expressed the sentiment that they didn't know how to relate to Benny or gain his confidence and trust. Benny didn't quite understand what workers wanted from him. "I'm here to do a job," he said. "My personal life is my own."

From Benny's perspective, and from the viewpoint of some of the other managers he had hired, Gadgets was a high-spirited but undisciplined company. Like a young colt, it needed to be broken and its energy needed to be harnessed and directed in more productive ways. "If Gadgets is going to succeed," Benny said to himself, "people have to become more professional. It's not personal, but everyone needs to grow up. I feel like everybody in this place expected Randy to know everything, and had to check with 'Dad' before they could do anything. The homegrown managers have good intentions, but they haven't been educated in modern procedures and haven't developed processes for making decisions. You don't need to talk about everything. The company needs to base its decisions on objective facts, and not on subjective spur-of-the-moment whims. And if I need to show people I mean business with an occasional firing, so be it."

Outside of several of the associates he had hired for upper management, Benny's opinion of the company's problems and prospects was not widely shared. Indeed, the prevailing attitude among many in the company, including several of the long-term managers, was that Benny was killing the company in his attempts to change it. And although his firing of Gloria was, in his mind, entirely justified, it triggered an attempt by workers to form a union, something the workers in the "old" Gadgets never believed they needed to protect their welfare.

Only several months into their retirement, Randy and Nancy received an emotional late-night telephone call from a long-time employee. She called to warn them that there was an upcoming meeting to discuss forming a union. Sure, Randy and Nancy were aware of some of the grumbling among the long-term employees at Gadgets, but they had assumed that it would merely be a matter of time before things calmed down and settled into a new routine. Clearly they had misjudged the seriousness of the situation. Randy couldn't believe that his own company would have such dissatisfied workers that they thought they needed a union. And he couldn't understand how Benny could have let things deteriorate so quickly.

First Aid for Gadgets

Randy and Nancy flew in from their retirement home several states away to put out the fire. They met with employees on-site and off-site, discussed concerns, and did their best to allay employees' fears. The idea of organizing a union, which appears to have been an effective attention-getting device anyway, was quickly forgotten. Randy and Nancy soothed concerns and reassured workers. Believing that they could trust the owners, the workers dropped their pursuit of unionization.

The owners talked the situation over with Benny, too. They were surprised and unsettled by his level of defensiveness and tendency to blame others. Benny's lack of savvy in handling this incident caused them to begin to wonder about Benny's judgment. Several months later, after Benny enacted a second round of dramatic firings of long-term company employees and a series of recriminations followed, Randy and Nancy removed him as CEO.

Martin, one of the managers who'd been hired from the outside but who blended a professional business orientation and an understanding of people, was named CEO. He had the background and personal savvy to win the trust of both the old-timers and the newcomers at Gadgets. Finally, it appeared that life at Gadgets was beginning to settle down. Then without warning, after only six months as CEO, Martin faxed in his resignation, "effective immediately due to personal reasons." The sense of normalcy that Gadgets had started to regain after Benny's departure quickly dissipated.

Retaking the Reins

Worried about the potential disintegration of the business, Randy returned to Gadgets as CEO. In Randy's terms, "I don't know who I could bring in who would understand how we do things here. Over the years, I've tried to bring people here along, but have been disappointed in them. I wanted to believe they could do it when they couldn't."

Randy recognized he was facing some serious challenges. The company he came back to was not the company he left. Many of the associates who had been with him from the beginning were gone, many bitterly. Some of the old-timers were glad to have Randy back, and expected things to go back to the "way they were." However, many members of the company were relatively new hires brought in by Benny to bring new professional practices and energy into the company, and they had no history with nor loyalty to Randy.

The core group of new managers was uncomfortable with Randy's informal leadership style. They felt that their expertise and knowledge were not valued and appreciated; they didn't know why they had to talk to Randy about everything, and didn't understand why Randy asked them to do jobs that were not "theirs." Indeed, Alan, a new customer services manager, believed that Randy was punishing him when he was asked to help with production tasks on the floor. Workers divided into coalitions, determined to protect themselves and their turf. Maria's, Andrew's, and their cohorts' ten hand signals for support were just one example of this self- and group protection.

At the end of his first month back as the company's CEO, Randy sat down to review the current state of the company and his options for returning it to profitability and relative harmony. "What should I do next?" he wondered.

How could he combine his commitment to—and preference for—a humane, hands-on, informal organization with his desire to grow the company into an expanded, professional, more profitable industry leader? How could he work with both the old-timers and the newly hired managers to create a cohesive management team and subsequently a cohesive organization? ✦

*This case has been developed based on real organization(s) and real organizational experiences. Names, facts, and situations have been changed to protect the privacy of individuals and organizations.

Chapter 3

How Do You Get Anything Done Around Here?

MARIAN L. HOUSER AND ASTRID SHEIL

Kate Elliott,* a new product development specialist at Donaldson Family Foods, Inc., paced in her office and shuffled papers on her desk. She had a lot of work to do, but she couldn't seem to concentrate. It had been one month since she presented a comprehensive proposal for product testing to SMART, the Senior Management Action Review Team. She needed an answer on whether she could move forward on test-marketing an all-in-one insulated portable cooking bag that had been developed as the anchor product for a new line of high-end, quick fix, specialty picnic foods. The planned product launch and the portable cooking bag were scheduled to coincide with Memorial Day weekend, the traditional start of picnic season. Although Memorial Day was still six months away, Kate knew that her window of opportunity for completing the test-marketing was closing quickly. If she missed the time frame scheduled for Memorial Day weekend, there was a good chance that annual sales projections would fall short. She didn't want to think about the consequences. Kate wondered why she could not get a straight answer. Could their dallying be the result of the famous "Black Hole" she had been warned about when she first joined Donaldson Family Foods ten months earlier?

The Beginning

When Kate received a call from an executive recruiter about a "great opportunity" at Donaldson Family Foods, her immediate reaction was "No thanks, not interested." A recent MBA graduate with two years' experience under her belt at a *Fortune* 500 food-manufacturing company, Kate was primed for the fast track. Her goal was to become one of the youngest national brand managers in the country by the time she was 28. All that Kate knew about Donaldson Family Foods was that it was a privately held family company that had been canning vegetables since 1899. The products had not changed in over 100 years—even the labels had not changed in 50 years. To Kate, Donaldson Family Foods was a low-growth, low-margin commodity business. It was stale and old, and she had no interest in applying there. Then she received a phone call from Jeff Donaldson, the president and CEO of his family business. Stunned by his forthright candor in calling her directly, Kate agreed to come for an interview.

Jeff Donaldson was the fourth generation to lead the family business. A graduate of Duke University with an MBA from Michigan, Donaldson was groomed from birth to take over the company. During high school and college he worked summers at the canning plants, driving forklifts, hosing down equipment, and changing the glue canisters for the labeling machines. After graduate school, he started as a shift supervisor, eventually working his way up to plant manager. Before rising to the office of the president, Donaldson had done a tour of duty in the marketing department and served as chief financial officer for six years. At 45, the man knew his business.

Kate was impressed by Donaldson's charisma and sincerity. "You're just the type of person I want on my team," he had told her. "I'm ready to move into the high-growth, prepackaged, specialty foods market. I need bright, energetic, and creative people who can take ideas from concept to completion without a lot of interference from management." It was that last phrase, *without a lot of interference from management,* that caught Kate's attention. Kate was ready to manage a portfolio. Donaldson dangled the ultimate carrot in front of her. "If you come on board with me, your first project will be to handle the introduction of our new portable cooking bag at the same time we launch our new prepackaged specialty picnic foods next year. You handle this right, and you'll be a national brand manager before you know it." Kate was hooked.

She liked everyone she met at the company, the money was good, the on-site workout facility and juice bar were an immediate bonus, and the opportunity to become a national brand manager was definitely the trump card. Kate could not think of one reason she should not join the company.

Early Warning Signs

One of the first things Kate noticed during her first weeks at Donaldson Family Foods was how lax everyone seemed to be about office hours. At 7:30 every morning, her car was generally the first in the parking lot. Most of the marketing and new product development people did not arrive until 9:00 A.M. By 5:15 P.M., the parking lot had cleared out, except for a few cars. Kate chalked up the late start and the early departures to the emphasis on family that Jeff had stressed in their first meeting. "This company was founded by my grandfather 100 years ago on the simple premise of neighbors working together to make a better life for themselves," Donaldson had told her. "No one is expected to put in a 70-hour workweek. Time with the family is important. Even our plants close on Sundays and major holidays so workers can be with their families."

It did not take Kate long to feel comfortable. During her first few weeks on the job, someone in the main office dropped by her office nearly every day to chat and welcome her aboard. The place was full of nice people, so it caught her by surprise when, after offering a problem-solving remark, she was singled out at a staff meeting for being "too aggressive."

Rick Clark, her immediate supervisor, told her, "Now, Kate, that might be how you talked to others at your last employment, but around here, we do not attack each other in staff meetings."

Embarrassed, Kate stammered, "I'm sorry . . . I wasn't trying to hurt anyone's feelings . . . was just trying to look at what the objections might be if . . ."

Clark cut her off with a wave of his hand. "We know you don't know any better yet, but you'll learn. We keep it nice and friendly around here in all our conversations. It's the Donaldson Family Foods way."

In her office later that morning, Kate replayed the exchange over and over in her mind. She was confused. Tom Kadzinsky, a veteran product development specialist, poked his head in the door. "Mind if I talk to you for a minute, Kate?" he asked.

The Culture Contradiction

Kate motioned for Tom to sit down. "Tom, what just happened to me in that meeting?" she queried.

"Ah, that was the official 'Welcome Aboard and Don't Rock the Boat Lecture' from Rick," he replied. "All of the relatively new people have gone through it, Kate." Kadzinsky shrugged.

"Do you mean we're not allowed to criticize or challenge anything in a staff meeting?" she asked.

"Yeah, that's pretty much it," he replied dryly. After a long silence, Tom continued, "I can see the wheels in your brain turning. You're trying to figure out what's going on here, right?"

"How do you get anything done around here?" she asked.

"Things get done eventually," Tom stressed. "This is a privately held company in a low-growth business. Because there's no big hurry, SMART—the Senior Management Action Review Team—always takes its time making decisions."

Kate was incredulous. "Wait a minute. Jeff Donaldson himself told me that the company was positioned to move into new, high-growth markets. If we're going to be competitive, we're going to have to make decisions in real time and get new products to market faster than our competition. All of that suggests decentralized decision making."

Tom smiled. "Yeah, it's even in our mission statement, but that's not the way things really work around here."

"Then why would they hire people like us? It makes no sense." Kate sighed. "I came here for the chance to be a national brand manager, to do cutting-edge work. I didn't come here to baby-sit a bunch of hundred-year-old products."

Tom looked out Kate's window onto the manicured lawn and landscaping in front of Donaldson Family Foods. "In my interview," Tom continued, "Donaldson promised that I would be in charge of branding a new line of Latin foods. I've been here three years and I have yet to roll out a single new product."

Kate sat silently, taking in this new disclosure.

"It's because of the Black Hole," Tom stated.

"What's that?" Kate asked.

"The *Black Hole* is the nickname the employees have given to the SMART group. In those weekly meetings of SMART, all initiatives, ideas, and proposals come to a grinding halt. Nothing moves forward until SMART has given its approval."

"How could there be a black hole when, according to Donaldson, the company hierarchy has been flattened to shorten the decision-making time?" she asked.

"Look, Kate," Tom offered as he turned to leave, "it's always a little frustrating at first here, but you'll get used to it, and why sweat it? The money's good, the hours can't be beat, and there is no pressure to perform. No one ever gets fired from Donaldson Family Foods."

Kate reached for her company manual. It was the first thing she had been given by the human resources manager when she joined the company. She opened to the inside cover and stared at the smiling, tan face of Jeff Donaldson. Even in photographs, he was charismatic, she thought. She reread the vision statement, next to his picture:

> *At Donaldson Family Foods, we are committed to being the number one innovator of high-end, specialty food products. We will reach this goal by employing the best and the brightest, adhering to the best management practices, and offering the best value for our customers, suppliers, and vendors. To this end, we strive to provide a safe and congenial workplace for all employees, offer personal and professional improvement programs, and compensate generously for performance. We provide a business environment in which innovation and creativity can flourish, and people at all levels of the organization are empowered to make decisions as if they owned the company.*

She agreed with every word in the vision statement. It sure looked good on paper.

The Project

The day after Kate's conversation with Tom, Jeff Donaldson dropped by her office. He flashed his winning grin as he sat in the plush visitor's chair across from her desk. "I just wanted to check up on you and see how you are getting along," he started.

"I'm doing great," Kate offered hurriedly.

"Good!" he replied. "I know you are ready to break out from the back of the pack and become a lead sled dog for Donaldson Family Foods!" Kate made a mental note of how Donaldson always peppered his conversations with metaphors about dogs. "She's a greyhound," he had told Kate when describing the CFO, Katherine Halburton. "I hired her straight out of business school. She made it to the front of the pack in less than five years."

Donaldson seemed to have a rating system for all his employees. He referred to some as greyhounds (fast, with a strong desire to win), St. Bernards (loyal, but not very productive), or strays and puppies. Kate wondered if he had already settled on a dog rating for her.

Donaldson continued. "I think it's time for you to take on the cooking bag project we talked about during your interview." Kate took out a pad of paper and jotted down notes while Jeff Donaldson shared his ideas with her. As he left her office an hour later, he offered one more suggestion. "Call Angie, my secretary, and make sure she puts you first on the agenda. Can you have the numbers ready in three weeks?"

"I'll be ready," Kate said confidently. All concerns regarding Tom's warnings about the Black Hole went out of her head.

Kate worked tirelessly, putting together the numbers and rationale for the new portable cooking bag. The centerpiece of the plan was the focus group research. She could not recommend the company move forward with production of the bags without strong evidence from the focus group research. With calendar in hand, she estimated when everything had to be completed to make a Memorial Day kickoff. Kate called the focus group research company and told them to have everything ready in one week. "This shouldn't take long," she told the owner of the research company. "I've got the budget, the timeline, and the rationale all worked out. I know it's a 'go.' I just need to get the final green light from Mr. Donaldson."

During her presentation, Kate fielded questions from the senior vice presidents. At the end, Donaldson announced, "Kate, this is really excellent work. We will have an answer for you shortly." She departed the meeting confident about her performance and the plan. She went back to wait for the answer from SMART. Inwardly, she laughed at how gullible she had been to believe there was a black hole.

The Black Hole Makes Its Appearance

At the end of the week after Kate had made her presentation to SMART, the phone rang in her office. It was the president of the research company. "Hello, Kate? This is Dave Seavers at Independent

Research. I've got a squad of people on standby waiting for your signal. What's the word? This is starting to cost me money." She felt terrible as she tried to stall for time. "I'm sorry, Dave. Jeff Donaldson has been out of touch this week with an emergency at the northern plant. I'll call you as soon as I have an answer. To be on the safe side, you better let everyone go for now."

Now, one month later in her office, Kate was lacking confidence with every breath. "This has got to be bad news," she fretted. "How could I have missed the mark so badly? Why doesn't one of them call me and at least tell me something?"

Kate drove home frustrated and tired from the lack of communication at Donaldson Family Foods. "This is not what I signed on for," she thought bitterly.

Monday morning, Kate called the president's secretary, Angie Parker, trying to sound confident.

"Hi, Angie. This is Kate Elliott in new product development. I need to set up an appointment with Mr. Donaldson as soon as possible."

"What's this regarding?" the president's secretary and gatekeeper asked coolly.

"Well, it's been one month since I presented the test marketing proposal at the weekly senior management meeting. I have a very tight deadline, and Mr. Donaldson assured me that he would get back to me promptly. I'm just following up because I have a lot of people on standby, waiting for the signal to begin. I don't have much time to spare if we're going to make the rollout in May. I just need to know where we are on this."

"Kate, if Mr. Donaldson said he would get back to you, I'm sure he will. Mr. Donaldson is in the Bahamas this week with clients and cannot be disturbed. When he returns next Monday, I will let him know you called."

"Monday! Angie, I really need an answer before then. Can't somebody else on SMART give me an answer?"

"I'm afraid you'll just have to wait until Mr. Donaldson returns."

Kate felt totally adrift. With each passing day, the chances of her making the Memorial Day weekend kickoff were fading quickly. "How could I have been so wrong about Jeff Donaldson and this place?" she thought. "Is he the consummate liar or was I naive to think I could make product development decisions on my own?"

Kate walked into the spacious break room, complete with fireplace and television, where employees gathered to chat, exchange pleasantries, and sample new products. The place looked the same as the day she started, but now she saw things with different eyes. "Jeff Donaldson may have flattened the organization, but he never empowered his people," she thought bitterly. "We're all just hanging around waiting to be told what to do."

Kate walked up to Tom Kadzinsky, who was pouring himself a second cup of coffee, the newspaper under his arm. "Does anything ever come out of the Black Hole?" Kate asked.

Tom looked at Kate sympathetically and said, "Yes, but generally not until you have completely abandoned the project and given up all hope on it."

Kate felt defeated. She stammered, "Why do you stay, Tom?"

"Kate, I may be here physically, but my heart and soul have left the building," Tom replied flatly. "I got my hand slapped so many times my first year, I quickly learned to keep my mouth shut, my thoughts to myself, and just do as little as possible. I have two kids in grade school, a wife, and they all like it here. There are worse things in life than not being fulfilled professionally. And I am one of many—just look at the parking lot. There are a lot of people with this organization who check out early every day."

There was a lag in the conversation and finally Tom said, "Come on, Kate. You'll get used to it, especially when you realize there's really nothing you can do about it."

Kate had given up a lot to come to Donaldson Family Foods. She thought about the friends and family she had left when she moved halfway across the country to take this job. What had seemed like such a promising career move now felt like a big mistake. "I don't know, Tom. I just don't know . . ." Her voice trailed off. ✦

*This case has been developed based on real organization(s) and real organizational experiences. Names, facts, and situations have been changed to protect the privacy of individuals and organizations.

Chapter 4

Downsizing at Tata Steel

Rajeev Kumar

"Every morning in Africa, a gazelle wakes up. It knows that it must run faster than the fastest lion or it will be killed.

Every morning a lion wakes up. It knows that it must run faster than the slowest gazelle or it will starve to death.

It does not matter whether you are a lion or a gazelle, when the sun comes up, you had better be running.

And for us in Indian industry, the sun came up in 1991 and it continues to become warmer and hotter."

Dr. Jamshed J. Irani, the Managing Director of Tata Steel, was addressing a gathering of distinguished industrialists at a seminar organized by the All India Management Association in September 1992. He was speaking about Tata Steel's response to the events of 1991, a critical period in India's economic history. Due to severe stagnation in the Indian economy, government controls and protections had been lifted, and his company was faced with a free economy and competition from manufacturers worldwide. He knew old philosophies and principles would have to be changed in order for his company to survive. And he believed downsizing was to be one of the essential strategies required to improve their profits, productivity, and competitiveness.

"In the past," Dr. Irani continued, "we had assured profits. Whatever we made, we sold. We had little domestic competition. We owned the raw materials. We had the technological edge. And we had no incentive to modernize. But now we are faced with new players, a glut in the industry, and competition in terms of quality, delivery, and cost. Now we must be agile and willing to change in the new environment."

Dr. Irani's voice increased in intensity. "The steel industry has been crying for decontrol and liberalisation for the past many years. Now that we have got it, we must face the challenges squarely and make the most of our opportunities."

The History of Tata Steel

Established in 1907, Tata Steel prided itself on its illustrious history of ethical industrial relations, providing workers with a productive, wholesome environment developed through the philanthropic- and welfare-oriented vision of Jamshetji Nusserwanji Tata, founder of the industrial house of Tatas. The company had routinely introduced welfare measures such as the 8-hour workday, leave with pay, and free medical aid decades before Indian legislation required them. Some measures, such as provision of schooling facilities for children, had simply been provided on philanthropic principle.

Tata Steel had always emphasized business ethics and social responsibility. The company's slogan, "We Also Make Steel," reflected the belief that its first commitment was to the community and society. Over the years, employees understood, and expected, a system of patronage would prevail. More and more people were hired in the '70s and '80s, but production remained level. The joke that made the rounds was this: "Tuesday, Wednesday, and Thursday were working days. We prepare on Friday to play. Play on Saturday and Sunday. And discuss the play on Monday."

Tata Steel Company Organisation

The company used a participative management style, relying on joint consultation and two-way communication to suggest, review, and introduce new programs, as well as to manage daily business. The three-tier system included the Joint Department Council (JDC) at the lowest level, the Joint Works Council (JWC) representing middle management, and the Joint Consultative Council of Management (JCCM), presided over by the Tata Steel Managing Director, Dr. Irani, and the highest representatives from both management and the union. All councils held regular meetings, thus enabling a continuous line of communication between labour and management.

Through this system, all workers were guaranteed a hearing and response to any grievances, as any worker, however menial his job, having any grievance could approach the JDC. The JDC also discussed various problems regarding machinery, productivity, safety, and personnel.

Officers in the company were also heard through regular sessions called *Dialogues,* chaired by one of the vice presidents or the managing director. In these meetings, officers could vent their grievances, offer their opinions and suggestions, and make demands. The discussions were typically free, frank, and uninhibited. Furthermore, the women employees of the company, senior citizens of Jamshedpur, and families of officers were also offered opportunities to participate in Dialogues.

Now that the company was faced with the need to move into a competitive era, these channels of communication would prove to be the mainstay in convincing all employees of the need for change.

A New Challenge

While social responsibility was still to be a core value, management was determined to change their unwritten slogan to "We Make Steel." As Dr. Irani put it, "The emphasis so far has been on creating jobs, not wealth. Now we will be forced to balance loyalty against productivity."

But how were they to reduce employees and keep the corporate image intact? Dr. Irani first decided to hold a public meeting for all employees, to try to communicate the big picture and explain the rationale for the changes to come.

The managing director explained, "We must find ways to compete. We will develop a long-term plan to *rightsize* our workforce. This will help us modernize, increase our productivity, and decrease our costs."

During the meeting, a worried employee queried, "Sir, the company has always followed a tradition of offering employment to a son of every Tata Steel employee. My sons will soon be of working age. Are you withdrawing that assurance?"

The managing director shot back, "My dear, you are worried about the employment of your sons! I am worried about keeping you on the job!"

The employees murmured their dissatisfaction and distress. Tata Steel had always taken care of them, from cradle to grave. For this they had given their time, energy, commitment, loyalty, and skills. Now they sensed they were about to be betrayed.

But Dr. Irani was relentless. "We must not let our past, however glorious, get in the way of our future," he bellowed.

Dr. Irani Plans

Dr. Irani retired to his study for some introspection. He knew resistance to change was natural. He would have to convince top management to support him and help him steer the change. He himself would have to spearhead the process. He was determined to take the responsibility for creating a shared vision, communicating the vision to others, overcoming obstacles, initiating change while creating opportunities for the rank and file, and still preserving the core values of the Tatas.

He set up a small handpicked group to plan and initiate the new business plan. This included three deputy managing directors, the vice president of human resources, the principal executive officer, the head of organisational learning and development, and the chief of corporate communication. He called them in for a meeting.

"Well, gentlemen, I have always advocated that Tata Steel change ahead of the times," Dr. Irani began. "You know we must alter our ways, become more fleet of foot and responsive to our customers."

"But, sir, despite market turbulence and the lifting of protections, we are still making profits. So why must we change now? In such haste?" asked one of the deputy managing directors.

"Ah, the inevitable question." Dr. Irani sighed. "We must change when we are strong, not when we are vulnerable and therefore appear even weaker. Our job is to make everyone—our stakeholders and our employees—see that change makes sense for the company and will benefit them. We must communicate, communicate, communicate. For change to happen, everyone in the company must cross the threshold of conviction. They must understand, Why change?

Why now? Where to? How to? What does it signify and mean to them?"

"But how can we convince them, if change includes downsizing?" asked the vice president of human resources.

"By changing their mindset, convincing them to see the world differently, getting them to see the opportunities that lie in our modernization," replied Irani. "Get them thinking about it. Get them used to the idea. Then make reduction an attractive proposition. So when we ask them to actually leave, they do not have to even think twice."

"I think we should launch an internal communications campaign," said Sanjay Singh, the chief of corporate communication. "I will deliver emphatic statements, full of promises, describing our company's intention to offer world-class products to the customer with world-class service. Then we will see changes in attitudes toward our work practices, our goal orientation, our customer satisfaction. But what do I say about downsizing?"

"Leave that to the line managers," interjected vice president of human resources Pandey. "First, you must give everyone a new vision of our company, to get the obstacles out of the way."

"To get the message across, speak from the heart. Do not let them think you are fabricating the figures. Show where we are behind, how we must improve," advised Dr. Irani. "And for God's sake, don't say anything that can be contradicted or shown to be untrue. Do not hold anything back. Do not exaggerate. Do not understate the problem. Keep repeating, refining, bringing the message up to date. Above all, repeat the message until everyone knows it by heart."

"We will need training and development for the line managers particularly," said Dr. Jittu Singh, chief of organisational learning and development.

"Yes absolutely," the managing director responded. "They are the ones who will deal with the redundant employees, as well as the survivors, face-to-face. They must be role models and examples of change. We must give them a training schedule that will help them handle the nuances of downsizing."

"Finally, remember these points," Dr. Irani concluded. "We must be credible and consistent. We must speak with one voice. We must be the first to change. We must assure the stakeholders that their expectations are being met. We must create a sense of urgency, but not panic. The change we are asking for is not superficial; ingrained habits must be questioned and discarded, and new ones learned. We must maintain communication while we break with the past."

Management and Trade Union Relations

On a cold Saturday morning in January 1993, Dr. Irani was heading for the collieries, where he was to address the executives and, later that evening, the supervisors of the trade union. During the day, he knew he'd have the opportunity to meet with the mineworkers, an encounter he always enjoyed, for he had deep admiration for their simplicity and congeniality. In return, the workers appreciated being able to air any grievances they had to such a high authority as Dr. Irani.

The relationship between management and labour had always been cordial. Indeed, there had been no labour strike at Tata Steel since 1928. A former president of the Tata Workers Union, V. G. Gopal, had once stated, "If we can find a way to discuss disputes, then there is no need for a strike. If we ask for reasonable things, management cannot deny them. Likewise, we the union do not feel we should ask for things that are unreasonable and create a confrontation. Over the years, we have learned to live with and trust each other."

Dr. Irani planned to tell the trade union executive committee about the plans for downsizing. A 1956 agreement between management and the union constrained both of their behaviors: Management was to treat employees equitably by not firing them should they become surplus, by training employees for transfer to new positions, and by guaranteeing wages. In return, the union had agreed not to interfere with management's business of modernizing the company and instituting various new business practices. Dr. Irani intended to honor the agreement.

But Dr. Irani knew that they still faced a pressing need to reduce the size of the company. He and his executive team had developed a thorough plan for downsizing. They would form a placement committee that would match individuals with alternative vacancies, or train surplus people for new positions and then deploy them, facilitating smooth transfers from one unit to another. Wages would be guaranteed, even if individuals were placed two to three steps below their existing grade. But most important, the emphasis would be on finding suitable workers for positions, to train them and post them, rather than on finding suitable positions for surplus workers. It was inevitable that some would be asked to leave.

Dr. Irani had always considered the trade union as a partner, and he hoped to use it again as a partner in communication, to assist in disseminating Tata Steel's strategy through the workforce. He did not expect the union to assist in the process of downsizing—no union worth its salt could go public and support that proposition—but it could help the workers see downsizing in a rational way, while the company itself communicated with individuals and negotiated terms. He hoped to convince the union that the reduction was necessary to save the company.

The Communication Plan

That same evening, Sanjay Singh, chief of corporate communication, was presenting his communication plan to the rest of the executive team at the office.

"We will stratify the audience, identify their information needs, and address each level directly," he said. "We will use all media—print, memoranda, intranet, email, teleconferencing, audiovisual, and our cable TV channel—to reach every employee and his or her family. We will establish the urgency of the need for change and promote their enthusiasm. We will invite employees to respond with ideas for management. We will welcome their emailed suggestions and questions and reply to each directly. We will increase the numbers of meetings at all levels of our system. Since we have over 40,000 employees at our lowest tier level, we have trained all managers to walk the talk and engage in face-to-face dialogue with all workers. We have also installed hotmail and suggestion boxes at the mines and collieries, our outstation locations."

"Finally," Singh continued, "we have also created on our intranet a dedicated website called Knowledge Management, where we will capture and store documented experiences of our process, thereby accumulating wisdom that will provide us with feedback and reference as we continue the process."

The Trade Union Meeting

At the same time, Dr. Irani was sharing the dais with Mr. Benjamin, the current president of the Tata Steel Workers Union. Benjamin was offering the support Dr. Irani had hoped for.

The president addressed the supervisors and workers. "Our first aim is profit. Our second aim is to get our share of the profit. The factory is like a cow that needs to be given fodder—the effect of our labour—so that it may deliver milk. Once you get milk, sharing can be resolved. But the first priority is to look after the cow."

He continued, "Why must the company downsize? We are on a big ship that has to cross the river. The ship is old and cannot sustain the load and may sink. Now another ship comes alongside. If some men get down and board the other ship, this ship will not sink and will reach its destination. Those who get down should also be looked after so that they can cross the river and reach their destination. Separation will not mean starvation."

Dr. Irani smiled as Benjamin exhorted his group: "The role of management and the union is that of a railway track. The company is the train that travels the track. If we do not cooperate, the train will derail."

Later, at a news conference, a journalist asked Benjamin why the union was so willing to support management's move. Benjamin replied, "Unlike many companies, our management makes our union stronger. They communicate with us. They keep their word. They share information, and they do not try to manipulate us. With this peace, progress is possible. Our message to the workers is that management and the union will look after them in all contingencies. We believe them that downsizing is necessary. For employees younger than 40, it is better to leave now, when reemployment possibilities are good. For those of us left, the larger the share of the pie."

Early Separation Schemes and Voluntary Retirement

Nonetheless, employees initially resisted separation. The first separation scheme coincided with the closing of the steel melting shop. Employees were offered voluntary retirement or separation with generous benefits—a monthly pension, repayable loans, grants for medical service and house rent, and an early loan against pension due. But of 800 personnel offered these benefits through a letter, only 4 accepted. They felt the compensation would not offset the loss they faced. Fortunately, management was able to redeploy these persons to a new unit.

Dr. Irani became the champion of the cause. He worked tirelessly to meet and speak with all concerned–workers, family members, media, senior citizens, and community members. The employees were convinced of his integrity.

The internal campaign emphasized terms such as benchmarking, productivity, customer focus, and competitiveness. All needed to be prepared for change. The underlying communication theme was "You are good, but it is the job slot that is not needed." As the human resources division argued, "Our aim was not to reduce numbers but to improve efficiency and effectiveness. Reduction was a consequence. We knew it would mean that."

Before the next separation scheme, the company interviewed and surveyed employees to understand their needs more thoroughly. This included profiles of their age, liabilities, dependents, housing and health needs, possibilities for self-employment, salaries, expectations, and skills. The new scheme was designed to meet their needs and expectations. It offered counseling in investment planning, socioeconomic concerns, and other issues. Tata Steel provided loans for buying a house or starting a new business. As the scheme more closely addressed the workers' needs, they were more receptive to the plan.

Between schemes, management used the time to capture more data about targeted groups and refine their offerings. They also persuaded employees that what was offered now might not be offered in the same form again. To further convenience employees, they carefully timed launching of new schemes to avoid marriage season, wage negotiation time, or the disruption of children's school programmes.

Line managers received ongoing training to address employees' feelings and emotions and to offer financial counseling. Bank officials were called in to educate employees in financial management. Rumors were captured and dispelled immediately. When employees feared that the company might not live up to its commitment five years down the line, Tata Steel provided the agreement on legal stamped paper to allay uneducated workers' concerns, even though in any case the agreement was legally enforceable.

Lifestyles of those who had separated were captured in print and video and relayed to those remaining with the company. Those who separated were encouraged to maintain relations with the company, receiving the in-house magazine, *Tisco News,* at their homes. When relatives of separated employees became distressed about their future security, joint bank accounts were opened at company cost to ensure that the spouse could access the pension money even if the employee died. A help line was made available for all former employees to assist them in settling into a new lifestyle.

Once an employee decided to take advantage of the separation agreement and notified the company in writing, the process was swift and easy, leaving little time for the employee to change his or her mind.

Some "hard nuts" hindered communication and declined to take any offer. Although senior management tried to persuade them face-to-face, a few never left but stayed with the company as excess baggage with little work and more pay.

Success for Tata Steel

From April 1994 to April 2001, Tata Steel reduced its workforce from 78,669 to 48,821, a downsizing of 38%. Of the numbers reduced, approximately one-third was due to normal attrition; two-thirds was due to early separation and voluntary retirement. At the same time, productivity reached an all-time high and profits soared. The heavy costs of separation were to be amortized over the next 10 years, and stakeholders received a considerably larger share of a bigger pie.

The rest of the industry groaned when they heard how employees had been compensated, but Dr. Irani, having managed the surplus manpower with a human touch, took satisfaction in the image of Tata Steel that he had nurtured. ✦

Chapter 5

Discord at the Music School

Terri Toles Patkin

"And here is where we keep the party supplies," the parent volunteer finished. "You'll want those pretty often, I imagine."

Carole's* head was spinning. She was only partly through her first day as music director at Bow-strings Music School and so far she'd met the piano and violin teachers, had lunch with the office staff (a confusing number of part-time and full-time workers and a few parent volunteers, too—she still hadn't sorted out exactly who was who), and had gotten a tour of the building. Along the way, she'd also gotten an earful about how everyone was hoping she'd be as strong a leader as Wendy, the school's founder.

Neither her years at the Conservatory nor her experiences with the Philharmonic had prepared her for this. Even though she had taught violin for some time, Carole had never had the responsibility for an entire music school. She hadn't even met the students yet, but she had already decided that teaching looked to be the easy part of the job.

That evening, still in her office, she leafed through several notebooks filled with old brochures, minutes of meetings, and photos, and reviewed what she knew so far about Bow-strings Music School. About 15 years ago, Wendy had expanded her home violin studio and moved into this sunny suite in an office park bordered by a playground. The school's location was convenient to highways and, most important, sat at the border of a small city and its most affluent suburb. Soon the sounds of young violinists playing "Twinkle Twinkle

Little Star" filled the air. Word spread quickly among eager parents, and the school expanded almost as soon as it moved into the building. Wendy's dynamic personality seemed to permeate every facet of the organization. Carole suspected that Wendy's recent family relocation across the country had come as a shock to the school, but she was sure that, in time, she could be a fine leader herself.

Carole was especially enthusiastic that Bow-strings was not just a music school, but a Suzuki music school. She herself had been trained in the Suzuki Method by one of the country's leading teachers, a mentor who had studied personally with the noted Dr. Shinichi Suzuki in Japan. Carole thought about Dr. Suzuki the next morning as she interviewed the parent of a prospective student.

"Dr. Suzuki believed that every child could learn music as naturally as they learn to speak their native language," she explained. "He also used music to help the children build positive character traits as well as musical accomplishment."

Carole hoped to keep the Bow-strings curriculum closely modeled on Suzuki's principles, and she was pleased to discover that Bow-strings already provided the atmosphere of cooperation and enthusiasm for learning that is the cornerstone of the Suzuki Method.

"I'm so glad that Bow-strings' atmosphere is so supportive," Carole said one day, as she and a long-time parent volunteer were stuffing envelopes with the monthly newsletter. "It's exactly what Dr. Suzuki must have had in mind."

"Who?" asked the parent as she gently stopped her toddler from trying to climb the piano. "I thought Wendy started the school. I didn't know anyone else was involved."

Carole started to explain, but she was interrupted by a phone call. By the time she'd chatted with the parents waiting for group class to start, fixed a broken violin, made a note on the calendar about Symphony auditions, and reminded several small boys not to chase one another through the hallways, the parent had gone home. She wondered whether others thought the methods were entirely Wendy's ideas.

If Carole had any doubts about Wendy's continuing influence in the school, they were quickly erased over the next several weeks by the parade of parents who made a point of dropping by to praise Wendy. As time passed, Carole found that she was hearing more and more about how her methods of running the school differed from Wendy's.

"Wendy always changed our lesson time around to accommodate our baseball practices," complained one mother after Carole explained that she couldn't keep changing their lesson time because it would have an impact on all the other students she taught.

"What do you mean, she needs to practice?" demanded another. "Wendy never worried about things like that. She just wanted her to love playing the violin."

Carole wondered how the child would be able to love playing the violin when she never picked it up in between lessons, but she didn't say anything.

When Carole asked the faculty why no one had given her a list of performers for the upcoming recital, they all looked astonished. "But Wendy always did that!" they chorused.

When Carole asked a parent volunteer to change the "Composer of the Month" bulletin board, the mother agreed enthusiastically. "I've always wanted to use my artistic talents to help the school! But Wendy used to do all the bulletin boards herself." The parent walked away still talking excitedly about her ideas.

One day, Carole noticed a problem. One family hadn't paid their tuition bill. Carole asked the office manager to contact them to find out what the problem was. "I'm uncomfortable doing that," the manager responded. "That's really your job. Wendy always did it."

Despite these difficulties, Carole could appreciate the energy of Wendy's influence, which she felt even now, three months later. The hallways were decorated with colorful hand-painted designs; photos of students joined those of world-class musicians on the bulletin board; families stayed after class to play and picnic on the field adjoining the school. Carole knew that it was unusual for a music school to have such a strong sense of community. Everyone seemed to know everyone else in the school, and Carole expected that she would one day share in the close support network the parents and teachers had developed with one another.

Carole had always enjoyed teaching, and the students at Bowstrings were a delight. She was surprised, however, to learn that their love of music was not matched by their skill. They didn't seem to know the basics. Carole wondered if her expectations were too high, but she was also frustrated by the emphasis on fun that seemed to leave little time to learn music. Wendy's students had grown to expect regular parties in group class, and Carole often had to end the class early because someone had brought in cupcakes or brownies to share with their music friends. When she asked in the monthly newsletter that people not bring food without consulting her, she felt snubbed all week by the parents, who seemed to stop talking whenever she passed by the small groups gathered in the waiting room.

Her opinions about the quality of her students' playing were confirmed during a chat with her stand partner during a break at Symphony rehearsal.

"I taught several Bow-strings students at a music camp last summer," he said, "and they were just awful. I certainly hope you're teaching them scales and etudes. Wendy didn't believe in that. 'Let the students find the joy,' she said, 'and save the hard work for later.'"

Carole was overwhelmed during her first weeks on the job, not only by the day-to-day demands of running a large school, but also by the disorganization she found in the office. Wendy's special tuition deals and lesson plans had all been done verbally, and there was no documentation to be found. Boxes of paperwork were shoved into corners, with registration forms and tuition checks mixed with tax statements, teacher résumés, and music catalogs. No one seemed to know how to do anything, since "Wendy always did that."

Carole decided that what the school needed most was organization. Although Wendy had apparently found the stream of toddlers and their parents dropping into the office to be energizing, Carole found it distracting. Rather than being at the constant beck and call of everyone, she began shutting the office door so that she could wade through the boxes and focus on what needed to be done. She posted office hours several hours a week, when parents, students, or staff could stop by and chat with her, so that she could then concentrate on their problems rather than thinking about paperwork. As she became more familiar with the school, Carole began compiling a binder of procedures for everyday activities like payroll, publicity, and concert planning. That way, she could delegate some tasks and focus on her own leadership priorities.

Sometimes, Carole felt as if the parents and teachers were almost challenging her to keep the school from going under in Wendy's absence, and she felt the weight of those expectations. In any case, she decided that since she could not duplicate Wendy's strong personality, she would earn the respect of the school community through her strong teaching and organizational skills. After all, those were what Wendy and the board of directors had mentioned when they had offered her the job in the first place.

Gradually she began to make changes in classes, too. Carole believed that fun and games were fine—*after* the student had learned some basic skills. She introduced scales and music theory into the group classes, and continued Wendy's habit of playing through the repertoire and having one or two students play a solo each week. Unfortunately, this left little time for the fun games like "hide the bow" that Wendy had so often had the children play while she took a quick phone call, nursed her baby in the office, or handled a parent's tuition problem. And there certainly wasn't time for anyone to serve cupcakes and clean up in the five minutes scheduled in between classes!

"Well!" exclaimed one of the parents after a particularly difficult lesson. "If I wanted this kind of atmosphere, I would have enrolled the kids at the music school downtown. We didn't come to a music school to learn scales."

"It's just not fun anymore," sighed a 10-year-old who was finishing up her math homework before her lesson.

"Why don't you give Wendy a call?" gently suggested one of the members of the school's board of directors. "She might have some great ideas for you."

But Carole saw that as a sign of failure, and besides, she wanted *less* of Wendy's input in the school, not more.

From her desk, Carole didn't notice that the parents sitting at the picnic table had begun to complain more and more. Enrollment dropped for the spring semester, but Carole assumed that it was simply normal attrition following the change in leadership. She introduced an orchestra program and a music history class, and she arranged field trips to see touring musicians perform. In order to fit these new activities into the school brochure, Carole excised what she saw as irrelevant material—Wendy's lengthy biography.

When some parents complained, she responded that it was unhealthy for the school to idolize the founder to such a great degree. "Saint Wendy!" she exploded when she returned to her office. "I don't see why I should be expected to do things her way all the time! And I'm certainly not going to call her to solve every little problem that comes up. If I just establish clear procedures, then everyone will know how to handle situations."

Carole began to see the rules as more and more important. In situations where Wendy would have made a decision based on the individual needs of the family, Carole referred to the policy manual and made no exceptions at all. The handshake sealing a teacher's employment was replaced by an ironclad contract. Ironically, the stronger Carole made the rules, the more the teachers and parents resisted them.

At the school's annual meeting in May, Carole was surprised when what she had anticipated as a routine "state of the school" address turned out to be a four-hour gripe session with emotional teachers, parents, and board of directors members besieging her from every side and questioning her every decision. There were even calls for her resignation! Even though some people appreciated her new, more organized style, others complained about the lack of a social atmosphere under Carole's leadership.

"All work and no play makes Jack a dull boy," intoned the chairwoman gravely.

"All play and no work makes Jack a lousy musician," Carole retorted under her breath.

Clearly, she had stepped on more toes than she had realized during her first months on the job, and changes would have to be made if she wanted to continue at Bow-strings Music School. Carole went into her office, closed the door, and began making a list. What had gone wrong? And what would she need to do to restore harmony to the music school? ✦

*This case has been developed based on real organization(s) and real organizational experiences. Names, facts, and situations have been changed to protect the privacy of individuals and organizations.

Chapter 6

Long-Distance Cultural Integration

Gerald L. Pepper and Gregory S. Larson

Jessica Mason,* human resources manager for Digiwise Technologies, was not easily ruffled. Today, however, as she drove to work on a hazy Colorado morning, she had to tell herself continually to settle down. The virtual meeting wasn't for three hours, and her presentation was ready. Still, she picked up her cell phone and put in a call to Kathy Ramos, her administrative assistant.

"Good morning, Jessica."

"Kathy, how did you know it was me?"

"Who else would be calling me at 7:30 A.M.?"

"Well, as long as I've got you on the line, could we double-check a few things for the meeting? First, what the heck time will it be in England?"

Kathy pulled out her preparation notes. "The meeting begins at 10:30 A.M. our time, which makes it 9:30 A.M. for California and Washington, 11:30 A.M. for Chicago, 12:30 P.M. for Florida, 4:30 P.M. in England, and 5:30 P.M. in Norway. Those international folks will want to be wrapping up for the day. Still, this beats the last virtual meeting we had, when they had to come to work at 10:30 P.M. just to participate."

"That's for sure. We don't want to make that mistake again. I hope they understood, though. These travel restrictions have made virtual meetings a way of life. We really don't have much choice. Although I don't miss the airports, I did get a good sense of what was going on when I made the trips."

"Virtual meeting," Kathy interrupted. "What an odd term. We might as well call it 'practically a meeting,' or an 'implied meeting.' I'm not even sure that it's a meeting at all."

"I think somebody got up on the wrong side of the bed this morning," Jessica teased. "Whether we like them or not, we have to make them work. Unrestricted travel is no longer an option. In spite of that, people still need to be kept up to date. And that's what we'll accomplish at today's meeting."

"Today's quarterly update, virtual meeting, you mean," clarified Kathy. "This is no run-of-the-mill gabfest."

"Thanks for reminding me," replied Jessica. "I wasn't anxious enough already. When I get in, I'd like to run over the meeting slides. I've got only 30 minutes to update everyone on the status of the acquisition at the one-year mark. I don't have a great feeling about how this is going to go. I can already see a dark cloud or two on the horizon."

Hitting the Ground Running

On paper, the acquisition of AI Cobb by Digiwise Technologies looked straightforward enough. Though still a relatively new company itself, Digiwise was healthy and growing. In 1999, CompuOptions (CO) created a new test and measurement company called Digiwise Technologies. In June 2000, Digiwise became a fully independent company, and the year 2000 saw Digiwise grow to about $13 billion in revenue and 51,000 employees, joining *Fortune* magazine's prestigious list of the 500 largest companies in the world. In July 2000, Digiwise completed its purchase of AI Cobb Technologies. AI Cobb was much smaller than Digiwise, employing 175 people, primarily in Chicago, Miami, and Oslo. AI Cobb joined Digiwise's Network Group Solutions Business Unit (NGS). The acquisition was made in an effort to increase the size of NGS's portfolio and market space in wireless services. AI Cobb offered Digiwise products and services that complemented its existing range. With the acquisition completed, AI Cobb no longer existed; it was part of Digiwise NGS.

After one year, the combined products and services were proving to be a good fit, and NGS had more growth potential than predicted. Jessica acknowledged this. However, as she had pointed out to the executive management team on more than one occasion, she also felt that Digiwise should have spent more time considering the cultural differences between the two companies. While she had expected a small, entrepreneurial company like Al Cobb to operate differently than a large company like Digiwise, Jessica realized that she had underestimated the challenge of merging these groups of workers into a single, unified workforce. From the beginning differences had arisen over decision-making practices, communication styles, work environments, and work procedures.

These difficulties were exacerbated by the geographic isolation of the units. Former Al Cobb employees—now Digiwise employees—worked from their ex-Al Cobb sites with Digiwise employees around the world. But they rarely met together physically, which required most of their communication to be electronic. Many workers complained that they were expected to contribute to long-term projects with coworkers whose faces they'd never seen. Now, after a year, many of these problems continued to surface in conversations Jessica had with employees and managers alike. She knew cultural integration was critical if the business unit and company were going to grow. Today's virtual meeting, attended by all the senior managers within NGS, was her chance to explain the problems and potential.

Making Decisions

As she did most mornings when she arrived at work, Jessica managed to balance an apple and a cup of coffee in her left hand and a laptop bag over her shoulder, all the while using her right hand to hold her cell phone to her ear. She nodded hello to the security guard as he smiled familiarly at her balancing act. This was an apt metaphor for her work life generally. At 120 emails and dozens of phone calls per day, not to mention numerous meetings, Jessica spent most of her time busily communicating with managers and employees throughout Digiwise, and sorting through that information. The information she gathered regarding the integration of ex-Al Cobb people, with their unique operating styles, key values, and identity, into Digiwise, revealed important differences between the two companies—differences that were a cause for concern.

When Jessica had settled into her office, she and Kathy pulled up Slide One.

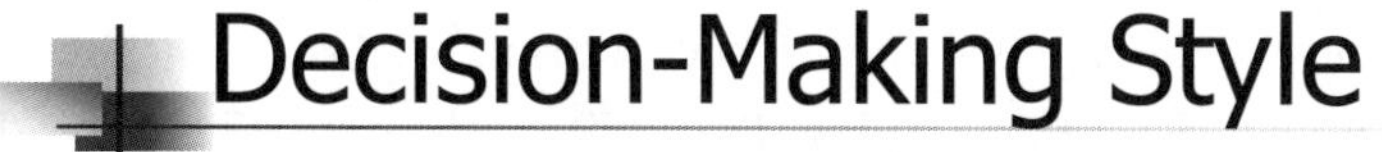

Maximum input vs. necessary input

Taking the best from both companies

Two-way communication

As she proofread the slide, Jessica suddenly recalled a focus group meeting she had conducted shortly after the acquisition. It was there that she first became aware of interesting differences between the decision-making styles of Al Cobb and Digiwise. The exchange had occurred between herself and focus group participant Bruce Johnson, an ex-Al Cobb employee.

Jessica asked, "Are you satisfied with your level of awareness of the decisions others are making in the company?"

Bruce's response caught her by surprise. "That is such a classic Digiwise question. This company spends more time worrying about whether everybody knows what everybody else thinks than it does making actual decisions."

"Don't people want to know what others are thinking on important matters? Don't more opinions lead to better decisions?" Jessica responded.

"For the most part, it wastes time," Bruce answered. "I get more emails and voicemails and updates than I could possibly care about on issues that aren't remotely part of my work responsibilities. Those, on top of the meetings I have to attend, all add up to a waste of time."

"You didn't have updates and meetings at Al Cobb?"

"Of course we did, but within reason. Decisions were made quickly. The process was more streamlined and overall more centralized. Fewer opinions were sought, because most decisions don't need maximum input."

"Earth to Jessica," Kathy chimed in. "Where were you just now?"

"Sorry," Jessica replied. "I was just thinking how important this issue is, and how difficult it would have been to discover, no matter how hard we would have looked, prior to the acquisition."

Kathy nodded in agreement. "Do you think the points on the slide are self-evident? It's not like you're going to be standing in front of the group, able to read their reactions."

"I think so. I need to get three things across in this slide. First, Digiwise values participative decision making, collaboration, and maximum input, while acknowledging that such a process means more time to make decisions. But when decisions get made, theoretically they are better and have more initial buy-in. On the other hand, Al Cobb had managed very well with a less participative, more streamlined, faster decision-making style. So, what Al Cobb called efficient, Digiwise might have called inflexible, and what Digiwise called collaborative, Al Cobb might have called wasting time."

"The slide does introduce that idea. What's your second point?" Kathy prodded.

"That there isn't a right way and a wrong way. We need to take the best from both decision-making styles and combine them into something that works for us. We can learn from each other."

"Even when those styles make planning and implementation more difficult? Or even if they contradict a Digiwise core value, such as participation?"

"Well, that's point three," Jessica responded. "If there's one thing this acquisition has made clear, it's that communication needs to be two-way. I still need more input from the ex-Al Cobb folks about decision-making procedures that they want changed within Digiwise. Hopefully, we can talk out a good balance. I can't tell you how many times I've floated an idea or proposal around only to have someone who used to work for Al Cobb assume a final decision had been made. I'm worried that we haven't done a good enough job communicating how we make decisions here."

Speaking of Values

Jessica and Kathy pulled up Slides Two and Three. Slide Two summarized the range of potentially competing values vying for prominence in the NGS Business Unit, whereas Slide Three summarized the complexity of values integration.

"Kind of a mess," Kathy offered.

"Indeed," Jessica agreed. "We're a business unit composed of members from three different countries. We have historical values stemming from Al Cobb's fast, successful, entrepreneurial growth, our own tremendous success as a spin-off from CO, and of course our long association as part of CompuOptions—only one of the most successful and beloved high-technology companies in history. Then, of course, we have ex-Al Cobb sites in Florida, Chicago, and Norway working daily with our sites in Washington, California, Colorado, and England. Each of these sites has its own track record, each is successful, each has its own operating style, each wants its own autonomy, and each knows that it has to conform somewhat to a unified set of operating values."

"Whose values is the question. Right?"

"Right," replied Jessica.

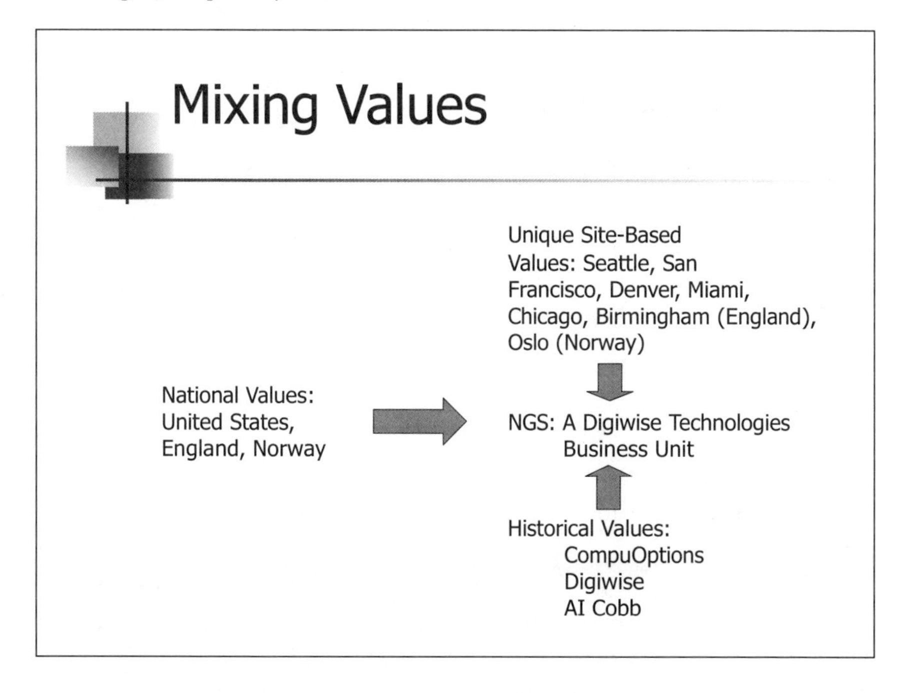

Jessica hoped that Slide Two would illustrate some of the complexity of values integration, if only in a general sense. She thought the slide might demonstrate to some employees who were getting impatient that the cultural integration was a large challenge that was not easily solved overnight.

"I do miss CO," Kathy reminisced as she looked at the slide.

"Not you too," Jessica cautioned. "I need you fully onboard with me."

Kathy had worked with CO for 15 years before moving over to Digiwise, and, like many employees, she had mixed feelings about the change. Digiwise had presented her with more opportunities for career growth, and she was very pleased with the quality of the managers who had come over from CO. Still, she had felt a sense of loss with the change. CO was legendary in the business world for both its products and quality of work life. Many of the CO values remained at Digiwise, but the company was also clearly trying to establish its own identity.

"What do you think of Slide Three?" Jessica asked, changing the subject.

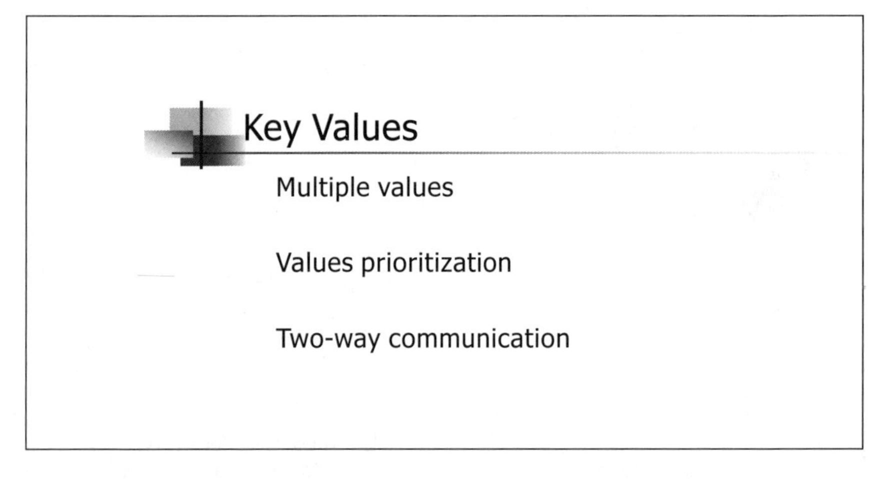

Kathy offered the obvious question that they both knew would be asked during the teleconference: "What's standing in the way of values integration?"

"Two things," Jessica responded. "First, for Al Cobb, site integration had always been tied to business effectiveness. Sites were left alone and operated on the assumption that as long as they made money, they would retain their autonomy, style, and uniqueness. For us at Digiwise, site integration is both functional and symbolic. We view integration as better for both business effectiveness and community building. We view ourselves as a large, diverse community, held together by common values and assumptions, despite being a multinational company."

"And the second reason?"

"Second, an integrated value system depends on agreement over whose values matter more. As we see, there is no lack of candidates for most important values. What needs to be made most clear to everyone is that a core set of values needs to be identified, so that the various sites share a common frame of reference. Without a shared, agreed-on set of values, we don't have heart as an organization."

"And let me guess," responded Kathy. "The means to constructing that shared set of values is via two-way communication."

"Right. For example, remember the infamous computer quandary? The one everybody in the company seems to refer to when we discuss value differences?"

Kathy nodded agreement. "That story has taken on a life of its own. And it's odd, because in that case, we really had no choice. Yet, as the story is told and retold, we seem to end up as a pushy, domineering bully of a company."

"That's the problem," added Jessica. "Granted, when we mandated a change in Chicago's and Miami's computers, the timing was awkward. The ink on the acquisition contract was barely dry, and there we were telling Al Cobb workers who had only recently been assigned brand-new computers that our IT function did not support their machines. It was impossible not to look like a bully there, even when we tried to give those machines away to employees as gifts. But, honestly, what choice was there?"

"We were in a no-win situation," Kathy agreed. "We're not in the habit of throwing away good computers, and I certainly don't think that we behaved unreasonably. All of our people have standard machines so that our IT function can plan replacement and service schedules with a reasonable amount of predictability and certainty. In the long run, we save a tremendous amount of money by having standard machines. Still, to them it smacked of a waste of money and, even worse, a power play early in the acquisition."

"There are other examples, but I think that this one gets the point across," Jessica added. "We need to do a better job of explaining the big picture, and this example is a place to start."

Jessica continued to look through her slides as the meeting approached.

Rough Going

"Now joining the meeting is . . ." came the recorded operator's voice.

"Amy Banks" completed the introduction by herself. Amy was the Miami manager, an ex-Al Cobb executive at an ex-Al Cobb site. She rounded out the meeting's participants. Jessica welcomed Amy, though secretly she was slightly aggravated that Amy was 6 minutes late, again, to a 45-minute teleconference. Because no one could see her anyway, she wrote a note to herself about sending out a memo on virtual meeting etiquette.

Jessica brought the meeting to order, reminded everyone of the agenda, and asked if everyone had her slides up on their computers. Dave Hanson, from Seattle, did not have the slides. Kathy, Jessica's assistant, was ready for this contingency and immediately emailed him a new copy. While waiting for the email to be received, Jessica decided to get a brief update from each of the sites. Phil Parks, from Birmingham, spoke first, commenting about production and asking a question about some recent benefits changes. While Jessica focused on Phil, she was positive she heard keyboard typing in the background by at least one of the other participants.

Amy Banks went next, but she didn't want to talk about production. Instead she confronted Jessica directly. "What in the world prompted you to distribute this memo about business casual dress standards? Is this for real?"

Jessica and Kathy looked at each other and sighed. "Here we go again," mouthed Kathy.

"What do you mean?" answered Jessica, stalling for time as she tried to find the memo in her laptop's files. Then she remembered. The *memo* referring to dress standards was actually only a bullet point included in a pre-agenda efax that was regularly distributed to all managers before virtual town hall meetings. The next town hall was in three weeks, and the purpose of the pre-agenda was to make sure that all managers had input into what would be discussed.

"Well, I mean a few things. Like, since when does anyone in Colorado care about how we dress in Florida? And why should you care? And how does what we wear, or not wear, affect what we get done? And what about process? Isn't this something that we all should have been consulted about? Florida is different from Chicago, or Colorado, or Norway. We may wear flowered shirts and some of us don't like shoes much, but we're good at what we do. . . ." ✦

*This case has been developed based on real organization(s) and real organizational experiences. Names, facts, and situations have been changed to protect the privacy of individuals and organizations.

Chapter 7

Why Does This Always Happen?

Philip Salem

Rosalie Garza* was waiting to meet her friends at Old Ebbitt Grill, one of Washington's oldest restaurants. She was the 58-year-old CEO of Hill Country Marketing, and this lunch would include discussion of a personnel matter. The friends at lunch included Ruth Castro, 52, head of the Texas region, headquartered in Dallas, and Patrice Carmady, 51, manager of the southeast region. Rosalie's two oldest friends, Laura Welch and Paula Sanchez, would also be at the lunch. When Rosalie became a manager in the 1970s, they were two of her first hires. These two still acted as senior account executives at the branch office now located in San Antonio. But both Rosalie and Ruth regularly consulted them about company matters. Laura and Paula had completed an investigation, at Patrice's request, about low-performing employees in the southeast region. The leather padded chairs and Victorian glass of the restaurant seemed like a sharp contrast to a discussion of employee performance.

Hill Country Marketing began as a small firm in San Antonio, Texas, after World War II. Its founding member, Linda Adams, turned over management of the firm in the mid-1970s and resigned from any official duties shortly thereafter. The consequent changes in management followed the growth of the company. Rosalie succeeded Linda and moved the headquarters to Washington, DC. The company now had four regions over the country's largest 15 states and several branch offices within each region.

The *Wall Street Journal* attributed the firm's growth to three things. First, the firm had been very sensitive to its clients. When there were problems, the firm compromised other factors to ensure a satisfied customer. Second, the firm had been innovative. The responsibilities of the account managers changed accordingly to include participating in problem-solving groups to create new marketing plans. Because Hill Country was one of the first companies to use digital technology, it was prepared for e-commerce and experienced the most rapid growth over the last 15 years. Finally, employees liked working for Hill Country Marketing. People were friendly and respectful of one another. Growth brought its own challenges, however.

Rosalie always cleared her desk before she left, stuffing her slim laptop, cell phone, and PDA into a briefcase that looked as if it were a medium-sized shoulder purse. As she turned to leave, Rosalie looked up from her desk and glanced at a postcard she had tacked to her bulletin board. The sentence "Every day do at least one thing that scares you" was displayed in white print on a black background. It was a stark reminder of the beginnings of Hill Country Marketing. Just a few years ago, Linda Adams, the founder of the firm, had given the postcard to Rosalie as a gift. Now retired, Linda had been visiting the Holocaust Museum, and she had dropped by unexpectedly to look over the renovated Washington offices and visit old friends. "Rosalie," Linda began, "not only does every CEO need to be reminded of this, but every person–period. You can get too cozy and forget that life doesn't mean much without risks." Rosalie liked the postcard because it reminded her not to get too cozy. She had just shut down her laptop and was thinking of the card again as Paula and Laura walked into the restaurant.

When everyone finally arrived, Rosalie would facilitate the luncheon discussion about the "Miami situation" and any other related topics. Of course, she would make the final decisions if needed. What was troubling her was that this matter had reached her desk, and that she had had to send Paula and Laura to investigate.

The Situation

Management of the Miami branch office wrestled with a common personnel problem. Matt Sanders, a senior account manager, was not performing. For five years, he had not recruited any new clients nor had he created or even suggested any new marketing plans. Over the period, there was an increase in complaints from his clients, and he was spending increasing amounts of time away from work tending to personal matters. The junior staff had become hostile.

Sara Bartles, manager of the department, had been a successful account manager. She was also a well-known author and trainer who mentored junior employees. She had dealt successfully with employee problems before by using the communication techniques she advocated in her training. She tried to deal with Matt by giving him positive feedback, encouraging him to improve rather than describing any of the negative feelings of the other staff.

"I don't know what more to do," she would later tell Paula. "My senior account managers suggested private meetings with Matt to get him going. I did that. I even designed smaller projects for him, ones that were easily doable, to help him feel better about himself and to empower him."

All efforts failed. In fact, Matt later told Laura, "Sara was singling me out. Everyone knew that. I was being punished."

The behaviors normally associated with effective interpersonal communication backfired. The entire situation became a crisis when Matt, who had been receiving poor evaluations from the rest of the staff and customers, actually asked Patrice Carmady, the southeast region's manager, for a raise.

Patrice consulted with Sara. Then Patrice called Rosalie. Rosalie was concerned enough to talk to Ruth, who had been Patrice's manager in San Antonio. Finally, Patrice, Ruth, and Rosalie met in Washington. They had met before in similar situations. Why does this always happen? How can it change? They decided to send Laura and Paula, respected by all involved, to investigate the situation.

The Investigation

When Laura and Paula arrived in Miami, Sara was there to greet them. She rushed them off to a happy hour attended by most of the account executives and part of the staff. Matt was not there.

"Say, didn't you hire Matt?" one of the account executives asked Paula.

"Not exactly—I did interview Matt for this job, and I did recommend him," said Paula.

"He might have been fine then, but he's a drag on the system now," said another employee.

"What ticks me off is that he gets the same raises—not commissions or bonuses—but the same raises that the rest of us get," added another.

"It's not Sara, either," said another. "What is she supposed to do if Patrice gives her only so much for raises?"

"Paula and I will have a chance to talk to all of you later this week," said Laura, ending the discussion of Matt during happy hour.

The next day, Laura and Paula attended the morning staff meeting. Sara distributed account information about the last month and discussed initiatives for the week. Matt seemed disinterested.

Toward the end of the meeting, Sam Marshall, one of the account mangers, voiced his concerns. "How the hell are we assigning accounts to account managers these days, anyway? I'm sick and tired of my account list. My clients are happy with us, but they haven't really bought anything new or bigger in a decade. Shouldn't the accounts be distributed more equally?" There were requests for data, a short discussion, and agreement to consider the matter next week. The meeting ended on time, with nearly everyone laughing and joking. Most people congratulated Sam on his victory and hurried off to meet clients.

After the meeting, Laura interviewed Matt. Matt had one of the larger offices in the company. Laura noticed off to the side a computer table with a very old computer on it. The main desk was wide and leather padded, with an executive leather padded chair. The desktop was crowded with family pictures and several pictures of the Hill Country account managers at their annual picnics. "Do they even make those anymore?" Laura asked as she motioned to the computer and chuckled.

"It does what I need it to do," Matt responded with a laugh. "It might even be one of the hand-me-downs from when you all started the company," Matt added. "We all know those stories about you all—taking chances, trying new things and all. Things were rougher then."

After telling one or two stories about his family, Matt finally focused on the issues he knew were at the top of Laura's agenda. Matt claimed Sara was out to get him. When Laura presented the data over the last year showing the downturn in Matt's performance, Matt claimed the numbers actually showed an upswing, considering economic conditions and problems in the office.

"This is the first time I've seen those numbers," said Matt. "Sara's just jealous because she knows how close I am to the rest of the staff," he argued. "Everyone else knows I'm doing well. Why would the staff have recommended me to mentor new employees?"

Laura then went to talk with Sam. Sam had the same office furniture but a more contemporary computer configuration. It was not the latest, however. There were fewer pictures on the desk, but there were the same company picnic photos. Laura looked more closely at the company photos, hoping she might learn how close Sam was to Matt. "Everyone seems so happy in these photos—does everyone go to the picnics?" Laura asked Sam. "Everyone," said Sam. "It's like a family picnic, and we have a blast."

Sam became more serious when he talked about Matt. "Matt's a good guy. He's great to have around here. He always has good things to say about everyone. I know he has been having some problems lately, but we all have problems from time to time."

Sam recognized Matt's poor performance, but he thought a negative evaluation of Matt might lead to other problems on the staff. No one had ever confronted Matt directly, as far as he knew, but others had said things to Sara about Matt.

"We don't want to hurt Matt's feelings—it would be like hurting your brother," said Sam. "We sure don't want those kinds of confrontations to be business as usual around here."

"Does anyone ever mention this lack of confrontation?" asked Laura.

"That would just cause conflict, and we don't have conflict here," said Sam coolly.

Meanwhile, Paula went to talk with Sara. When Paula arrived at Sara's office, Sara's administrative assistant told her that Sara was running a bit late, but Paula could wait in Sara's office. Paula noted how comfortable the office seemed, not realizing it was similar to the other offices. When Paula met with the executives in Washington, DC, she even commented on how the leather padded chairs at the restaurant were almost as comfortable as the one in the Miami office. There was no computer visible in the room, and only a picture of Sara's family was on her desk. She did not notice the company photos on the wall at first, but later she would discover they were the same photos others had. Also on the wall were photos of employees hugging Sara as they were giving her some token of appreciation.

Sara began the meeting by noting that Sam's outburst during the meeting was not normal. "We try to deal with the facts," she said. "Besides, nothing is going to change—Sam won his battle, and we will go through the motions of a review. The whole thing will be over by next month."

Laura noticed that when anyone spoke during the meeting, no one else challenged their opinion. People either ignored the comments or simply voiced their own unquestioned opinions. Was this because Laura and Paula were there?

"We're family here, and everyone is happy," Sara said reassuringly. "Everything is under control, except for Matt."

Laura asked Sara whether she had ever directly confronted Matt with his performance data. Sara said she had initially encouraged Matt, but at their last meeting together she had confronted him.

"When I told him his work had been slipping, Matt denied any loss of performance. Then he said, 'I've heard enough of this, and I'm not talking about this anymore.' And he stormed out of the room."

Sara blamed this last meeting for the current tension. Sara said she had not discussed this with Matt again, although she had invited him to meet again. Sara also had avoided discussing this with other staff for fear of the damage it would do to her image and the image of the Miami unit. Eventually, she had to discuss the matter with Patrice, which ultimately led to Paula being sent to Miami.

The remaining interviews followed similar patterns. One other thing emerged across the interviews. "We haven't been running smoothly since this whole thing blew up—glad the top brass sent some grease," said one employee. "We need you here because we can't keep performing like this," said another. Perhaps the most common remark was "I hope you can work this thing out between Sara and Matt." Communication about the situation was sufficiently ambiguous to allow everyone to perceive most actions as reinforcing their own positions, even though the positions were contradictory. Everyone was right.

As Rosalie Garza listened to the report, she had the uneasy feeling that she had heard all this before. Although this situation involved a particular sequence of events occurring in the Miami branch office, the situation seemed similar to situations in other branch offices in some odd ways. "Why does this always happen?" she thought. What could she do about the Miami office? *What* "always happens"? Can it be prevented? How? ✦

*This case has been developed based on real organization(s) and real organizational experiences. Names, facts, and situations have been changed to protect the privacy of individuals and organizations.

Section 2

Virtual Communication in Organizations

Briefing Paper

Virtual Communication in Organizations

The transformation of civilization through the fusion of computing and communications technologies has been predicted for at least 50 years. Now the revolution has truly begun. The impact will be as profound as was the shift from an agrarian to an industrial society.

—Michael L. Dertouzos,
Scientific American,
September 1991

Although important disagreements exist regarding the future of organizational life, scholars and practitioners agree we live in turbulent times characterized by ongoing change. Few have escaped the workquakes of the past decades. Downsizing, reengineering, unprecedented competition, rapidly changing technologies, and globalization are but a few of the factors affecting almost everyone. Most agree sophisticated communications technologies enabling virtual communication will both enable and constrain future organizational practices, processes, and individual experiences. Handy (1995), in discussing the evolving virtual organizational experience, describes transitions in a sense of place from the physical to the virtual and identifies challenges associated with eliminating from the concept of work a physical location and ongoing interpersonal interactions. The virtual organization and individuals using the technologies of today and tomorrow are challenged by extensive geographic distances, asynchronicity across time zones, resistance to change, diverse national and regional cultures, protecting personal freedom and privacy, and understanding the boundaries and limitations of information technology.

Many claim that increased technological access with resulting access to information will increase democratic processes in organizations. Others argue that this is a form of technological determinism because important distinctions exist between access to information and genuine knowledge to influence planning and decision making. One of the most fundamental challenges for virtual communication is creating values, attitudes, and behaviors for information sharing. Traditional organizations have been structured to protect and control information. Individuals are seen as owners of information, and information ownership equates with degrees of organizational power. No technology exists which, in and of itself, changes these attitudes and behaviors.

Leadership is challenged to balance between technology and face-to-face interaction. The load of organizational communication increases as the 24-hour workday becomes a reality. Managers must adapt to managing individuals and groups whom they rarely if ever see. Trust between employees and leadership replaces traditional managerial controls. Individuals face many of the challenges attributed to organizational leadership. In point of fact, virtual communication increasingly blurs distinctions between individual contributors and leadership. Workers are challenged to develop and continue to develop individual competencies related to information access and use. Assisted by virtual communications technologies, individuals and teams assume extensive problem-solving and decision-making powers, increasing their overall communication load. Workers face issues of trust, motivation to share information, technical competencies, and degrees of organizational commitment in more unstable work settings, as well as the potential for personal alienation.

Virtual communication, supported through a myriad of technological innovations, is often high risk, with potential for creative engagement of the workforce as well as potential for significant resistance to change. The challenge, then, to facilitating technological innovation is to increase the likelihood of acceptance of change while preparing those impacted for maximal use. Issues of skill requirements, training needs, the mix of workers needed, and the spatial location of jobs all are indicative of technological change and the dynamic character of virtual communication processes. Virtual communication supported by complex technologies influences information control and supports or dismantles hierarchical structures. Virtual communication is related to powershifts within organizations and competition between organizations. Traditional communication strategies of the past have emerged from relatively homogeneous organizations. Strategies for the future will be based on diversity—of employee populations, customers and markets, values, approaches, and sociopolitical world views. Problem solving and decision making will require new and improved processes. Most of us will work with technologically assisted decision tools, yet these processes are genuinely artificial intelligence and only well utilized when in the hands of capable human communicators.

Virtual communication influences organizations of today and tomorrow. It is both an exciting and difficult time. Information abounds and power is shifting, but knowledge is more than information and power. Knowledge, in the organizational sense, is the application of information to problems of organizing, innovating, and communicating.

Suggested Readings

Dertouzos, M. (1991). Communications, computers and networks. *Scientific American 265*(3), 62–69.

Fulk, J., & Collins-Jarvis, L. (2001). Wired meeting: Technological mediation of organizational gatherings. In F. M. Jablin & L. L. Putnam (Eds.), *The new handbook of organizational communication: Advances in theory, research, and methods* (pp. 624–664). Thousand Oaks, CA: Sage.

Handy, C. (1995). Trust and the virtual organization. *Harvard Business Review,* May-June, 40–50.

Mantovani, G. (1996). *New communication environments: From everyday to virtual.* London: Taylor & Francis.

Rice, R. E., & Gattiker, U. E. (1999). In F. M. Jablin & L. L. Putnam (Eds.), *The new handbook of organizational communication: Advances in theory, research, and methods* (pp. 544-581). Thousand Oaks, CA: Sage.

Roberts, K. H., & Grabowski, M. (1996). Organizations, technology, and structuring. In S. R. Clegg, C. Hardy, & W. R. Nord (Eds.), *Handbook of organization studies* (pp. 408–423). Thousand Oaks, CA: Sage.

Scott, C. R. (1999). Communication technology and group communication. In L. R. Frey, D. S. Gouran, & M. S. Poole (Eds.), *The handbook of group communication theory and research* (pp. 432–472). Thousand Oaks, CA: Sage.

Shockley-Zalabak, P. (2002). Protean places: Teams across time and space. *Journal of Applied Communication Research, 30,* 231–250.

Shockley-Zalabak, P., & Burmester, S. (2001). *The power of networked teams.* New York: Oxford.

Toffler, A. (1990). *Powershift.* New York: Bantam. ✦

Chapter 8

Where Do We Go From Here?

Edward C. Brewer

Phil Sanders,* a middle-aged male who was old enough to be Trish's father, opted to forgo the early retirement option and stay with the company. Both Phil and Trish had been with Liatco Enterprises for about five years, with Phil coming to the company a month after Trish was hired. Trish, inventory and production director, had a college degree; Phil, research and sales director, had more education and experience than Trish. Phil was known in the organization for being somewhat aloof and for having research ideas that were progressive yet often unrealistic, given the resources of the organization.

Suddenly Colleagues

The year 2000 had marked a transition of ownership. The transition was an emotional one for Liatco Enterprises, a supplier of fire protection equipment, whose western Kentucky office dealt primarily with fire extinguishers. A staff of 94 had been reduced to 12 and then expanded to 40. As a result, remaining staff members took on additional work responsibilities. This, of course, caused stress and tension in the office. The early retirement and buyout had been offered to senior members of the staff. Several younger staff members had benefited from the retirement offers due to the vacancies created by the departing employees. Trish Copeland, who at 28 was one of the youngest members of the staff, found herself 1 of the 12 out of the original 94 employees who were able to keep their jobs. Twenty-eight new employees soon joined these 12 to compose the new staff of the western Kentucky regional office.

Phil's career rank was higher than Trish's, but both of their positions had the same promotion potential. Phil, however, saw himself as Trish's superior. Even though he and Trish were suddenly on equal footing as colleagues, Phil continued to treat Trish as a subordinate. They shared a cubicle with about eight feet between their desks, but Trish tried to keep to herself as much as possible because she was somewhat intimidated by Phil. Though their conversations were limited, Phil sought to maintain control.

"Did you get the Eldridge file?"

"Yes," Trish replied, "but do you have the numbers from last month's inventory?"

"No, you'll receive them when I have time to get to them, but I want that Eldridge file on my desk by noon."

There were no pleasantries and no casual exchanges. Sometimes they would email each other instead of speaking, even though only a matter of feet separated their desks.

A Trio of Decision Makers

As the organization began to adapt to the new ownership, procedures had to be examined and refined. One such procedure was the inventory system, known as STAR, which had some glitches that needed to be worked out for it to be considered timely and accurate. The western Kentucky office was considered a demonstration laboratory for the organization; thus the office was expected to set the standards and procedures that the other regional offices would eventually follow. The western Kentucky office had special authority to make modifications to various systems (such as the inventory management system) that would promote consistency within the organization as well as help to integrate all offices into a central system. Phil and Trish, along with their boss, Marshall, would be attending a presentation on Monday at organizational headquarters in Phoenix, Arizona, to discuss inventory management possibilities.

Marshall Barrone, who was 60, had been with the organization for only a few months. While he had the legitimate authority as manager, Marshall had not yet earned the respect of Phil and Trish. In fact,

Phil thought that he should have been promoted to the manager's position. The relationships among the three were strained. Just last night Marshall had asked Phil, "Have you sent the new brochures to the printer yet?"

Phil responded rather sarcastically, "I am good at my job and take care of my responsibilities in a timely manner."

Trish just rolled her eyes. It seemed as if Marshall could never get a straight answer from Phil, and he was never sure if Trish's nonverbal indications of aggravation were directed at Phil, or him, or both. Conversations were always related to business, never personal issues.

The morning of the meeting all three had arrived at the airport separately. They had not ridden together, even though they all lived within two miles of one another. Before he left, Phil had told his wife, "Marshall doesn't understand our business well enough yet, and Trish is just a kid."

Actually, it wasn't just Trish's age that bothered him. He had never been happy that a woman held her position. "I think I should be going alone. I am the most qualified person to make this decision as to what inventory system we should be using." He sulked all the way to the airport and dreaded the four-hour plane trip.

Trish, too, had concerns. She told her husband that morning, "Phil doesn't respect me and I don't know what Marshall thinks about the inventory system, or even how he feels about us." Trish continued, "I am the best person to decide what system we should use to keep track of our inventory. After all, I am the inventory and production director." She stopped to get a cup of coffee at Two Sisters Café on her way to the airport and ran into Marshall doing the same thing.

"Good morning, Trish," Marshall said.

"Morning," Trish replied.

They paid for their coffees and headed to their separate vehicles.

"See you at the airport," Marshall said.

"OK" was Trish's only reply.

Two hours later they were on the plane together. The secretary had made the reservations, so they were sitting together in seats 3A, 3B, and 3C. Trish had the window seat and felt somewhat claustrophobic. Marshall was in the middle seat, and Phil had the aisle seat. Marshall finally broke the uncomfortable silence with the words "Good morning." Phil and Trish responded in unison, "Morning." They didn't speak for the remainder of the flight. Trish read the *Wall Street Journal.* Phil perused the *New York Times.* Marshall pulled out a novel entitled *Blood Ties.* He wondered if the process of deciding on what inventory system to use would be as brutal as some of the scenes in his book.

When they arrived in Phoenix, they were forced to talk to one another as they arranged for the rental car to make the drive to the national office. It was a half-hour drive to their destination.

Trish asked Marshall, "Who is making the presentation today?"

Marshall replied, "Jerry Matthews, from MB Consulting, is presenting an inventory management option for us to consider."

Phil added, "I understand he is a very good speaker and has an excellent product."

"Yeah, I heard that too," Marshall replied.

For the remainder of the drive they discussed how different the landscape in Arizona was from their western Kentucky home. This was probably the first time the three of them had discussed anything besides business, but it seemed to be a safe topic that didn't require much self-disclosure.

The meeting began at 10:00 A.M. and was over about noon. At the luncheon that followed, Trish and Phil mingled with some of the friends they had made within the organization over the past five years. Trish sat at a table with friends from the Phoenix and Cleveland offices. Phil had lunch with some golfing buddies from the Houston office. Marshall attended a luncheon meeting for managers. The three met in the main lobby at 2:00 P.M., as they had agreed earlier. They drove to the airport to catch a 4:30 P.M. flight. Because of the difference in time zones, this flight would get them home around 9:30 P.M. A delay at the airport in Memphis put them home closer to 11:00 P.M.

Marshall thought that during the flight home they could discuss the presentation. "I think we should stick with our current STAR system and just make the needed adjustments," Marshall stated. "John has made it clear that he does not support any system that would require double entries." John Brown was the district manager and Marshall's immediate boss.

"I agree," Trish added. "Our staff is already overworked with all of the cutbacks and extra work due to the transition."

Phil responded in a slightly irritated voice. "I think we should adopt the REPS system that Jerry introduced and use the STAR system to do the things REPS can't do."

"Well, let's sleep on it and discuss it together in the office in the morning," Marshall replied.

"Fine," Phil said in an obviously aggravated manner.

"We are all tired," Trish suggested. "Perhaps discussing it in the morning after a good night's sleep is a good idea." Trish didn't respect Marshall's authority, but she happened to agree with his sentiments and felt vindicated that her choice was right and was going to be accepted by Marshall. It felt good to think that her arrogant coworker, Phil, would be put in his place.

Electronic Escapade

After a short night's sleep, Trish arrived in the office 15 minutes early, at 7:45 A.M. She was surprised to see Phil already at his desk. Phil, who had arrived 45 minutes earlier that morning, had been busy typing on his computer. He was in the break room pouring himself a cup of coffee, smiling smugly, when Trish sat at her desk and turned on her computer. She checked her email messages, as was her practice every morning. When she got to a message from Phil, which had been sent only moments earlier, she turned visibly red. She could feel the heat in her cheeks as her anger flared. Phil had sent an email to Jerry, the consultant, and had copied Trish and Marshall. The email read, in part:

> The decision to go with the solution proposed by Trish and Marshall is not exportable to other divisions. Therefore, the western Kentucky office has forgone its responsibility as a demonstration laboratory in favor of the simplest solution for western Kentucky. . . . Other divisions will have to rely on REPS while western Kentucky, in effect, will ignore the problem of keeping a system that is incompatible with those of the other divisions. Thus, sharing inventory information becomes problematic.

Trish was angry because, rather than wait and talk things through to make local recommendations together, Phil had come in early and put his thoughts into an email, basically denouncing the decision to choose STAR that he expected Marshall would make, while at the same time insulting her (and Marshall, for that matter) in addition to demeaning her perspective. Trish's reactive response was to immediately fire off an email of her own to Phil to defend her position, copying all the recipients of Phil's email:

> I hate to be reactive instead of proactive, but that seems to be my survival mode these days. I agree with much of what Phil said, but I do have specific reservations and concerns, not the least of which is

> that I'm NOT prepared to throw in the towel on western Kentucky's demonstration effort and put faith in REPS to give us the inventory data we need, especially since NONE of us at western Kentucky has spent any time using it and we're not ANY more sure of its accuracy than that of STAR. And NONE of western Kentucky's staff has time to do the double entry required by REPS. I won't give up the certainty of STAR for the maybe of REPS providing the data we need.

Trish had even put some words in capital letters to express her assertiveness. Although Phil and Trish had yet to sit down with Marshall and discuss this issue, both presumed that it was quite clear what Marshall's decision was going to be.

Tuesday was the morning Marshall's Rotary Club met for breakfast, so he didn't arrive in the office until 8:30 A.M. "Good morning," he said as he greeted Sue, the receptionist. Sue nodded acknowledgment as she talked on the phone and handed Marshall his messages. Marshall glanced at the yellow slips of paper as he headed to his office. Three messages were from various sales representatives who hoped to become his source for office supplies, and one was from the national office in Phoenix, reminding him of a conference call that afternoon at 3:00 P.M. He turned on his computer, sat down at his desk, and reached for the local paper. By the time he had perused the headlines, his computer was up and running. It was time to check his email messages. He intended to meet with Phil and Trish in the conference room at 10:00 A.M. to discuss the inventory management system and the reasons to stick with the STAR system.

Within minutes Marshall could feel his blood pressure rise and his cheeks flush as he burned with anger. He had just finished reading both Phil and Trish's email messages, and he was livid. Not only had Phil denounced what he expected Marshall's decision would be, but he had also included outsiders in his insult. Marshall quickly fired off a response to Phil and copied Trish:

> While I can understand your sentiments and respect your right to disagree with me, I resent your inclusion of outsiders in this discussion. I loathe the idea of any double entry effort and the wastefulness that causes. Even when we disagree, we should present a united front to other regional offices, and especially to outsiders. We will discuss this issue in the conference room at 10:00 A.M.

Phil didn't wait until 10:00 A.M. to respond. He sent off another caustic email further deriding Marshall's decision and more fully outlining his feelings concerning Trish's ineptness. He copied everyone from his first message and added Jerry's associate at the consulting firm, the district manager, John, and two friends from the Houston office:

> It seems that Marshall hasn't fully considered the consequences of the STAR system and Trish doesn't seem to understand inventory management at all. What a shame it would be to make such a foolish decision because of one or two hardheaded employees who fail to fully understand our business.

Within minutes Trish had composed and sent a response, feeling that she needed to defend herself. She replied to all who had received Phil's last email and added two of her friends in Phoenix:

> It seems obvious that the person who is hardheaded and has not fully considered the consequences of both the STAR and REPS systems is Phil. In fact, if Phil truly understood our inventory, perhaps he would be able to see the problems associated with REPS. Maybe Phil should stick to marketing and research.

By 9:45 A.M. (just over two hours from Phil's first email message) the conflict had escalated to include about a dozen people, most of whom should not have been privy to the discussion. At 9:55 A.M., John, the district manager, sent a scathing reply concerning the unprofessional conduct. John, however, sent his email only to Phil, Trish, and Marshall:

> The correspondence of this morning has been disheartening. I am deeply disappointed in the unprofessional conduct of the western Kentucky office. Most alarming, however, is the fact that these messages have been shared with people not only outside of your office but also outside the Liatco organization. I should hope that you would want to present a united front to both your colleagues and those who are not a part of our company. You represent Liatco to the world, and this is not the type of impression I want you to make. I can only hope that you will agree. The items discussed electronically this morning should have taken place in private in the western Kentucky office. Only after you had hashed out the details should you have shared—in a united way—your decision and the reasons for that decision. I will be in Phoenix the remainder of this week, but I will meet with Marshall sometime at the beginning of next week. In the meantime, I expect you to take care of this matter in a professional manner among yourselves. Limit your use of email to the western Kentucky office until I have met with Marshall.

It was now time for Marshall to go to the conference room for the scheduled meeting with Phil and Trish. ✦

*This case has been developed based on real organization(s) and real organizational experiences. Names, facts, and situations have been changed to protect the privacy of individuals and organizations.

Chapter 9

Caught in the Intranet

Jensen Chung

Jean Kopel* was stunned, staring blankly at the computer screen. She looked at the email again. Yes, it was about her. President Scott Longman of the Tempflo Asian-Pacific branch was admitting in public that, in hiring Jean, he had hired the wrong person to be director of the Engineering Department.

The Tempflo Company had set up an intranet three months before. Since then, several blunders had occurred on the email system. Because the IT group used a different configuration for the email *REPLY* command, several colleagues had inadvertently sent personal messages to the entire company. Jean had been amused initially, especially by romantic or flirtatious notes sent to her and everyone else by mistake. But, with this latest blunder, she was no longer amused. Apparently in response to complaints about her from the engineers in the Browser Group, Scott had sent an email saying:

> . . . Thank you for your information and feedback. I was surprised to know that a manager from the U.S. headquarters would have such a level of incompetence. I will see to it that she improves. As the Asian-Pacific branch's president, who was instrumental in bringing her over, I apologize to you. We will be more careful in the future when selecting managers from headquarters. . . .

"This is horrendous," Jean thought. She reflected on how Scott had appeared so nice to her from day one. She had solved so many problems for him. Yet, as soon as a few employees ganged up on her, he yielded to their pressure. All along, she had believed that with the two of them working together, they could transform this branch. How naive she had been, Jean suddenly realized.

Jean resisted the impulse to send Scott Longman a nasty message. She decided to take a shower and wait until the next day to get more information before reacting. She told herself to just cool down and sleep before dealing with the humiliation. But Jean could not stop worrying about what Scott had done. How could she? Even a shower, which normally stimulated her to think of innovative solutions (including the one that had helped her win the $85,000 patent for the company), did not help. The warm water proved no respite from Scott's treachery.

Was I Sold Out?

Jean pondered her working and social relationship with Scott Longman. The day she arrived in this Pacific Rim country, Scott had taken her to dinner and told her that she was the first woman to be hired by the branch since headquarters had delegated the authority to hire and fire managers of local branches. He also said that he had argued on her behalf to convince the hiring panel that she was the best choice to head the Engineering Department, which consisted of the software section and the hardware section. To help her settle in, Scott had asked the Department of Human Resources in the branch to assign a person to take care of her housing, transportation, and other adjustment needs. He had been so thoughtful, even bringing hangers and phone cards from his own home to her.

Jean had been trying to reciprocate by supporting Scott. Since the intranet was built for the company, employees in the hardware section (called "Hardies") had accessed a lot of files that had not been made public before. Hardies started expressing particular interest in many policy issues, including opposition to the proposed collaboration project between the Asian-Pacific branch and a local semiconductor provider. In several spontaneous instant-messaging conferences, they had become unusually vocal, and Jean had been striving to come up with all kinds of arguments to support Scott's proposals.

About 30 expatriates from the U.S. headquarters had been transferred to the local branch, and they often socialized after work in groups of four or five. After the intranet was installed, most of the 30 "Yankees" frequently used multimedia facilities to engage in instant messaging, discussing both job-related business and social topics.

They gradually formed a clique, communicating much more frequently than before. President Scott Longman had not been included in their chat group. Jean was in the group but never initiated and seldom joined the conversations.

Most of these expatriates, particularly supervisors, managers, and engineers, did not like Scott's management style. In their chat rooms, for example, they often made fun of Scott's habit of routinely inviting individual employees to lunch with him at a nearby restaurant. "Who goes to lunch?" had become an often-cracked inside joke among the expatriates, who ate their homemade sandwiches at their desks. They argued that Scott should spend the money and time in social functions with local businesspeople, not with employees. "Scott should lunch with clients, not us," a supervisor once whined.

Furthermore, since the intranet allowed employees more access to shared files, lower level employees could now browse the spreadsheet analyses on the electronic resources. Engineers in the software section ("Softies") pointed out that rank-and-file colleagues knew more about clients' problems than Scott did.

After hearing this complaint about Scott's not having enough contacts with clients, Jean had managed to connect her engineering department with a local university and cosponsored two open-to-the-public workshops. The two workshops attracted media attention and were successfully publicized. Three hundred people, including Tempflo employees, attended the workshops to learn about state-of-the-art animation techniques, audio file resources, and network administration. As far as Jean knew, at least one business deal was struck as a result of the workshops, even though generating businesses had not been the main purpose of the workshops. She gave sole credit to Scott by purposefully working behind the scenes while Scott hosted the workshops.

One week after the workshops, Jean was browsing the branch president's monthly reports to headquarters, which she had never accessed, and came across Scott's report to headquarters about the success of the workshops. She noticed that her name was left out. Although somewhat disappointed and a bit suspicious of Scott's motivation, Jean didn't make a fuss. She told herself that she should be a good team player and it was all right to let the leader take the credit.

Now, however, having re-read this most recent and damaging email, Jean reconsidered her earlier suspicions. Perhaps they were reasonable. Other curious incidents had occurred. Two months ago, for example, she had expressed to Scott some reservations about Lucy, who supervised the Browser Group (the "Browsers"), a special task force consisting of engineers from both the software and the hardware sections, who were researching and developing browsers. Jean had casually mentioned to Scott that Lucy lacked enthusiasm in conveying to Jean the needs and expectations of the Browsers. Coincidence or not, a couple of days after Jean had made this remark to Scott, Lucy became quite cold to her.

Jean had hoped to have a good relationship with Lucy. Lucy, a local-born employee, was the most senior in the hardware section and was the only local in the Browser Group who had ever worked in U.S. headquarters, albeit for only a year. Jean had noticed that many engineers would look up to Lucy when making decisions at the project group meetings. Jean also observed that, unlike other locals, Lucy always spoke English at work (which was appreciated by this group of multinational colleagues), but she spoke the local language with her resident colleagues after work. Indeed, Lucy provided a bridge between cultures. A week before the incident of Scott's damaging email, Jean had inadvertently learned that Lucy had invited all the local Browsers to her home for a party celebrating a culture festival, a fact Jean had learned because of another misdirected email—a Browser had mistakenly included Jean in his emailed apology to Lucy for not being able to attend the gathering.

Jean reflected more upon this. Although the spoken and written language used in the Asian-Pacific branch was English, local employees spoke their own language among themselves. Scott had been living in this Asian-Pacific country 10 years and could speak the local language fluently. Jean had once mentioned to Scott that she was not fluent in the local language, but he reassured her, "Oh, forget it. No need to spend time on that. I would rather you learned more Java language than the local tongue." At the time, she had thanked him for his reassuring words. But in light of this new evidence, she suspected that he was being cagey, perhaps keeping her separated from the local employees by language so that he could solidify that role for himself.

After the long shower, Jean tried to put herself to sleep. Instead of counting sheep, she worked on translating an executive summary into the local language. The translation didn't succeed in putting her to sleep, either.

At 4 A.M., Jean took a tablet of melatonin, provided by Scott, who said it would put her to sleep when work anxieties caused insomnia.

He had said, "Guess what, its antioxidants can keep you young, too." However, the melatonin didn't work. She got up and did some yoga stretches, a practice that she had taken up also at Scott's recommendation.

Jean decided to read the email again when she discovered a new message appeared right after Scott Longman's "apology" to the group. A former U.S. colleague, now in the hardware section, was forwarding Scott's apology message to her. In the postscript to the message, the man explained to Jean that employees in the Browser Group had obtained some of Jean's personnel evaluation criteria from the intranet and had subsequently complained to Scott that Jean evaluated subordinates "solely on results, ignoring their effort."

"Evaluating based on how hard they work rather than how the job gets done?" Jean pondered, bewildered. The company manual never mentioned effort but rather results. "Is that an unwritten practice in this branch? How come I have never heard of it?" Jean was perplexed.

The President Promised to Fix

At work the next morning, Jean could not concentrate. At 11:00, she received a phone call from the colleague who had forwarded Scott's message to her last night. After speaking with him, Jean decided to write Scott a very simple email, saying:

> Scott, I was shocked by a colleague's phone call informing me of your response to the complaints of a few Browser group members about me.

Upon pressing the *SEND* button, Jean had second thoughts as to whether it was wise to communicate through email instead of confronting Scott face-to-face. She then calmed herself by the thought that her message was crafted tactfully: She had made no mention of knowing the Browsers' complaints. Nor had she mentioned having read the entire content of Scott's message, thinking this would test his candidness. She had been polite in her wording.

Half an hour later, Scott replied:

> Jean, I'm terribly sorry. I apologize. After answering hundreds of email messages, I was so tired last night when I responded to the complaint from the Browser Group that my message was quite hasty. I realize that my reply to them was a big gaffe. Let's talk. I will

cancel my lunch engagement today. Let's have lunch together and discuss this matter. Scott

Scott's email struck Jean as insincere. She reasoned, "If he was so sorry, why hadn't he picked up the phone and called me?" But then, by the same token, she had to question her own motivation for emailing rather than phoning herself.

Presently, Jean did phone Scott's direct line. She declined his offer for lunch, saying she preferred to meet in his office.

With a mask of a smile, Jean walked into Scott's office past two secretaries, who didn't return her smile. This struck Jean as unusual. Normally, the secretaries would have greeted her with broad smiles. And normally Jean would have had a mug of coffee in her hand when walking into Scott's office, particularly when discussing relatively trivial business. This time, she went empty-handed.

Scott opened his office door to greet Jean before she could even knock. He started to invite her into his private conference room but hesitated. He instead asked Jean to sit down on the sofa by his desk. Again, he apologized. He explained that he had piggybacked the wrong message for replying to the Browsers, and the *REPLY* command in that email system had been set up to reply to all employees in the company, so unfortunately everyone had read his message demeaning Jean. Jean demanded a second message from Scott to the Browsers retracting his statements. She had also come in planning to demand a formal letter of apology, but she decided to hold off that demand for the time being. For his part, Scott, although clearly embarrassed, argued that as the Browsers were still very upset, he should let them calm down before he sent them the message Jean demanded. "I promise to write the second message after Christmas. It's only three weeks away anyway," Scott lowered his voice beseechingly. Jean reluctantly agreed.

It Wasn't a Revolt, But...

Returning to her office, Jean found several email messages from friends at the U.S. headquarters asking "What the heck's going on?" Obviously, Scott's "hired the wrong person" message to the Browsers had reached other parts of the company. Jean fell into depression again—until getting a phone call from Nancy Mooney, inviting her to meet for dinner.

Nine years older than Jean, Nancy had been Jean's classmate in communication classes during their college years together. At that time, Nancy was a software engineer, Jean a communication major. Later, after working as a human resources officer for a few years, Jean had studied computer programming. With Jean's move to Tempflo, the two had found themselves working together again; Nancy Mooney was the director of human resources. During an email chat session, one engineer in the branch had nicknamed Nancy "The Moon," as opposed to "The Sun" for President Scott and "Star" for Jean. Nancy accepted the nickname by using it as her email signature.

That evening at the restaurant, the first question Jean asked Nancy was if she had read Scott's message to the Browsers.

"That's why I called you. . . . I could understand how you must be feeling," answered Nancy. "On a positive note, if you had heard other people's comments about Scott's message last night, you certainly would feel much better. Jean, it's not your fault, this whole faux pas. I would focus now on how to repair the damage."

After Jean explained that Scott had promised to send a second message of correction, Nancy suggested that Jean look into the cause of the complaint.

"I already did," said Jean, beaming. "This afternoon I wrote myself a 12-page memo trying to identify the root causes of the mutiny. They can be a potential list of complaints, too."

"You go, girl! That'll be another chapter of the textbook you said you've been writing for yourself, right?!"

Jean smiled in agreement. Her friend Nancy was like a beloved older sister.

"Jean, I'm reminded of the days when we were in that corporate communication class together. When a bunch of guys were arguing with the professor about her grading scale, you were busy writing down several options for managing the conflict from the perspective of a professor. What an attitude!"

Jean's expression showed her appreciation for Nancy's compliment on that long-past incident. After a pause, she returned to the present matter, saying, "To avoid similar reply-all blunders, I'm proposing a negotiation with the intranet provider to set up some safeguards. They should be able to come up with message-retracting capabilities after a warning signal. Or they can increase training in intranet email protocols."

Nancy praised Jean's problem-solving ideas and leadership skills and asked her if she went out to lunch with colleagues.

"Don't we folks from America bring our sandwiches for lunch?" Jean sighed.

"Yes, but not every day. Besides, you are different from other Yankees, especially from other techies. You are leading all kinds of people. I mean, folks from all kinds of backgrounds. Most Yankees don't have the same role as you do. They don't need to communicate as much as you do."

Taking a deep breath, Jean looked up to the ceiling, laughing. "Com-mu-ni-cate!" She raised her voice, almost shouting. "Compared with senior colleagues or senior professionals, I spend more time exchanging information and opinions with professionals in other companies. Now that we have an intranet in place, we rely on that system to communicate with each other. It allows us to communicate with a whole range of people throughout the company. Sharing information has sparked more dialogue, as we both know."

"And more power to employees, too," Nancy intoned.

"There you go. The more information employees share, the more questions they raise, and the more managers have to justify. I feel I have more bosses than before the Intranet Era."

"That's all right, Jean. Remember managing up?"

"Yes, managing-up bosses . . . there is another new big boss."

"Who?" Nancy raised her eyebrow.

"The intranet. I feel these communication tools are increasing our communication needs! We thought we had brought in servants; we actually have brought in masters—making us do more."

"I agree. The intranet is like laundry machines and microwave ovens. They save us a whole lot of time but at the same time push us to do even more work."

Nancy continued, "What the Browsers were complaining about is debatable, but if you chatted with them over a lunch or a dinner, don't you think debates might become discussions? Most of them are locals after all, you know; thus they are people of consequence to this branch location."

Resting her chin on her hands, Jean contemplated Nancy's suggestion. It sounded a familiar ring. Suddenly she remembered that a colleague had told her that Scott spent half a year eating out with local colleagues when he assumed his duties as president. "Maybe," she thought, "he was doing the smart thing, even though some of our Yankees made fun of it."

The two friends conversed throughout dinner. On parting that evening Nancy said, "Since Scott has given his word to send a corrective message, you should continue in good form." She added, "The revolt won't bring you down. After all, it isn't a revolt."

He Is My Trusted President No More

A month after Christmas, Jean went to Scott's office with a gloomy look. She asked when he would write his promised overturn message.

He looked perplexed. "Oh, I'm sorry. I thought we had put that matter to rest when you said 'It's all right' the other day."

"When did I say that?"

"When I mentioned the issue to you in my email message about my contact with the Browsers."

Now she remembered. In that message, Scott had admitted to her that, according to his individual interviews with the Browsers, not every Browser had agreed to the complaint about her that was sent to him. Scott had then repeated his apology to Jean, adding his intentions to make it clear that some Browsers disagreed with the complaint. Jean had emailed back, "That's all right."

Apparently "That's all right" had been misinterpreted by Scott. What she had meant was that it was all right for him to clarify the issue in his retraction.

The following day, all concerned finally received Scott's email, as promised to Jean. She read the long-awaited message with some relief, but her distrust of Scott remained. She forwarded his email to Nancy, with a brief note mentioning her reservations about Scott's character.

A Turning Point

A month later, Jean was suddenly transferred back to the U.S. headquarters with the tentative title of senior programmer, pending a new position. The title was a demotion back to the position she had held for six years prior to going to Asia. Scott appointed Lucy, the head of the hardware section and the leader of the Browser Group, to be acting director of the Engineering Department.

To ease her transition back to headquarters, Jean was granted a two-week vacation.

When Jean returned to work, a friend at the headquarters' Human Resources Department told her privately that, in an earlier proposal by the personnel vice president, Jean had been in line to succeed Scott Longman when he retired. After the two successful workshops, headquarters has been very impressed with her accomplishments.

"The vice president overseeing your department learned of your accomplishments through informal intranet discussions," the friend said, "but then that email incident caused a series of personnel chain reactions." The friend then added, "Thanks to the intranet, folks here know pretty much about what's going on out there in the branches."

Jean was frustrated and angry, but then she learned more developing news that lifted her spirits: While Jean was on vacation, her friend and mentor Nancy was also transferred back to U.S. headquarters, promoted to become one of three vice presidents overseeing Human Resources, Training, and Corporate Communication for the entire company.

Physically rejuvenated by the two-week vacation, Jean returned to her office and logged on the computer.

She went first to a message from Nancy that read:

> Hi Jean,
>
> I have nominated you to be one of the candidates for the position of the Director of Human Resources. You will need to be interviewed and to make a presentation pretty soon. Come by ASAP for details.
>
> Nancy ✦

*This case has been developed based on real organization(s) and real organizational experiences. Names, facts, and situations have been changed to protect the privacy of individuals and organizations.

Chapter 10

The Challenges of Radical Change

Andrew J. Flanagin

Introduction

Choruses of "nice to meet you" were ringing through the office as the introductions took place. As I was presenting my coworker Cheryl* to the departmental manager, I caught a glimpse across the office of Mary, a longtime employee of the government organization that had brought me in as a computer systems consultant. As I was beginning, "Cheryl, this is . . . ," I saw Mary reaching toward her computer monitor with a brush dripping with Wite-Out® to correct a typo she had made. It was a combination of the formal introduction process I was in the midst of, coupled with the hesitation that an outsider instinctively feels, that stopped me from yelling out.

Now somewhat distracted, I proceeded with the introduction ritual, while at the same time wondering whether my task was to be even more difficult than I had been led to believe. Although Mary had caught herself before actually touching up her computer monitor with the white liquid, it suggested that there was a long way to go before workers here would accept the changes to come. How was I supposed to implement a completely new computerized work process system in a department where some employees were obviously fairly new to computers? Could it be that the average employee still habitually used Wite-Out® rather than the backspace key? If so, how would they ever accept the dramatic changes that I was in charge of implementing? How would I convince them that the new system was better than the manual one they had used for decades and that change was good?

The Consulting Practice and Work Processes at Personnel Services

Consulting firms normally bid against each other in order to procure a consulting contract. Usually, a detailed bid is derived from a set of specifications that is drawn up to reflect the nature of the work to be performed for the client. Consultants' bids typically include the scope of work to be performed, a time frame for completion, specific products or *deliverables* that will be part of the job, the qualifications of the firm and possibly of the individuals who will work on the project, and a cost estimate for the work to be done. Through such a process, several consulting firms had competed for a contract to automate and modify the functions of Personnel Services, a large governmental organization.

The overarching task of Personnel Services was to process applicants for the agency's several open job positions (there were 524 separate job titles and, at any given time, dozens of positions that needed to be filled). More specifically, Personnel Services had three main responsibilities: job classification, test development and administration, and recruitment and staffing. Thus, workers in Personnel Services were in charge of classifying all of the agency's jobs by defining the responsibilities of and qualifications for each, developing appropriate assessment criteria in order to evaluate the qualifications of many job applicants, and recruiting internal and external job applicants and selecting the best candidate(s) from among them.

The first two of these tasks—job classification and test development—involved specific education and training and were handled by a very small proportion of the Personnel Services staff. By contrast, job recruitment and staffing required the efforts of approximately three dozen employees at any given time. Mary, whom I had met on my first day in the office as she nearly marked up her computer monitor with Wite-Out,® was a typical employee in the Personnel Services department. Her job was to log in and track job applicants as part of the recruitment and staffing process. At the time, this process was done manually on note cards and files, as it had been done for the past 20 years or more. All job processing was performed using paper records where a file was created for each individual, which was then passed physically from person to person in the department in order to track the progress of each applicant through the job selection process. Old files were sorted manually and stored in huge filing cabinets. After applicants were recommended for interviews based on their test results, departments would interview them and make the final hiring decision; then Personnel Services would finalize the process, filling the position and closing the job request. Like other personnel workers, Mary spent the majority of her time doing data entry and shepherding batches of job applicants through the lengthy testing and evaluation process.

Based on our bid, Leeds and Associates, a medium-sized management systems consulting firm, had been awarded the contract for the project at Personnel Services. The new applicant tracking system, or ATS as it was dubbed, would replace the manual job recruitment and staffing system that had been used at Personnel Services for the last several decades. The ATS, however, would not rely on paper records at all but would instead be entirely computerized. This was to be a radical change for the Personnel Services department.

The Consultant's Role

At the time, I was a fairly new consultant who had been out of college for only a few years and had just completed my first year working for Leeds. Although I had been involved with perhaps a dozen different consulting projects at this point in my career, this was my first project to manage. As manager, I had full responsibility to bring the project in successfully: on time, on budget, and to the satisfaction of the client. I was the leader of the three-person design team that had approximately six months to complete the redesign and implementation of the work process system that Leeds had contracted to supply. In this case, the cost and time deadlines were very strict, since data from the system had to tie in with a parallel system from another department by a specific date and because any cost overruns would require a special meeting of a legislative body in order to be approved.

My areas of expertise were in software design and work process engineering, with an emphasis on database systems. In other words, I designed and built software that kept track of large amounts of data, enabling many users to dynamically access and update information from remote locations, whether in different parts of the same building or different parts of the world. Although the technical side of the job could be complex, it was also rather straightforward. Networked computers, database systems, and computer programming languages were the tools that were used to accomplish the necessary communication and information sharing tasks. In this respect, my job was like that of an air traffic controller: To avoid conflicts, I had to know where everything was at all times and make sure that the pieces fit together in a very specific manner.

The most interesting part of the job, however, was the work process reengineering portion of my work. In this role my job was to assess and modify the range of tasks that constituted the basic functions that workers performed in the completion of the organization's mission, of which they were only one part. This aspect of the job was also the most difficult because it dealt fundamentally with social change. In essence, work process reengineering involved locating the most appropriate areas for change in an organization (if any) and then convincing people who are typically entrenched in certain ways of working that there may be advantages to doing their jobs differently. Ultimately, this process required working closely with both management and employees in order to understand organizational objectives, the nature of people's work, and the underlying processes that were important for accomplishing organizational and individual goals. My job was made more difficult by virtue of the fact that, as an external consultant, I was an organizational outsider and was at least initially regarded with a certain degree of distrust.

Implementation of the ATS

The ATS implementation was particularly challenging, since several of the workers had never done any of their jobs via computer, working instead exclusively with handwritten or typed files that they moved physically from place to place. Furthermore, in addition to automating existing processes, the ATS was also to include a number of new reports and processes that would capitalize on the novel data that would be a fundamental part of the system. Finally, it was anticipated that the ATS would also initiate a number of entirely new functions that could not be predicted until after workers began to appreciate the capabilities of the new system and to recognize the potential changes that were possible.

Past experience had taught me that the most successful implementations of new systems capitalized as much as possible on existing ways of doing things. For example, such mundane strategies as using existing terminology in new environments to make people more comfortable had proven effective in the past. I recalled, for instance, an office automation project where I had named one portion of the process the "brown folder" function, mimicking the brown folders that had been used to store completed files. This made the new way of doing things more intuitive and familiar to the workers, which led them to accept the changes more easily. I had also learned that taking the input of employees seriously was crucial, as was finding ways to make workers a part of the change process. I knew that this helped reduce the shock of change, provide some sense of ownership of the new methods, and diminish the extent to which they perceived me as an outsider who was inflicting my ways of working upon their own.

The Organizational Environment of Personnel Services

Most of the workers in Personnel Services had been with the department for a very long time, many starting immediately after high school and working their way up the hierarchy for as long as 30 years or more. Although the division offered free skills training as part of a staff education program, the vast majority of employees did not take advantage of this opportunity, preferring to continue in their positions long-term or until the few opportunities for advancement in their own department eventually became available. Thus, due to long tenures and low turnover, employees in the Personnel Services department were extremely familiar with one another, having worked together in close quarters for many years.

Like any group of people under similar circumstances, cliques of workers had developed and some people were better respected than others. For example, Monica, who had been in the department for about 10 years, was friendly, well liked by almost everyone, and highly regarded for her thorough understanding of job procedures and her computer knowledge. Although she was relatively new to the department, she was admired for her sense of humor, her approachable nature, and her high knowledge level. In fact, when discrepancies arose as to how to properly interpret nuances of the job selection criteria, Monica was one of a handful of people to whom others turned for advice. Furthermore, on several occasions Monica had been called on to settle personal conflicts between workers that had gotten out of hand. So although she was not the highest ranking among the employees, she was clearly among the most respected, both professionally and socially. As one employee noted, "Monica is the one who really holds this place together." There were a few other employees like her in the department who were clearly regarded quite favorably by the vast majority of workers.

Implementing Change at Personnel Services

As my first task, I began to interview a number of workers to get a clearer sense of their work roles and the ways in which their various tasks fit together to process job applicants. Among the first people I spoke with was Betty, a clerk typist whose job was to enter and process new applicants. Betty was helpful in teaching me about what her job involved, but it was clear she was skeptical of the ATS. Eventually, as Betty and I talked more, she came to share her opinions quite openly. One day, she put her cards on the table. I still recall her words vividly: "We don't need any new system and there's no way in hell we'll use it if it is ever built." When I asked her to explain why she felt the ATS would not be used, she told me that there was no need to alter a method that in her view had been working efficiently for decades. In her words, "If it ain't broke, don't fix it."

Unfortunately, Betty was not alone in this view. As the days progressed, I heard the ATS described as "unnecessary," "a waste of time," and as "another of Linda's pet projects that we'll never use," referring to the manager of the division who had made the decision to adopt the ATS in the first place. Perhaps the most extreme position I heard was from Sharon, a senior clerk who was a few years away from retirement, who said to me one day in the hallway, "You know, if you do build this ATS, I'll boycott it . . . it's just a few more years for me here, and I'm not about to learn a whole new way of doing things." Overall, although there was also support for the new system, employees seemed not to share their manager's view that the current method of processing applications was cumbersome and inefficient. Furthermore, they did not comprehend the extent to which their department was lagging behind others in the organization and how they desperately needed to automate and update their work processes in order to better mesh with other units.

Betty and other workers also made me aware of another fact: The project had been oversold to the minority of workers who were receptive to the ATS. For example, one day I was interviewing Mark, a fairly new employee at Personnel Services. Mark mentioned that he was looking forward to a reporting feature that I knew was beyond the scope of the ATS, and I had to tell him that it would not actually support this function. The look of disappointment on his face was obvious as he replied, "Oh, that's too bad, I thought it would. That would have helped me a lot." Similarly, there were times I had to tell other workers that things they had been told that the ATS could do were not possible, even with modification to the current design. I got reactions ranging from a blunt and disappointed "Oh" to "Well, I wish they hadn't told us it would do that then."

Clearly, many features that employees perceived to be part of the ATS were actually beyond its capabilities, a misunderstanding that I feared might be in part responsible for their support of the system. In view of the resistance to the ATS by many employees who were quite set in their work methods, the potential disappointment that supportive employees might feel when the completed ATS did not meet their lofty expectations, and the strict budget and time frame we had to work within, I was skeptical that the project could ever succeed. I could not help hearing Betty's words from our last formal session together over and over again: "Good luck with the project. Maybe you can make it work." At this point, I was having plenty of doubt.

The Future of Implementation at Personnel Services

Thus, just a few days into the project, I was facing what appeared to be insurmountable obstacles to the successful implementation of the ATS. Furthermore, on a personal and professional level, I was a junior consultant in my first role as a project manager, and I was facing failure. From past experience, I was certain that no matter how good the software and hardware were, people would not use the system unless they were convinced of its value to them personally. Also, I knew that the key to its acceptance was not only the value of the ATS itself. Rather, people operate within social climates of complex relations that influence their reactions to things, such as the implementation of new technologies. If the ATS project were to succeed, these things would have to be taken into account and dealt with directly. Still, I wasn't certain how to garner the commitment of the employees and convince them that it was in their best interest to support the ATS project. Given these obstacles, I couldn't help but wonder if Personnel Services was destined to retain the methods of the past rather than embracing those of the future, even if the old and new methods clashed like Wite-Out® on a computer monitor.

It was under these circumstances that I walked to a downtown restaurant one afternoon to meet Dick Leeds, the president and founder of the company, for our monthly meeting. We greeted each other and took seats at a table by the window, looking out across the downtown skyline. After we had settled in, chatted a bit, and ordered our lunch, Dick posed the inevitable question, "So, how is the Personnel Services project coming along?" I took a deep breath and began. . . . ✦

*This case has been developed based on real organization(s) and real organizational experiences. Names, facts, and situations have been changed to protect the privacy of individuals and organizations.

Chapter 11

Knowledge Is Power

MELINDA M. VILLAGRAN AND MARY HOFFMAN

Katie Morris* hit the key to send an instant message to her mom. "Just wanted to let you know I am settled in and start work tomorrow. I am so excited that I found a job where I can use my tech skills and help protect the environment."

The next day Katie was set to begin her new position at Green Solutions—one of the most innovative companies in the country. The company marketed technology for use in environmental engineering projects. Katie's position would enable her to assist in the creation of communication plans for Third World nations that were trying to ensure a supply of pure, potable water and to protect their wetlands and other natural habitats.

Katie's interests in the environment and in technology began when she was a child. Growing up, she had often taken walks and spent time watching the herons and egrets that shared the wetland near her home. In college, she especially enjoyed working in an online learning team, something the recruiter had told her was common practice at Green Solutions.

After graduating at the top of her class, she felt Green Solutions was a great place for an environmentally conscious, techno-savvy professional. She knew preserving wetlands would be a meaningful way for her to use her interest in communication technology.

At her interview, Katie had asked about the hardware and software used by the company. The recruiter had assured her, "Oh, we are state of the art in that area. I mean, how could we sell technology if we weren't on top of it ourselves?" He presented an image of Green Solutions as a thoroughly modern company with excellent profits over the last several years.

On her first day at her new job, Katie was introduced to Ned Benson. Ned was the Director of Communication Projects and her new supervisor. Ned shook Katie's hand and said, "I'm so glad you have joined our team."

As Ned introduced Katie to her new colleagues, she was surprised by how many people said, "Oh, you're so lucky to work with Ned. If you do everything just like he does, you'll do great." She was further impressed as she listened to Ned talk about the types of projects he had been part of for Green Solutions. He had been with the company for 20 years, during which time he had built relationships with countless corporate executives, engineers, and government agencies. He had helped solve real environmental problems all over the world.

Clearly, Ned had earned his title and position in the company. He spent years marketing corporate products and building coalitions among groups to tackle environmental issues. Even though they were just getting acquainted, Katie already respected Ned. She admired his rapport with many of his colleagues and his ability to speak with people at all levels of the company.

In the first few days of her training, Katie tediously filled out forms, memorized training manuals, and completed screening tests. During training, she noted many areas where her technological experience could improve company operations. She decided to send Ned an email outlining her ideas:

> To: Ned Benson GreenSol.org
> From: Katie Morris GreenSol.org
> Subject: Tech Ideas
>
> Ned: I have some really great ideas for how we can improve orientation. I thought you would want to hear them. I can create an interactive website for new employees so they can do their training at home. I can either create the website using html or use whatever web editor you work with. We would need a couple of portables with remote access to the LAN. We might also need to expand server capability. I would be happy to spearhead this project if it is something you are interested in. Love working here. ☺ KM

Katie had spent a lot of time thinking about this project, and she was disappointed when she never heard from Ned. She was eager to contribute to the company, and when her initial training was completed, she was ready to begin the work she had been trained to do.

Gradually, after a couple of weeks in her position, Katie realized that although Green Solutions used technology in their external products for clients, a fairly large portion of the staff had little or no expertise with the most basic office technology applications. At meetings, Katie saw lots of people with weekly planners, but almost nobody had a handheld PC except her. She was shocked when a coworker asked her to fax something because he did not know how to use the fax machine. She was especially surprised at the number of people who did not appear to even use their computers!

It had been weeks since she had sent her idea to Ned, and still she had heard nothing. It dawned on her that maybe he hadn't responded to her email because he rarely used his computer. Indeed, he had an assistant who handled most correspondence through dictation and snail-mail letters or memos. One afternoon, Katie mentioned to Ned that she had sent him a project update as an attachment.

"What was it attached to?" Ned asked. "I haven't seen anything like that in my box."

Katie couldn't believe what she was hearing. She said, "I sent it to your email."

"Oh, that!" Ned joked, adding, "You know, I really prefer the personal touch that a typed letter offers."

Katie thought, "Wow, is Ned ever lucky to have Donovan. Otherwise, nothing technological would get done in his office."

Donovan Adler was Ned's assistant. Although Donovan had been at Green Solutions nearly as long as Ned, he was excited about learning new technology, and he regularly attended workshops and training seminars outside the office. One day he told Katie, "In all the years I have been working with Ned, I have come to the conclusion that although he is great with people, he is totally dependent on me when it comes to technology."

Donovan knew virtually everything about computer software and hardware, fax machines, data retrieval systems, and telephone and video conferencing. Donovan's expertise had the effect of making Ned look good inside and outside the company. In fact, few people perceived a problem with Ned's lack of computer knowledge. It seemed that few people even knew about Ned's technophobia.

Donovan was so capable that he was promoted to become the internal information systems specialist for the entire company shortly after Katie arrived at Green Solutions. Donovan left Katie's office to move to New York, and Ned hired a new assistant who had significantly less experience than Donovan with office systems. At Donovan's going-away party, Katie told him with a wink, "I know who really runs this place, and we're gonna miss him."

Donovan answered, "Call me if you need me. I'll be as much help as I can from New York."

Katie spent the next three months settling into her job, but she became increasingly frustrated and concerned about the leadership of the office after Donovan's departure. Then Green Solutions named a new vice president, Leigh Peyton. One of the first things Ms. Peyton did was to hold a team meeting via teleconference of all employees. During the meeting, Ms. Peyton announced her intent to "make Green Solutions as technologically efficient on the inside as it is on the outside."

In a confidential memo sent to the president of Green Solutions following the teleconference, Ms. Peyton noted, "While many of our executives excel in knowledge and expertise that is important to the attainment of company goals, they are hindering corporate functioning by their lack of knowledge about basic office technologies. Among other initiatives, we will move immediately to institute virtual teams so that the appropriate personnel can collaborate on a regular basis."

A company-wide email appeared the next week:

To: Employees@GreenSol.org
From: Leigh Peyton <Peyton@GreenSol.org>
Subject: Tech Updates

In keeping with our new commitment to make Green Solutions as technologically efficient on the inside as it is on the outside, we announce the following initiatives:

- In the next 90 days all employees must complete the email proficiency test located on the corporate website.
- Handheld PCs have been purchased for all employees. All handhelds must be synched during working hours so that employees receive corporate data in a timely manner. Handhelds will also be used for all scheduling and calendar maintenance.
- All computers are to use the same software systems for easy transfer of information. Data retrieval systems will be enacted to ensure accountability of all internal office information.

(continued)

(continued)

- Those without necessary skills should complete a copy of the needs assessment to let headquarters know what types of training will be necessary.

We are serious about these changes—failure to comply in a timely manner may lead to disciplinary action or dismissal of noncompliant employees.

Katie was excited, but she worried about how Ned would handle the changes. Knowing that Ned probably didn't get the email, she printed out a copy of it and took it to Ned's office. "I know you're busy," she said, "so I thought you might want a copy of this email."

As Ned read it, his face got red, and he sputtered, "Handhelds? Data retrieval? Needs assessment?—I'll tell them what I need—the only thing I need is to be allowed to do my job the way I've always done it. Maybe we don't need better machines to run this office, maybe we need better people."

Katie realized that she would have to help Ned transition to the new system. She thought a first step was to show him how to log on to a website that offered basic computer information and instruction.

Ned was reluctant to admit his shortcomings, but as he looked at the website Katie recommended, he realized that he didn't even know where to begin—even the language was unfamiliar. To him, trying to go online to learn about computers was frustrating, confusing, and a waste of his valuable time. He resigned himself to getting help, but he was not sure if he had the skills, or the desire, to make the transition to using technology.

Katie was surprised to be invited to participate in a teleconference with Ms. Peyton the next week. Ms. Peyton explained that, after viewing the needs assessment data, she realized there were lots of people in the organization who needed technological training. To supplement the formal training to come, Green Solutions enlisted the help of Katie and others at the meeting to aid in the transition.

Katie realized that this was an opportunity for her to take a leadership role to ensure compliance with the new policy. Finally, she would be able to use her experience with virtual teams, since she would be training people from several different Green Solutions locations. She was anxious about her new responsibilities but excited to have the opportunity. She decided to share her concerns with Donovan, since he had offered to help:

To: Donovan@GreenSol.org
From: Katie@GreenSol.org
Subject: Help!

Donovan: I guess you know that Ned is going to have to change his attitude about computers. Can you believe they put me in charge of training all these people who have been here forever? I just got here—I can't be a leader. It is unbelievable to me that I am now more knowledgeable about some aspects of Green Solutions than the Director of Communication projects! It seems like the balance of power has shifted here with this new policy. How am I going to coerce Ned into joining us in the 21st century? I am afraid if he doesn't do this, his job could be in jeopardy—and I think the organization really needs him. Any ideas for how I can supervise my supervisor during this change?

Hope things are going well in NYC. Thanks, KM

✦

*This case has been developed based on real organization(s) and real organizational experiences. Names, facts, and situations have been changed to protect the privacy of individuals and organizations.

Chapter 12

Left Out of the Loop

NIRANJALA D. WEERAKKODY

"Oh, I am not important enough to get email access!" said Cathy Johnston,* the unit manager of vocational therapy, to Graham Brown.

Graham had recently taken over as manager of Nirogee Centre, a state government-owned residential care facility for the intellectually disabled located in the small, rural Australian town of Guthrie. Nirogee consisted of six direct care units, which were residences for the intellectually disabled clients, and three nondirect care units, such as catering, housekeeping, and vocational and hydrotherapy units.

Graham had been visiting each unit at Nirogee during his first week in his new job, accompanied by his assistant, Narelle Ford. Narelle had been at Nirogee since it was established 23 years ago and had served as the administrative assistant to the centre's manager for the last 12 years. Having been born and raised in Guthrie, she was also a local, like most of the Nirogee employees. She introduced Graham to the centre's staff as they went around.

Cathy appeared happy to see Graham and Narelle visiting her unit, especially to meet her and her staff. They all seemed surprised to see them there. Greeting them, Cathy beamed and said, "It is so great to see you." During her meeting with Graham, she made some suggestions for improvement in her unit, which Graham thought were useful.

He said, "Cathy, why don't you email me your suggestions as a memo? Then I will see if the budget can handle them."

It was then that Graham learned that Cathy did not have access to email as he, Narelle, and other staff in the administration building did.

He wondered what Cathy meant by "not being important enough" to be part of the network.

On their way back to the administration building, Graham asked Narelle for some explanation. "Why did people look so surprised to see us?" he asked.

"Well, the former manager, Jonathan McLeod, was very unpopular. He didn't care about anything. In his three years here, the guy may have left his office maybe twice, three times, tops. So that's probably why people were surprised," Narelle said.

On being appointed to Nirogee, Graham had heard from a friend at the head office, located 70 kilometers from Guthrie, that his predecessor had been ineffective and staff morale at Nirogee was very low. That is why Graham had decided to visit each unit at Nirogee as soon as he arrived to meet staff and see things for himself.

"If Cathy does not have email access, wouldn't there be problems with her and her staff not receiving important documents and memos sent from the head office to Nirogee, which are only sent via the intranet?" Graham asked himself. He knew that at least some of the direct care managers had email access, as he had received some email messages from them already. So he wondered why Cathy didn't have intranet access, when the direct care managers equal to her in rank did. He thought he knew just the person to ask.

The Inner Circle

Returning to his office, Graham called Peter Nash. "Peter, can you spare some time today to brief me on something?"

Over coffee, Peter answered Graham's questions about the intranet. Like Narelle and most of the others at Nirogee, Peter was a local. He had also been at Nirogee most of his working life. He was a nursing professional who had started life in direct care and moved up to become a unit manager. Now he was a sector manager who supervised three of the six direct care units. Graham had known Peter over the past few years, having met him at various official gatherings at the head office. Peter's friendliness was evident in his explanations.

"Six months ago, the head office decided to link us—I mean Nirogee—to their intranet. Then they decided that all memos, policy documents, procedural manuals, almost everything from them to us would only be sent over the intranet. We had no say in the matter.

Before that, everything came in the regular mail. The thing is, everyone at the head office has a computer. But we have only 20 computers for nine units and about 200 staff. Even then, most of these are in the administration building for administration staff. Of course, every direct care manager has a networked computer. But only the managers and deputy managers can touch them because they are in the managers' offices. The catering manager has a computer, but the head office didn't network it to the intranet. And that's it."

"Hmm," thought Graham. "So the only people who can access the intranet are direct care unit managers, deputy managers, and the administration staff."

The Outer Circle

"So what about the other staff without intranet access?" Graham asked Peter.

"Well, Marilyn Wright, the secretary in the administration building, is supposed to print out all emails from the head office and send them to nondirect care units. The unit managers in direct care must print them out and post them on the bulletin boards for other staff to read. But, you see, sometimes poor Marilyn is too busy with other work and forgets to print them or send them out. After the intranet, we all get so much more correspondence. It's an information overload in a way," Peter explained.

"So is it just the nondirect care staff who are affected?" Graham asked.

"Actually, no. It is worse for the direct care guys," Peter replied. "The head office gave us only one training session for the intranet. As usual, they said there was no money for any new computers or additional training. Some managers missed this training because they were on leave, on a rostered day off, or on a different shift. Or some don't like the intranet, period. These guys, both male and female, won't use the intranet. They ask their deputy managers to do it, because they are younger. Then the deputies complain about having to spend too much time fiddling with a computer when their real job is to work with the residents. After all, they had specially trained to become nurses of the intellectually disabled because that's what they wanted to do. When the deputies spend too much time on the computer, other staff in direct care have to carry the deputies' workload, and they are complaining. So actually, nobody's happy. And, just like Marilyn, the deputies also sometimes forget to print out all emails from the head office," Peter laughed.

Nobody's Happy

The picture was gradually becoming clear to Graham. He remembered Meaghan Swann, a direct care manager in her late 50s, talking to him about the intranet. "It's so impersonal. I prefer to use the phone or talk to people face-to-face. That's why I refuse to use it."

Graham mentioned this to Peter. "Oh, Meaghan was not there for the training. She was on her annual leave at the time," Peter remembered.

Graham also recalled Anita Devlin, a middle-aged junior level caregiver in Meaghan's unit, having told him, "If they give me the training and a computer I can use, I will use the intranet." So Graham knew that, unlike Meaghan, Anita was eager to use the intranet but had no access to it.

The next day, Graham called Cathy Johnston in vocational therapy and asked her about problems she faced with not having email access. She had reason to be upset. "My staff and I miss getting many important memos from the head office because we don't have a computer or the intranet. And this happens all the time."

Graham also remembered a conversation he'd had with Wayne Harris when Wayne came to take measurements for a new bookshelf in Graham's office. Wayne was a carpenter attached to housekeeping and a committee member of his trade union branch at Nirogee. Referring to the computer in Graham's office, he had said, "Boss, it would be nice if we in indirect care had computers, too. We can network the nondirect care units in-house at no cost at all. Just get us the computers and the software from the head office. I took this computer training course they had in town last year, so I can handle email, too."

"This guy is in his late 50s and has no higher education, but he is no technophobe," thought Graham.

You Are Dispensable

"It was not fair to give intranet access only to the direct care units. I am sure it made indirect care people feel terrible," Peter had continued during their coffee together. "You know, last year when the head office was talking about outsourcing nondirect care functions at Nirogee, it pretty much scared the daylights out of the indirect care staff. It was like they were dispensable. Nirogee is Guthrie's biggest single employer. Sometimes, two or three persons from the same family work here. A lot of other people do casual work for us. Almost half the town has worked here at some time. So when staff here are worried or unhappy, the town grapevine goes crazy with all kinds of rumours, mostly about the centre closing down, and then people write letters to the editor in the local newspaper. The 'no computers, no intranet for you' situation is actually saying that indirect care has no status here. Direct care staff generally earn more because they are health care professionals, while those in indirect care are less likely to have degrees. So they already feel discounted. I don't blame them for getting upset," Peter went on.

Who Decides and Why?

While going round the centre, Graham had also seen a brand-new, state-of-the-art video-conferencing facility setup in one of the meeting rooms in the administration building. He thought this was unusual, especially when the head office was so tightfisted about almost everything, not just about the costs related to the intranet.

When Graham raised the issue of the intranet with Allan Lockwood, the manager of catering, Allan had said, "The video-conferencing setup cost $33,000. We didn't ask for it and I don't think we needed one either. But the same head office that set it up here can't give us a few more lousy computers to network the indirect care units or funds for a another half-day training course for the direct care managers who missed the first one. They were too cheap to even network my existing computer."

After making a few inquiries, Graham found that the video-conferencing facility had so far been used only once, two months after installation. Another month had passed since then. When he had later mentioned this to Peter, Peter had explained, "The facility was for the head office staff to conduct meetings. They don't want to travel the 70 kilometers to Nirogee. Actually, the video-conferencing setup should have gone to Pottshill. Those poor guys spend five hours each way traveling for meetings to the head office, and they have to do it every two months. But they have nothing, not even the intranet or a voicepoint setup, for audio conferencing."

Pottshill was a small remote town where a branch of the state department that owns Nirogee was staffed by five persons. Graham had met some of them at a meeting at the head office once, during his previous job with the department. He felt sorry for them.

The Physical Layout

Graham also noticed that Nirogee's physical layout did not encourage contact between direct and nondirect care staff because all buildings at the centre were located far apart on a large acreage of uneven terrain. Graham found that he had to walk considerable distances to get from the administration building to both direct and indirect care buildings. He asked Narelle, who was accompanying him on these visits, why the buildings were set up so far apart.

"The original plan was to build 30 to 40 direct care units. So they built the original 6 units far apart, hoping to add the others later. But they didn't build any more units," she replied.

"Next time, I will drive myself between buildings to save time," Graham noted.

No Social Activities

Narelle had casually mentioned to Graham that, at work, she rarely got to see any staff from units other than administration. "In the past, everyone had to sign in at the administration unit so that people at least saw other staff who are not working in the same unit. Now that staff sign in within their own units, we rarely see people from other work areas."

The centre had had no social gatherings that included the entire staff in years. Each direct care unit had its own Christmas party for residents and their families, but they didn't include indirect care staff.

"The only time I meet people in direct care at work is when it is my turn to take the food over for the residents. Then everyone is in a hurry, and we talk only about work stuff. There's no time for chit-chat," Steve O'Connell, from catering, had remarked when Graham visited the kitchen a few days ago.

Nirogee had no common staff room for people to gather. Staff took their meals in their own units, and no one had bought food from the cafeteria since the meal subsidy was removed. In direct care, staff needed to take staggered breaks to accommodate the residents' need for round-the-clock care. So they, too, got few opportunities for socializing with each other at work.

The Nature of Work

The workloads of direct care staff were heavy and stressful because some of the residents would suddenly "act up." The work involved with reporting and documenting such incidents had increased in recent times due to new legal requirements. This work took precedence over other tasks, such as those involving the intranet, for both unit managers and their deputies. Recently, the head office had placed several mental patients convicted of crimes, rather than clients with intellectual disabilities, which added to the staff's stress levels and workloads. This was in spite of a long waiting list of intellectually disabled persons in the state who needed residential care. Once again, Nirogee had no say in the matter. Graham knew that the current state government that ran Nirogee was well-known for its commitment to economic rationalization.

Do Something!

So what could Graham do to solve the intranet issue and the staff's low morale? What were his options? He thought an additional computer and a printer provided in each direct care unit, accessible to all staff, would reduce the problems created by managers and deputies failing to print emails for other staff. Each nondirect care unit too could be provided with a computer networked to the intranet that would allow all staff in those units to access the intranet messages from the head office independently. And this could be accompanied with training to use the intranet for all permanent staff. How about some social activities involving the entire staff at the centre?

Graham thought about calling a staff meeting of all managers, deputies, and representatives from other levels in both direct and nondirect care to discuss the issues. Maybe they could appoint a committee to provide suggestions to improve the situation.

Most of all, how could Graham convince the head office of the need to provide sufficient access to the intranet for all staff at the Nirogee Centre and counter their arguments about funding shortages? What could he do to improve staff morale and make sure people in indirect care, such as Cathy Johnston, didn't feel left out and unimportant?

"I have been here a long time, just like the direct care managers," Cathy had told Graham. "I am not trying to be a troublemaker, but why shouldn't I be treated the same as other managers?"

She had a point. ✦

*This case has been developed based on real organization(s) and real organizational experiences. Names, facts, and situations have been changed to protect the privacy of individuals and organizations.

Section 3

Teamwork and Group Processes

Briefing Paper

Teamwork and Group Processes

Every organization has many groups or teams, whether they are called task forces, committees, ad hoc groups, executive or management teams, crews, or boards. Are there really differences among these groups and teams, or are these merely differences in terminology? That's a difficult question to answer because each group is unique—depending on its size, the degree of interdependence among members, the degree to which members identify with one another as a group, the group's goals, and the manner in which the group is structured.

Organizations use teams for many reasons. Sometimes teams are used because the organization is structured into group and team units. In other instances, teams are used because there is greater support for decisions when the group as a whole makes them. But the most frequent reason given for using teams and groups in organizations is that the goal or the task of the group is so difficult, complex, or time-consuming that it is beyond the capacity of one person.

A group or team is a fundamental unit of all organizations. We expect to be a member of a group or team at work. Although each team is embedded within an organizational culture, each team creates its unique culture, or *groupness,* as its members work together using verbal and nonverbal communication to establish rules and norms about its practices and procedures.

One approach for considering the influence of the individuals in the team, and the team itself as an interacting unit, as well as the influences of the organization of which the team is a part, is structuration theory. The theory emphasizes how team members structure their groups by actively using rules and resources. Rules are viewed as organizational constraints, directing employees in how to think and act. Resources are messages (that is, about what or how teamwork should be done), symbols (for example, organizational title), possessions (for example, money), or attributes (for example, leadership qualities) used to control the actions of the group. In essence, every communicative act among group members contributes to the creation and re-creation of the ongoing and continuous structuring process. The structuring process implies that groups operate as social systems through patterns of verbal and nonverbal communication and building of relationships. Structuration theory also implies that a team's culture is never really its own. Instead, a team must manage the tensions among the multiple group structures nested within the organizational culture. Although each group establishes its own unique structure (rules and resources), that structure is shaped and influenced by the organizational or macro environment.

A second perspective for analyzing organizational teams is the systems perspective. Many organizations are composed of several groups, or systems, all of which are interdependent for the organization to function effectively and achieve its goals. Systems theory proponents argue that systems are either open or closed. For a system to survive, it must be open to information from both the internal and external environments. Open systems are said to be permeable as boundaries are blurred or minimized; this allows the various groups to exchange and process relevant information. However, not all elements of the system are equal. As a system becomes more complex it becomes necessary for various components (or groups) to specialize and differentiate themselves from other components. In this way, interdependence is created at the same time the hierarchical ordering of the systems becomes visible. Systems theory serves as a method for understanding and managing behavior in organizational settings.

Relatedly, it can be helpful to consider the formal and informal communication networks used within a group or used by a group with other individuals and teams in the organization. The study of communication networks focuses on the patterns and directions of the communication process as they occur in a system. The patterns emerge based on how information is transmitted or exchanged between the different components of the system. Describing the existing networks in the group, or the networks used by the group with other components of the organization, is a way to understand how communication moves, influences others, and is effective or ineffective.

The skills, talents, and attitudes of each group member will have a significant impact on the group. Indeed, the influences of diversity that individual members bring to the team setting are often overlooked and underutilized. What kinds of differences (for example, age, class, gender, race or ethnicity, and professional or disciplinary expertise) and whether that aspect of diversity is salient to group members will influence group goals and the processes a team uses to reach those goals. In short, whereas there is plenty of research indicating that homogeneous groups may perform better, heterogeneous groups can lead to better quality decisions because of the different informational inputs that people can bring to the table for discussion. People who have weak ties to each other and have sources of information that are unavailable or unused by other team members have access to much more data than those who have strong ties to each other and redundant data, information sources, and viewpoints.

Team members are selected, elected, appointed, or emerge in formal roles, such as leader and secretary or recorder. In addition to whatever formal roles the group needs, members also emerge in informal roles to satisfy the task and relationship maintenance needs of the group. The formal and informal roles that members adhere to influence the group's leadership effectiveness and its ability to manage conflict, make decisions, and solve problems.

As with any group of people, teams may run into problems. They may be unable to fully use the knowledge of their team members, or they may find it difficult to come to a shared understanding of goals, methods, and priorities. Despite these problems, organizations rely heavily on groups and teams to provide leadership, make decisions, solve problems, manage conflicts, and create innovative ideas, solutions, products, and services. As a member of an organization, you are likely to be a member of a team or even lead or supervise a team. Understanding the role of communication in shaping group process will help you succeed in being an effective group member.

Suggested Readings

Arnold, V. (1996). Organizational development: Making teams work. *HR Focus, 73*(2), 12–14.

Cohen, S. G., & Bailey, D. E. (1997). What makes teams work: Group effectiveness research from the shop floor to the executive suite. *Journal of Management, 23,* 239–291.

Guzzo, R. A., & Dickson, M. W. (1996). Teams in organizations: Recent research on performance and effectiveness. *Annual Review of Psychology, 47,* 307–339.

Hackman, J. R. (Ed.). (1990). *Groups that work (and those that don't): Creating conditions for effective teamwork.* San Francisco: Jossey-Bass.

Hackman, J. R. (1992). Group influences on individuals in organizations. In M. D. Dunnette & L. M. Hough (Eds.), *Handbook of industrial and organizational psychology* (pp. 199–267). Palo Alto, CA: Consulting Psychologists Press.

Hirokawa, R. Y., & Salazar, A. J. (1999). Task-group communication and decision-making performance. In L. R. Frey, D. S. Gouran, & M. S. Poole (Eds.), *The handbook of group communication theory and research* (pp. 167–191). Thousand Oaks, CA: Sage.

Keyton, J. (2002). *Communicating in groups: Developing relationships for effective decision making* (2nd ed.). Boston: McGraw-Hill.

Kolb, J. A. (1995). Leader behaviors affecting team performance: Similarities and differences between leader/member assessments. *The Journal of Business Communication, 32,* 233–248.

Monge, P. R., & Contractor, N. S. (2001). Emergence of communication networks. In F. M. Jablin & L. L. Putnam (Eds.), *Handbook of organizational communication* (pp. 440–502). Thousand Oaks, CA: Sage.

Murnighan, J. K., & Conlon, D. E. (1991). The dynamics of intense work groups: A study of British String Quartets. *Administrative Science Quarterly, 36,* 165–186.

Stohl, C. (1995). *Organizational communication: Connectedness in action.* Thousand Oaks, CA: Sage.

Tracy, K., & Ashcraft, C. (2001). Crafting policies about controversial values: How wording disputes manage a group dilemma. *Journal of Applied Communication Research, 29,* 297–316.

Zorn, T. E., Jr., & Tompson, G. H. (2002). Communication in top management teams. In L. R. Frey (Ed.), *New directions in group communication* (pp. 253–272). Thousand Oaks, CA: Sage. ✦

Chapter 13

The Fun Team

Carolyn M. Anderson and Heather L. Walter

In the beginning, the Internet group had been largely an unnoticed unit at BC Financial Services.* The group members were viewed as computer geeks and were pretty much left alone to create and manage the corporation's websites. BC, a *Fortune* 500 company, is a financial services business with locations throughout the United States. The majority of business is conducted through call centers where shifts of employees staff telephone banks 24 hours a day, seven days a week. Independent sales representatives also generate company revenue through direct sales to customers. However, in the wake of technological advances, business on the Internet was becoming a viable third source of revenue for BC.

Customer inquiries to BC's website soared as a growing number of savvy customers logged on to the Web and comparison shopped for services and prices. Customers could easily use the Web to sign up for financial services by clicking through a series of easy-to-follow links. Thus, the Internet group members attributed their initial successes to cutting-edge and user-friendly websites designed to fit BC's organizational and customers' needs.

As sales grew, members of the small Internet group began to bend under the weight of their success. They found themselves overworked and ill prepared to handle the volume of sales inquiries and the corresponding increase in customer complaints about response-time delays. Another challenge for them was tied to the growth of competitors, as it did not take them long to catch up by using creative websites of their own. The Internet group's slipping e-commerce market share triggered action by Alex Smart.

Alex Smart founded BC over 45 years ago guided by a conservative philosophy; he ran a tight ship and kept a watchful eye over the company. Believing that the e-commerce way of doing business represented the next growth market, he could not ignore the Internet group's disappointing last two quarterly reports. Alex picked up the telephone and dialed Chris Johnson's telephone extension. "Chris, Alex here," he said. "Come to my office at two o'clock. I have an important job for you."

Chris entered Alex's office promptly at two o'clock. No one dared to be late when beckoned by Alex. Chris came to BC with an impressive résumé. He was a talented 30-year-old MBA graduate from a top school with work experience at a premier consulting firm in Chicago. Alex paid outlandish dollars for talented people with top-notch analytic skills, demonstrated competency working in groups, strong leadership potential, and competent communication skills. In two years at BC, personnel evaluations reflected the fact that Chris was an outstanding performer who was assimilating with ease into BC's culture. There was no question that Chris was on the fast track.

Motioning Chris to sit down, Alex said, "I want you to take charge of the Internet group, fix the problems, get them back on track, and see to it that the unit grows. Our share of the e-commerce business market should be climbing upward, not stagnant or slipping downward."

Chris' Challenge: Building a Successful Team

Chris was a workaholic, but days and nights became a blur in the weeks after the meeting with Alex. The potential for e-commerce growth was attractive. Chris knew that since websites are easily accessible to competitors as well as customers, staying ahead of the market share game called for innovative strategies that won customers and kept them happy. That was the only formulation for staying a step ahead of competitors.

Chris' first challenge was to evaluate the operations of the existing Internet group, including their day-to-day routines. The 10 members were a youngish bunch. All had graduated college with computer science and media technology degrees; not one member had a business degree. As a result, the team was weak in business skills. Chris first analyzed the group's profit-and-loss numbers, evaluated customer complaints, and surveyed competitors' online presence. The reality check of strengths and weaknesses for the group was worse than Chris imagined. To confront the day-to-day volume and customer complaints alone, Chris reasoned that additional team members were needed. He believed these new hires should also have strong business and analytical skills. The existing group could no longer handle the workload driven by the demands of technology-savvy customers. Adding people would address a short-term fix in the Internet group and meet initial growth objectives for BC. No two ways about it, there would be long days and weekend work for everyone until the unit attained a more attractive market share position.

Pat Kinisky popped his head in Chris' doorway. "How's Captain Picard, leader of the new generation bunch?" Chris and Pat had met at the new employee orientation two years ago. They became fast friends as well as coworkers, providing each other with support while climbing the ladder at BC.

"In some respects, all right. Alex approved my strategic plan, including my hiring five new people. I don't know, though; integrating strong business types into an existing group of computer geeks could be disastrous."

Pat laughed. "You could always force the old ones and the new ones to get along by threatening to beam them to extinction."

Chris laughed at Pat's sense of humor. "That's a thought, Pat. We need the talents of individuals who are committed to fixing and growing our business. Yet no one can force any individual to be a member of a cohesive group." Pat grew more serious.

"Oh, stop worrying, my friend. Hire newbies with strong communication and group skills and let them work it out."

Chris sat back in the gray leather chair to think about alternatives for fixing and growing the Internet group. Earlier on a yellow pad Chris had jotted down three strategies: (1) change jobs and routines, (2) integrate the new hires, and (3) motivate the group to work as a team. After mulling them over again, he still felt that these strategies were key ones.

When Chris and Pat were walking to the subway after work that day, Chris shared the strategies with Pat. Chris summed up their conversation by adding, "I think that for us to regain a number one position, a lot hinges on how well this group gels and if Alex stands behind us."

Later that night, while tossing and turning, Chris thought about what Pat had said earlier about hiring the right people. Of course, Pat was right. Chris should hire competent business people with good communication and group skills. That combination should spell success. But Chris also knew that not all groups reach their goals and that group success is not automatic just because the right people are in place.

Within the month, five new hires had been selected. Chris had also evaluated the 10 current members of the group. He had also told them about changes in their jobs and routines. Chris had made sure to ask for their input and listen carefully to what they had to say. The group also had to move. The space they were in was too small for adding new team members.

By the end of the month, the Internet group had moved to the fourth floor of the newest satellite building across the street from BC's headquarters. The boxes were unpacked, the phones working, and the computers up and running when the newcomers came on board. To facilitate the changes, Chris called a meeting of the Internet group the first day all of the new group members reported to work.

The Internet Group Culture

Chris opened the meeting with introductions. Two of the newcomers, Lei and J.T., demonstrated that they were especially good sports by adding some humorous things about themselves that made others laugh. Then Chris turned the group members' attention to the goal. Sounding a bit paternalistic but enthusiastic, Chris said, "Now is the time for us to confront the challenges of our task. Our mission is clear. We are to once again be the undisputed leader in market share in the financial services world of e-business." The group members clapped and hooted and hollered in agreement.

Chris added, "As I see it, first we need to change the way we have been doing things and quickly fix any problems in order to stop our competitors from chipping away at our market share. With the problems remedied, we can concentrate on growth." Chris knew that understanding the urgency of the situation would be a critical first step. Members would have to work together and work quickly. Taking on a coach's voice, Chris said, "OK, everyone, let's break into subgroups and generate ideas on how we can become the team that will reach our goals."

The sound of voices filled the conference room as the newcomers got to know the Internet group's existing members. From their conversations, Chris could tell that they were already generating ideas. Chris was pleased. Things seemed to be going along fine. Everyone was participating and demonstrating a willingness to work together.

Yet Chris felt uneasy when thinking about the larger picture. Although Alex sanctioned the strategic plans Chris had presented, the Internet group was a very small unit representing a substantial portion of revenue for BC. The group's mission was dependent on new technology that was constantly changing. Chris believed that the growth of this unit represented, and would require, a fundamental shift in BC's organizational culture. Thinking back to their conversations, Chris perceived that Alex was committed to the idea of growth, but he also knew that the unit's changes were only one part of organizational life at BC. And BC was no different from other large corporations. Day-to-day operations were fraught with red tape, politics, power struggles, and competitiveness among workers at all levels. Chris was well aware that these forces could be potential barriers to the group's success.

The Fun Team

For starters, the Internet group members agreed on one thing. Lei phrased it best. "We need an innovative, zany, and fun workplace that reflects who we are. We need a culture that reflects who we are, and that's a first-rate team." By the end of the meeting a subgroup formed to generate ideas on how to create a fun workplace. They called themselves the *Fun Team,* and Lei emerged as the Fun Team's leader.

Under Alex's directive, all BC's offices were modernistic glass structures strung together in a campuslike look. Interior walls were stark white, furniture black, carpet gray, and workstations lined with gray panels. Alex had hired an artist friend to paint or select all the artwork for the corporation's many buildings. Employees were restricted in what could hang on walls and adorn desks. Alex had human resources include a statement about these parameters in the employee handbook. After all, they were dealing with customers' money and he wanted the BC look to represent a prosperous yet traditional organization.

Chris told Pat about the Fun Team over lunch. Pat took on a professorial look and began reciting from memory: "According to Professor Allen, transforming the workplace to a fun environment emerges from the need employees have to cope with stress. Alas, overworked employees have little time for coworker camaraderie. Aside from time pressures, another factor might be the environment. Is the workplace conducive to kinship?"

Chris smiled at the story and asked Pat, "Does the environment at BC stimulate camaraderie?"

Pat retorted, "You should let your Fun Team answer that question."

The Foosball Table

At the next Fun Team meeting, Lei said, "We need to liven up the fourth floor. Don't you think it's depressing looking at white walls and gray carpet every day? Our workspace should communicate that the new generation group works here." The Fun Team members agreed. They liked the idea of transforming the fourth floor into a unique new look and agreed to brainstorm ideas.

At the next meeting, the Fun Team discussed ideas for the large empty space in front of the elevators that welcomed them and visitors to the fourth floor. J.T. joked, "Why not make that space a playground?" After the laughter settled down, the members started to seriously talk about it. By the end of the meeting, they agreed to meet after work at a nearby toy store to generate ideas.

Inside the store, Lei spied what she thought was a great idea—"Look, gang, here's a foosball table. Just $3,000." The members hovered around it, falling in love with it and with the idea. At work the next day, they located two websites for foosball enthusiasts.

To win the entire group's approval, Lei presented the arguments. "Playing games with coworkers reduces stress without having to leave the area. We'll get to know each other better, and build trust and camaraderie. And, best of all, we'll be known as the group with the foosball table." The vote was unanimous. The Internet group members wanted a foosball table.

"Whatever makes the group work harder and be happy is great by me," Chris told Lei. "I understand the link between symbols and bonding. And, for your information, I love to play foosball." Chris ordered the table and paid for it out of department funds.

Paint, Carpet, and Furniture

Partially prompted by Chris' acceptance of the foosball table, the Fun Team continued thinking about and sharing ideas for office improvements. They read office design magazines, searched the Web for carpet and furniture ideas, and visited paint stores for color swatches. Within the week, they had created mock office displays with color themes of mellow yellow, vibrant blue, hunter green, and spring violet. The mock displays featured movable furniture, which they argued allowed for easier communication flow among team members.

Lei told the Internet group members, "Let's study the displays for the next week or so and then we'll vote." Group members liked all four mock displays. Since there were four task areas within the unit, each task area could have its own theme. Everyone was enthusiastic about the potential changes. By the end of the week a vote didn't seem necessary, and Lei asked Chris to fill out the necessary paperwork. Chris did it right away and sent along the invoices to the controller's office.

Chris was encouraged. The new Internet group of geeks and business types was gelling nicely and working productively. Customer complaints were being handled in a more timely fashion, and they were trying new ways to handle the volume of inquiries and sales. Chris ordered box lunches for everyone to celebrate progress on the tasks and their unique new workspace. Excitement was high for the Internet group members as they congratulated themselves on having a foosball table and a creative new work environment.

Trouble Ahead

When the foosball table arrived, Lei and J.T. assembled it and posted a schedule for lessons and tournaments. Winners of tournaments would keep the trophy on their desks until they lost. The group agreed that employees from other units could sign up to play against the Internet members. After just a few invitations to other employees to play, the rumor spread fast through BC's grapevine—the Internet group had a foosball table.

But euphoria among the Internet group was short-lived. All hell broke loose when the invoice for the foosball table came across Comptroller Ed Parker's desk. Ed was second in command to Alex. He screamed through the phone at Chris. "Employees should be working, damn it, not playing games. My phone is ringing off the hook with managers demanding to know what the hell this is all about. Their subordinates are whining about not having a foosball table. Chris, get rid of it now!" Before Chris could speak, Ed slammed down the phone.

Chris sat quietly for several minutes and then called Pat. After relating the phone call with Ed, Chris said, "OK, Pat. Any ideas?"

Pat chuckled. "Come on, Chris. Ed's the management type, afraid of change. Why not tell him it's only one small ripple in a tiny unit's space? We're talking about a place where 15 people and a manager work. Tell him it's the wave of the e-commerce future. He'll get over it."

Chris snapped back, "I don't know, Pat. I've never seen Ed upset like this before. In fact, I've never heard of him ever yelling at someone before."

Just a few minutes after Chris hung up the phone from talking with Pat, Ed stormed into the office, throwing the invoices for the fourth floor's carpet, furniture, and paint on the desk. Ed's face was flushed. As his voice cracked, he screamed in Chris' face. "Are you mad? Let employees decide which chairs to sit on or colors they want? People come and go around here. If I approve this crap for your pea-sized unit, holy hell will break loose. The phone is ringing enough over that foosball thing. Now you want more chaos around here over damn carpet, furniture, and paint. You're history, Chris. I'll see you fry over this fiasco. I'll make damn sure Alex won't approve this."

Chris knew that Ed was not joking. Chris picked up the phone to call Alex, but Alex's assistant, Emily, said he was away at a family funeral. Emily refused to give Chris the number or say when Alex would return. Chris finally hung up the phone after a few failed attempts to change her mind. Chris dialed Pat's office.

Pat listened to Chris give a blow-by-blow description of Ed's outburst.

Pat's voice was serious this time. "Chris, Alex adores you. He'll be supportive. Come on, we're young blood around here. Tell Ed where he can go." But after a pause, "Good luck, dear friend."

Chris didn't have to tell the Internet group members what had happened. The open office environment allowed them to overhear Ed's screaming words. And they could tell from the look on Chris' face that something was seriously wrong.

When Chris walked out of his cubicle they were standing as a group ready to confront him. He could tell that they were outraged and angry. The foosball table and new fourth floor look was their group's vision. Lei and J.T. threatened to quit. A few other members mumbled about getting out of the prison they worked in.

Chris faced a dilemma. If people quit, the unit would suffer. Then, too, Alex might heed Ed's words and make Chris history. Chris had never thought about being fired from BC. In the meantime, work was on hold. The phones were ringing and ringing. Even worse, no one was following business activity on BC's website. ✦

*This case has been developed based on real organization(s) and real organizational experiences. Names, facts, and situations have been changed to protect the privacy of individuals and organizations.

Chapter 14

Engineering Difference

Patrice M. Buzzanell, Edward J. Coyle, Leah H. Jamieson, and William C. Oakes

The EPICS* faculty and industry advisers lingered in the meeting room—several engineers on one side and a couple of liberal arts faculty advisers talking to one another as they put on their coats and gathered their materials together on the other side. Kathleen, the codirector and cofounder of EPICS, Engineering Projects in Community Service, started putting her slides in folders and placed her handouts and pens in a box for storage. She looked up and caught Trevor's goodbye wave. She smiled and waved back at Trevor, a project engineer from HP who co-advised the wetlands team with an environmental engineering professor.

Kathleen continued smiling as she watched the rest of the faculty and industry advisers leave. She thought back to the time years ago when she and some other engineering faculty, especially Colin, first thought about developing EPICS. She and Colin were convinced that creating multidisciplinary design teams to tackle real social and local community problems over several semesters would give their engineering students an incredible advantage. EPICS would enable students to appreciate the contributions of diverse work group members and help them see how their design work touched lives in ways that classroom lectures simply couldn't convey. She remembered the excitement that she and Colin first felt when they proposed their idea to their department, then the faculty, and finally the college administration. EPICS became a reality. Many engineering alumni and recruiters praised their foresight.

Foresight! She wished she really had some foresight. Kathleen was still convinced that this kind of service learning could have immediate and long-term benefits for her engineering students and for local non-profit organizations. But she wondered how she and the two other codirectors could work around some of the contradictions that seemed to develop in each team. Diverse work teams were supposed to be valuable in the workplace because different group members had fresh ideas and nonredundant sources of information. She was certain that multidisciplinary teams were the right way to go. But she kept hearing about and seeing problems in her own and other EPICS teams, especially in integrating engineering students with students from other disciplines. What could she do to encourage team members to share information more readily? How could she get them to work together more effectively? How could she and other advisers point out the negative effects of stereotyping and in-group/out-group communication without causing students and their advisers to resent each other?

Kathleen was deep in thought when Joe, one of the EPICS codirectors, came up beside her. She closed the Ethernet connection to the EPICS website and turned to Joe. "So, how do you think the advisers' orientation went?" she asked.

Joe rubbed his eyes and frowned. He responded thoughtfully, "Pairing up returning and new advisers was a good idea. Opening the session with introductions and statements of best and worst EPICS experiences also worked well. The new advisers seemed to enjoy hearing the returning advisers talk, and they seemed to like the idea of sharing their reasons for getting involved in EPICS."

"But I don't know about the rest of the orientation," Kathleen interrupted. "I'm talking about the part about diversity. I guess it went as well as these sessions usually do."

Joe became more animated. "I *wish* I knew how to get *all* of our students and advisers fully engaged in the team processes. I wish I knew how to show the advisers that their behavior either facilitates or hinders the process, especially when it comes to stereotyping and all." Joe shook his head in frustration and said, "You did a great job with the examples today, Kathleen. And we always talk about advisers' expectations influencing design and product outcomes. And they just look bored. Their eyes glass over. You know the look."

Kathleen nodded.

Joe continued, "I guess they figure that it's not their job as adviser to monitor the students' behaviors. Too many of the advisers think it's the student leaders' job to keep their team members on track. But what the advisers don't see is that they are just as guilty as our students! I don't know. I feel like I am beating my head against a brick wall. I really do enjoy codirecting this program with you, Kathleen, but there are times when I think EPICS needs someone with some different skills to lead it."

"You're not going to start that again," Kathleen laughed. "Besides, I am hoping that our grant proposal to study our multidisciplinary team processes will go through. Having a team of researchers investigate how our teams work—or don't," she said, raising her eyebrows, "would help us structure EPICS more effectively, I think."

Joe mouthed "yes" silently in agreement.

Kathleen resumed, "If we get the grant, we can pull in expertise that we don't have. We definitely need some input from communication and psychology faculty, but we can't ask them to just donate time to us."

After a pause, Kathleen continued, "Joe, did you notice that some of the faculty actually paid attention to Bart's story about the team he advised a couple of years ago? Did you see the look of horror on Vanessa's face when Bart talked about the junior who changed his major from Computer Science to Communication and then the other students on his team acted as though he had no technical expertise? Even I had to start laughing when Bart recounted how the students wouldn't consult this guy even on technical aspects that he had designed just the semester before. And then the team members would say to him, 'Now that you're a communication major, you can write the team proposal and design our presentation.' They wouldn't even talk to him about anything technical.

"Vanessa looked as though she couldn't decide whether to laugh or cry. I am sure she is wondering why she decided to join this crazy bunch of engineers and advise a team with me. If I don't see her later, I'd better call her. I don't want to lose our *one* communication adviser before this team even begins!"

Bonnie, the EPICS administrative coordinator, came back into the room with an empty cart, and obviously overheard what Kathleen and Joe were talking about. As she separated out team project brochures into different piles, Bonnie interjected, "Oh, Vanessa will be fine. Watching her sit there with her mouth open was more fun than I've had in a while."

Bonnie grinned and stacked the EPICS pamphlets and advising manuals on the cart to return to her office. "I meant to tell you, Kathleen, that I walked Vanessa through the labs and signed out a digital camera and a laptop to her. Do you want me to do anything else?"

"I think that's about it," Kathleen responded. "Vanessa is on our email distribution list, right? You know, Bonnie, I can't imagine directing EPICS without you. Joe and I simply couldn't handle all the details and the traveling that we do."

"I'll second that," Joe remarked.

"Well, if I'm so valuable, why don't you help me load the laptops on this cart," Bonnie replied. "By the way, you didn't tell them my favorite story. That's the high point of these orientations for me."

"I know which one that is! It's the one about the woman with the power tools," Joe exclaimed.

"Nope. Try again," Bonnie said.

"Wait, let me hear," Vanessa called out as she came into the room. "I want to hear about the power tools."

"Have you noticed how everyone seems to be talking about power tools? Must be all those home improvement shows," Joe laughed. "What are you doing back here?"

"I was walking over to the liberal arts building when I realized that I must have left my keys here. Has anyone seen them?" Vanessa asked as she scanned the room for her keys.

"Ah! This is a familiar question! I remember the first time we met a couple of months ago. You, Joe, your department head, and I talked about your involvement in EPICS for about an hour—then you left for another meeting. But you returned after a couple of minutes because you thought you left your keys in the conference room. And the keys were in your laptop carrying case. You amaze me—you never seem to be worried when you misplace your keys. I'd be frantic!" Kathleen said.

"Well, I know that I'll locate them, so I don't panic! And there they are!" As Vanessa grabbed her keys from a nearby table, she turned to Joe. "I still want to hear about the student with the power tools. What happened?"

Joe got a big grin on his face and replied, "This female visual design student signed up for a team a few semesters ago. Of course, the male engineering students figured that she didn't know a thing about designing or building stuff. So they were going to have her facilitate the team's brainstorming and write parts of the team report—you know, the usual *soft* stuff that every nonengineer is supposed to be good at!"

Vanessa rolled her eyes and brushed a strand of hair from her face.

Joe went on with his story. "Well, the guys were saying that they didn't know where to get their hands on certain tools. She listened to them for a while, then finally said that she not only had those particular tools but an entire set of power tools. The guys almost fell out of their chairs. Then it occurred to them that she might actually know how to use the tools. They were in shock. She ended up being the only one who could actually construct the project they designed."

Joe stopped for a moment and said, "Bonnie, do you want me to stack the PDAs over here?"

"Sure," Bonnie said. "But you still haven't guessed what my favorite story is. Talk about engineers."

"Talk about engineers . . . that's for sure," Vanessa interrupted, then added, "I was talking to some other advisers as we were leaving the meeting a little while ago. I found out that one team really started to produce some terrific results when the audiology and sociology students decided to pick up technical expertise. Now they are fully involved in programming and website development. Before that, they were assigned report writing and bringing in snacks for their meetings on Wednesday afternoons. Only the engineering students remained . . ."

"Okay, okay . . . doesn't anyone want to hear what I have to say?" Bonnie asked.

"Do we have a choice?" Joe laughed.

"Sure you do," Bonnie said. "Just don't expect your equipment orders to go through on time."

"We'd *love* to hear your story, Bonnie," Kathleen quickly inserted.

"That's what I expected," Bonnie replied, and turned to Vanessa. "Vanessa, you wouldn't believe this one team a few years ago. It was the team setting up a database for homeless people in Lafayette and surrounding areas. Colin was co-advising it. You know that Colin is one of the cofounders of EPICS with Kathleen, and that he's the other codirector?"

Bonnie waited a moment for Vanessa to nod, then went on. "Anyway, it must have been around 1995 and the team started with all engineers. Then they got some sociology students and a sociology professor as their adviser. You remember, Kathleen? It was Eric Martin who advised the team with Colin.

"Anyway, I went to the first meeting to bring along some team member forms and pass out lab keys and software we purchased for the team. I walked into their meeting room and all the technical types are at one end of the table and the sociology folks are at the other end. The students were all talking among themselves, but separated into two distinct groups. The engineers were all guys. There were two females and one male in the sociology group. This not-talking-outside-of-their-own-little-group kept up for a couple of weeks. Colin tried everything he could think of to get the two sides to talk to each other. In desperation, he finally paid for a team party out of his own pocket. The party helped—but not much.

"It turned out that the male sociology student actually had been homeless at one point in his life and was pretty mature—he was in his 40s. His name was Bob. Bob was really interested in making a difference for homeless people."

"The women were another story. Eric didn't really like to intervene. He thought that an adviser should be a passive observer, not an active facilitator. In the meantime, Colin was pulling out his hair. Because they were sociology majors, Colin suggested that the women look at some legal issues and do some research on social policy issues. But the women weren't interested. One finally admitted that she just wanted an A so that she could keep her perfect GPA. She thought EPICS would look good on her résumé. We never did figure out what the other woman was doing on the team. Neither of them ever spoke at meetings outside of the sociology subgroup.

"So the technical types gave all this trivial work to the women. And then they'd ignore them. In fact, the guys started this little clique that would go out drinking. They invited Bob, but he declined because he was a recovering alcoholic. Even though he wasn't part of the engineer subgroup, the techies considered Bob one of the gang. I guess because he was a guy.

"Bob really took charge of things. He ended up doing stuff that no other team had done. He started a web-based newsletter to keep all the agencies posted on legal issues and other changes relevant to the homeless project. He ended up working for one of the agencies. He really made a difference in the community.

"But Colin never did figure out what he could have done differently to get that team integrated. And Eric was no help."

"That's interesting. I can't imagine *not* getting involved as an adviser," said Vanessa. "When you showed me all the stuff that EPICS students built for kids with cerebral palsy, Bonnie, you sold me on the program. I'm really looking forward to working with my first team. And thanks for setting up today's meeting. It made a huge difference to me to meet our community partner and some of the returning students."

Vanessa glanced at her watch. "You know what? It's getting pretty late and I'm starved. I could go for a pizza right now. Any chance we could charge it to EPICS, Bonnie?"

"Not a chance! Good try," Bonnie responded. "I'm ready for pizza, too. Are we done here, Kathleen and Joe?"

"I think so," Kathleen replied as she finished stacking her notes. "I agree with Vanessa about involvement. But I still don't know what we could have done differently with the homeless team. The same issues are there in other forms on most of our teams. We could really use your expertise, Vanessa, to help us figure out what we can try to do to improve team communication. Our students do well with their presentations after some coaching. It's the internal team and adviser-student interactions that we could use some help with."

"Yeah, I'd like to work through a new team dynamics exercise, if you have the time in the next couple of days, Vanessa" Joe said.

"Sure! I can handle the *soft* stuff. You know us communication types," Vanessa joked. "But seriously, at some point can we talk about how teams' internal dynamics are being influenced by the nature of the problem assigned to them? I can't just wave a wand, and students aren't going to transform their interaction because of one exercise. You know that."

"Yeah," Joe sighed. "I wish it was that easy."

"Your saying that, Vanessa, reminded me of something," Kathleen said, "we had our meeting with the senior design students. Four of them admitted that they signed up for EPICS rather than a regular engineering design class because they thought it would be an easy A with all this teamwork."

"We can do what we did last semester," Joe responded. "We went through everything to make sure that every student who signed up for senior design credit contributed something technical and unique. That seemed to work."

"Yes, it did seem to work," Kathleen said slowly, "but we do need to be careful." Kathleen turned her attention to Bonnie and said, "Bonnie, I talked to the student whose adviser gave him a C last semester."

Kathleen glanced at Joe to get his attention and said, "I think you should hear about this, Joe, in case you have to handle it when I'm out of town."

Kathleen continued, "The kid was not a mechanical, computer, or electrical engineer, so he did the team leadership and project management work. *All* the peer evaluations from other team members said he did a great job in facilitating the team and helping the group produce its outcome. His design notebook was in good order. His lab attendance and other assignments were fine. But he got a C.

"You'll never guess what the adviser—it's Dick, you know—said to him. Dick told this kid that he didn't think that he did what was required because he didn't do any *real* engineering work. Dick literally said to him, 'All students must be evaluated on their technical contributions no matter what other team functions they fulfill.' Anyway, Dick gave him a C. And the student is upset. Can you believe it?"

"That the student's upset or that Dick gave him a C?" Joe responded. "Don't you remember the *other* Dick issue?"

Vanessa looked puzzled, but Kathleen and Bonnie just groaned.

Joe explained, "Dick is the same faculty member who got into a heated argument with one of the social work faculty at an advisers' meeting because he thought that this adviser wasn't qualified to lead the students in a discussion of ethical issues. Dick said that it wasn't within the other adviser's expertise and that a faculty adviser shouldn't lead a discussion on an area in which he had no background. There are an awful lot of engineers who have very one-dimensional views of advisers' and students' capabilities. It gets old."

"It sure does get old," Kathleen agreed.

"While you ladies try to figure out the answers to all our student and adviser problems, I am heading home. Enjoy your pizza thing. I'm coaching soccer tonight," said Joe as he turned to leave.

"Wait a second! You need to give me your travel form before you leave for Chicago tomorrow afternoon," Bonnie reminded Joe. "I'm not covering for you if you forget. The business office will be after me if you don't start getting those travel forms to me early enough for them to process before you leave."

"Do I ever forget anything?" Joe asked. "I'll stop by your office tomorrow morning with a completed and signed form. I'll come early so that we can start processing the forms for the other million trips I'm making this semester.

"And to show you what a good guy I am," Joe continued, "I'll even hold the door open for you ladies while you push Bonnie's carts."

"Such a gentleman," Vanessa commented as she grabbed some PDAs. "Have a good trip!"

Joe said goodbye and started running down the hall.

Vanessa turned to the two women. "Now, Kathleen, what are you going to do with the team members who won't talk to each other?"

"I'm hoping you can help me answer that," Kathleen grumbled. "If they continue with this behavior this semester, then I'm going to write an order to have the facilities and maintenance people come and bolt the chairs down in a circle formation. Bonnie, do you think I could get approval for that?"

Bonnie shook her head "no" and said, "I haven't heard about this team. What's up?"

Kathleen explained, "The subgroups continued to sit in separate bunches despite my telling them every week for an entire semester to move the chairs into one big group. I think that they just figured that there was no reason to talk in the large group since they split the task into subparts. The subgroups had no clue what the others were doing, and it showed in their presentation to community partners. I hope it changes this semester. I am still so irritated with them. And I'm so tired of trying to think of ways to convince them that they actually need to talk to each other.

"But," Kathleen brightened, "that's enough about my team. You know what? I could really go for a beer with my pizza. Let's go to the Brewmeister!"

"Sounds great!" Vanessa agreed. "I love their deep-fried beer-battered pickles. Kathleen, if it's okay with you, I'm going to write up some of our discussions as a case. I'm teaching our undergraduate organizational communication class this semester. We're just about to get into team processes and related issues."

Bonnie asked, "Am I going to be featured in this case?"

"Absolutely," Vanessa said.

"Good! Make me the tall, gorgeous, blonde administrative assistant who drives a fancy red sports car," Bonnie laughed.

Kathleen laughed too and said, "It would be a big help for me to find out how we can do the multidisciplinary part of our teams better. Some advisers think that getting everyone involved just isn't their job—especially if the team makes some engineering advances on the project by the end of the semester. They consider the multidisciplinary part a nuisance. You know the problem, create a great bridge that takes you nowhere. So whatever you and your students could suggest would be a great help."

"Okay. Let me think about it and get back to you," Vanessa responded. "Maybe my org com class can make a formal presentation to you with their ideas and the theoretical background on group process. They are a good group—smart and motivated. Simply a joy to teach! In the meantime, let's go for pizza, pickles, and beer! But—on one condition."

"What's that?" Kathleen and Bonnie asked.

"No more EPICS talk—unless it's talk about all the good stuff that is going on with the teams," Vanessa replied.

"Agreed," said Bonnie and Kathleen.

As she turned to leave following Bonnie and Kathleen, this time with her keys in her hand, Vanessa wondered what she had gotten herself into. ✦

*EPICS stands for Engineering Projects in Community Service. Cofounded in 1995 by Leah Jamieson and Ed Coyle, professors in the School of Electrical and Computer Engineering at Purdue University, EPICS now has 24 teams and around 340 students enrolled for the Spring 2003 semester. EPICS programs have begun at other sites, including Notre Dame, Iowa State, Penn State University, the University of Wisconsin (Madison), Georgia Tech, Case Western Reserve University, the University of Illinois (Urbana-Champaign), the University of Puerto Rico (Mayaquez), and Butler University.

All the names of people and teams in this case have been changed. However, the EPICS website at Purdue University (<http://epics.ecn.purdue.edu>) lists current team projects, goals (to broaden students' educations and to provide services to not-for-profit organizations), descriptions of the unique course structure (multiyear student involvement in ongoing design teams that incorporate diverse disciplines), and other details. Currently, students come from 20 different departments. Advisers are from eight different departments at Purdue University as well as from local companies.

On the Purdue University website, under the "About EPICS" button, readers can locate a bibliography of publications about this program (e.g., Oakes, Krull, Coyle, Jamieson, & Kong, 2000). For each of the 24 teams, videotapes of the most recent presentations are located on the EPICS website. Project reports without technical appendixes (for intellectual property reasons) are available on the same site.

Chapter 15

Maintaining Faith

Christine S. Davis

"What a day!" Suzanne Whitaker* exclaimed to her husband as she entered the door. She was exhausted. She had been the executive director of the Interfaith Center for Aging for 14 months and had never felt so frustrated in a job before.

"Remember the good you're doing there," Jake gently reminded her as he helped her with her briefcase and coat.

Suzanne tried to focus on why she had joined the organization in the first place. It was a ministry for older adults. The Interfaith Center provided services to seniors—generally those who were relatively healthy for their ages. The center's mission was to give retired, widowed, and lonely seniors a place to go, make friends, and develop meaning in their lives. After almost 20 years of being a cog in the corporate wheel, Suzanne had seen this job as an opportunity to use her administrative skills to make the world a better place. But for now, she was just tired!

As Suzanne was sorting through the mail, she described what had happened that day at the senior center. "You know my great idea to have a *Mom's Cooking* cookbook? They don't want to do it. None of them cook! See, that's the problem! They don't act like old people are supposed to act!"

Jake smiled. He knew she was exaggerating but not far from the truth. The truth was, Suzanne worked with over 200 older adult volunteers who did not fit Suzanne's expectations about senior citizens.

"They are so stubborn! No matter what my idea is, even if most of the volunteers like it, there will be five people to *always* tell me what's wrong with it!"

After feeding the dog, Suzanne went into the kitchen to start working on dinner. As she did, she reflected on her decision to take this job—this job that she thought would be different. She had imagined that working for a nonprofit would be less stressful, more rewarding, and more meaningful than working in the corporate world. Now she realized that she had just traded one set of frustrations for another.

"I had another chat with Angela," Suzanne began in a complaining voice.

"Uh-huh," Jake said expectantly as he began the salads while she microwaved yesterday's leftovers. He knew that Angela was one of her key volunteers and a board member, and that she always spoke her mind.

"She went off again on how Cindy used to be such a terrible executive director. I used to take that as a compliment to me, but now I just wonder if that's what they're going to say about me when I finally leave."

"Tell me again what they didn't like about Cindy?" Jake asked supportively.

"I don't know, there were always conflicts. They're always complaining that she didn't get enough work done. You know, her position was only part-time. It seems to me that she got done as much as she could. That place will work you to death if you let it!" Jake caught her eye and smiled, trying to calm her mood.

"Angela's always complaining about something. Today she accused me of trying to take over her job as public relations chairperson! Honestly! I was just trying to get a press release out. She said I had an ego issue!" Suzanne vented.

"Can't you just discourage Angela from volunteering there anymore?" Jake suggested helpfully.

Suzanne sighed. It would certainly make her life easier. However, at the Interfaith Center volunteering was viewed as one of the primary vehicles for making seniors feel useful. Volunteers helped because they received companionship and a sense of belonging, feeling needed, and doing good.

Jake knew that. He was just trying to ease Suzanne out of her stressed mood.

The Interfaith Center had a variety of programs and services, typically divided into two categories, educational programs and service programs. Educational programs included a mini-university for seniors, support groups, health seminars, and a health fair. Service programs included transportation, visitation, respite care, and handyperson assistance.

At the Interfaith Center, there were three types of older adults involved. There were the volunteers who worked on their fundraisers, sat on committees, and helped clients. There were program participants, who attended their educational programming. And there were the clients, who were the recipients of the service programs. But in reality, everything wasn't so neatly divided, as many of the seniors fell into all three categories.

Leading the Volunteers

Suzanne had a fitful night's sleep, and went to work early the next morning. She was trying to finish the monthly newsletter and was pressed for time. The newsletter, which went out to all the volunteers, clients, and donors, was the primary way the Interfaith Center communicated with each of these groups. This month's newsletter advertised their upcoming Annual Volunteer Appreciation Luncheon; plugged their membership drive; promoted volunteering; thanked donors; announced the death of one of their office volunteers; publicized a cooking class; and issued invitations to a support group, a trip to see a play, a bridge group, a health fair, and an art studio.

Margaret, the Friday morning office volunteer, was already there. "Good morning!" she greeted Suzanne cheerfully. Margaret always had a ready smile for everyone.

"How's David?" Suzanne asked her. Her husband suffered from a chronic illness, and Suzanne worried about both of them.

Margaret sighed and shook her head. "Not a good day yesterday." She seemed to purposely change the subject. "Remember the committee meeting this morning. Do you want me to sit in and take notes?"

Suzanne nodded appreciatively and scanned her desk for the materials she would need for the meeting.

The Fundraising Committee Meeting

Angela was the first to arrive for the meeting and selected her seat at the opposite end of the table from where Suzanne normally sat, even when she wasn't chairing a committee. Well groomed, with a strong southern accent, her presence commanded a room. She could be intimidating to other volunteers. The last time she and Margaret were at the same meeting, Margaret told her to "quit being crabby!" Suzanne was sure that Angela was trying to intimidate her as well, but mostly Suzanne was frustrated by her outbursts.

There were 10 volunteers on this fundraising committee and they were working on their current goal, planning their next fundraising event. Clark, the committee chair, had called in with a sudden family emergency, so Suzanne called the meeting to order and went through the agenda. "Okay, we want to come up with ideas for our newest fundraiser," she began enthusiastically. Everyone nodded. "Why don't we talk about our goals for the fundraiser and then brainstorm for ideas?" Everyone nodded.

Just as Suzanne opened her mouth to speak again, Angela interrupted. "Shut up," she said sharply. "You are talking too much." Suzanne bit her tongue and said nothing as she felt a flush go up her neck. Nobody said a word. The room was still. After a moment, Angela spoke again. "Why don't you let someone else talk?" Suzanne remained quiet, but not a sound was heard from anyone.

"Typical," thought Suzanne. "No one ever comes to my rescue."

Finally, Suzanne asked tentatively, "Angela, what would you like someone to say?"

Angela took the bait. "I think we need to come up with ideas for the fundraiser." Suzanne looked around the room. Everyone was suddenly intent on their notebooks.

"Angela," Suzanne said, in as positive a voice as she could muster, but she knew her voice was still shaky, "would it be all right if we first decided on our goals for the fundraiser?"

"Yes," Angela said with an air of satisfaction. The meeting continued in its original format even though Suzanne noticed that no one directed a comment to Angela. But who could blame them? She didn't either.

The Mini-University

Suzanne was still thinking about Angela's behavior the next morning when the Interfaith Center held their mini-university. The 9 A.M. session consisted of three choices of courses: Faith in Our Chaotic World, Storytelling for Grandparents, and Fall Gardening. The 10:30 A.M. choices were Conversational French, Tai Chi, and Political Activism for Seniors. The afternoon choices were Digital Photography, Advanced Needlework, and Bridge for Beginners. Suzanne was proud of the university and pleased with the 125 who signed up to attend.

Lunch was served before the afternoon sessions and consisted of beef tips, green beans, a roll, and iced tea. Suzanne was delighted to see several new faces in the crowd, so she stood at the door to the Fellowship Hall to welcome each person as they came into the luncheon. When Angela came through the doorway at the end of the crowd, she amazed Suzanne by giving her a hug and calling her "darling." A little startled, Suzanne had to compose herself. The seniors were waiting for her to take her seat at the head table.

As lunch was winding down, Suzanne checked to see where Angela was sitting. She wanted to avoid making eye contact with her during her announcements. Suzanne was still playing Angela's change in character over in her mind when she began reading the announcements. "Don't forget that our support groups are starting up again next month. And in two weeks, we're having a seminar on skin cancer prevention. We have a day trip coming up to go to the glass factory in Mayodan for a tour. Remember to sign up for our cooking class on making gingerbread houses. We still need more volunteers to sort books for our book sale. Thank you to the folks at Brighton Gardens for our refreshments at this morning's break. And we're looking for someone to volunteer to videotape these mini-university sessions, so we can let others take part when they can't be here in person."

Suzanne liked it when the mini-university drew this large a group. The luncheons in between sessions were one of the few opportunities they had to get together as a whole group, to solicit feedback from a wide variety of volunteers and clients, and to communicate upcoming events. In one way, the mini-universities were examples of the center operating most effectively. She could use the luncheons to emphasize a shared culture and vision. Unfortunately, the Interfaith Center only had three mini-universities throughout the year, so there were many times when there was no way to communicate to so many people, except through the newsletter.

Identifying New Volunteers

As people were chatting after the lunch break, waiting for the afternoon sessions to begin, Liz came up to talk to Suzanne. She was an attractive woman who looked to be in her mid-60s, with short gray hair and wearing a coordinated pantsuit. "I want to start volunteering," she began hesitantly. "What do I have to do?"

Suzanne motioned to a chair and invited Liz to join her. "What type of volunteering do you want to do?" she asked.

"Anything!" Liz replied, brightening. "I used to be a secretary, but I'm retired now and I'm so lonely! I moved here to be near my daughter, but then her husband was transferred shortly after I arrived and now I'm here all alone!" Liz's eyes filled with tears as she looked at Suzanne with a hopeful look.

Suzanne nodded. She had heard this story many times before. "I'm so glad you found us," she said sympathetically. "You know, I need an office volunteer for Wednesday mornings. Do you think you'd be interested?"

Liz's face lit up. "Do I need to fill out an application or go through training or anything?"

"No, just tell me you'll do it, then show up. I'll explain to you what to do then."

Liz squeezed Suzanne's hand. "You know, now I have something to tell my daughter when I talk to her."

Suzanne sighed. Now she remembered why she took this job.

Back in the office after the last mini-university session, Suzanne found Betty waiting for her. "You said to stop by today. Is this a good time?"

Suzanne smiled. Betty was a longtime volunteer who put in many hours for the Interfaith Center. Suzanne wanted Betty to chair the rummage sale. She knew Betty would be resistant, but she had arguments ready. "Betty," she began optimistically, "you know it's time to begin planning for our rummage sale."

Betty nodded, clearly wary. "And I always help out with the sale," she interjected.

"You're a great help," Suzanne acknowledged. "As a matter of fact, you're so knowledgeable about the sale that I'm hoping we can count on you to be the chairperson."

Betty made a face. "You know I don't like to be in charge of things."

Suzanne had expected this reply. Most of the volunteers didn't like to be put in charge of committees. She was ready with an answer. "What if I asked Barbara to cochair it with you? The two of you have always worked well together, and that way neither of you would be doing it all yourself." She saw Betty softening. "Besides, you know that you'll have plenty of help from the other volunteers. And, of course, from me!"

Betty nodded hesitantly. "Can I get the office volunteers to help me send out notices about the sale?"

"Of course," Suzanne agreed, inwardly relieved.

"We'll need to start planning it soon," Betty added, with an efficient tone to her voice.

Suzanne got out her calendar. "How about if we meet next Wednesday to lay it all out?"

Betty nodded. She was in.

Volunteer Appreciation Luncheon

It was December and the weather was quite chilly. Parking was a problem, but this didn't keep the seniors away from this event. The Interfaith Center's Annual Volunteer Appreciation Luncheon was an event people didn't want to miss. Other than their mini-university classes, it was the only time throughout the year when everyone got together. It was a grand occasion. The Fellowship Hall had been transformed. Fresh flowers topped the tablecloths, and Christmas music wafted in the background. Suzanne smoothed her red suit and took a deep breath. Even though she had given hundreds of speeches in her career, she was nervous today. This was her one chance all year to thank all the volunteers for their hundreds of hours of hard work. This was the prom, the Academy Awards, the State of the Union Address, and a Christmas party all rolled into one event. She took her seat at the head table and looked around. There were about 300 people there, mostly gray haired, mostly dressed in holiday colors. She mentally practiced her speech as the caterer served the meal. She watched him serve the special vegetarian meal to Linda and Marie. Linda always complained about the meal; if it wasn't vegetarian, that was cause to complain. If it was vegetarian, it wasn't balanced enough, or tasty enough, or healthy enough, or something. Suzanne refocused her attention on the rest of the room. Everyone was laughing, chatting, eating, enjoying themselves. Suzanne relaxed and rose to begin the awards presentation.

"Today," she began, speaking powerfully and pausing dramatically, "we're here to honor and thank *you,* the volunteers who so selflessly give their time, energy, and work. *You* are our stars. *You,* the volunteers, consistently give us your best efforts. *You* are what make our team successful!" She picked up a large gold star paperweight and held it up for everyone to see. "This award is for our Volunteer of the Year. As you know, our Volunteer of the Year was selected by *you. You,* the members, nominated and then voted for our Volunteer of the Year. This is quite an honor, to be recognized by the other volunteers, the people who see how hard you work and the people who have been the recipients of your caring and sharing."

She looked down at her notes and continued. "Our Volunteer of the Year gave us 250 hours this year! She is a joy to work with. She has volunteered for our book sale and our rummage sale, and she is an office volunteer. Every time our doors are open, she is there helping out. I am very pleased to announce our volunteer of the year."

Suzanne paused dramatically. "Barbara Brooks!" Barbara jumped up, clearly excited and pleased. The room burst into applause. "Barbara, come up and get your award!" Suzanne gave Barbara a hug as she presented the paperweight. Cameras flashed. As Barbara returned to her seat, Suzanne continued with the awards.

"Next, I'd like to recognize our star volunteers. These volunteers have all worked at least 100 hours this year. All of our star volunteers will receive this gold star pin. Please come forward as I call your name." She smiled and gestured toward the audience as she announced the first name. "Paul Bledsoe." She spoke as Paul walked to the front of the room. "Paul is our most active handyperson volunteer. He was cochairperson of our golf tournament. Paul is always willing to help out." Suzanne shook Paul's hand firmly, then pinned the star onto his lapel. "Congratulations, Paul."

They paused to have their picture taken; then Suzanne continued calling out the names of the other six seniors who received the star volunteer award. Each received a gold star pin and had their picture taken with Suzanne. Not wanting anyone to feel left out, Suzanne had planned it so everyone received some recognition. Others who had volunteered during the year received a lapel pin. Even those who had just begun volunteering received a certificate for their participation. Suzanne had spent many hours compiling the information about volunteer hours and activities. She wanted to make sure that everyone who volunteered at the center received some sort of recognition. She looked at the beaming faces and felt the positive energy and unity in the room. Clearly, her time putting together the information had paid off.

The Board Meeting

Jane popped her head into the office and found Suzanne bent over the copier, fixing a paper jam. Suzanne saw Jane and stifled an exasperated curse directed at the copy machine. Jane Langston was Interfaith's board president and was here for the board meeting. "Is the agenda ready yet?" she asked Suzanne.

"I'm copying it right now, but you can look at it," Suzanne said as she handed Jane the original and Jane looked it over. She read:

Board Meeting Agenda

Topic	Time
1. Call to order (Jane Langston)	1:00
2. Prayer (Art Graves)	2:00
3. Approval of November minutes (Jane Langston)	4:00
4. Treasurer's Report (Clark Wyss)	5:00
5. Director's Report (Suzanne Whitaker)	35:00
6. Committee Reports (Committee chairs)	10:00
7. Other Business (Jane Langston)	2:00
a. Time of next board meeting	
8. Adjourn (Jane Langston)	1:00

Jane was a vice president at a bank that had a history of supporting the center. She smoothed the front of her corporate blue suit as she approved the agenda. "Looks good to me! Thanks for putting it together."

"Jane," Suzanne said hesitantly as she began the copying again, "I need to talk to you about something." She hated to bring up serious matters here in the open office, but Jane was seldom available between board meetings. "You know, Jane, I've been here for almost year and a half, and I still haven't received a performance evaluation."

This topic really made Suzanne angry. Jane had been putting her off for months, and Suzanne was overdue for a raise. Suzanne knew that Jane's company wouldn't stand for her delaying employee evaluations like that.

Jane patted her arm condescendingly. "Yeah, we do need to do that. I'll call you to schedule something. By the way, you're doing a great job." She walked out of the room. When Jane was safely out of range, Suzanne rolled her eyes and continued fiddling with the copy machine.

Most of the board members were seated at the table when Suzanne walked into the conference room. The 12-person board consisted of 6 Interfaith Center volunteers and 6 businesspeople and community leaders. As with other nonprofits, Suzanne wasn't a member of the board. In fact, technically she reported to them. It was an odd combination, Suzanne thought, gray hair and comfortable clothes mingled with blue suits and daytimers. Warm greetings filled the room as she passed out the agendas. Some board members got up to get another helping of coffee and doughnuts.

The friendly chatter stopped as Jane called the meeting to order. "Art, will you please start us with a prayer?" she asked.

"You know," Art directed his gaze at Suzanne as he complained, "I never said I would do the prayer every time. I think we should take turns."

Suzanne sighed. Art was a retired minister. She never thought she'd hear a minister complain about praying.

Art prayed, "Lord, thank you for bringing us here together, and bless what we do here today. In Jesus' name we pray. Amen."

Suzanne cringed. The Interfaith Center was supposed to be nondenominational. She was sure that she would hear about the reference to Jesus after the meeting. Jane called for approval of the last month's minutes, and Clark gave his treasurer's report.

The next item on the agenda was Suzanne's Director's Report. At Jane's nod, Suzanne passed out copies of the 15-page report and began with the first item. "Since our last board meeting, I have sent out two grant proposals. The first was to our local community foundation to obtain funding for a feasibility study for a new senior center. We discussed this at our last board meeting. I asked for $15,500. We should hear if we were successful by the end of January. I also sent a grant proposal to the state to fund our visitation program. We should hear about that in January also."

Suzanne looked around the table. Frank was frowning. "Why are we doing a feasibility study?" he asked firmly.

"We discussed this at the last board meeting. We agreed that having our own space was a goal we wanted to work toward," Suzanne answered, trying to suppress a flash of exasperation.

"I don't think we should be moving in that direction," Frank argued.

"But the board agreed at our last meeting that we would pursue this," Suzanne persisted. She glanced over at Jane, waiting for her show of support. Jane had voted for the study at the last board meeting, and Suzanne had thought she supported the proposal. But Jane didn't jump to defend Suzanne, the funding for the feasibility study, or even the idea of having their own space. At best, Suzanne thought Jane had a reserved, noncommittal look on her face.

"I think we're moving too fast. We need to discuss it some more." This last argument came from Dell, a longtime volunteer.

Suzanne stiffened. She felt blindsided. "Here they go again, changing things after they had agreed to them," she thought angrily.

"Maybe we need to rethink this," said Angela resolutely. "It seems like you are trying to railroad this through."

Suzanne took a deep breath, feeling left out on a limb by herself. Jane finally spoke up. "Well, all we're doing now is asking for money for a feasibility study. We won't be taking any action until the study is done."

Suzanne looked around the room. Heads were nodding, Jane made no further comments, and no one offered another argument, so she continued with the next item. "I would like to rework our mission statement. My sense is that it is not very meaningful to our membership. I doubt that most people can recite it. I think it's important for everyone on our team to have the same understanding of what we stand for. I'd like to get together a task force to rewrite it."

She had their full attention again. Dell spoke first, with a defiant edge to her voice. "I was with this organization 12 years ago, in the beginning, when we wrote that mission statement. A lot of hard work went into it. I don't think we should just throw it out!"

Frank spoke up next. "I don't think we can change the mission statement without a vote of the entire membership!"

Angela echoed the sentiment. "You can't just go changing things like that!" Heads nodded in agreement.

Jane spoke up. "Why don't we think about it and discuss it at a later meeting?"

Suzanne moved on to the next item in the report. "I'd like to begin including financial information in our newsletter. Someone asked me the other day why we needed donations." She continued, "Since we were such a small organization, I'm afraid people think that we don't have any expenses. I'd like to put our most recent financial statement in the newsletter to let everyone know where their money goes. And it will help everyone connected with Interfaith to understand where we are financially, and where we are going." This was another touchy subject, and she braced for one more fight.

"Are we allowed to show our financial information to the public?" asked Sharon.

"As a matter of fact," answered Suzanne, "as a nonprofit, I don't think we're allowed not to." Heads nodded thoughtfully.

"I don't think we should tell people too much," Will added.

"I think Suzanne's got a point," said Clark convincingly. He and Suzanne had already discussed the topic and its possible opposition before the meeting. "We accept money from the public and we serve the public. We should show them how we spent the money."

Frank agreed. "That makes sense to me."

Jane voiced her support. "I think it's a good idea too. Shall we vote on it?" The vote was unanimously in favor.

Suzanne moved on. "We have an opportunity to hire a student intern from the university. They'll work eight hours a week, mostly helping in the office. Because we can get an intern through the AmeriCorps program, we'll have to pay only $3 of their $8 hourly wage. It's a great deal."

Angela spoke up this time. "Why do we need another employee? Would this person have anything to do?"

Suzanne took another deep breath and tried to control the flush moving up her neck. "Well, I need help in getting all the work done that I have to do. You can see in the Director's Report all the things I am involved in."

"We always used to get the job done and Cindy only worked part-time," interjected Angela.

"Yes, but the workload has grown a lot since I've been here," countered Suzanne.

"It's only $3 an hour," said Jane.

"We can afford it," offered Clark.

Lib showed her support. "I move to hire the intern," she said. That vote was unanimous.

Suzanne ran through the rest of the Director's Report, pointing out all the work she had accomplished since the last board meeting.

The next item on the agenda was committee reports. Given by the volunteer chairpersons of each committee, they were brief and perfunctory.

The board members filed out of the room, exactly on time. "Here," said Angela hurriedly as she handed a paper to Suzanne. "You'll need this for the public relations committee meeting tomorrow. Please have someone type it up for me. Oh, and I can't be there, but I wrote a description of what you need to accomplish."

Suzanne sighed as she took the paper from Angela and looked around the empty conference room. Dirty coffee cups, napkins, and leftover doughnuts littered the table. She tucked Angela's paper under her arm as she gathered the trash and picked up the coffee cups to wash them. What would she tell Jake tonight? ✦

*This case has been developed based on real organization(s) and real organizational experiences. Names, facts, and situations have been changed to protect the privacy of individuals and organizations.

Chapter 16

Teaming Up for Change

Maryanne Wanca-Thibault and Adelina Gomez

In 1995, during a weekly staff meeting, Lieutenant Jack Whitson,[1] a police detective with the Castle Springs Police Department, addressed his concerns and frustrations to the others present. "I am very frustrated. As the city grows, the number of domestic violence cases in our community continues to increase. Nothing we do seems to reduce our caseload numbers."

He continued, "We go by the book; we respond to calls and take the necessary information from both parties, and then we determine if the case merits charging one or both parties involved. But then it's out of our hands until the violence happens again. There has to be a better way."

Janet Garcia, the deputy district attorney, agreed. "Our court cases are so backlogged that by the time we reach the court date the victim often decides to drop the charges."

Sue Mackenzie, the domestic violence victim's advocate, added, "My frustration is in trying to provide the victims with support services to keep them safe while the perpetrators are trying to get them to drop the charges. Usually, they end up right back in the same abusive relationship."

Frustrated with the high volume of domestic violence cases and a bureaucracy in which professionals from across many units did not routinely or formally share information, these three individuals determined that it was time to take action and change the status quo.

As the meeting continued, they began to discuss a possible approach to the domestic violence issue—an approach that had not been tried before. Jack envisioned a collaborative team approach to the problem. "It's obvious," he said, "that we can do a better job of working together and sharing information about our cases. We just have to put the mechanism for it in place."

Jack, Janet, and Sue all knew that it would be a challenge to change the attitudes and values of groups who traditionally had worked on the same side, but not always together or with the same information.

Sue countered, "I agree that we have our work cut out for us, but if we are able to convince our colleagues to reorganize into a more efficient and holistic method of dealing with victims and perpetrators, we might get the support we need. Let's face it, we spend so much time trying to handle all of the calls we receive that we really can't focus on things like containment, education, and protection of the victims and their families. A collaborative approach would provide a central source for dealing with all of the issues related to domestic violence."

Janet said, "I agree. It would be great if the new model could better incorporate community policing. But I hesitate to add that, since you know how resistant the old-timers have been to that."

Jack responded, "I wish we had a system where we would regularly rotate police, judicial, and social service personnel through the team. When they leave the team they could go back to their home agencies with a new perspective on working collaboratively. Of course, that means we will have to provide ongoing training for individuals. We haven't traditionally used a collaborative approach in law enforcement. We tend to work independently of social services and the justice system when it comes to handling domestic violence. From my experience, other agencies work in about the same way. Everybody does their thing, independent of others in the system who also work with domestic violence."

"Yes, I agree," said Janet. "Simply putting a collaborative team in place won't accomplish what we want it to. We are going to have to learn how to collaborate, if we plan to make this work."

Creating DVERT

It took many more meetings and a great deal more discussion, but in 1996, funded by a federal grant from the Department of Justice and with support from members of local law enforcement agencies, the judicial system, and social services agencies, DVERT (Domestic Violence Enhanced Response Team) was created.

The objective of the DVERT team was to identify and work with individuals who pose a significant risk to their past or present partners because of acts or threats of domestic violence. Under DVERT, a number of community agencies would become real partners and combine forces to identify suspects who fit the profile of abusers. If the DVERT team determined that the level of violence necessitated intervention, the team added the case to their load, meaning that both victim and perpetrator were subject to follow-up meetings with the team.

The Stakeholders

Detective Jack Whitson, the DVERT program manager, sat in his office behind closed doors and replayed the events of the morning's yearly board meeting in his head. "This is 2002," he thought. "We've successfully operated DVERT for five years. We've certainly had our ups and downs, and there has been plenty of change during that time. But our future's at stake. We are really going to have to pull together to make some decisions and it's not going to be easy." He knew that frustration was running high among a number of the DVERT board members, and he was going to have to address their concerns in the afternoon session.

Jack was a pragmatic man. He was known to face challenges head-on, and creating and managing a multidisciplinary program like DVERT had certainly tested his leadership skills. But for Jack it always came back to the program's mission: "to work in partnership with community agencies to enhance the safety of victims of domestic violence and their children, while ensuring appropriate containment of offenders." In his mind, regardless of any other differences the agencies had, this was a value they all shared.

The 14-member advisory board of directors (Figure 16.1) was somewhat unique. Each member represented a community agency or group with a vested interest in domestic violence containment and prevention. In addition to the clients, these community members were key stakeholders in the organization. Depending on their expertise, agencies were responsible for negotiating and providing their expertise, manpower, and other resource support to DVERT. The 8

Figure 16.1
DVERT Partnering Agencies

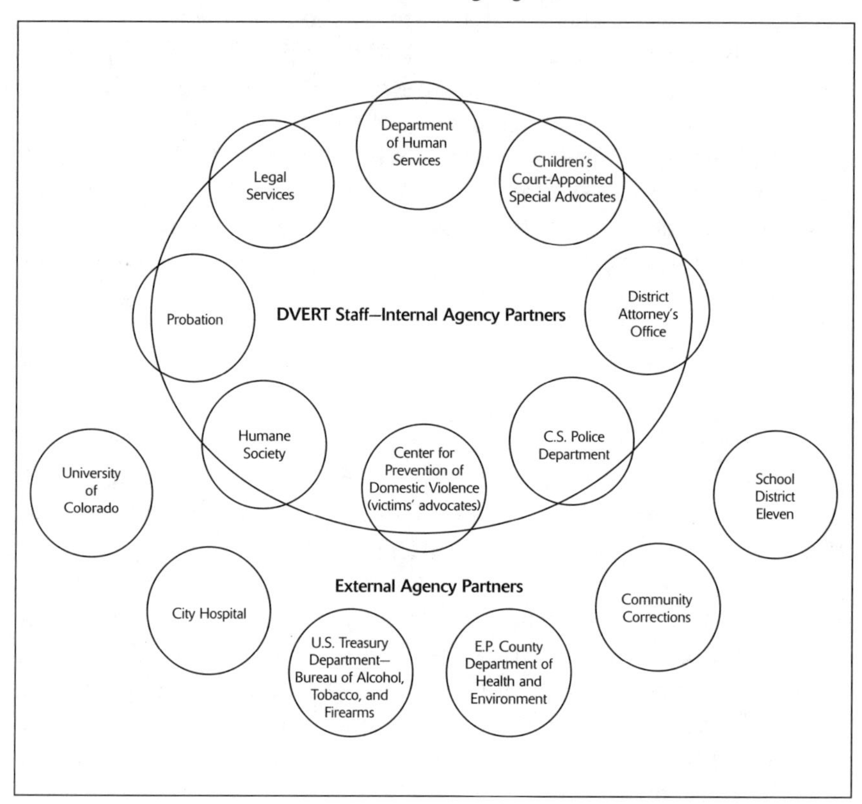

internal partnering agencies provided permanent and rotational manpower in the form of victim advocates, police officers, court-appointed children's advocates, a district attorney, and animal advocates[2] who actually worked on a daily basis with full-time DVERT staff. The 6 remaining external agencies acted as consultants and provided expertise and support to the DVERT staff. Generally, the external agencies had more limited interaction with the full-time staff, although a number of them were involved in weekly staffing meetings, where caseload decisions were made. However, all representatives of the board met at least once a year to discuss their ongoing roles and contributions to the program. The diversity of the agencies represented allowed DVERT to address the variety of concerns associated with the containment and prevention of domestic violence. Jack saw the challenge as making certain that each agency maintained its commitment to DVERT's organizational mission and values. This was tough, given that each agency representative also felt allegiance to other people and projects.

DVERT's structural form was different from most public sector organizations that rely on traditional hierarchical designs. In this case, the organization was characterized as a flat organization composed of teams with defined accountabilities and responsibilities (Figure 16.2). There were two full-time managers under Jack's direction. The first managed operational issues regarding caseload. Under this manager were two full-time team leaders who, along with their multidisciplinary teams, assessed and investigated the domestic violence cases brought to DVERT. The second manager handled research and development issues (i.e., training, grants, crime analysis) for the organization. In this high participation environment, decision making was always considered a collaborative process involving all of the appropriate stakeholders.

In the early days of the program there had been many turf battles. It was bound to happen. Most of these groups had rarely collaborated with each other in the past and now found it challenging to share office space, let alone ideas and decision making. It was not unusual for someone from human services to complain that "we don't even share the same language" when speaking of other team members. In particular, many of the rotational staff found that in order to do their jobs, they had to develop a better understanding of what other agencies around them were doing. That resulted in a great deal of negotiation and adjustment on everyone's part. Subsequently, there was an ongoing perception among many of the staff and partners that the program was always evolving.

An unwritten credo among staff was that the one thing you could expect at DVERT was change. This situation was difficult for many of the staff, who had worked in organizations where standards and policies were firmly in place. In those first several years the program lost a number of full-time staff who had a hard time dealing with the change and collaborative decision making. Moreover, many people who had volunteered for a rotation at DVERT left after their three-month commitment, disillusioned with the process. However, in the past two years the membership at DVERT had stabilized, and some members had asked to stay on for more than a single rotation. Some rotational staff had even moved into permanent positions.

Figure 16.2
DVERT's Organizational Chart

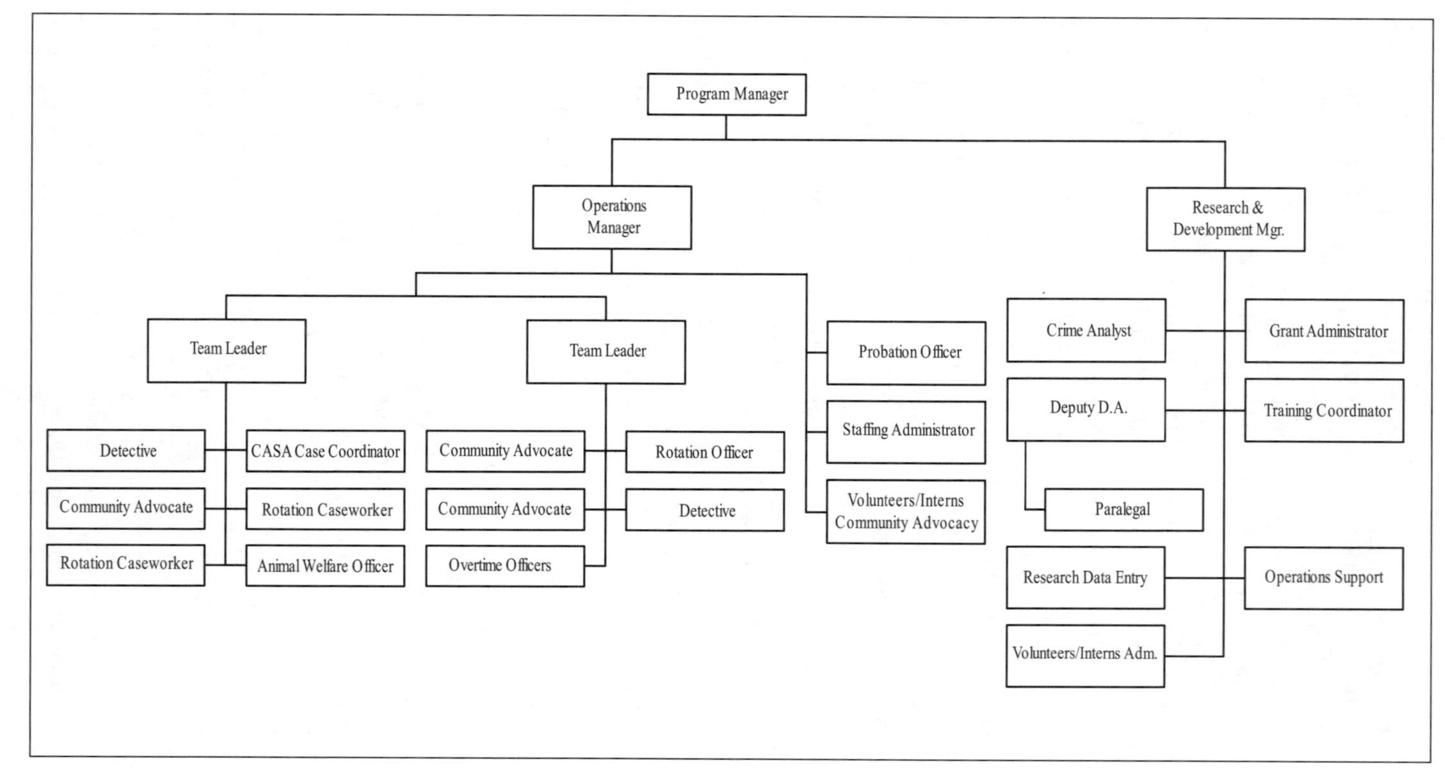

Coming from a law enforcement background, even Jack could clearly see how the diversity of organizational values affected DVERT's climate. In his leadership role he often found it a challenge to help the group manage change and to work through the differences that arose. But from his perspective, that diversity and the ability to quickly adapt to the external and internal environment, if channeled correctly, was the underlying strength of this collaborative approach toward domestic violence.

From Whitson's perspective he thought now that the program was moving into its sixth year, they had moved beyond that stage of *muscle flexing* and were working together more effectively. However, it was clear from this morning's discussion that a number of partners were looking to make some changes. While he encouraged planned change as a strategic management tool, he also realized the importance of maintaining continuity when things worked well. In Jack's mind the question was whether these changes were right for DVERT at this time.

The Issues

During the morning session of the board meeting, Jack had been prepared for questions from disgruntled members. He started by reviewing the issues that would likely emerge. He summarized, "Our first issue is centered on increasing financial support for DVERT."

Kirby Jones, the humane society representative, interjected, "I thought all the funding that we would need would be covered by the federal grant."

"Much of it is," Jack responded, "but we still need to consider other options for ongoing funding. Our grants are getting smaller every year."

Sue Mackenzie, the domestic violence victim's advocate, interrupted, "VAWA or Violence Against Women Association is a potential funding source."

Janet Garcia, the deputy district attorney, added, "We also need to identify other grant sources to help sustain DVERT. We have been extremely fortunate to have had significant monetary support to maintain the program."

"Yes," said Jack, "and let's not forget the rotation staff, which some partners are providing on an ongoing basis, as well as the furniture, office space, and supplies that are donated. Those are critical operating resources." Several members nodded in acknowledgment.

At this point, Jack interrupted the discussion to explain that there were still two key issues left to discuss. "We can't forget the most important issues here," he said. "We touched on funding. The second issue is growth of the program, meaning the expansion of cases that the program can comfortably handle. The third issue is whether or not to expand the partner base."

Elliott Richards, a board representative from the probation department, interrupted. "I'm not convinced that we are informed enough to act on any of these issues. First, our decreasing budget already affects the level of services we can provide for our clients. How will we be able to increase services without increasing the budget?"

One of the major arguments among the partners was the issue of quality versus quantity. Many felt that it was the role of DVERT to handle only the most serious and ultimately lethal domestic violence cases, whereas other members felt that DVERT should not distinguish between the levels of lethality and should strive to serve as many victims as possible.

Elliott continued, "Moreover, the current economic climate makes the development of the program tenuous, at best. And the way I see it, we will have to really struggle to increase funding without increasing the number of partners we currently have on the board. It's obvious we have to add new partners."

Jack tried to remain neutral at this point and declined to respond to Elliott's comment, but he knew that there was political pressure from some local leaders and politicians for DVERT to address the entire gamut of domestic violence issues. There was a growing perception in the community that domestic violence was out of control and better methods of containment and prevention should be made available. Jack was very familiar with the argument and had recently had a number of discussions with the police chief, the mayor, and several state and federal legislators about the direction in which the program was headed. Yet, while there was pressure to grow, there had been no additional promise of community or state funding in the near future to help defray the costs of the program.

Jack knew that a number of the smaller organizational partners were beginning to worry about their continued participation in DVERT. They, too, had experienced budget cutbacks. In many ways, the cutbacks were harder to absorb in these smaller agencies. Despite these worries, these were also the groups who were adamant about maintaining the quality of the program.

The larger community and state agencies that partnered with DVERT saw the issue from another perspective. Many of these partners (e.g., human services, district attorney's office, Center for the Prevention of Domestic Violence) were feeling political pressure and felt that the response should be to serve the broadest client base possible. They believed that taking on more cases and perhaps not spending as much time on any particular case would be advantageous in two ways. First, it would expose more clients to DVERT. Second, that exposure would translate into higher visibility and provide a strong argument for increased funding sources.

While there was disagreement on how the first two issues should be handled, there was almost total agreement on the third. The partners were all lobbying for adding more external agencies to the advisory board as a means of maintaining, if not increasing, current funding levels. Over the years, Jack and his staff had grappled with the appropriate size for the advisory board. As the group leader, he knew the inherent difficulties of working with a large group. It had not been easy to create a culture for this team, which already represented 14 agencies. He was fairly adamant that adding new partners during a time when the group was already divided on significant issues would be problematic. However, adding partners just to increase funding was a disaster waiting to happen, he thought. In the past, Jack had successfully argued his position against adding partners. But, based on this current discussion, it was becoming clear that maintaining his stance against adding new members would be more difficult in light of the other issues the group was facing. Based on the board's discussion, Jack knew he would have to carefully consider the possibilities, and he struggled with what he would say in the afternoon session.

But for now, Jack needed to get back to the team's lunch meeting. Not wanting to waste time, he had invited two consultants to present some of the findings of their communication audit of DVERT. Specifically, Jack has asked to them focus on their findings about leadership and the team's communication effectiveness. Given the decisions that were before them, he hoped they would hear something that would help the group make these decisions about DVERT's future.

The Consultants' Findings

On the way to the luncheon meeting, Janet and Elliott talked about what they thought the study would reveal. Janet said, "I've been concerned about what to expect from the study. On one hand, the DVERT program would not have survived as long as it has without Jack's leadership and guidance. He is the guiding force that has propelled the program and driven the rest of us to work diligently. On the other hand, my informal conversations with others suggest that he spends too much time micromanaging the group. It's almost as if he believes that without him overseeing everything, the program will fail."

Elliott agreed. "I know what you mean. He is an extraordinary manager, but I was honest on the survey in my evaluation of his leadership style, good and bad; I hope others were too. I wonder how he'll react to the consultants' presentation?"

The consultants' presentation confirmed what many of the partners had known all along. One of the strengths of the DVERT program was the group's leadership. In her report, one of the consultants indicated that Jack had been described by others as a "charismatic leader," a "visionary," "goal-oriented," "someone who promotes collaboration and emphasizes success," and an "individual who is committed to serving clients and the community." Jack was also seen as someone who motivated others to perform to their highest abilities. One write-in comment went so far as to identify Jack as the ideal representative for the program. It was true. Jack had gained national recognition for DVERT, due largely to his ability to obtain funding, create a sense of trust among the organizational representatives, and surround himself with high-caliber people.

Ironically, these qualities also created the greatest concerns for some of the partners. As the consultants continued their report to the group, they acknowledged that while the group's leadership was a source of strength for the program, it was also a source of frustration for some of the team members. One of the consultants reported, "Some of the partners felt that performance expectations were too high, and the small number of staff made it tough to handle the expected workload. Others expressed concerns that team members were always expected to be open and insightful while being poised for continual change. There was also the belief that there was too much micromanaging, which resulted in too much attention to day-to-day details and too little attention to the big picture."

The board members continued to listen intently as the consultants presented their findings on DVERT's communication effectiveness. One of the consultants said, "I can tell you that this organization really has some positive perceptions about its communication. That's not to say that there aren't some issues that need to be worked on. The next six slides underscore our key findings."

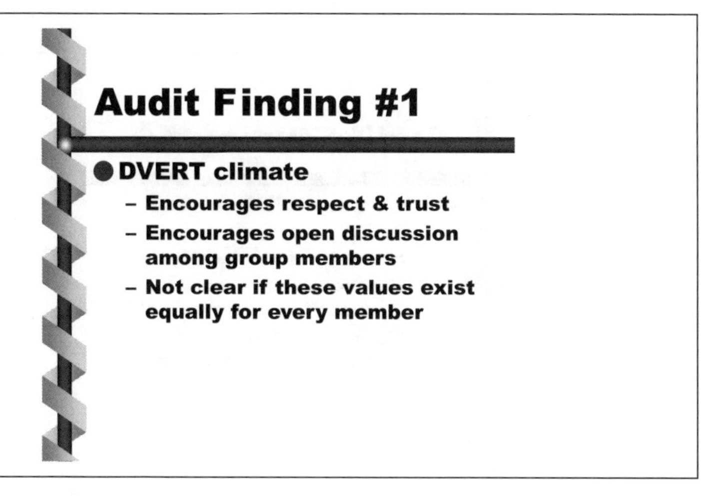

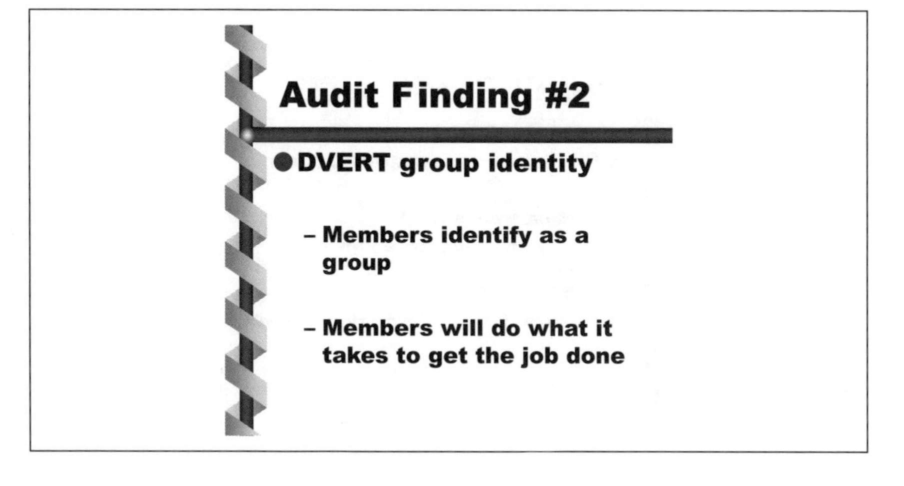

Audit Finding #3
Members' perceptions
– Members see themselves and their coworkers as highly skilled and capable
– Members feel like they are making a difference

Audit Finding #4
Views on collaboration
– Group works collaboratively, rather than cooperatively
– Members desire more input from staff in decision making
– Members believe constructive feedback from management is lacking

Audit Finding #5
One-on-one communication
– Most frequently used channel
– Does not guarantee all members receive necessary information
– More timely information needed

Audit Finding #6

- **Job satisfaction**
  - **Members like their jobs**
  - **Feel overworked**
  - **Lack resources to be most effective**
    - **Computer technology outdated**
    - **Not everyone has a computer**
    - **Hinders timely information gathering**
    - **Hinders communication w/staff**

At the end of the presentation, board members asked a few general questions and thanked the consultants for their efforts. Shortly thereafter Jack and the partners reconvened for the afternoon session. Jack opened the meeting by asking the group, "Now we have some insight into the communication in this organization. So how do you propose that we proceed? What is best for the team?" ✦

Endnotes

1. This case has been developed based on real organization(s) and real organizational experiences. Names, facts, and situations have been changed to protect the privacy of individuals and organizations.
2. In the literature on domestic violence, animal abuse is one of the precursors to human abuse. Moreover, animal abuse often continues in an abusive cycle. Subsequently, the humane society is an integral part of the DVERT team.

Section 4

Decision Making and Problem Solving

Briefing Paper

Decision Making and Problem Solving

Although the terms *decision making* and *problem solving* are often used interchangeably, each of the processes is unique. Decision making is the selection of one alternative from many while problem solving is the generation of probable alternative solutions. Both require the sharing of information and the use of analysis, reasoning, and judgment. In organizations, individuals and teams can engage in decision-making and problem-solving processes. Obviously, team members would interact to make a decision or identify solutions. And it would be highly unusual for an individual charged with the responsibility to make decisions or solve problems to do so without getting information from or consulting with others.

When groups or teams are given decision-making or problem-solving responsibilities, they are likely to use standard agenda, consensus, voting, ranking, or brainstorming (or nominal group technique) procedures. While the focus of group decision making and problem solving is primarily on the task, it is also important for group members to attend to the relationships among group members. How can a group know which procedure to use? Proponents of the functional theory of decision making suggest that a group should select a procedure based on its ability to help the group (a) thoroughly discuss the problem, (b) develop the criteria by which solutions can be judged, (c) propose alternatives, (d) assess the positive aspects of each solution, and (e) assess the negative aspects of each solution. In addition to decision making and problem solving, groups are often also responsible for implementing decisions or assessing them once implemented.

Any number of elements can positively or negatively influence a group during decision making or problem solving. For example, a group's process will be based on the norms the group has established or more generalized norms of the organization or culture. Thus, decision making and problem solving are not something that groups do. Rather, decisions and solutions emerge from the sequences and patterns of speech among group members.

Some groups and teams find it helpful to use a facilitator. There are two types of facilitation: basic and developmental. A facilitator can be used temporarily to help a group discuss issues and make decisions through a number of techniques, including agenda setting, agreement on ground rules, monitoring group process, and consensus building. Or a facilitator can be used permanently to improve a group's process. In developmental facilitation, the facilitator helps the group learn how to work together more effectively by focusing on group dynamics. Facilitators can be either internal or external to the group. Internal facilitators know the group's members and norms but may be biased by their experiences with the group; external facilitators are more neutral because they are not an ongoing part of the group.

Facilitators can perform a wide variety of tasks for a group including preparing the agenda, setting up the meeting space, and helping the group determine the ground rules that will govern the discussion and decision making. Facilitators generally do not assist the group in its decision making or problem solving. Rather, a facilitator's role is to help the group stay on task by asking questions, recording group ideas and decisions, summarizing the group's progress, and intervening when the group gets off track or conflicts emerge.

Individuals, usually high-level leaders, are more likely to take on, or be given, decision-making and problem-solving responsibilities in organizations when the decision centers on an organizational crisis or other time- or issue-sensitive problem. As a result, other organizational members will often view their decision-making and problem-solving actions as indicative of their leadership skills. When a leader makes decisions or solves problems skillfully, he or she has the potential to broaden and elevate the interests of followers, generate awareness and acceptance of the organization's mission, and motivate followers to look beyond their own self-interest for the good of others. These are the hallmarks of a transformational leader. In essence, transformational leaders are charismatic leaders who provide vision and direction for followers. They communicate high standards and inspire and challenge employees to better themselves, as well as encourage employees to engage in critical thinking and problem solving.

Regardless of who generates the solutions or makes the decisions, both processes will create change or adaptation for the organization. Communication is critical in persuading others in the group or the organization to consider and finally commit to the change. Whether small or large, a decision or solution that requires change is likely to create the need for other changes as well. Usually there are forces inside and outside the organization pushing or resisting change.

How decisions or solutions are communicated are key to effective organizational practice. In some cases, decisions or solutions are transmitted via an information-transfer model, in which communication is viewed as a tool or conduit, with the sender controlling the message. Alternately, decisions and solutions can be communicated via a transactional model, in which individuals are simultaneously senders and receivers who interpret the meaning of messages based upon the present situation, their individual experiences, history, and organizational and cultural influences. As a result, multiple interpretations are to be expected, given that each receiver will interpret the message according to personal experiences and perceptions.

Suggested Readings

Aakhus, M. (2001). Technocratic and design stances toward communication expertise: How DGSS facilitators understand their work. *Journal of Applied Communication Research, 29,* 341–371.

Axley, S. R. (1984). Managerial and organizational communication in terms of the conduit metaphor. *Academy of Management Review, 9,* 428–437.

Coopman, S. J. (2001). Democracy, performance, and outcomes in interdisciplinary health care teams. *The Journal of Business Communication, 38,* 261–294.

Hirokawa, R. Y. (1988). Group communication and decision-making performance: A continued test of the functional perspective. *Human Communication Research, 14,* 487–515.

Kotter, J. P. (1990). *A force for change: How leadership differs from management.* New York: Free Press.

Miller, S. J., Hickson, D. J., & Wilson, D. C. (1996). Decision-making in organizations. In S. R. Clegg, C. Hardy, & W. R. Nord (Eds.), *Handbook of organization studies* (pp. 293–312). Thousand Oaks, CA: Sage.

Mitroff, I. I., & Anagos, G. (2000). *Managing crises before they happen: What every executive and manager needs to know about crisis management.* New York: AMACOM.

Rees, F. (2001). *How to lead work teams: Facilitation skills.* San Francisco, CA: Jossey-Bass/Pfeffer.

Stevenson, W. B., & Gilly, M. C. (1991). Information processing and problem solving: The migration of problems through formal positions and networks of ties. *Academy of Management Journal, 34,* 918–928.

Sunwolf, & Seibold, D. R. (1999). The impact of formal procedures on group processes, members, and task outcomes. In L. R. Frey., D. S. Gouran, & M. S. Poole (Eds.), *The handbook of group communication theory and research* (pp. 395–431). Thousand Oaks, CA: Sage.

Tichy, N., & Devanna, M. A. (1997). *The transformational leader: The key to global competitiveness.* New York: John Wiley & Sons.

Tropman, J. E. (1996). *Making meetings work.* Thousands Oaks, CA: Sage.

Ulmer, R. R. (2001). Effective crisis management through established stakeholder relationships. *Management Communication Quarterly, 14,* 590–615. ✦

Chapter 17

T Link Enterprises

Trudy A. Milburn

At 7:30 A.M. Eastern Standard Time, people began to fill the conference room. A continental breakfast had been set up in the corner of the room. Helping himself to coffee, Michael St. John,* the Western European market director, began. "I was with T Link way back when we were just making cable connectors. And now look at us, positioning ourselves as a provider of global networking communication services." Michael continued without really expecting anyone to answer him. "Do you think it's possible we'll accomplish anything in a two-day meeting? We have too many issues that are unique to each region and can't be resolved easily. And it's not as if everyone is going to be here."

Yao Gia, the Asian and Pacific Rim market director, looked down at his pastry. Not sure that he should answer, but feeling like someone should because a question was posed, Yao answered quietly, "I believe we will hear updates on each territory. The difference I see is that this time the memo stated we will try to create a standard and efficient global system."

Michael asked, "Well, what about the feasibility team? Weren't they exploring regions in Africa?"

"Um, yes." Speaking rapidly but still softly, Yao continued, "I understood that if they could not produce specific projections by the first of the month, and did not have a well-developed action plan, they would not be invited to the meeting."

"I don't believe it."

"Well, that's what I understand. Excuse me, can you confirm the time this meeting was to begin?" asked Yao.

"It was scheduled to begin at 8 A.M., but you know that someone is always late."

Dottie Corran, the North American market director, walked over to join the conversation. Pausing from her cup of coffee, she injected, "I hear Wilkins isn't going to make it."

"From what I know," Michael said, "his biggest account—almost 60% of his entire sales—demanded a meeting with him in Estonia tomorrow morning. I think our competitors are trying to move in on us there." They began taking seats around the large conference table.

Down the hallway, Abigail Craft, vice president of marketing and sales, was approached by her assistant, Lenny. He handed her a note from the feasibility team. It read:

> We found out you were holding a meeting to discuss global sales and were hoping we could sit in. Even though we have yet to complete our profitability and growth analysis of the region, we believe that we would make a valuable contribution to the meeting overall and feel that not being included may appear to be a slight to certain members of our organization.

Abigail looked into the room, then turned to her assistant, folded the note signed by the vice president of product extension services, who also led the feasibility team, and said, "Where is Mr. Castelanos? We can't begin without him."

Lenny answered, "He hasn't called in. I can try to find out." Abigail shook her head disgustedly as she walked in. Seeing the others, she gave them a courtesy hello by nodding her head and then began setting out papers.

Five minutes later, Andreas Castelanos, the Latin American market director, walked in. He approached Abigail and said, "Excuse me, Vice President Craft, I apologize for my tardiness," and took a seat at the far end of the large conference table next to Dottie. "*Buenos dais,* Mrs. Corran, how are you? How is your husband?"

Dottie replied, "I'm doing well, thank you. How's business?" she asked, trying to change the subject.

"I cannot complain," said Andreas, nodding his head down and holding it in a respectful position. "How are your children? Aren't they still in grade school?"

"Yes, James is 11 now and Tess is 6. How was your flight here?"

Andreas responded, "Oh, thank you for asking. It was a nice flight. I was thinking about the meeting on the way over in preparation for our discussion of our cultural differences, as the vice president requested. Tell me, how is it with your Hispanic customers in California? I was wondering if those tensions were among your most pressing issues. I'm interested in hearing more about your view on them."

Dottie asked in a surprised voice, "Well, who are you talking to? Who's telling you that? I speak to my reps on a weekly basis, and that's not what I'm hearing."

"Pardon me." He stood up quickly to get some coffee.

At 8:10 A.M. Abigail motioned to her assistant to get Henry Wilkins, the Eastern Europe and Russian market director, on the phone for the conference call. Once Lenny confirmed that Henry was on the line, Abigail began the meeting by matter-of-factly thanking everyone for attending, and then launched into her opening remarks.

"I have asked all of you here today to capitalize on all of our successes these past three years with the intention of creating a system whereby successful sales and marketing techniques in one region can become standardized and meshed into a global sales model. As I mentioned in the memo, this will facilitate the training of additional salespeople as we increase market share in each region. As we all have experienced, turnover has been quite high. That, coupled with our intentions to increase services around the globe, will mean that we will be training substantial numbers of new employees over the next 18 months. Recall, as well, that I intend to start transferring successful sales reps and sales supervisory staff to new regions. I have every intention of making T Link truly a global enterprise."

T Link Enterprises began operations in the 1970s making cable connections. Since then it had expanded into providing global networking communication services, including cellular, broadband, and IP networks for both consumers and businesses. From Abigail's perspective the last five years had been the period of the most dramatic change—both in the technology T Link had developed and marketed and in sales. Sales had increased from $50 million to $100 million in the last two years alone, following unprecedented technological advances that T Link had successfully moved from business to consumer applications. More important, in America and Europe, T Link had excelled in persuading consumer customers to buy value-added services after signing up for their initial cellular phone service contracts. In developing regions of the world, T Link had been successful in establishing the networks that allowed cellular phone service to be viable where broadband and IP networks were not. In different ways in different parts of the world, T Link had established itself as an industry leader. Hoping to capitalize on both their consumer and business markets, T Link now planned to continue adding multimedia products and services.

Abigail continued, "Most importantly, though, we need to create a global sales model to explore untapped opportunities. And that's the primary thrust of today's meeting. Thus far, we have been operating under a model in place since the company began. Initially we hired sales reps in each region and asked them to use their contacts to sell our services. We didn't think so much about strategic sales. Being the first in the market, we were able to focus on quick growth to create brand awareness and service capabilities as rapidly as possible. Now that we have established a number one—and number two, depending on the region—market share, we need to take stock of staying profitable in our current regions, as well as developing untapped markets."

She paused for emphasis. "The way we are going to do this," Abigail said firmly, "is to take the next two days to examine our differences and create an overall sales strategy as well as a process that will help us meet our targeted growth rates."

On a signal from Abigail, Lenny handed out copies of Abigail's slide presentation. Before the market directors could flip through the handouts, Abigail indicated for Lenny to dim the lights. The first slide was projected on the screen at the end of the room. Before addressing the group again, Abigail turned to the speakerphone and asked, "Henry, can you view these online now?"

After a short delay, Henry responded, "Yes, thank you. Abigail, I'm sorry I was late getting connected to the meeting, but I just returned from my client meeting. And I'm sorry to say, I can't stay online long. I'm meeting with the client once again in about 45 minutes. My presentation to the director of purchasing is tomorrow."

Abigail didn't respond. She turned her attention to the slide on the screen, which the market directors were reading.

1. Given that there are language and other communication differences, do we create one system and then translate it into different languages?

OR

2. Do we think about how sales might be conducted differently in other countries and try to create localized versions?

OR

3. Do we incorporate the best of what works in each country into one global sales process?

Speaking loudly and distinctly, Abigail brought her listeners' attention back to the meeting. "Okay, let's start by going around and having each person define the top three concerns for their region."

Looking around to see who was going to start, Dottie finally initiated the discussion. "Our issues relate to customer service in the business market. After we make an initial sale, the sales staff—especially in some of our southern California areas—have difficulty closing on the value-added components. Los Angeles is a particular problem. For example, our staff members are Korean and our clients are primarily African American. Based on my troubleshooting trips, I find that staff and clients describe different scenarios. And I simply do not know how to resolve it. African American clients often describe our staff as being suspicious of them, often making them wait for an extended time before helping them. When I interviewed the staff to try to discover the reasons for the difficulties, they described the clients' behavior as impolite. I really don't know what to do. So I have simply been visiting each site, listening to and watching what is happening as staff interact with clients."

Abigail asked, "Can you describe a typical interaction?"

Dottie replied: "Well, companies place orders for a variety of business network connection services. Our clients' employees then come to the service centers to get particular items. And you know that many of our clients are unsure of exactly which switches and connectors they need. Of course, the sales staff pull the contracts, where this is all specified. Because the technical specifications are part of the contract, they don't understand why the individuals picking up the parts have difficulty making specific requests. It also seems that some of our clients want to engage in small talk and our staff members do not respond to that very well. After watching one such interaction, I pressed a staff member to say something about what just happened. He hesitantly indicated that he thought the client was loud and aggressive."

Abigail looked up to ask the others, "What's happening in other areas?"

Although she had just described one problem, Dottie spoke up once again, intending to keep anyone else from speaking. She wanted to continue with the problems she was facing. "We have also noticed a similar kind of interaction problem between our Arab American staff and customers in the Detroit area. Customers seem to want to engage in much more small talk. And sometimes they ask for directions to install the component. Of course, our sales staff can't answer those types of questions."

Seeing the annoyed expression on Abigail's face, Dottie decided these two examples were enough.

Yao was the next to explain his experiences. "Well, I apologize if this is not related, but we have some issues with our Japanese sales reps when they interact with Chinese customers. They become frustrated that decisions have to be made by an entire group rather than by one person. It seems to take forever for a client to come to a decision."

Andreas interrupted Yao. "Abigail, we have issues with gaining respect. Our reps in Mexico seem to have some difficulty when they talk with clients in Argentina. Sales there have been weak lately due to economic circumstances, I am sorry to report. The reps have trouble with the form of address. It is very confusing to them. Instead of speaking to them formally, Argentineans use the familiar form *vos,* which is similar to our *tu,* when they should be using a more polite form, such as *usted.* Granted, the Spanish language is spoken differently in the two countries, but this simple matter of addressing one another seems to create a lot of tension during the sales process."

"Okay, thank you for that input." Abigail turned again to address the speakerphone. "Henry, now what can you tell us from your perspective?"

Silence. About 30 seconds went by before Abigail asked if the connection was working.

Finally, those in the meeting room heard Henry. "Yes, we have a connection," he confirmed apologetically. There was a pause again, for about 10 seconds. "The issues for us here in Eastern Europe are a bit different—perhaps an example would clarify. When I call on Russian clients, they simply demand a lower price than we are offering. Of course, many reps report that they need to pay small bribes to be directed to the right person.

"And, because products made for Russia and most of the newly independent states require a different electrical connection, there are similar problems when our Russian clients talk with the product development team in New Jersey."

"Okay," Abigail responded, "but product development isn't really the issue here today. We are trying to answer the question of how we create customer relationships so that we can sell value-added services to our customers and create long-term sales for ourselves."

Henry replied, "Yes, I understand that."

Launching once again into her idea and pointing at the screen, Abigail said assertively, "The issue now becomes how we use what we have learned locally to shape our global sales force. For example, do we simply insert a cultural summary for each nation—for instance, as a chapter at the end of a training manual? Or, more ideally, I believe, do we integrate these differences into our sales process and create a new approach?"

Eagerly, Michael chimed in, "Well, I think we should just let each region continue to operate independently. They seem to be doing all right and then we don't offend anyone."

"Um, no. Um, I think the point she is trying to make is that integration will bring efficiency," Yao added hesitantly.

Before Yao could continue, Andreas commented, "Yes, yes. The efficiencies will produce a definite cost advantage if we can all work within the same sales model."

"Please excuse me," Yao interjected, and after a pause continued, "I was going to say that while efficiencies can be produced by a consistent sales process, I do not think that we can effectively integrate all of our cultural differences into a standard training program or even a training manual."

Not seeing anyone else who wanted to contribute, Abigail moved the conversation along. "Okay, good dialogue. I have a suggestion. For the sake of trying to determine if we can create one global model that works, let's start with an understanding of how our differences fit into our current sales process."

Abigail motioned to Lenny and a new slide appeared.

1. Timeline of sales process
2. Channels/media
3. Communication issues in face-to-face sales interactions
    - Forms of address
    - Use of pauses and silence
    - Turn taking and interruptions
    - Frequency and quantity of conversation
    - Purpose of interaction
        - Information exchange
        - Demonstration of product

Before anyone could respond or ask a question, another slide was shown.

Customer
- Needs
- Expectations
- Value chain
    - Where do our products and services fit into their business or personal use?
    - Transaction model or relationship model?
    - Focus on products and services?

Again, before anyone could comment, Abigail directed the group's conversation. "Let's continue to talk about where in this process our cultural differences are most acute. Also, how do pricing, implementation, and delivery affect our customer relationships? Who would like to start?"

Michael spoke up. "I'll start. Which slide are we supposed to be addressing? And why weren't the people on the feasibility team included in today's meeting?" ✦

*This case has been developed based on real organization(s) and real organizational experiences. Names, facts, and situations have been changed to protect the privacy of individuals and organizations.

Chapter 18

For the Good of Many

Nancy M. Schullery and Melissa Gibson Hancox

A delay in orders compels the layoff of the company's most productive manufacturing team—or does it? Company founder and CEO Howard Crane* has an innovative solution for this crisis that can benefit the organization, the employees, and the community. But can he and his management team make it work? So far, the solution has triggered only more organizational crisis.

The Crisis

"What do you mean they don't want to go, Anne?"

Howard Crane, my boss, the founder and CEO of Wister Manufacturing, fought to control the drop of his jaw. As I struggled to find words to answer him, he tiredly sank into his desk chair. It had been a long two days. As director of human resources and training at Wister, I was in the thick of our second internal organizational crisis in less than 48 hours. Wister, a 50-person auto parts manufacturing company, was facing an unforeseen downtime in orders that threatened the jobs of 19 employees. Many of these particular employees were the least senior of our assembly workers but had set a model for productivity. They had finished their latest assembly job *one whole month* ahead of schedule, a record in the company. However, we had hit a schedule delay: Our largest customer had just pushed back its next order for an additional two months, so now we were faced with up to 90 days downtime, instead of the 30 days we had expected. The delay created a crisis for our small company, which had no other major orders right now and expected none in the near term. Laying off the employees seemed like the only option, until—just yesterday—we devised an innovative solution. However, all too soon Jason Loomis, chief financial officer, and I found that the employees didn't want any part of our proposed solution.

The Monday Morning Blues

My Monday morning had started like any other, but little did I know that I'd soon be facing the worst organizational crisis in my six years at Wister. Bleary-eyed, I stumbled into my office at 8:10 A.M. only to hear the bad news. My assistant confirmed that the 19-member employee team would not have any work for the next 90 days. My boss, Howard, called 15 minutes later to schedule an emergency meeting.

"Anne, this is big. We have to sit down and figure something out. I need to see you and Jason in the conference room now!"

Howard tried to smile as he nervously passed around the box of jelly doughnuts he had picked up on the way to the office, and we began to discuss the situation. We all knew we needed a win-win solution to this organizational crisis. Also, we all wanted a systematic way to manage this crisis and effectively respond to this challenge. However, we all came in with slightly different perspectives and agendas.

From my vantage point in HR, I looked at the problem from a human capital perspective. This team of employees was the most productive team at Wister Manufacturing, despite many obstacles. Many in the group spoke English only as a second language and came from diverse backgrounds (African American, Caucasian, Hispanic/Latino, and Vietnamese). They had worked together only a year at Wister. Yet, they had finished the latest job in record time by becoming familiar with one another's strengths and tapping each worker's unique talents. It seemed unthinkable that the best workers in the company would be forced out of their jobs because of their own success. The irony pained me: the apparent *reward* was so out of step with their efforts.

Further complicating the issue from a human resources perspective was the fact that Big Falls, the small midwestern community where the company was located, boasted a 3.2% unemployment rate, typical of the prosperous economy shown in that region of the state. I knew we ran a big risk if these employees were laid off: sending a negative message to other employees that the company didn't value productivity. Without a solution we would likely lose these productive workers to competitive manufacturers. As a small company, we couldn't afford to just throw away the accumulated training our company had invested in its employees. And, as their company trainer, I had to admit that this group was exceptional. It had been slow going initially, due to the language barriers, but the nonnative English speakers were particularly motivated to prove themselves. In all my six years at Wister, this group of employees stood out for how quickly they caught on to their new jobs and how tirelessly they worked. Maybe many of them tried harder because they were single parents—sole support of themselves and three or four kids, in some cases.

Jason's perspective was different. Middle-aged and squarely built, Jason was a product of this predominantly Dutch community and had worked with Howard for nearly 15 years. He was well aware of the difficult times the company had gone through and knew Howard would want a solution that considered the workers' needs, but he had to be practical. After all, company profits were his stock in trade. As the CFO, Jason tended to favor what we all knew to be the obvious solution—downsize, lay off these employees for 90 days until orders picked up. Layoffs of the least senior employees were typical in the auto industry and worked well with the schedule of our largest customer, Jobson & Jobson, a car seat manufacturer. Jason's boss, however, had a slightly different view.

Howard's perspective was based on 26 years of industry experience. He was well aware that layoffs were typical in small to medium-sized companies like his, but the typical outcome had no appeal. Howard had witnessed tremendous downsizing of the auto parts industry, starting 20 years ago with layoffs of over a million employees in the 1980s alone, as the industry shed hierarchy and streamlined operations. A total of 90,000 jobs had been forever lost in the $200 billion auto parts industry, and hundreds of firms the same size as Howard's had gone belly-up. Howard had never expressed a desire for early retirement, much less bankruptcy, I thought.

I roused myself from my thoughts just in time to catch Howard recapping why he wanted to avoid a layoff: the group's productivity, the risk of losing the employees permanently to competitors, the motivation the employees had shown, and his history of taking care of this company's workers. The typical solution, to lay off or downsize the employees, did not appeal to me and especially not to Howard.

He had built a successful company from a small family operation and felt proud of the strong organizational culture he had helped create. I knew that he read a lot to keep up with the industry, but it was Howard's nature that brought an extra ingredient.

Howard took great pride in having helped shape a culture in which employees were valued and respected. He and Nora, his wife of 28 years, and his entire family showed the employees their appreciation every Thanksgiving. Nora, an excellent cook, fixed the traditional turkey dinner and all the trimmings. For the last 23 years, Nora and their children had spent several days before the holiday preparing the appetizers, vegetable casseroles, and desserts. At Christmas time, everyone had the week off, and employees never worked on their birthdays. He prided himself on his willingness to listen to employee ideas (which had brought the company increased profits) and concerns (which he saw as showing respect for and developing trust with his employees). Indeed, Howard had always been one of those rare bosses who defied the typical *Dilbert* cartoon image of a contemporary manager.

The Best Laid Plans

Faced with the unwelcome situation of high inventory and no major orders, Howard believed that he had come up with a clever way out of Wister's crisis. In a time when management had been accused of losing confidence, and even doubted its ability to create instead of cut, Howard's idea showed true leadership. As Jason and I waited with anticipation, Howard said, "You know, I think this is an opportunity to respond to our changing work environment, to maybe even transform the way we think about working here."

Jason asked, "What do you mean, transform?"

Howard didn't answer. Instead, he abruptly quit pacing and said, "I was just wondering what on earth we're going to do, and I thought, 'Hey, that's it!'" Then, turning to Jason, he asked, "Can we do this?"

Jason seemed to know what Howard meant. Howard was asking if the company could afford to pay the 19 employees for the next three months, even if the employee team assembled nothing. Jason didn't look happy, but he answered, "We could for a while," his voice lingering on that last word.

Howard pressed: "A while?"

"Well, yeah, three or four months, probably, assuming all our other orders are on schedule," Jason responded.

Turning to me, Howard finally explained his idea. "I'm thinking we'll pay our most productive team over the next three months, but instead of working here, the employees will spend their workday time at nonprofit organizations in the community, we'll loan them our workers. You know, being socially responsible," he said.

I nodded. "We talked about this in the graduate class I'm taking. Corporate social responsibility is a big thing now—but I haven't heard of anyone loaning labor to nonprofits. This sounds like a win-win solution all the way round."

"My favorite part of this," Howard continued, "is that we can demonstrate we're a family." Howard had to agree when Jason raised another important consideration.

"And it will keep our best workers on the payroll and out of the clutches of our competitors." We all nodded as Jason continued. "You know, we have a chance here to send a solid goodwill message to the entire Big Falls area, since we'll be providing paychecks for these folks while they're making improvements around the community. We can only guesstimate the value of that kind of thing."

As the implications sunk in, I saw another advantage. "This way the workers will keep their health insurance for their kids and stay off unemployment." Last but certainly not least, paying the employees to work at nonprofits would allow employee relationships to continue, not only with each other but with us, and with Wister, as committed employees. We sat grinning at each other, impressed with ourselves and the solution.

Finally, Howard asked (without really expecting an answer), "How can I do anything else? A layoff would betray employee trust, after these workers have struggled so hard to contribute and succeed." Howard concluded the meeting with the comment, "OK, we're agreed. Let the nonprofits know we have people for them—and let me know the plan."

An Unseen Hurdle

As Jason and I returned to our offices, I was bursting with enthusiasm. "This is the most exciting program we've done since I've been here. Let's split the list and get started on those calls."

Jason agreed. "Yeah, let's get this thing solved so we can get back to work."

Jason and I began contacting a list of 18 local community organizations. Soon I heard his voice coming from down the quiet hall. "Well, if you can't do it, you can't do it. We want the solution to be a good one for everybody. Right. Thanks for your frankness. Bye."

Soon, Jason's discouraged face appeared at my door. "All I'm getting is, 'Thanks, but no thanks.' How 'bout you?"

I had to admit my luck was the same. Although most nonprofit organizations vie for volunteers and every one of the 18 organizations reacted positively to the program in concept, none was prepared to take on 19 volunteers for 40 hours per week for three months. Bob Dillard, director of the local United Way, pointed out the reality of nonprofit labor: "It takes a lot to organize volunteers and see productive results from their work. We would have to make sure that this was a mutually beneficial process so your employees wouldn't get abused and we wouldn't get abused." Most of our community contacts, recognizing the same problem, reluctantly declined to participate.

However, after what seemed like endless phone calls, by 3:00 P.M. we eventually identified eight community sites that agreed to participate. The local Habitat for Humanity, YWCA, and YMCA offered to provide the majority of assignments for the employees. At Habitat for Humanity, employees could work for three days a week and then choose another nonprofit agency on the list for their remaining two days. Now that enough nonprofit sites were secured, it was time to inform the employees of the solution. I proudly drafted a memo to employees announcing the plan and asked Monica, Howard's secretary, to see that the 19 employees received it when they came to work Tuesday morning. Monica also agreed to post an announcement on the bulletin board in the employee lounge. Jason and I left the building with a sense of smug satisfaction for the great plan we had organized and set in motion, all in one day.

Tuesday Morning—Reality Check

When I strolled into work this morning, I immediately sensed the tension. Employees glared sideways at me from corners, whispering as I passed. I realized that they had read the *loaned labor* memos, and it wasn't long before their reaction became clear: "No way!" I was shocked and taken aback by the variety and intensity of the negative comments.

As word spread, a line formed outside my office door, and the stream of employees with complaints seemed continuous and unending. Just when I thought the complaints were over, Carlos Toscano, a 15-month employee, leaned against my office door and said, "What they should do is give us a bonus for sticking with this place. We don't get paid enough to begin with."

Phan Doc, another worker, chimed in, "I don't see why we have to go out there and work like that. I could be getting unemployment."

As they walked away, I found myself seething with anger. "How could they even think about a bonus? Don't they realize they're lucky to have jobs?"

I was muttering to myself as Kalena Johnson, a 10-year employee, plopped down in my visitor's chair and said, "Look, my car pool comes to Wister. I don't have no car to be driving all over the county to work for these other people."

"I'll work on it, Kalena. We're still trying to iron out the wrinkles," I said, now only half convinced myself. As soon as she had left, I grabbed the phone and dialed Jason's extension. "I can't take this anymore. Let's have lunch and discuss this. Meet you at Big Mack's Diner at 11:30."

Tuesday Afternoon—Figuring It Out

As I slid into the booth at Big Mack's, I could see the look of despair on Jason's face. Our waitress turned over my coffee cup and splashed it full of java as my words, rapid-fire, spilled out to Jason. "You're not going to believe this. The employees think our brilliant solution sucks!"

"Tell me about it," said Jason. "This morning Luisa Sanchez came to my office saying that she can't work in the community because the nonprofits don't open until nine in the morning and she's used to working 7:00 A.M. to 3:00 P.M. She has her entire schedule built around when her kids get on and off the school bus. She says she can't afford to disrupt her family like that."

I shared with Jason the problems I had heard; then we sat munching our sandwiches and pondering what we were now facing. A major implementation challenge had surfaced: conflicts with personal schedules and transportation. The nonprofits often didn't start operations until two or three hours after our plant opened. Luisa Sanchez's experience was typical of the single mothers among our employees: The employees had each gone to substantial effort to find effective child care providers and arrange transportation to day care as needed before or after school. Understandably enough, they were reluctant to disrupt their interwoven schedules.

And the children were not the only ones with transportation problems. Many employees had no way to get to the designated nonprofit destinations. Most did not own cars and relied on a limited city bus system or neighborhood car pools to get to Wister's plant. Taxicabs in the small community were rare and expensive. To Jason and me, the once-attractive solution now loomed as another huge problem. So our second internal crisis had arrived. If that were the only problem.

Behind the facade of schedule complaints, we could see the reluctance of many employees to leave their known environment, where they were part of a successful manufacturing team, and go out on their own to an unfamiliar setting to do unspecified work. At the nonprofits, they didn't know what they might be asked to do: anything from putting up plasterboard, to installing a sink for a new home, to dealing with mounds of paperwork in the nonprofit offices. And, as one employee reported, "I don't know anything about building a house!"

On top of the logistical challenges and fears of unspecified, changeable work responsibilities was another concern. The employees were confused. They had never heard of or seen a company bestowing such an unusual solution as the loaned labor program. Instead of getting the gratitude we expected, we were finding that employees were suspicious, alarmed, and concerned about the impact on their personal and work lives. In school I had studied the ways in which employee resistance to change can be a normal part of organizational functioning, but now I was seeing it up close, and it was hard not to take it personally. The employees' comments forced our attention to more subtle issues that would need resolution, beginning with employees' suspicions of the program and including the employees' substantial resistance to change, a resistance often based on lack of trust.

Organizational change naturally elicits fear and uncertainty on the part of employees. In this case, the problem was compounded with the repeated layoffs and job losses in the industry, which had conditioned workers to expect similar treatment in this, now comparable, situation. Despite the benevolent nature of Howard's proposal and his intentions, employees were upset and confused by the lack of explanation accompanying the announcement. In my haste to get the word out, I had committed the same sin most other organizations do while in the thick of change—limited communication. And now it seemed that we were going to pay for it.

Back at the office, Jason and I continued to field mostly negative comments from workers, many of whom came looking for further explanation about the plan. By late in the afternoon, I found Jason in the employee lounge and said, "We've got to get the word out, and the first person who needs to know is Howard. He has to explain why we're doing this, or the rumors will take on a life of their own." Without an explanation in their brief announcements, workers couldn't believe the loaned labor solution was real or that it would actually be implemented. Employees wanted their information from the top; they needed to understand the changes better, and Howard needed their commitment. "Oh, why didn't I word that memo differently," I thought, as Jason and I gathered our forces to tell the boss. "After all, I'm supposed to know something about communicating crisis information to employees." Aloud, I said, "Jason, didn't Howard say something about leaving early tonight?" We hurried down the hall to his office and found the door open; Howard was packing his briefcase as he always did before going home.

To Be or Not to Be?

When he heard our news, Howard's mouth seemed stuck, wide-open. He appeared dumbfounded by the unexpected problems with his presumed win-win solution. "Wh . . . wh . . . what are you saying?" he stammered. "I feel as though I've been stabbed in the back!"

I tried to explain. "We need to look at this again. The employees are worried about several things. One, how they're going to get to these other work sites; two, what they're going to do when they get there; and three, what's going to happen to their kids while their parents are working all over the county."

Jason chimed in, "It all sounded great when we talked about it, but the problem is that there've been so many layoffs in the industry—and a lot of those jobs have just gone away. Our people think we're gonna do the same thing, and before that happens we're putting them in some sort of twisted routine that's gonna turn their lives upside down before they *really* get laid off. They're not willing to go through the hassle."

Howard was quiet, listening as we explained. Finally, he spoke slowly, as if forming the thoughts while he spoke. "Well, maybe we should just forget the whole idea. I thought we had come up with something worthwhile. I really thought the employees would see the same vision I see, that this solution could be good for so many. Maybe we should just forget the whole idea and lay off those 19 employees for the 90 days. It sure would be easier. Or . . ." he paused, reflecting, "maybe we should try to convince our reluctant employees?" Then, a bit hurt, he mused, ". . . or I could just order them to go to the nonprofits and let the chips fall where they may. After all, if they don't believe that we have their best interests at heart, maybe we're wasting our time," he rationalized.

Howard's disappointment was clear. He's not just worried about losing employees, I thought. He really did hate to see them, and us, miss this opportunity to do some long-term good. By having our employees work in the same community that had been so good to Wister over the years, we could give back so much. If we could only pull this off, it would be a truly unique solution and absolutely transform what had been a crisis into a wide-ranging benefit.

"Howard," I said quietly, "you can still do something about this. Do you remember that article in *Harvard Business Review* that I gave you to read last month? The one that talked about transformational leaders? You know, leaders who get their organizations pumped up about their vision—whatever it happened to be."

"Yes, that rings a bell. Transformational leadership, yes," Howard mused, growing quiet as he realized the challenge that awaited. "Somehow, I'll have to help them figure a way to get there."

I couldn't help but think that, given the current employee mood, Howard had his work cut out for him.

Jason looked at the two of us quizzically. "How're you gonna do that?" he asked.

Howard seemed to be thinking aloud as he replied, "I remember reading that the real movers and shakers out there make such things happen by enlisting their followers in achieving a vision. Whatever noble cause the leaders have chosen, somehow they manage to spell out a way to actually make it happen. They get their employees to follow."

Jason and I exchanged discreet glances. Clearly, Howard would have to be very eloquent to enlist *these* followers, even when the noble cause was helping out at nonprofit organizations.

Howard grew more excited as he continued. "I'm convinced that once the employees actually get out there and work with the nonprofits, they'll feel good about doing their part."

Then Howard's jaw set as it often did when he felt strongly about something and he continued, quickly outlining the issues. "How can we communicate the potential solution to the employees? And how can we make loaned labor work for them? Will they trust us?" Then, hardly able to restrain his delight at his strategic brainstorm, he confided to us, "You know, there's no way to demonstrate respect for the employees like empowering them to help solve the challenges that they've raised."

Surprised, Jason blurted, "But they expect answers from us!"

I nodded, noting, "This plan has a challenge around every corner, it seems. Maybe we all need a little time to think about it."

Howard glanced at the clock; it was almost 4:15 P.M. He had promised Nora that he would attend their daughter Jessica's school play tonight. "Let's sleep on it," he said. Howard hurriedly closed his briefcase and left for home. Jason and I looked at each other, shrugged in unison, and wondered how Wister's crisis would ever be resolved. ✦

*This case has been developed based on real organization(s) and real organizational experiences. Names, facts, and situations have been changed to protect the privacy of individuals and organizations.

Chapter 19

A Matter of Perspective

PAAIGE K. TURNER AND ROBERT L. KRIZEK

The Metropolitan Medical Group,* or MMG, is the practice arm of a private university's medical school. This was the first time that MMG experienced significant revenue loss, which interestingly followed three years of declining levels of patient satisfaction. Perhaps even more interesting, the onset of the decline in patient satisfaction coincided with the divestiture of the hospital to a national health care conglomerate. While a major component of the MMG's mission has always been to provide a clinical environment for medical interns and residents, it had become increasingly clear that this mission would be in jeopardy if MMG could not cover its costs. The administration of MMG, which in the past had relied on reactive cost-cutting measures to address decreases in revenue, decided that a more proactive strategy needed to be devised if they were going to halt this trend in declining revenues.

The thinking on the part of the administration was that declining patient satisfaction and revenue loss were inextricably linked. As part of a larger project to address these two related issues, Mike Taslow, the CEO of MMG, hired Betty McDaniel as the director of patient care. This was a new position for the MMG. In their initial interview, Mike told Betty that he wanted patients to have a *seamless experience* at MMG. "Patients should expect the same procedures, the same treatment from our staff, and the same efficiency from all the various departments of the MMG," Mike explained.

When he offered Betty the job, Mike challenged her to first assess the problems surrounding reduced patient satisfaction and then solve them, always keeping in mind his vision of a seamless experience. Betty, in accepting the position, agreed to present her ideas for improving patient satisfaction in three months. She was confident that the three-month time frame would be enough for her to develop a preliminary plan of action.

Prior to accepting this position, Betty had spent nine years as part of the practice management team at an affluent suburban medical center owned and operated by a competing regional health care system. Although Betty had considerable experience dealing with issues of patient satisfaction, she had never operated in an environment that included a medical school or in one that drew a substantial number of its patients from an urban population. Consequently, during her first few weeks on the job, Betty set out to gather information about the organization and the various factors that were affecting patient satisfaction.

Understanding the Issues

Betty quickly learned that there were many issues at a teaching facility with which she never had to deal at the suburban medical center. For example, since they were associated with a medical school, MMG doctors not only saw patients, they also taught classes and supervised medical students. These multiple and conflicting roles reduced the number of days and hours that doctors were actually available to see patients. Also, in order to facilitate learning, residents were sometimes present when the physicians saw the patients; other times they were not. Patients never seemed to know what to expect or even who was a *real* doctor and who wasn't. In addition, since the administration divided the practice according to academic departments (i.e., surgery, internal medicine), different department heads oversaw each area within MMG without the coordination of an overall practice manager.

Finally, Betty learned that while its midtown location made MMG easily accessible to a large urban population, the flight of many white-collar, middle-class professionals to the suburbs resulted in a patient population that was primarily lower-income individuals and families, often without health insurance. In addition to their medical issues, these individuals often had other concerns that could affect their satisfaction with their visits to the MMG. For example, many of these individuals had limited health coverage and even those with health insurance frequently had to take time off from their hourly jobs to visit the doctor. Betty, like many of the newer hires at MMG, had not worked with a clientele with these types of concerns.

During this time, while she was getting the lay of the land, Betty decided to observe actual interactions between the MMG staff and their patients to see how they could be potentially influencing patient satisfaction. She sat in the waiting area watching people arrive for their appointments and checking in with the intake desk. She listened to their conversations with one another and took notes discretely.

The Office Visit

It was a Wednesday afternoon about 2:15 as Betty walked past the waiting area for internal medicine. The two dozen or so brown and gold cloth chairs were about 75% filled with patients and family members. As she passed, Betty noticed that a 40-something woman and the intake nurse, Carolyn, were having some difficulty in confirming an appointment. Being relatively new and not knowing proper protocol in these matters, Betty elected to stand back and simply observe.

"Are you sure your appointment is today, Ms. Dillard? I can't seem to locate your name. You wouldn't happen to have your appointment card with you, would you?"

Ms. Dillard searched her billfold and then her purse, dumping its contents onto the narrow counter in front of Carolyn's window. A few pieces of paper and some change fell to the carpeted floor. "I can't seem to find it. I'm sorry, but I'm sure my appointment was for today at 2:30. I hope this doesn't cause a problem—I have to get back to work soon."

Carolyn seemed sympathetic. "I'm sure we'll get this cleared up," she said. "Just have a seat and I'll check to see if maybe your appointment was made with another department. Did you talk to us or to central scheduling?"

"I don't remember, but I'm sure it was for today."

From her position Betty could hear Carolyn on the phone saying, "She's very nice. Could you check and see if she has an appointment in your department?"

After a few minutes, maybe 10, Jacqueline, a receptionist from acute care, entered the waiting room and escorted Ms. Dillard over to acute care and sat her down in that waiting area. Betty could overhear

Jacqueline saying calmly, "We're sorry for the confusion. I'm sure we'll get it straightened out." Jacqueline excused herself and went back to her office to check on the appointment.

A short time later Ms. Dillard and Jacqueline returned to Carolyn's intake window, and after a brief three-way conversation Ms. Dillard, somewhat jokingly, turned to another waiting patient and said, "I don't want to have to get ugly today." As Betty was taking notes, she wrote down that the patient had been there for over 30 minutes and it was still unclear if she had an appointment and if she would be able to see her doctor.

Carolyn slid her window shut, and Ms. Dillard began talking to other patients around her. Each of the waiting patients took a turn telling their MMG horror stories. At some point Ms. Dillard said rather loudly, "I'm wondering what they're talking about back there. Just get me in to my appointment. I took time off work today and had my sister give me a ride just so I could be here."

Just then Carolyn slid the window open once more to call Ms. Dillard over. "Again I apologize for the confusion. We're trying to figure out what happened. I should have an answer in a few more minutes."

"This is a big problem. I'm not going to deal with this anymore!" Ms. Dillard said to anyone who would listen. "I don't need a doctor I can't get to see. If she doesn't see me today, I'll . . ." In the middle of her speech, Ms. Dillard was called to the window.

Betty was tempted to intervene, to go over and offer her help. But she didn't, wanting to see how the intake receptionist would handle the patient.

Carolyn shook her head and said, "I'm afraid there is some confusion. Your doctor works with residents today; she doesn't see patients except those scheduled as patients of her residents."

"So what can be done? I took off from work today and my sister gave me a ride. I wouldn't have done this if someone hadn't scheduled me an appointment."

Carolyn continued. "Again I apologize for the confusion. Let me give you a couple of options. The doctor is in clinic with her residents, and as I said she doesn't see her own patients when she's with her residents. Clinic is finished at five o'clock and she can see you then."

Betty wrote in her notes that it had been almost an hour at this point.

"I can't wait until then. I have to get back to work. Let me talk to the doctor," Ms. Dillard pleaded. "Last time she fit me in when you said there were no appointments."

"We could schedule you for another day," Carolyn offered.

"Can I get another doctor? Is there another doctor I can see? She seems real good, but if I can't see her . . ." Ms. Dillard turned to another patient, one of her complaint group. "I had to wait to see her the first time I came here. Now this for my second visit."

"Again I apologize for your inconvenience."

"I've had a lot of problems with this place. Today I left work to get here. I guess I'll have to find another doctor. Or maybe I can go to the nurse where I work. I think they let us see her sometimes, even when it's not work related. Maybe she can recommend a doctor for me to see."

She grabbed her purse and stormed off, looking for her sister.

The next day at lunch Betty discovered from Joyce, one of Carolyn's intake associates, that Ms. Dillard actually had an appointment scheduled for the same time and date the following month. "It was her fault," said Joyce. "We weren't wrong here. It wasn't our mistake." Betty also discovered that Carolyn hadn't informed her immediate supervisor about the incident. She wondered if there was a mechanism in place for reporting these types of patient issues.

Making Sense of It All: From the Patient's Perspective

Betty's experience with issues of patient satisfaction and her basic instincts told her that assessing and solving MMG's problems would be more difficult than she first thought. But she had told Mike Taslow that she would have an initial plan at the three-month mark, which now was only six weeks away. She decided that her best strategy at this point would be to hold some one-on-one conversations with patients to hear what they had to say directly, and decided that she would begin interviewing patients the next day.

Getting off the elevator on the second floor, Betty identified a woman who she presumed to be a patient, as her wrist was bandaged, and introduced herself. "Hello, my name is Betty McDaniel. I'm the director of patient care. I'm trying to improve patient care here at MMG and would like to get your opinion on how we are doing."

Startled by the abrupt introduction, it wasn't clear if the woman would agree to respond to Betty's introduction. Finally, she said, "My name is Miriam."

"Miriam, if you wouldn't mind, why don't we sit over here so that you can be more comfortable and we won't be in the way," Betty offered as she motioned toward some chairs in an adjacent waiting area. "Please tell me, how did you happen to get started coming to the MMG?"

"I work only a few blocks away and going to MMG would be convenient. I just never took the time to come over here. But everyone I talk to always says how wonderful the doctors are at MMG, and I wasn't that happy with my own doctor. I just didn't take the time to switch. But then I hurt my wrist and my boss, of all people, suggested that I come here to see them. She had hurt her wrist playing sports—tennis—and said how great her doctor was."

"So you started coming here because of our doctors' reputations?"

"Yes, but you folks have some problems. The first time I called to make an appointment I had to push about 10 different buttons on the phone just to talk with someone. When I finally spoke with someone, I was told that I would have to wait four to six weeks to see a doctor. But since I had heard such good things, I decided to go ahead and wait even though my wrist hurt now. They told me about acute care, but what they told me didn't make sense. Then about a week or two before my appointment I got a letter saying that my appointment had been moved, but they moved it to a time when I work. I called the nurse and she checked with the doctor. They managed to fit me in at a better time. I thought that was really nice of her and, of course, the doctor. I remember thinking that I understood a little better why people spoke so highly of the doctors at the MMG."

Betty asked her to continue, to tell her more specifics about her experiences when she arrived at the MMG.

"Well, I went upstairs to sign in but had to go back downstairs to register. No one told me to register downstairs, not even the receptionist in the lobby. I was on time for my appointment, 1:15 I think, but going downstairs took some time and I got back up to my doctor's a little late. The waiting room was OK, a little crowded, but I've seen worse. They had some magazines set out, but nothing I was interested in.

"Anyway, after signing in I waited in the waiting room for about 15 minutes and finally asked how much longer. The woman didn't even look up from what she was doing. She just told me that the doctor was with other patients and she would see me as soon as possible. I just wish I would have known how long that would be. I mean, I was afraid to go to the bathroom. While I was there waiting, this guy sitting next to me told me that on clinic days you could sign in early and they would see you first.

"At about 1:45 or 1:50 a nurse took me into the exam room, I sat for another 45 minutes—just the exam table and me. No books, no nothing! It felt like they had forgotten about me. Eventually, a doctor came in, at least I thought she was a doctor and she asked me a bunch of questions and then told me that my doctor would be there in a little bit. I thought she was my doctor, but she wasn't. I'm not sure who she was. After 10 minutes or so another doctor came in and asked all the same questions. She also asked a lot about my work and what I do all day. She was really nice and figured out that I had, and still have, some inflammation in my wrist. She suggested that I get an X-ray to be sure that was all. I could tell she really cared about me and wanted me to get better. She told me that I needed an order to take to their X-ray department and that the woman at the intake window would make it for me. From the woman's response I guessed that this was something she normally didn't do.

"When I got back to work I was complaining about the cost of parking and my boss asked why I didn't get my parking ticket validated. You know why—no one told me! I don't have money to throw away. I don't know. I really like my doctor, but . . ." Miriam paused as if waiting for Betty to respond.

"How would you rate your satisfaction with your visit to MMG?"

"On a scale of 1 to 10 I'd give it about an 8. The doctor was a 10, the appointment process was close to zero, and the rest was about average, maybe a 5 or 6."

A day or two later Betty talked with Roz, a patient at the MMG for the past three years.

"I never understand how you schedule appointment times. The doctors are always late, at least 20 or 30 minutes, or even an hour behind on most days. And waiting for me—you know, a single mom—is difficult. I have to bring my kids with me, since I don't have any day care. That's tough. Especially if the appointment is around lunchtime, when my kids get really hungry. The first couple of times I came here I looked for a lunchroom or something to get them a snack, but there were signs everywhere saying that there was no food or drink allowed. I don't know what that was about, since I can always smell food cooking in the back, like popcorn or chicken or something. Now I sneak in a couple of snacks, you know what I mean, just in case the kids get hungry."

"Please continue. These are the kinds of things I need to hear," Betty said to encourage Roz to tell her more.

"And then some departments, I don't remember the names, have a few toys for the kids in the waiting areas, but others don't. Don't they think people have kids?"

"Is there anything else beside the appointment times that you don't understand?" Betty questioned.

"Well, there's referral. One woman I talked to when I was in the waiting room one day called it referral hell! She was right. I needed a referral to see some specialist and when I went to the referral office, the office on the first floor, and knocked, no one answered. I mean I could hear them in there. Then, as I was waiting for the elevator, someone came out and I asked him about getting a referral. They told me that I had to call the office. So I went into the registration office and called, but no one answered. I called back when I got home and then once I did get through they told me I needed something from my insurance, but when I called my insurance they told me I needed a referral number. It's all too complicated."

At that point Betty jumped in and said, "Well, it's my job to make this all a little less complicated. Please tell me, how would your rate your satisfaction with the MMG?"

"If you mean with my doctor, I guess about a 7. He's getting better with me, but at times he just doesn't listen to me. If you mean everything else, I've got to be honest: I wouldn't rate it that good. The phone system makes me mad because I can't talk to anyone and every department, every doctor, seems to have a different set of rules. And don't get me started telling you about how I got lost trying to find another part of MMG over on the other side of the hospital. You probably don't want me to go there."

Making Sense of It All: From the Staff's Perspective

Although Betty felt she had a fairly good idea of what problems looked like from the perspective of the employees of MMG, she decided to sit down with a number of them and hear what they had to say. She hoped that they might provide her with some ideas for developing her plan. Now she had only three more weeks to finalize her plan to present to Mike.

"Jennifer, I want to thank you for taking some time to talk with me. As you know, I've been charged with the task of improving patient satisfaction and I would like your help. Any thoughts?"

Jennifer, a department coordinator, started right in. "I know that we have to do something. Our patient satisfaction ratings are falling. We do these recall phone surveys from our list of recent patients, and we can see that our numbers keep slipping. Actually, we don't need our patients to tell us we're slipping; all we have to do is look at our bottom line. We lost a lot of money this past year."

Betty asked her what she thought was the problem.

"What I think patients want and what we need to give them is this seamless experience that administration has talked about. Gee, I'd like a seamless experience when I see my doctor here. But that's easier said than done. I think we first need to educate our patients about how we do things here," Jennifer explained.

"Can you tell me why you think we need to start there?" Betty asked.

"I mean, some people show up and expect us to see them without an appointment or even if their health insurance doesn't cover our office. One of the biggest problems we have is walk-ins late in the day and no-shows. I think people see us as a free clinic, and they can just come when they please or just not show up for an appointment if it's not convenient. Sometimes we have to move their appointments because the doctors have an emergency or need to teach a class. But sometimes our patients tell us little white lies that create problems for us. I mean, they will say that they can't get off work or something, but if they could get off for the first appointment, why not the next? It isn't everyone, just some people. I know I probably shouldn't say this, but I really wouldn't be upset if those individuals left. They tend to see us as a drop-in clinic rather than a medical practice. We need to somehow explain to them the difference. We need to educate these people so they understand what we are, how we operate, or things will never be seamless."

"What would help, specifically, to improve patient satisfaction?"

"What would really help me do my job would be access to an electronic medical record system. Sometimes I have to go to two or three different departments to find someone's file, and that takes a lot of my time. And I have to do it. If I send the intake nurse, then there isn't anyone to greet patients as they arrive.

"There's another problem," Jennifer continued. "People don't understand how what they're doing affects other departments. We have no communication between departments. If I need to solve a problem, I just go to a friend in the department and have them fix it. And then patients need to understand that we aren't always in control of what happens. We have only one person working referrals, and in order to get referrals they need to be on the phone calling insurance companies and doctors' offices. So if they are on the phone trying to get referrals, they can't answer the phone, let alone answer the door. One thing that we are really proud of is the fact that our patients don't wait very long before we get them into an exam room. Usually they are only in the waiting room 10 to 20 minutes. Patients need to understand that we have ways of doing things so that we can ensure they get quality health care."

Betty talked with a department head, Dr. Penev, that day as well.

"Our employees and staff do a wonderful job, but we are overcrowded. We have multiple staff members in one office, and you can never find a place to sit down in the waiting area. Sure, we have our problems, they kind of percolate up. I mean, my secretary will get a call from a patient that there is a problem and I get on the phone with them. Usually we can fix it with a quick call. For example, a quick call can get an appointment set up or a report forwarded. But I also talk to a lot of people in the halls and on the phone who really like and appreciate their doctors and the rest of our staff. Sure, I get satisfaction reports from MMG and sometimes the numbers drop, but I know that my patients are satisfied.

"We provide world-class health care," he boasted. "Our doctors have national reputations. We can provide almost every service right here within MMG. Yeah, you may have to go to a different building and I know that it can be difficult, but we take care of our patients and our students. We just need more room."

At the three-month deadline, Betty scheduled a meeting with Mike Taslow. As they sat down, the first thing Mike asked was, "Okay, why aren't the patients satisfied?" ✦

*This case has been developed based on real organization(s) and real organizational experiences. Names, facts, and situations have been changed to protect the privacy of individuals and organizations.

Chapter 20

The 'Expert' Facilitator

MARY E. VIELHABER

"Marlene,* what do you think about having an external consultant facilitate our strategic planning session?" asked Mitch Johnson, the vice president of finance for the Midwest Energy Company. Mitch posed this question as he and Marlene Lewis, the director for banking relations, met to discuss the upcoming departmental strategic planning session.

"That sounds like a great idea to me, Mitch. You and I want to be actively involved in the discussion rather than leading it, so it probably would be better to have a facilitator help us."

Deregulation of the electrical utility industry had led to new competitive pressures for all electrical utility companies. Both Mitch and Marlene knew that the energy companies that would survive in this new environment had to meet customer demands by cutting costs and providing reliable, safe energy. Mitch and Marlene also knew that the finance department had to make changes in how it managed the company's cash and pension investments. Marlene, in particular, was keenly aware that there would be considerable resistance. Some employees always seemed to cling to the old ways of doing business.

"There's a consultant I know named Tom Davison," said Mitch. "I think he would do a good job for us. Last summer, he worked with the top-level executives at our teambuilding retreat. I am not sure if he does facilitation, but I'll check with him."

Several days later, Mitch mentioned to Marlene that he had hired Tom Davison to facilitate the strategic planning session. "I told Tom that the goal for the departmental strategic planning session was to come up with a strategic plan that could move the department forward in the new deregulated environment. I asked Tom to meet with a smaller committee to prepare for the session. Then I asked Bill Edwards, the director of risk management, and Susan Maher, the director of pension investment, and four of our top financial analysts to work with Tom to prepare for the departmental session."

The Strategic Planning Session

As members of the finance department came into the conference room on the day scheduled for the strategic planning session, Marlene noticed the room and the refreshments were all set. There were six round tables with six chairs at each table. Marlene greeted Tom. "Hi, Tom. I'm Marlene Lewis. Is everything ready for today?" As Tom looked around the room, he replied, "I think so."

Tom continued, "I met several times with the six people who were on the preparation committee, but I wasn't able to schedule much time with Mitch. Clearly, he is one busy guy. We talked by phone yesterday, and he seems fine with the agenda I developed for today."

Just then, Mitch walked in and greeted Tom. Marlene excused herself as Tom and Mitch chatted with each other.

By 9:10 A.M., most people had arrived and sat down. The seating was typical. The financial analysts sat together; the directors were at another table; the assistant directors were at another table; the administrative assistants were at a table in the back of the room; and the last two tables had a mix of the people who arrived late. Marlene sat with the directors and waited for things to get started.

As Marlene sat down, she noticed at each place there was a small wireless keypad the size of a television remote control. The keypads would allow each person to register individual responses of strongly agree, agree, neutral, disagree, or strongly disagree. Marlene assumed that Tom planned to gauge their reactions to ideas with these feedback mechanisms. Next to each wireless keypad, there was a cardboard tent that had a number corresponding to the number on the keypad.

Prior to the meeting, everyone had received an email with the starting time (9:00 A.M. sharp!) and the ending time (4:00 P.M.). The notice said that this meeting was to develop the strategic plan that would guide the department for the next three to five years. Since there was no written agenda, Marlene was really not sure how the day would be spent.

Finally, at about 9:20 A.M., Mitch Johnson began the session with some opening remarks. "I want to thank everyone for coming. This is a very important meeting for the finance department. We are going to begin a strategic planning process today that will culminate in a three- to five-year strategic plan for the department. I want each of you to contribute your thoughts and ideas openly today. The contributions of each member of the staff are valuable.

"Prior to today's session, a committee from the department met and they generated some ideas about our mission, vision, goals, strategies, and action plans. Our goal today is to build on those ideas and to reach some common understanding as a department about where we are going and how we plan to get there.

"This plan is important because with all of the change that is going on in our company and our industry, we don't want to be over a barrel and have to dig our way out of a hole."

Marlene chuckled to herself as she thought about the way Mitch mixed metaphors. Mitch continued, "To help us reach consensus today, I have asked Tom Davison to facilitate our session. Tom has his own consulting business and I have seen his work. Last summer Tom ran an outdoor teambuilding session for our executive team." Then, turning to Tom, he said, "Tom, are you still doing those ropes courses?"

Tom nodded and said, "Yes. Those are still quite popular for teambuilding. For those of you who are not familiar with ropes courses, they are experiential training courses that are held outdoors. Typically, a variety of team exercises are used that require all of the team members to tackle some physical challenge like climbing over a wall or crossing over a fast-running steam on a narrow plank. The goal is to develop trust and confidence in each other as you take on outdoor challenges as a team. The thought is that the trust and confidence will then be transferred to working together on business issues."

After a brief pause, Tom began the session by thanking Mitch and then said, "To start today's session, I would like each of you to get up, walk around, and introduce yourself to two people you don't know."

The group laughed. We know each other all too well, Marlene thought. We meet quarterly as a group, and there have been no new hires in the last two years. Hesitant, but willing to respond to Tom's request, Marlene introduced herself to Susan Maher, sitting next to her, even though she knew Susan well after working with her for seven years. In fact, Susan and Marlene were both on Mitch's executive team, so they met together every week for several hours. Following her lead, others got up and shook hands with colleagues, imitating what Marlene had modeled. Anyone listening to these *introductions* would have noticed that people were faking it. Yet people played along and pretended to enjoy meeting colleagues they already were quite familiar with. Meanwhile, Tom did not seem to notice that his icebreaker wasn't accomplishing much at all.

As people shook hands, Marlene heard the song "Celebration," a popular tune from the early eighties playing in the background. Obviously, Tom chose some very upbeat but dated music to get the day started. Marlene also noticed that Mitch must have slipped out of the room when the introductions started. Mitch wasn't someone who could fake an introduction just to be polite. He probably thought he could take a quick break, check his phone messages, and get back before the real discussions began.

Getting Down to Business

When it became clear that everyone had exhausted the introductions, Tom continued. "Well, now that you have had an opportunity to meet some new people, I would like to get started. Today we have a lot to cover. We will be developing our mission, vision, goals, strategies, and action plans for the next three to five years. I know this may sound like a lot, but I have some technology here that will allow us to move more quickly through these topics. My job is to help you find the most expedient way to reach consensus."

Taking a wireless keypad in his hand and holding it up for everyone to see, Tom continued, "At each of your places, you will find a wireless keypad for voting. This mechanism will allow you to vote anonymously on ideas today. After you vote, the totals will be displayed on this large screen in the front of the room. To test this out, please answer the two questions that you can see on the screen up front with strongly agree, agree, neutral, disagree, or strongly disagree."

> Question 1: If I was independently wealthy and I did not need to work for a living, I would still work.
>
> Question 2: If I was independently wealthy and I did not need to work for a living, I would still work for *this* company.
>
> Strongly agree—agree—neutral—disagree—strongly disagree

"Now let's look at the results."

Marlene was not surprised. A large majority (65%) agreed that they would still work even if they were independently wealthy. However, an even larger majority (75%) disagreed that they would work for this company. Marlene knew that recent rumors about a reorganization had made most people concerned about whether their jobs were secure. There were also rumors of a merger with another, larger energy company. These rumors were especially troublesome, since people were speculating that the larger company would keep their own finance department and Marlene and her colleagues would be replaced.

Tom briefly commented on the results from the voting. When he asked for questions, the participants looked around nervously. No one asked a question or offered a comment about the results. Moving on, Tom explained that the group would continue to use the wireless keypads to determine team consensus on a variety of issues.

As Marlene thought about the rumors, and her colleagues' obvious reaction to them, Tom put a mission statement on the screen. He explained, "This mission statement was drafted by a few of your colleagues in the department." Since most of the people in the room were seeing the mission statement for the first time, they carefully read the words on the screen.

Tom continued, "Now, I want you to vote on this statement. Again, choose one of the following responses: strongly agree, agree, neutral, disagree, or strongly disagree."

Ralph, a supervisor in the cashier's office, raised his hand and asked, "Tom, can we discuss this statement before we vote?"

Tom quickly replied, "No, I just want you to vote so we can see if we have consensus."

Ralph frowned and looked around the room to others for support. No one said anything, so he continued. "That doesn't make sense to me. How can we vote when we have not talked about this mission statement at all? I'm not even sure what the statement means."

Tom looked away from Ralph and directed his attention back to the group. "After we have tallied the votes, we can discuss the statement. Will everyone please vote now?"

When the results appeared on the screen, it was clear that just over half of the participants either agreed or strongly agreed with the mission statement. Tom summed up the results by saying, "Just over

50% of you either strongly agree or agree with the draft of the mission statement. You will also notice that another 20% are neutral. While this is not a strong consensus, the results show that most people agree with the mission statement proposed."

Without asking for questions or comments, Tom moved on. Next, he put up a vision statement and asked the participants to vote. This seemed really odd to Marlene, and she suspected others were uncomfortable as well. How can we decide our vision when we have not all bought into the mission statement? Marlene decided that she would abstain from voting. She looked around and saw confusion on some of the faces. In fact, many of the individuals at the meeting seemed to be preoccupied with something else. Some were attending to their PDAs, and some were looking over papers they had brought with them.

Tom looked at his computer screen and announced firmly, "It looks like not everyone has voted. Please vote now."

There was a brief pause, followed by another request to vote on the vision. When it didn't look like people were responding, Tom turned to his laptop computer and pushed a key. As he turned back to the audience, the numbers of the keypads that had not been used appeared on the large screen in the front of the room. Since the numbers on the tent cards at each person's place were also large, most people could glance around the table and see who had not voted. Marlene's number was there. And so was Ralph's number.

Tom again announced, "These five people have not voted. Will each of you vote now?"

An undercurrent of whispering became obvious. Finally Ralph stood up and said, "I object, Tom. You said that this voting would be anonymous. Why are you singling us out? I honestly feel that I cannot vote on a vision statement until I have had an opportunity to talk the mission statement over with colleagues."

Marlene looked around the room and wondered why Mitch still had not returned to the room. She wondered if anyone else, including Tom, had noticed his absence.

Tom again looked away from Ralph and explained to the group, "This is not a final vote. I just want everyone to let us know how they are feeling."

"I would be glad to tell you how I am feeling, but you said we can't discuss the mission statement yet," Ralph interrupted.

Tom turned to the group and asked, "How many of you would like to stop and discuss the mission statement?"

Hands went up. Marlene thought it looked like more than half the people there had their hands up. She did notice, however, that all of the committee members who had worked with Tom to prepare for the session did not raise their hands.

"It looks like the majority are happy with the voting," Tom concluded.

Not to be deterred, Ralph continued, "It looked pretty even to me. Maybe we should count hands."

Again, Tom seemed to ignore Ralph as he turned to the group and asked, "Do you want to continue?"

Marlene could see by Ralph's expression that he was angry as he continued. "I thought my contribution was supposed to be valued. Where is Mitch? What are we doing here?"

Marlene sighed. This meeting would be a disaster if Tom did not take control immediately. Just then, Mitch walked back into the room.

Tom turned to Mitch and said, "Mitch, we seem to have some disagreement about the process you and I discussed for today. I planned for the group to vote on the draft statements for the mission, vision, goals, strategies, and action plans. Then I thought we would discuss them and vote again. I want them to vote to find out how many people agree. If we all agree, there is no need to discuss the statements. What do you want to do, Mitch?"

Clearly, Mitch had little idea of the controversy that was brewing as he answered, "Tom, you are the facilitator, you decide."

Before Tom could say another word, Ralph and two other people who had not voted and whose numbers had appeared on the screen got up and walked out of the room.

Marlene wondered what she should do. She knew that Ralph and others, including herself, were frustrated by the process, not necessarily the ideas. What could she say to help Tom understand that he needed to stop and resolve this misunderstanding before the group could continue with a productive discussion of strategic planning? ✦

*This case has been developed based on real organization(s) and real organizational experiences. Names, facts, and situations have been changed to protect the privacy of individuals and organizations.

Chapter 21

A Decision to Change

Theodore E. Zorn, Jr.

Bill Inglis* closed his office door and slumped into his office chair. He knew he wouldn't have long to relax before he heard from at least one member of the Knowledge Link Task Force. The task force, of which he was chair, had just adjourned its seventh meeting. They had worked hard over the past five months—from June to October—in their attempt to create a plan for establishing knowledge management (KM) systems for the company. This was a particularly frustrating meeting, since the task force had just been told at the meeting by Tom Kirk, director of engineering, that their project would have to be scaled down dramatically.

The task force members had taken the news quietly, but some—particularly Don Lucas, the project champion and the key driver of the project from its earliest stages—had expressed their anger and frustration as soon as Tom left the meeting. Bill had suggested the task force adjourn the meeting, think about next steps, and reconvene later. Now he and the task force were faced with the difficult decision of what to do. Should they define some more limited objectives and do their best to make these successful, knowing it was a far cry from what they thought was needed? Or should they tell top management what many of them were thinking, that if they were serious about becoming a company that managed (rather than squandered) its intellectual capital, top management needed to quit being an obstacle and start being a role model.

Bill had been with Black Cap Engineering and Construction for 10 years now. A civil engineer by training, he had substantial experience as a project manager. Thus, after the Knowledge Link project had been initiated by Don Lucas and approved by upper management, he was asked to serve as project manager. He didn't know much about knowledge management systems when the project started, but his reputation as a results-oriented project manager led to his appointment on such projects regularly. Black Cap Engineering was primarily in the business of building roads and bridges. The name of the company was a play on words, referring to the company's core business of building *black capped* or asphalt roads, as well as to the New Zealand national cricket team (the Black Caps). The company started as a branch of the New Zealand government, but in the wave of privatising that occurred in the late 1980s, the government sold it so that it was now a publicly listed, fully private company. There were two major divisions of the company: engineering, responsible for design and problem solving, and construction, responsible for the actual construction and repair of roads and bridges.

In the mid-1990s, Black Cap, like many New Zealand companies, had gone through several waves of reengineering and subsequent downsizing. It had reduced its numbers from over 700 employees at its peak in 1994 to just over 300 in 2000. It had sold off a major part of its construction division and maintained a minimal staff of construction workers. Now, Black Cap hired contractors—many of whom were formerly part of the construction division—to do the majority of the actual building.

The Origins of Knowledge Management at Black Cap Engineering

While the terms *organizational knowledge* and *knowledge management* had begun creeping into the company's language several years earlier, the knowledge management initiative got its real start in February. That's when Ed Willis, a senior executive, phoned Don Lucas, the information systems manager. Don recounted the conversation:

> Ed: What do you know about knowledge management?
>
> Don: Not too much. Just what I've been reading in the trade magazines, and what I've been told by consultants. Basically, it's an attempt to strategically identify, store, and take maximum advantage of the company's knowledge resources—its expertise, which may be stored in databases, documents, and even in employees' heads.
>
> Ed: Right, and it usually involves specially designed information systems, which is why I thought you'd know something about it.

Don: Some of the big companies have really gotten into it in a big way. The big consulting firms are pushing it as the next big thing.

Ed: Yeah, I know. I've been hearing that from the PricewaterhouseCoopers chaps we brought in to work with us on our outsourcing project last year. They say we've got to take KM more seriously if we're going to remain competitive.

Don: Well, I'd jump at the chance to look into it further. There are quite a few vendors selling KM technology, and of course the big consulting firms will gladly come in and help us design the systems we need.

Ed: Yeah, well, let's hold off calling them in just yet. I was thinking of attending a seminar on knowledge management that's being held in Auckland next month, but I don't know if I'm going to have the time. How would you feel about going?

Don: Yeah, I'd be quite keen to go.

Ed: Great. And if you think it's worth pursuing, you could present an overview to the MG [management group] when you return. Before we could begin any substantial effort, of course, we'll need to get the MG to commit a budget for it.

After the Seminar

Don attended the seminar and as a result was even more excited about the prospects for knowledge management at Black Cap. "It just makes so much sense," he told his wife the night he returned from the seminar. "The main competitive advantage companies in today's economy have is their expertise, their intellectual capital. Why wouldn't we take stock of what we know and figure out how to store it and make it accessible to our staff?"

Don was given 15 minutes on the agenda of an April 2000 meeting of the MG, or management group, the company's top management team. As he prepared his presentation, Don thought to himself, "I have to convince them first that KM is not just some technology, but requires a change in our organizational culture. The KM experts say we need to find a way to tap into the tacit knowledge that people have in their heads and in their work practices. I also need to demonstrate a clear plan of action." So, for his brief presentation to the MG, Don chose the information about KM for his PowerPoint® presentation that he thought would be most convincing.

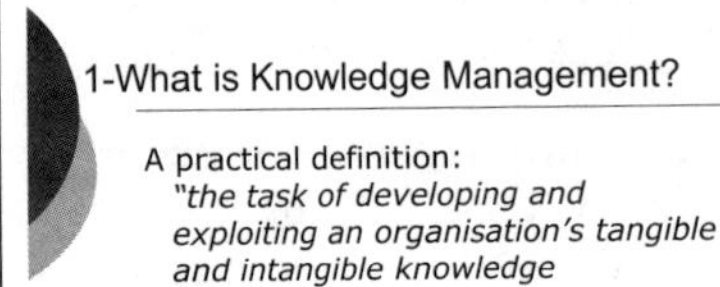

2-Why Knowledge Management?

corporate amnesia
companies forget what they know.
30% of documents never found again.

myopia
knowledge remains in departmental "silos."
no sharing; information is power.

anorexia
we don't feed the knowledge we have.

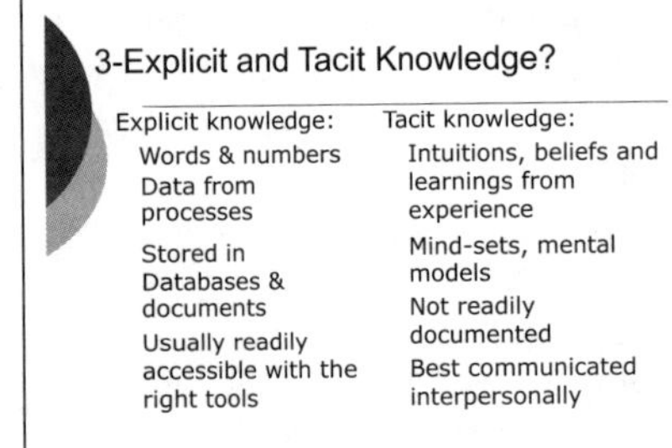

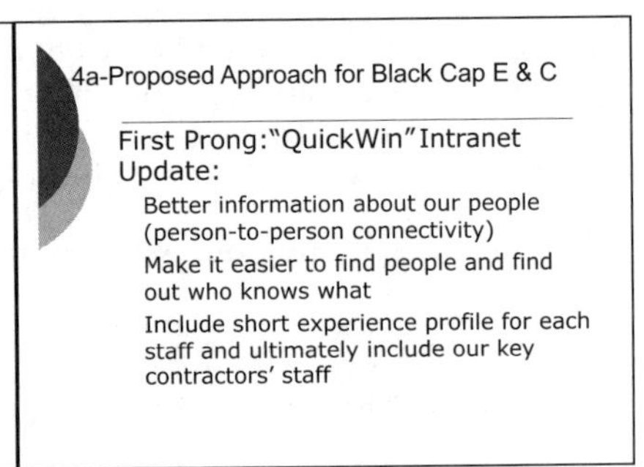

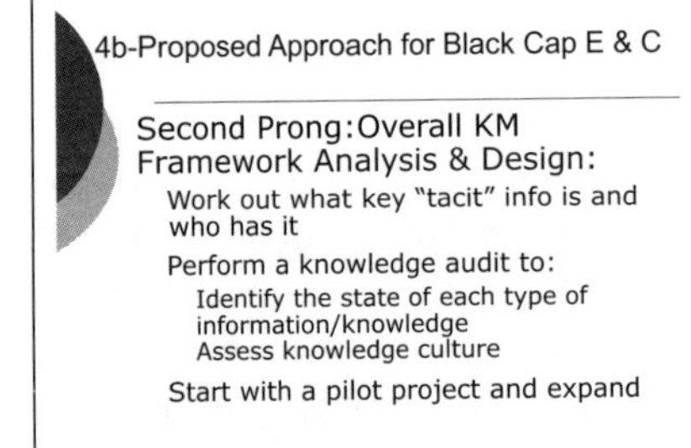

Final thought

"Knowledge Management is expensive (but so is stupidity!)"

(T. H. Davenport)

The MG had asked a number of tough questions. "What's the return on investment?" "How do you measure whether you've been successful?" "How do we know this isn't just the 'flavour of the month'?" While Don didn't have specific answers to all of their questions, he suggested that measuring the success of the effort required starting with a knowledge audit to establish a baseline. That way, the company would be able to assess changes in practices and results.

He was also able to convince them of the reality of the problems that KM was purported to solve by pointing out some specific dilemmas the company had faced. For example, he reminded them, "Remember earlier this year when Stuart Tamahere left the company? Everyone in the public affairs department panicked because Stuart had such a wealth of knowledge about government practices. Stuart had all that stored in his head, just like any other experienced professional. And it all went out the door when he left. We've lost a lot of people—some of whom we didn't want to lose—with our downsizing and outsourcing initiatives in the past few years. If we had done a better job of capturing and storing what they knew, we wouldn't have been so vulnerable."

After some discussion, the MG decided there was enough of a good idea here to ask Don to write up a project justification. Don consulted with Tom Kirk and agreed that Bill Inglis would be a good choice for project manager. After getting Bill's buy-in, Don and Bill developed and submitted the project justification form to the MG, along with a requested budget of $100,000 for the remainder of the fiscal year.

Planning for Knowledge Management: Creation of the Knowledge-Link Task Force

In May, Don received a response to his project justification. It was in typical form—a brief memo from the secretary of the MG. The memo simply stated, "We agree to provide $40,000 in funding to support the project in the short term, which will provide the opportunity for a project team to explore the feasibility of implementing a full-scale knowledge initiative. We will reconsider funding it fully later in the year, once the team has developed more specific proposals, objectives, timelines, and ROI estimates."

Project Justification Form

Project Title: "Knowledge Link"

<u>Scope of Work</u>

1. Undertake a knowledge/information audit throughout the engineering division, including staff interviews and review of information holdings. Identify and communicate the available subject matter experts for key business processes and any missing areas of knowledge/skill that we need to obtain or outsource. (continued)

(continued)

2. Implement a restructured information storage system for paper and electronic files.
3. Implement an improved intranet structure to simplify information searches.

What will the project achieve?

1. Find previously unidentified knowledge/skills and information, not readily available to other staff, that may be possessed by individuals. Identify any missing areas of knowledge or skills that we need to obtain (either by employment, upskilling, or outsourcing).
2. Time savings in searching for electronic and/or hard copy information.
3. Make the existing knowledge base of engineering more accessible, which is important as an enabler for our in-house and external consulting activities.

Who will perform the work?

1. Knowledge audit: External consultant (will require availability of a large proportion of engineering staff for interviews).
2. Restructured information storage:
   - LAN/database/intranet/search engine—IT contractors.
   - File recoding or database entry—support services staff responsible for library, archive, and file records, with assistance from temporary staff.

When will the work be performed?

July 2000 to April 2001.

Alternatives considered

1. Base option (do nothing). Continue with existing plans to revise records filing and electronic filing without a knowledge audit. This would not provide benefits of understanding the business needs of staff and the hidden knowledge potential that is believed to exist. It would also not identify any areas of weakness that we need to build on.
2. Proceed to a wholesale EDMS (Electronic Document Management System) architecture. This is extremely costly, requires a clear understanding of knowledge and information requirements to begin with, and does not in itself deliver the cultural changes necessary to effective sharing of knowledge and information. For full benefit, a complete change in document-handling processes is required, and the project as proposed will provide a good platform for future development into EDMS when it becomes cost-effective.

(continued)

Signatures (continued)

Project Champion

Don Lucas

Project Manager______________________________

Bill Inglis

Director______________________________

Tom Kirk

Don discussed this response with Bill shortly afterward. Don explained that he had mixed feelings about the memo. "I was happy they thought enough of the project to fund it partially, but I'm concerned that we might never be able to provide the sort of tangible measures that would satisfy them. After all, the MG is almost all engineers, and they're used to dealing with concrete, steel, and asphalt, not fuzzy things like knowledge and intellectual capital."

Bill laughed. "Well, I'm one of those engineers, and I think you're right. But we can't expect them to give us hundreds of thousands of dollars if we can't be fairly specific about what the company is going to get in return."

Bill, too, had mixed feelings from the beginning. He thought KM was a good idea. After all, it made sense to identify the company's expertise, their intellectual capital as the KM gurus called it. It made sense to try to capture expertise and make it available to staff as they go about solving problems and making decisions. But he also empathized with the MG's wish for specifics. As an engineer himself, he felt a lot more comfortable dealing with engineering projects than with "HR and IT projects"—which is what he considered KM.

And he also empathized with his boss, Tom Kirk, who had said to Bill when he was first assigned to be project manager, "This whole knowledge management idea sounds a bit esoteric to me. I want you to see if there's something tangible there. If not, let's can it and move on." That suited Bill fine, since he was very committed to a systems approach to project management: identify the objectives very precisely, identify measurable outcomes, and set up systems to achieve them.

Within a week after receiving the MG's statement of initial support, Bill and Don had identified appropriate members of the task force and set up a meeting, to be chaired by Bill as project manager. They wanted members who represented multiple divisions of the company, especially people in roles they thought would be key to making KM work. So, in addition to Bill and Don, the members included Christine Post, the newly appointed human resources manager; Janet Harrison, strategy and business systems adviser; Cliff Anglesea, environmental engineering manager; and Vikram Singh, an information technology specialist who worked closely with Don.

The Knowledge-Link Task Force's First Meeting

Getting ready for the meeting, Bill contemplated what this team needed to get a good start. So, before the meeting, he sent an email to the task force members with a suggested agenda, and he attached electronic copies of the project justification form and the response memo from the MG.

The suggested agenda items were the following:

1. Overview of task force charter—led by Bill
2. Presentation on knowledge management—led by Don
3. Creation of a formal task force charter—led by Bill

When everyone arrived for the first meeting, Bill worked through the agenda. He started by saying, "As most of you know by now, we've been asked to consider whether and how to do a better job of knowledge management in the company, or specifically, the engineering division for now. You each received the project justification that Don wrote up, and Don's going to give us the overview of KM that he presented to the MG, just to get us all on the same page as to what KM is and what we can do with it. Then, the third item I have on the agenda for today is the creation of a formal project charter for our task force. Don and I have made an initial stab at this, just to give us a starting point to work from. I thought we'd see where we can get to today, then bring the draft document back to our individual departments for feedback, and try to revise and sign off on the charter at our next meeting, in three weeks or so."

There were nods of approval, but not much discussion, not even questions. So Bill invited Don to make his presentation. After the presentation, a lively discussion ensued about the possibilities for implementing KM at Black Cap E&C.

"I don't mean to be cynical," said Janet, "but I think we as a company are terrible at sharing knowledge, and it starts at the top. I mean, what you're describing, Don, sounds fantastic, but can you really imagine people sharing knowledge freely in the way you're describing it? I mean, I can't even get the MG to give me enough information to draft a decent strategic plan!"

Cliff reinforced her point. "I know what you mean. I'm supposed to be representing the company in environmental negotiations with the government, and I feel like I'm working in the dark half the time."

Janet added, "Right, and what you're talking about is a real culture change."

"You're right, it is," replied Don. "And I don't pretend it's going to be easy. But if we're going to truly manage our intellectual capital—and not just continue hiding it or letting it walk out the door—then we . . ."

Vikram interrupted Don. "It's more like we *push* it out the door, from what I can see of the company's record of downsizing over the past few years."

"Right." Don continued, "That's exactly the sort of thing we have to change. We've failed to recognize what we're losing with those staff departures, and we've failed to recognize the value of the knowledge we have here now."

"And you expect the same management that authorised those downsizings and that keeps us guessing about what's happening in the company to accept a change to a knowledge-sharing organization?" Janet chimed in as she rolled her eyes and shook her head.

Christine added, "Not only accept, but *lead.* I'm new here, so there's much I don't know about this company. But you don't get culture change without top management setting an example. After 20 years in HR and organizational development, I've seen lots of failed attempts at changing organizational cultures."

Bill thought it best to turn this conversation around. "Right. Well, folks, as we can see, this is potentially a very ambitious—maybe even too ambitious—project. What we have to decide is what we want to attempt to do, and try to agree on some objectives and a plan."

At this point, Bill passed out the draft project charter. The group generally responded positively and worked for 20 minutes or so to edit it to their liking. Then they agreed to take the charter to their own departments for feedback and meet again in three weeks.

The KM Implementation Process Begins

By the end of the second meeting, the task force members had agreed on a project charter.

Knowledge-Link Project

Project Charter Approved by Management Group

Title: KNOWLEDGE-LINK ★ Knowledge ★ People ★ Information

Objectives

- To identify critical knowledge and facilitate access to and use of existing information.

Scope: To Include

- tacit knowledge from all engineering staff.
- existing paper and electronic files and information across engineering division.
- consideration of the database framework.

Methodology

- Project Management
  1. Use the project task force as a steering committee to decide how the project is implemented and to communicate closely with all staff to facilitate change to a culture of trust and knowledge sharing.
  2. Closely monitor costs and review projected costs.
  3. Establish a methodology for assessing the success of the project in terms of the objectives and business value.
  4. Integrate the results of past and current projects (e.g., engineering business systems project; filing system in the environmental section; establishment of intranet drive for common access to files).
  5. Complete the project closeout report by June 30, 2001.
- Investigations
  1. Audit the existing knowledge, information sources, and requirements throughout engineering and establish gaps.
  2. Investigate solutions for storing and presenting information, and to reduce identified gaps in knowledge and information.
  3. Investigate the physical environment for knowledge transfer.
- Report on the outcome of investigations and make recommendations

(continued)

(continued)

- Implementation
  1. Implement selected recommendations.
  2. Restructure as necessary the information storage systems for paper and electronic files.
  3. Communicate the revised framework and philosophy to all engineering staff.
  4. Post-project monitoring and review.

Additionally, over the next two months, the group met four more times and took several actions.

The KM Seminar

In July, they hired a consultant to present a half-day seminar on KM to the task force and to other interested members of the organization. Don and Vikram were the primary organisers of the seminar. Since these two had a large network of colleagues in the IT field, the task force members agreed that they were in the best position to identify an appropriate consultant to work with. Don sent invitations to the entire MG to attend the seminar, as well as to midlevel managers—in other words, the people considered key to the success of the KM initiative. Unfortunately, because of their busy schedules, two MG members declined the invitation and two others canceled at the last minute. Thus, Tom Kirk and Ed Willis were the only MG members who attended, and each of them had to leave the session on a couple of occasions to handle pressing business issues. In fact, Tom ended up missing more than half the session. The seminar was very informative for the task force members and the half dozen or so middle managers who attended.

The task force members were appreciative of Don and Vikram's efforts. But Janet and Cliff shook their heads and exchanged knowing glances when told about the MG members who declined to attend and those who canceled.

Connecting KM With Departmental Goals

In July and August members of the task force took turns reporting on how projects they were working on in their departments might interface with the KM initiative. It became apparent that almost every department had its own specialised information management systems that worked in isolation from the others. For example, Janet reported that her group was currently in the process of overhauling the engineering division's primary management information system (MIS). She suggested, and other members of the task force agreed, that it was critical for that project to align with the KM initiative, since so much critical information was stored and processed in the MIS.

In September, the group agreed to write a bulletin outlining their plans and progress and to circulate it to all members of the engineering division. The bulletin was intended to educate staff on KM, to get their buy-in, and ultimately to begin changing the culture to be more KM-friendly. Vikram drafted the first bulletin. After some discussion, the group agreed that Bill should edit it to make it simpler, less technical.

Also in September, the task force reached agreement with a local management professor to conduct a knowledge audit for the engineering division. The objectives for the audit were defined as (a) assessing the extent to which the organization records, shares, and uses knowledge resources and (b) identifying areas where knowledge can be managed more effectively both within the organization and at its interfaces.

The management professor, Scott Corner, was invited to attend the sixth meeting of the task force. He had been contacted initially by Vikram and had had several conversations with Bill before the meeting. Thus, he came to the meeting with a draft plan for the knowledge audit.

After Scott was introduced, Vikram led off the meeting with, "I know he has some questions he'd like to ask us."

"Thanks, Vikram. I guess the big question is, how and why did this knowledge management project get initiated?"

Cliff was the first to respond. "Oh, that's easy. A bandwagon rode by and we hopped on."

Everyone except Scott laughed. Seizing the opportunity, Bill provided a quick history of the project. When he finished, he asked,

"Scott, maybe you could tell us a bit more about your plan for the knowledge audit."

"Okay. I've made the plan fairly generic at this point, because I need to be clearer about your goals for the knowledge audit."

Janet said, "So do we, Scott." Everyone in the group but Don laughed.

"That's the problem, really," Cliff explained.

Don attempted to take the group's discussion to a more serious level. "Well, if you take a look at our project charter, what we've said is that our goals for the audit are to examine existing knowledge, information sources, and requirements throughout the engineering division and then establish where the gaps are. That's it really, to identify what knowledge we need in order to function well and what's easily available, and then to identify the gaps between the two."

Bill added, "Scott, I think the plan you have on paper looks good as a starting point. As I understand it, you plan to start with interviews and focus groups of key people focusing on what knowledge they think is essential and where they get what they need."

"Exactly. Plus some other things like what they see as current attitudes and practices toward sharing knowledge and what they think could be changed to make critical knowledge more accessible."

The group supported the plan and agreed that Bill would check the plan out with Tom Kirk. Then, assuming Kirk approved it, Bill would work with Scott to begin the audit. The meeting was winding down, but it was obvious that not all of the members were satisfied.

Vikram asked, "Isn't there anything more we can do in the meantime? I mean, what does the task force do while the audit is taking place?"

Bill said, "Well, continue to report progress to and get feedback from our teams for one thing."

Don confirmed Bill's response. "Right. I know some of you have told me you haven't been doing that, and we absolutely *have* to. It's critical to winning support and making the changes we hope to make."

"That's fine," said Cliff as he looked around the room to determine if others had similar sentiments. "But we've been at this for four months now, and I'm still not sure where it's all going. It seems like a massive project just doing the technical stuff—aligning all these databases and information systems. It's bigger than what we can hope to manage with the resources we have. Besides, the softer side—changing the culture—is probably going to be harder still, given the ingrained practices here."

Christine quickly agreed with Cliff. "I know what you mean, Cliff. I think that if we could make this happen, it could be huge. We could make this company great if we could pull it off. But I don't know if we can. We really need top management to step forward."

"Listen, nobody said change is easy," Don cautioned them. "But if we don't do this and do it right, this company is just going to be mediocre. We keep talking about being world class and innovation leaders. Let's get the MG in here and tell them what they need to do."

After a brief pause, Janet asked suspiciously, "So, we're going to tell the CEO how he has to change, ay?" Nervous laughter kept anyone from answering.

Scott jumped in. "If I can add my opinion here, getting top management support is absolutely critical. But there are two choices: Get their buy-in before you move forward, or get some tangible results, then sell them based on your initial success."

After several seconds of silence, Bill suggested, "Uh, well, we could ask Tom Kirk to meet with us and talk through some of these issues."

After several more seconds of silence, Don agreed. "Yes, let's do that. Maybe he can advise us on how to frame this for the MG."

Bill concluded the meeting. "Okay, then, let's meet again at our regular time one week from today and ask Tom to come along. Scott, could you join us, and perhaps take that opportunity to address any questions Tom has about the audit?"

The End of the Line for Knowledge Link

When Bill invited Tom to the meeting, Tom seemed to be a bit cagey in his response: "Um, I'll see. I'm still not sure about that project. I'll let you know if I can make it." It turned out to be three weeks before the meeting could be scheduled. Because of other commitments, Scott wasn't able to attend.

Tom looked quite grim as people arrived for the meeting, not smiling and not making eye contact with others. He kept his focus on some papers he had brought with him. When Bill officially opened the meeting, he reminded the group that they had asked Tom to come in and discuss some of the thornier aspects of implementing KM.

"Our hope is that you can give us some guidance on how we can broach some difficult issues with the MG, Tom. In particular, we want to focus on how to get their buy-in."

Tom, however, held up a hand as if to say he had something to say first. "I'm sorry to be the bearer of bad tidings, but the MG has decided not to continue funding this project, at least not in the way originally envisioned in Don's project justification. I've been keeping up with your, uh, progress over the last four months through discussions with Bill and through your meeting minutes. I've shared my concerns with the MG, and we're convinced that this project isn't likely to produce the sort of tangible outcomes needed to justify the time and cost. Besides, there have been some new developments that are demanding our attention. We agree there are some specific things that need addressing, like upgrading the intranet, so we're willing to provide a small amount of funding for that. But I'd like you to rethink the scope of this project to focus on some specific improvements with immediate payoffs. Now, I'm prepared to take any questions you have, but I'm afraid that's the bottom line for now."

No one asked questions, so Tom excused himself from the meeting. When Tom left, however, the questions and comments started flying.

Don's face was red, but he was the first to talk. "What a load of crap!"

Janet agreed, shaking her head and rolling her eyes. "See what I mean? These guys don't plan to change, and the only change they're going to support is if it means everybody else changing, but not them."

"Well, hold on a minute. Let's look at it from the MG's point of view," said Bill.

Immediately Christine added, "Bill's right. We should . . ."

Interrupting her, Don broke in, "The MG's point of view? Okay, I see a committed group of people trying to make this a better company!"

Cliff turned to face Don. "Oh, come on, Don. We've just been too pie-in-the-sky for them to buy into this."

"Well, maybe it wouldn't be pie-in-the-sky if everyone would do what we agree to," claimed Don.

"Absolutely," Vikram said decidedly.

Looking both bewildered and angry, Cliff asked, "And what's that supposed to mean?"

Trying to regain control, Bill pleaded, "Look, people, hold on a minute. I know you're frustrated. We've put a lot of time and effort into this to have the rug pulled from under our feet. Let's call it a day and think about this, then get together in a week or so to see what we want to do."

The meeting ended with some heavy sighs and grumbling.

Now Bill was back in his office. He knew it wouldn't be long before Don came knocking, wanting to blow off steam if not actually conspire to storm the boardroom for the MG's next meeting. What should he advise the group? He wasn't sure. He realized he stood to lose quite a bit of credibility in the eyes of a number of people as a result of this. But maybe it could still be salvaged. Maybe. ✦

*This case has been developed based on real organization(s) and real organizational experiences. Names, facts, and situations have been changed to protect the privacy of individuals and organizations.

Section 5

The Individual and the Organization

Briefing Paper

The Individual and the Organization

Working in organizations is an important experience of life for almost everyone, so important, in fact, that for most people organizational experiences influence how we evaluate self-worth and achievements. Yet understanding these experiences is as complex and varied as the experiences themselves. An individual's organizational experiences result from the attitudes, beliefs, preferences, and abilities the individual brings to the organization; how the organization seeks to influence the individual; and what types of organizational relationships the individual develops. Each person brings to an organization his or her personal needs, self-concept, predispositions for behavior, communication competencies, expectations, skills, and past experiences. Individuals develop relationships with others both within and without the organization. These relationships become primary information sources about all aspects of organizational life. The organization in turn establishes goals, policies, procedures, reward systems, and less overtly defined leadership and control processes that influence individual expectations and job experiences.

Individuals are influenced in all aspects of life by the somewhat ambiguous concept of motivation, the internal synthesis of experiences thought to influence behavior. Social scientists take many different approaches to describe the concept of motivation for behavior. Abraham Maslow, for example, contends that behavior is influenced by internal needs. Frederick Herzberg, on the other hand, describes behavior as a result of both internal and external motivators, and B. F. Skinner views reinforcement from the external environment as the primary influence on behavior. Gerald Salancik and Jeffrey Pfeffer provide an important link between motivation and communication when they propose that workers' job attitudes are a function of their organizational communication activities. Regardless of differences in perspective, most scholars agree that individuals have a complex mix of internal and external motivators that influence individual responses to managing information, problem identification, conflict management, and behavior regulation.

Individuals also differ with regard to preferences to assume or avoid leadership responsibilities. Whereas most individuals assume defined task responsibilities for job assignments, more variation exists with regard to communication responsibilities and participation. Some prefer intense interpersonal communication relationships and others prefer the use of technology; some seek public visibility in group and presentation settings and others avoid these responsibilities altogether.

Individuals also bring to organizational experiences diverse value systems and ethical frameworks. These frameworks contribute to evaluations of organizational experiences and serve as guides for behavior. Although certainly subjective assessments, values can be described as organized systems of attitudes that define for individuals the relative worth of a quality or object. Values, therefore, become part of complex attitude sets that influence behavior. Members of organizations also develop value systems represented through complex cultural processes. Organizational values not only influence the behaviors of current members but also contribute to the type of person who gets hired and the types of career experiences employees are likely to have. There is danger, of course, in thinking that individuals and organizations have singular sets of values reflecting closely held beliefs. As with individuals, most organizations have diverse functions, leadership practices, and histories, all contributing to differences in what is desirable and important. A large body of research, however, continues to demonstrate that value congruence (the similarity between individual and organizational values) between employees and their organizations has a significant effect on organizational commitment, employee work satisfaction, and turnover.

Related to the concept of values, ethics are the standards by which behaviors are evaluated for their morality—their rightness or wrongness. When applied to human communication, ethics are the moral principles that guide judgments about the good and bad, right and wrong, of communication, not just communication effectiveness or efficiency. From this perspective it is fair to say that values influence what individuals will determine is ethical. Values are measures of importance, whereas ethics represent judgments about right and wrong. This close relationship between importance and right and wrong is thought to be a powerful influence on individual behavior, how individuals evaluate the behavior of others, and overall organizational experiences.

In addition to organizational value systems, goals, policies, procedures, ethical standards, and reward systems, organizations engage in a variety of important communication-based influence processes for creating and changing organizational events. These processes assist individuals in determining who and what are viewed as influential, the way people seek to influence others, and how people respond to influence. Questions about the influence process in organizations focus on how individuals identify with their organizations, how organizations attempt to socialize members, and how power is used.

Most organizations encourage members to identify with the organization. It is likely that when people perceive the goals of an organization as compatible with their individual goals, they are identifying with the organization. The person who identifies is likely to accept the organization's decisional premises or reasoning. Generally speaking, the person who identifies with the organization is more likely to be positively influenced by the organization. Closely associated with identification is the influence process of socialization, or active organizational attempts to help members learn appropriate behaviors, norms, and values. The socialization process attempts to help new members understand how their interests overlap with those of the organization. Socialization efforts provide job or task information, describe how the individual's position fits into the organization, and establish social or interpersonal relationships.

An additional communication dynamic that influences behavior is the use of power. In its most general sense, power has been defined as an attempt to influence another person's behavior to produce desired outcomes. As such, power is a neutral term subject to positive use as well as abuse. The power process occurs through communication and is related to resources, dependencies, and alternatives. Power is embedded in leadership processes; yet both managers and individuals have power resources. The manager has the formal authority established by the chain of command. The manager controls information flow and performance evaluation. Individuals control technical performance, have access to important information, and have vital firsthand information about the progress of work. Both are dependent on each other. The manager directs, but without compliance and performance, no work is accomplished. Power is one of the central issues for leadership and primary to the functioning of organizations as well as to individual experiences.

Suggested Readings

Bahniuk, M. H., Hill, S. E. K., & Darus, H. J. (1996). The relationship of power-gaining communication strategies to career success. *Western Journal of Communication, 60,* 358–378.

Cummings, H. W., Long, L. W., and Lewis, M. L. (1983). *Managing communication in organizations: An introduction.* Dubuque, IA: Gorsuch Scarisbrick.

Flauto, F. J. (1999). Walking the talk: The relationship between leadership and communication competence. *Journal of Leadership Studies, 6,* 86–97.

Gibson, M. K., & Papa, M. J. (2000). The mud, the blood, and the beer guys: Organizational osmosis in blue-collar work groups. *Journal of Applied Communication Research, 28,* 68–88.

Herzberg, F. (1966). *Work and the nature of man.* Cleveland, OH: World.

Maslow, A. (1954). *Motivation and personality.* New York: Harper and Row.

Meyer, J. C. (1995). Tell me a story: Eliciting organizational values from narratives. *Communication Quarterly, 43,* 210–224.

Salancik, G., & Pfeffer, J. (1978). A social information processing approach to job attitudes and task design. *Administrative Science Quarterly, 23,* 224–253.

Schrodt, P. (2002). The relationship between organizational identification and organizational culture: Employee perceptions of culture and identification in a retail sales organization. *Communication Studies, 53,* 189–202.

Scott, E. D. (2002). Organizational moral values. *Business Ethics Quarterly, 12,* 33–55.

Shockley-Zalabak, P. (2002). *Fundamentals of organizational communication: Knowledge, sensitivity, skills, values.* Boston: Allyn and Bacon.

Skinner, B. F. (1953). *Science and human behavior.* New York: Macmillan.

Winiecki, K. L., & Ayres, J. (1999). Communication apprehension and receiver apprehension in the workplace. *Communication Quarterly, 47,* 430–440. ✦

Chapter 22

The First Day at Work

Organizational Socialization and the Dimension Drama

JULIE A. DAVIS

"Yeah, Mom, I'm excited about starting my new job. I'm pretty nervous, too. You know, this is my first real job. Everything else's been waiting tables. I don't really know what to expect. Today's all orientation, so I won't even be in the building I'll work in, but it'll be fun to learn about Dimension.* Everybody who works for the company goes through this training program. They even fly out trainers to other cities when they hire a bunch of new people. Wait, here's the turnoff now. Gotta go, Mom. I'll talk to you tonight." Paige Martin smiled as she turned off her cell phone. "Mothers," she thought. "No matter how old you get, they insist on treating you like a kid. Then again, I'm still pretty close to *being* a kid."

As Paige parked in front of a low-slung brick building, she took a deep breath and thought about how far she'd come. Two months ago she was a senior at State University, about 50 miles away. Between worrying about exams and packing up her apartment, she knew she had to find a job, but she wasn't sure where. Now here she was, about to start her new job at Dimension Telecommunications, a local, long-distance, and wireless telephone provider headquartered in Denver, Colorado, where 20,000 of its 48,000 employees worked, scattered among 24 buildings in a 50-mile area. Paige took a deep breath and walked toward the building.

Once inside, Paige followed signs pointing her to an older woman making ID cards. "Are you here for the orientation?" the woman, whose badge labeled her as Margaret Adams, asked.

"Yes, it's my first day," Paige said, trying not to look as nervous as she felt.

"Step right up here so I can take your mug shot," Margaret said and snapped the picture. "Your badge will be ready at lunch. Breakfast is set up right over there," she added, pointing toward a row of tables. "Enjoy it. It may be the last free meal you get from Dimension. Welcome to the company. You're going to like it."

"That was weird," Paige thought, as she headed for a large spread of pastries and fruit. "I wonder if everyone sends out mixed messages like that," she thought, pouring herself a glass of orange juice. Noticing that everyone else was going inside, Paige walked into the meeting room. "This looks familiar. I thought I was done with classrooms," she thought, eyeing the long rows of tables facing the front of the room, where a TV/VCR, dry erase board, and flip pad stood. Paige slipped into the last open seat, between a woman who looked a few years older than Paige and a man in his mid-30s. At each seat was a sheet of white paper, a marker, a black cloth briefcase with the Dimension logo on the side, and a red and white booklet with "The Dimension Drama" emblazoned across the front. Everyone also received a folder full of papers, brochures, and a pen, all also bearing the Dimension logo.

Before Paige had time to do more than smile hello to her seatmates, an energetic man in his mid-40s walked into the room.

"Good morning, folks," he said. "Let's get this show on the road. I'm Peter Geller and I'll be facilitating your training today. I'm really excited about this program. Eleven years ago, when I first started here at Dimension, we didn't have anything like this. My orientation consisted of, 'This is your desk, the restrooms and vending machines are down the hall, here's Shirley and she'll tell you what to do. Let me know if you have any questions.'"

Paige and the rest of the new hires laughed at his skeptical expression.

"In fact," Peter continued, "I didn't know too much about Dimension until I started facilitating these training sessions two years ago, and I'd been here for nine years before that. Now you get the opportunity to learn about the company from the very beginning. This morning, we're going to talk a little about Dimension's history, mission, goals, and values. This afternoon, after lunch, which Dimension provides for you, we'll talk about benefits and company policies. Before we get started, take the paper in front of you and fold it into a nameplate," he said, demonstrating what he meant for them to do. "Take the marker and put your name on both sides, so both I and the rest of the group can see."

Paige smiled as she wrote on her nameplate. "This is new," she thought. "No one at the restaurants really ever cared about the rest of the group knowing who we were. In fact, my supervisor had to look at my name tag for the first two months I was there. She would never have encouraged us to get to know each other on the first day. She thought we spent too much time talking to each other as it was."

"Tom," Peter asked, pointing at a young man near the door, "would you turn out the lights for us please? Mr. Duncan will begin our meeting this morning."

Once the lights went out, Peter quickly turned on the VCR and a balding man in his late 50s appeared and began to speak.

> I'm Jim Duncan, CEO of Dimension Telecommunications. Let me be the first to welcome you to Dimension Telecommunications. Today's session will introduce you to the elements that provide all of us with our direction—Dimension's mission, goals, and values. Associates are impressed and inspired by them.
>
> You know that it's rare in the history of American business that any company has the opportunities before it that we now have at Dimension. So let's be determined that 10 years from now it will be said that we fully seized this moment in our history by taking full advantage of these opportunities. And let it also be said that it wasn't just the efforts of a few, but rather it was the efforts of all the Dimension associates in building this great company of ours. Our future here at Dimension is most certainly a bright one, and our future is you.

After the lights came on, Peter stood before the group again. "Mr. Duncan is right. We're all inspired and guided by Dimension's mission, goals, and values, but we're also inspired by Dimension's history. This next section will talk a little about Dimension's history, and then start talking about its vision and goals. Tom, please get the lights again."

On the screen, the Dimension logo appeared and a soothing voice began to speak:

> The year was 1903 and the place was Last Chance, Colorado. For more than a decade, the Bell Company was the only game in town and they knew it. Enter D. K. Green, who founded his own telephone company, giving the residents of this tiny midwestern town their first viable alternative for telephone service and the local Bell Company its first taste of real competition. On February 1, 1904, D. K. Green opened his first long-distance circuit—a line connecting Last Chance with nearby Cope, Colorado—50 miles as the crow flies—and serving towns in between. Within a few years, the local Bell Company finally gave up trying to compete with the upstart, but Green's company was only beginning to grow. Today, Dimension continues to live and grow with that same independent spirit demonstrated by D. K. Green in Last Chance, Colorado, almost 100 years ago.
>
> That independent spirit, the ability to defeat the leaders in the industry and then become one of them, influences our vision for Dimension. Our vision is to be a world-class telecommunications company—the standard by which others are measured. Just like D. K. Green's little phone company set the standard customers used to judge Bell, so Dimension wants to be the model customers use to judge our competitors, and just like Ma Bell, our competitors can't compare.

"Wow," Paige thought, scribbling notes furiously on the pad Dimension gave her. "I didn't think anyone could outdo Bell in phone service back then. I didn't even think anyone tried." Then she turned her attention back to the video.

> Dimension works toward this vision by reaching three interlocking goals: exceptional customer satisfaction; inspired, innovative, and empowered employees; and superior financial results.

Peter jumped up and turned off the tape. "All right, everybody. Turn to page six of your workbook," Peter said, holding up the red and white booklet included in the briefcase. "Write down what you think it means to provide exceptional customer satisfaction, and three ways Dimension will be able to improve customer satisfaction. After you've written them down, turn to the other people at your table, introduce yourself, and compare notes. Then see if you can come up with other ways to help customers."

Paige looked down at her workbook and wrinkled her brow. "Exceptional customer satisfaction, hmmm. Phone service is one of those things I don't want to think about. Customers will be satisfied if they never have to think about the phone or the phone company. On the other hand, they won't be satisfied if the product doesn't work or if it's too expensive," she thought. "So simple, reliable, and affordable phone service will make them happy."

After filling out her form, Paige looked up to see the other people at her table waiting for her. The 30-something man stuck out his hand.

"Hi, I'm John Reuter. I've worked for Dimension for the past five years as a contractor, but I was just hired on full time, so I have to go through this training."

The woman on Paige's other side smiled. "I'm Kelly Smith. This is my first job in telecomm, but I've been working for Yikes! Jeans across town for a couple of years. I liked it there, but I heard Dimension was a good place to work and thought it would be more secure than Yikes! So here I am."

Paige smiled nervously. "I'm Paige Martin. I just graduated from State U in May and this is my first job." Looking at John, she asked, "What do you think of Dimension?"

"It's all right. It's not all sweetness and light like they'd have you believe, but it pays the bills. Kelly, what did you say provided great customer satisfaction?"

"Speed, speed, and more speed. People want fast connections, quick responses, and their complaints solved quickly," Kelly replied. "They also want their bills to be simple and right, the first time. Sometimes bills don't look right, but they're so complex no one knows for sure. It takes forever to get through on customer service lines, and then people are rude or can't answer simple questions."

Paige nodded agreement. "That makes sense," she said. "I just want the phone to work and be easy to use. I also don't want to pay an arm and a leg for the service I want."

"Those are good ideas," John commented, "but you're thinking like a residential customer, not a telecomm company. The big money's in wireless and business services. Those customers are interested in new products. Cell phones that act like radios and provide chat rooms, prepaid phone cards to give to their own customers, and multiple lines in one building or on one phone. Kelly, you're right about speed. When something goes down, they want it fixed fast. If the phones don't work, they can't do their business."

"But business customers are only part of the business, John," Paige offered. "I know when I pick up the phone, I just want it to work. I don't want the company calling me or sending me info about expensive products."

"Welcome to the work world, Paige," John laughed. "The focus is on what makes the company money, not what customers like. Leaving them alone doesn't grow the business or get new customers."

"How can Dimension have exceptional customer satisfaction if it doesn't give all its customers what they want?" asked Paige.

Before John or Kelly could answer, Peter called from the front of the room, "OK, everyone, let's talk a little about customer service. What's one way to delight our customers? Bill?"

"Relationships," said a man in his early 40s from the back of the room. "Know what the customer wants before he does. Tell him about new products when they first come out and show him how those products will help him."

"Make sure the different departments know each other, too," chimed in Meg, a woman in her late 20s sitting on the other side of the room. "Customers get upset when they have to keep making the same complaint over and over again. They also want consistent information from different parts of the company."

"Excellent ideas, everyone," Peter said. "If we want our customers to be delighted by Dimension, we have to give them something our competitors can't. Going the extra mile, knowing them, and working extra hours so they'll meet their deadlines. Thinking about the customer's needs before our own will give them exceptional satisfaction. Now, look on page 8 about inspired, innovative, and empowered employees. Do the same thing, define it and then spin and buzz with your table about those ideas and new ideas."

After going through two more spin and buzz sessions and listening to the rest of the new hires, Paige felt even more confused. "This is hard," she thought. "All my experience with phones is talking on them and paying the bills. I don't know how to think like a company. OK, go to great ends to serve the customer, share information so everyone who works at Dimension can make decisions and come up with new ideas to help the customer, and get new products and customers while reducing costs. That sounds good, but how am I supposed to do all of that at once?"

"You have some great ideas about ways to help customers, fellow employees, and Dimension's bottom line," Peter said at the end of the final group discussion. "But just trying to meet each goal isn't enough. In fact, associates who focus on one goal at the expense of the others tend to run into trouble. For instance, what if you had a customer who wanted to surprise his wife by having us rent a helicopter to deliver a prepaid card while they were on a backpacking trip? The customer would be thrilled, whoever authorized this would be empowered, boy would he ever be empowered," Peter laughed, "but we'd take a bath financially. Whoever tried this wouldn't get very far in the company. While this type of service makes for a good story, it doesn't balance our goals, or do Dimension any good."

"Instead, you want to use other ways, more innovative and cost-effective ways, to provide excellent customer satisfaction. One customer wrote a letter about an associate who did just that. Let me read it to you," John said, unfolding a sheet of paper.

> When our contract was up with BB&E, we welcomed bids from all major carriers. This time, the rates were very competitive. Ultimately, the decision came down to a company that had given us good service, BB&E, or Dimension. After a long decision process, we decided to sign with Dimension. This decision was based on how well Dave Short presented himself and your company. Dave found out what we needed and put together a package that gave it to us, plus some services we didn't even know existed. He came across as being honest, trustworthy, hardworking, and fair—and willing to do anything for his customer and his company. It has been a pleasure working with Dimension. I hope this relationship continues.

"See," Peter said, "Dave was able to please the customer, come up with an innovative package, and gain a new customer, balancing all three goals. On that note, let's take a break. There are drinks outside. Take about 20 minutes to stretch your legs and grab a drink. Then we'll talk about Dimension's values before lunch."

As she picked up her purse and walked out of the conference room, Paige saw Kelly and John talking to each other next to the beverage table. "Hi," she said. "What do you think of the training so far?" she asked, picking up a diet cola.

"I couldn't believe that last story," John said. "I know Dave Short, and he killed himself for that contract. He begged his boss to let him add services to the deal that would have clinched it a lot earlier. They wouldn't go for it. Instead, he had to come in on weekends and make long-distance calls from home. That's Dimension for you, spend all of your time and energy but guard their pocketbook with your life. All in the name of balance."

"Don't be melodramatic, John," Kelly said. "All companies are like that. They give you a paycheck and want a lot in return. Frankly, this sounds better than my last job, where salespeople turned in record contracts and management wanted to know why they weren't higher.

At least here customer satisfaction and employee morale matter. Other places are a lot worse."

"Hah!" John exclaimed. "Did you see the date on that letter? Dave finalized that contract six months before the customer bothered to write that letter. Who knows how long it took Customer Service to pass it along to him, if he ever saw it. If he hadn't closed that deal, he'd have heard about it immediately, but when you do something right, it takes forever for anyone to notice.

"You know," John grumbled, turning reflective, "I just hate hypocrites. We're supposed to balance their goals, but all they're interested in is the bottom line. That's the only reason for the other goals—exceptionally satisfied customers buy more and empowered innovative employees sell more and come up with new products for Dimension to sell. There's no balance involved. It's all about money. The sooner you figure that out, the better off you'll be."

"But that's good for us," commented Kelly. "Companies that make money can spend more on benefits and don't have as many layoffs, plus the stock price goes up. The more they make, the more I make. I have student loans to pay off and could use the money."

"Money's nice, but isn't there more to life?" asked Paige. "I mean, I have student loans, too, but I want to help people, like Dave did in the letter. I also want to be a part of something important. Can't we have it all?"

"John, you've scared her. Yes, Paige, you can feel good about your work and still make enough to live well. We just all want more than we have. Besides, some people are just cynical and grumpy in the morning," Kelly said with a sidelong glance at John, who snorted and walked away. "If you go into something with a bad attitude, you're guaranteed to hate it. Don't listen to him. Keep an open mind about work. Whether you love it or hate it, you've got to work. Dimension has a good reputation in this town. Don't worry. You'll be OK," Kelly said and headed off down the hall.

"Great, now what do I do?" Paige thought, watching Kelly's retreat down the hall. "At least waiting tables I could tell immediately if people were happy. If there was a problem, I could generally fix it. People would be surprised how many problems a free dessert will solve. I really like working with people. I like talking to them and getting them what they want. If they aren't happy, they let me know with a lousy tip, but I get to start over with another table just as fast. Not knowing what customers want or if they're happy for months will be depressing.

"Big corporations just may not be right for me," she thought, staring into her soda can as if looking for answers. "I've been here three hours and I've only met two people, and they work in different buildings than I will. We may never see each other again. At the restaurant, we were all able to help each other out, too. This place is just so big . . . I don't know what to think or who to believe. I'm not even sure I think like a businessperson, especially not like someone who's supposed to be Dimension's future. What have I gotten myself into? Will I be happy here or should I start looking again?" Just then, Paige noticed people heading back into the conference room. Putting down her soda can, she followed them in and sat down, waiting for the next phase of the orientation to begin. ✦

*This case has been developed based on real organization(s) and real organizational experiences. Names, facts, and situations have been changed to protect the privacy of individuals and organizations.

Chapter 23

Dr. Jekyll and Pastor Clyde

G. L. Forward

Jason Ford* was casually chatting with friends after church when Pastor Clyde Barnes approached. "Hey, Jason, have you got a few minutes?" he asked.

"Sure, Pastor Barnes. What's up?"

"Well, first call me Pastor Clyde or just Clyde," he said, smiling. "Most people do and I like it that way. I've been thinking about something and wanted to run it by you. Stan Parker, one of our board members, attends the same adult Bible class that you and your wife attend and he told me about your program in organizational communication at the university. I think you can help us," he said earnestly.

For the next several minutes, Pastor Clyde outlined some ideas about conducting a congregational self-study and quizzed Jason about his studies and experience. Jason responded to the pastor's inquiries, asking a few questions of his own but mostly listening, occasionally nodding in agreement. After the conversation had wound down, the pastor took a deep breath and stated with finality, "Jason, I've decided the church needs to do this and I think you're the ideal person to do it! I'll provide you with an office to use, secretarial support, office supplies and postage, and a $1,200 stipend for your time and expertise."

This last piece of news put a smile on Jason's face! At the same time, his mind raced in a dozen different directions, thinking about all he would need to do and the best way to go about doing it. Pastor Clyde broke his reverie by adding, "Jason, I'd like for you to begin as soon as possible, this week if you can. Technically, an arrangement like this needs to be approved by the church board, but they won't meet for another month and I don't want to wait that long. But don't worry. The church needs to do this and you'll get paid. I don't think anyone will buck me on this. Besides, I can always make the board see reason later if anyone dares object!" At that point Jason and Pastor Clyde concluded with a handshake and a promise to meet again within the next couple of days to get things rolling.

A Great Opportunity

Jason and his wife Darla had a lot to talk about in the car on the way home that Sunday. In many ways Jason was an ideal candidate to conduct the sort of project outlined by Pastor Clyde. When the Fords moved to Springdale eight months before, they had planned to visit several area churches before deciding on a new church home. However, they attended North Willow Community Church on their first Sunday in the city and never visited anywhere else. As Jason had explained to his neighbors, "The people were friendly, the services inspirational, and the preaching short! There just wasn't a reason to look anywhere else." In addition, the Fords enjoyed Pastor Clyde's ministry. As they noted, the pastor seemed genuine and caring, the services warm and inviting, and the messages designed to help people.

Jason also found it easy to relate to many members of the congregation. The location of the church made it convenient for several parishioners who were employed at the university, and others, like Jason, were graduate students. Beginning graduate school at 39 meant Jason was a little older than most of these other students. Nonetheless, he had resigned his job and moved to Springdale to work on a graduate degree in organizational communication. He was fascinated by organizational dynamics and knew the study proposed by the pastor would allow him to explore them in detail. And, as luck would have it, he had just completed a course in survey research as a part of his program, so he felt ready to tackle the challenges of this assignment.

Perhaps most important of all, Jason was also an ordained minister in the same Protestant denomination as Pastor Clyde. When he moved to Springdale he had almost 10 years of pastoral experience. Pastor Clyde was aware of Jason's ministry background and educational work at the university and thought the combination of the two would uniquely qualify him for this assignment.

Defining the Assignment

Two days after their initial conversation, Jason and Pastor Clyde met to discuss the congregational survey. Pastor Clyde greeted Jason warmly and got both of them coffee as they started to talk. Although Jason estimated that Pastor Clyde was about 12 years older than he, they seemed to have a lot in common and he was looking forward to working with the pastor on this project. The two engaged in small talk until Pastor Clyde handed Jason a cup of coffee. Then Jason, who was always very task-oriented and anxious to get to work, took control of the conversation: "Well, I think the place to begin is to hear more about why you think a survey is a good idea right now."

The pastor's demeanor seemed to change. "There's just something wrong with the congregation," he blurted out, "and I need to find out what it is!" He went on to explain that attendance, giving, and lay involvement had all declined or stagnated within the last several months. "Maybe we just grew too big too fast, and we're experiencing the inevitable growing pains, but I'm having difficulty finding people willing to serve on the church board. Not only that," he continued, "but there's been significant turnover in paid staff in the last year and some people on the board are starting to grumble. You know there are always some malcontents who like to point fingers and criticize the pastor. The bottom line is, I'm starting my fourth year here and I've got to take control of this situation before it gets out of hand."

As a result of this meeting, Jason agreed to design and administer a comprehensive survey assessing all aspects of the church's programs, policies, personnel, congregational beliefs and values, and demographic characteristics. At the conclusion of this three-month process, Jason was to present his findings and recommendations to the church board in a half-day seminar. Following his presentation to the church board, a one-hour summary session was to be presented to the entire congregation during a special Sunday night meeting to be held a couple of weeks later and open to anyone who cared to attend.

Although Pastor Clyde had told Jason to begin work on the project right away, the pastor waited for official board approval before announcing the study to the congregation. In spite of this, word of the project began to leak out well before the official announcement. It seemed to Jason that everybody had an opinion about the survey. Some seemed excited and energized by the prospect. Stan, a member of the church board, hinted ominously, "It's about time someone asked us what we thought." Irene, a member of Jason's adult Bible class, warned, "You're just stirring things up. You're asking for criticism and so you're going to get it. No good can come of this." An even larger group seemed indifferent, claiming nothing significant would happen because "people just say what they think you want to hear on those things anyway!" Jason either ignored or deflected these comments, stating, "I'm doing this by the book; the results will speak for themselves."

Background Information

Prior to designing the actual survey to be used, Jason investigated the historical background of the church. North Willow Community Church was begun just nine years before. A core group of nearly 100 members had sought and received permission from the bishop to leave the downtown congregation they were attending in order to plant a new church in the fast-growing northwest corner of the city. Over the course of the previous nine years, the congregation had purchased and renovated an abandoned public school building, increased average attendance to nearly 300, hired a senior pastor and two full-time associates, and organized a successful day care program. In addition, the church now operated on an annual budget exceeding $850,000. Nonetheless, what started as an innovative, highly cohesive group of people with a strong organizational culture had now become a much larger, diverse, somewhat transient congregation. At present there seemed to be little feeling of shared history due to an almost constant churning of new families arriving and old ones leaving. Jason knew that churches, like other kinds of organizations, often cycle through predictable stages of advance and decline in response to changes in the environment. He thought, "Maybe this *is* just a case of growing pains!"

Issues With Pastor Clyde

As the project got under way, Jason inserted weekly announcements in the church bulletin and provided updates from the platform each Sunday morning. These announcements stressed the rationale, content, and procedures for the self-study that all congregation members would soon receive in the mail. These announcements were designed to reduce uncertainty about the study, ensure members anonymity and confidentiality, and help increase the survey return rate. "You will not be asked to sign your survey, no other identifying data will be added, and no one but me will ever see the returned surveys," Jason promised the church members in accordance with standard procedures for protecting research subjects. In fact, Jason sometimes wished his research professor were a member of the congregation so that she could see how smoothly and professionally the survey was proceeding.

Every church member 16 years of age or older was sent a survey packet in the mail. Three weeks after the initial mailing, a second packet was mailed to those who had not yet returned a survey. As a result of the weekly reminders and second mailing, 72% of the adult church membership had participated in the study.

As the surveys were received and the data were tabulated, some clear and disturbing patterns began to emerge. Jason's initial euphoria began to fade. A number of relatively minor issues dealing with church policies and procedures that were consistently mentioned (e.g., regular reporting of church income, nominating committee membership and procedures, introduction of persons on the platform for worship functions, and so forth) could be easily addressed and corrected. However, one issue emerged that dwarfed all the others in significance. The picture that emerged, especially from the open-ended questions, was of a pastor with a very caring public persona who was reported, in private interactions, to be manipulative, deceitful, and verbally abusive. In fact, the survey data made it clear that the major impediment to effectiveness in the church was Pastor Clyde's leadership and interpersonal communication style. This was indicated by the following comments taken from the surveys:

> There is widespread dissatisfaction with Pastor Clyde. He seems unaware of his own unhealthy needs and behavior. His outbursts are having a negative effect on morale.

> There is no way to handle honest concerns about the church in a constructive way. If you disagree with the pastor, he is either defensive or responds harshly.

> The pastor needs to be more receptive when people confront him. Many have left our church because they are intimidated by his reactions.

> It is difficult for me to have respect for Pastor Clyde because of the poor way he has treated me and others. I used to serve on the church board, but *never* again!
>
> The pastor needs to be more flexible and less dictatorial!
>
> I work here at the day care center and see how badly the pastor treats the workers.
>
> He's a control freak! I can't continue to attend here as long as Pastor Barnes remains.

Jason was surprised and confused by the comments he was reading. The pastor had seemed a little irritated when Jason refused to discuss the surveys that were coming in, but Jason really hadn't seen the kind of behavior these people were describing. Maybe Pastor Clyde was more distant and less friendly toward him, but he rationalized that everyone was busy and what mattered now was the finished project anyway.

Jason was further surprised when Pastor Clyde asked him to come into his office one morning. The pastor seemed agitated and upset. He abruptly began, "I understand some people are upset about the church board nominating process."

In fact, several people had mentioned that issue in the surveys Jason received. "How could Pastor Clyde know that?" Jason thought. His weekly announcements had guaranteed absolute confidentiality and anonymity to those who provided data, and the surveys were kept in the locked church office he was using for this project. The answer seemed obvious and Jason panicked. Pastors are human like everybody else, but this was inexcusable! He made some feeble excuse to end the meeting and left the pastor's office abruptly.

Although he did not confront the pastor with his suspicions directly, he immediately spoke to the church secretary. "Oh yes, I've seen him in your office on a number of occasions looking through the surveys and other material on your desk."

Jason shot daggers back at the secretary. "Why didn't you tell me this before!"

"I thought you knew," she stuttered. "I assumed you told him it was OK."

Jason turned without speaking and quickly hurried back to his office. He removed all the surveys from the desk and took them home, where they could be kept securely until they were no longer needed. Later Jason would shred them. Jason never confronted Pastor Clyde about this breach of protocol and, in fact, avoided him whenever possible. What had once been an easygoing and friendly collaboration about church matters became a strained and distant relationship.

Finally, Jason was done with the data tabulation and analysis. A devastating portrait of Pastor Clyde emerged, centered on a pastoral leadership style viewed by many congregation members as deceitful, abusive, manipulative, and demoralizing. Jason completed his written report according to the original timetable and made an appointment to share it with the pastor. The meeting was tense and awkward for both Jason and Pastor Clyde. Gone were the handshakes, smiles, easy conversation, and camaraderie they had earlier shared. At one point the discussion focused on this specific question from the survey:

> The pastor's leadership style is helping the church function as it should.

The results of that question were as follows:

Strongly Disagree	Disagree	Neutral	Agree	Strongly Agree
19%	27%	24%	29%	1%

Jason stated that, as a former pastor, he was very concerned that 70% of the respondents were neutral or negative on that issue.

Pastor Clyde replied, "You can't tell the congregation that. When you get to that question, all you can say is that the largest percentage of respondents agree."

Jason was shocked, "I don't think I can do that," he said. "I think we need to share all the responses for each category of a question. What you say may be technically correct, but it's twisting the facts."

Pastor Clyde's normally composed demeanor seemed to transform before Jason's eyes. "Are you calling me a liar?" he shouted. "Look, some people are out to get me and instead of helping me you're letting yourself be used by them."

Shaken, Jason replied, "I'm not letting myself be used by anyone—I was hired to conduct a survey and I'm just reporting the results. I didn't ask for those answers, but it's what I got."

"You can't get out of it that easy," Clyde snarled. "I know some things about you that you might not want to get around!"

Stunned, Jason said he needed to go to class and asked for the dates of the board seminar and congregational meeting.

Pastor Clyde paused to regain emotional control and said, "I've decided to cancel the congregational meeting, but you'll hear from me concerning the board seminar." Jason was then paid the agreed-upon stipend of $1,200 and dismissed.

A Crisis Looms

Two weeks after submitting his 30-page report to Pastor Clyde, Jason received a phone call from Stan, a member of the church board. Stan asked Jason when he would complete and submit his report. "We're kinda anxious to see the results," he added.

Jason told Stan that he had already submitted a written report and that he should speak to the pastor about obtaining a copy for each of the 12 board members. One week after that conversation Jason received another call from Stan, who told him he was looking at a copy of the report but that "it didn't make much sense." He asked to come over to Jason's home and arrived 40 minutes later. Stan then produced a copy of the report that he had received from Pastor Clyde. Stan asked, "Is this what you submitted to the pastor?"

What Jason discovered was a partial report of about 22 pages from which Pastor Clyde had awkwardly excised all comments that directly or indirectly referred to him or his leadership style.

"That's what I thought," Stan said. "He's not going to get away with this!" Stan took back his copy of the report and left.

A couple of days after his meeting with Stan, Jason received a call from the secretary of the church board. He said he wanted to arrange the details of the half-day board seminar at which Jason would deliver his findings and respond to questions from board members. Although the Fords continued to attend North Willow Community Church, Jason and Pastor Clyde had not had a conversation since meeting in the pastor's office several weeks earlier. Once the board meeting was called to order, Pastor Clyde asked if he could read a statement. In that statement Pastor Clyde said the board should never have approved a survey such as this and argued that it was inappropriate to challenge or question the "Shepherd whom God had called" and stated, amid tears, that "I never claimed to be perfect but am doing my best." The board secretary affirmed that no one was there to attack anyone but that "the board still needs to hear and discuss the report. We paid for it and deserve this much." At this point the pastor stood up, looked around the room, and said, "Well, if you want to rip me apart, you can do it without me sitting here." With that said, he left the room.

After hearing the full report, many people on the board confirmed that they thought the survey had uncovered the source of congregational disillusionment and demoralization and brought into focus long-standing interpersonal problems with the pastor. "Look," Carl said, "we've had plenty of hints about this behavior before, but we either ignored them or made excuses, hoping things would get better. Well, things won't get better till we do something about Pastor Clyde!"

Stan immediately agreed, but not everyone did. A minority of the board now attacked Jason. They argued that this method of data collection was inappropriate in the church and constituted a violation of the biblical admonition to approach someone in private if there were concerns that needed to be addressed.

Jason answered, "I did what you hired me to do, and I think much useful information has been uncovered."

He was thanked for his time and excused while the board continued its deliberation.

Aftermath

Jason later learned that the board concluded there was a persistent, long-term pattern of manipulative, disingenuous, and verbally abusive behavior on the part of Pastor Clyde. This behavior characterized numerous interpersonal relationships involving both laypersons and paid staff. The board then debated its options. The board secretary confided that he had contacted the bishop and offered to provide a copy of the report for feedback. The bishop declined, saying, "This is an internal matter and needs to be handled by you. I have full confidence in Pastor Barnes. I wouldn't have recommended him to you four years ago if I didn't."

Another member, Janice, said, "Well, it seems to me that we have two options. We can simply say that Pastor Clyde has lost the confidence of the board and we recommend that he resign, or we can agree that he stay here but only if he enters into counseling to help him explore his communication behavior and find other ways to deal with lay leaders and church staff. We need to decide which of these options is best!"

Betty, who had been silent until now, said, "I find all this to be very upsetting. To be fair to the pastor, I think we need to do something about Jason Ford, too, some kind of censure for starting this whole mess in the first place."

At that suggestion, some board members rolled their eyes and grimaced, but others nodded at Betty in agreement. Animated conversations ensued as small clusters of board members began talking to the persons closest to them. The secretary rapped on the table and asked for attention. "Well," he stated, "there's lots at stake and lots to decide . . . we'd better get at it!" ✦

*This case has been developed based on real organization(s) and real organizational experiences. Names, facts, and situations have been changed to protect the privacy of individuals and organizations.

Chapter 24

When a Good Thing Goes Bad

Anne P. Hubbell

When Karen Morgan* was about to start her senior year in college, her mother died of cystic fibrosis. Karen knew that her mother's death at age 45 was the exception to the rule. More commonly, cystic fibrosis strikes children and ends their lives while they are teenagers or young adults. Despite this, Karen felt cheated at her mother's death. She wouldn't be able to tell her mom about her college experiences or see her beaming face as she walked across the graduation stage. Karen wouldn't have a grandmother for her own children. She was left with an emptiness that she did not know how to fill. When she returned to school, she felt even more alone. With her family it was okay to talk or not to talk about missing her mother. At school, few people understood what she was going through.

"I am so sorry about your mom," seemed to be the common refrain, but it never seemed to touch how deeply Karen hurt. "Sorry" was not enough. She constantly thought to herself, "Someday I am going to do something about this disease." She went on to receive an M.D. and a Ph.D. in molecular biology so she could study cystic fibrosis. She received a prestigious fellowship and then accepted a position at a prestigious medical school. Here Dr. Karen Morgan continued researching and teaching about cystic fibrosis and other genetic disorders. Her entire life was dedicated to the search for a drug that could help others with cystic fibrosis live long, healthy, and productive lives.

Hope in the Form of a Bottle

When Stolltech, a midsized pharmaceutical company, released the drug Cyclofam, Karen was excited and overjoyed. She had been reading about the drug as it went through animal and then human testing and then received FDA (Federal Drug Administration) approval for patients with cystic fibrosis. It was proved that the drug could help cystic fibrosis patients have a better quality of life. Young patients taking the drug were able to gain weight, breathe easier, and sometimes even play like normal children. Hospital visits were decreased as well, and children with the disease lived almost normal lives. What had not been proven yet was whether their lives were extended through the use of the drug, which was Karen's primary interest.

A Chance Meeting

Pharmaceutical companies often ask physicians who understand their product as well as Dr. Morgan understood Cyclofam to make presentations to other physicians and health care professionals. The presentations generally cover disease states and how medications or procedures address those disease states. The physicians who do this are paid honorariums and are considered to be highly reputable and knowledgeable. Dr. Morgan was an especially desirable speaker because of her M.D. and Ph.D. in molecular biology. Although Karen did not prescribe medicines in her role as a researcher, she well understood the biomechanics of the product through her reading and her own research, and she knew how a product like Cyclofam influenced the body on a cellular level.

Charles, one of the sales representatives from Stolltech, asked Karen to be a speaker for a physicians' program sponsored by the company. Karen agreed to speak to the physicians and worked diligently on her presentation.

As she was speaking to the group of 20 physicians at the program, she noticed one extremely well-dressed man sitting at the back of the room. He was attractive, with black hair and dark brown eyes. "Such kind and sad eyes," she thought. "I wonder if he knows someone who died from this disease."

When she finished her presentation, Charles brought the man she had been wondering about up to the front of the room and introduced him to Karen as José. "I was impressed by your presentation," he said with an easy smile, and Karen immediately liked him.

"Thank you. You could say that I have spent most of my adult life thinking about this."

"It shows. Tell me, could we talk more about your research?" He handed her a business card. Charles had neglected to tell Karen that this well-dressed man was José Ambrose, the CEO of Stolltech.

A Partnership Is Formed

José and Karen spent many hours in person, on email, and on the phone discussing her research and his goals for Stolltech. They became friends as well as professional associates.

One day, over a lunchtime talk on the phone, Karen said, "So, I know a lot about Cyclofam. Tell me about Stolltech."

"Stolltech's main products are pharmaceuticals that have demonstrated an ability to extend the life of individuals with cystic fibrosis. We are also working on new products that promise to do the same with other diseases that primarily affect children. Our company has been growing rapidly, which we are really proud of. We have a 1,000 sales representatives and a staff of 500 in the home office. The manufacturing of the company's products occurs in a separate facility employing 1,000 people. I try to get to know as many people there as I can."

"I know about these things—I have read your annual report." She smiled into the phone. "What about the company? What is it about?"

"Oh, well, it was started by Jeremy Carr, in his basement, so to speak. He started the company by making vitamins in his basement and selling them to doctors." He smiled at the comment and continued on with his response. "Stolltech is not the original name; the company used to be called Carr Pharmaceuticals, after Jeremy. When Jeremy died in 1993, the marketing company thought we should sound more like a biotech company. We had a big competition for the best new name and one associate came up with Stolltech—I think he won something like a thousand dollars for the new name. We sure had some funny suggestions, though. That was great."

"How do you manage so many people?" Karen asked. She liked working in smaller research teams. One aspect of the research process that she did not enjoy was managing others.

"I had a good role model. Jeremy Carr worked hard to create a climate focused on trust and openness; I followed his lead. I ask my closest associates to report any issues that come up—whether they be out in the field with the sales representatives, at the factory, or in the home office. Sometimes I call associates personally to help them resolve issues."

Over their continuing conversations, José told Karen about the other ways that he led his company. He had yearly meetings including all of the sales representatives and many of the home office staff members. At the meetings they would break out into discussion groups and talk about how things were going and what more could be done. José and his senior associates would go from group to group and listen and take notes. They then discussed what they heard and often created task groups to follow up on major issues.

José also regularly visited the manufacturing facility and talked with managers and people on the line. In those facilities, associates received quarterly evaluations by their superiors and were asked to express ideas and discuss areas in which they would like more training. They were encouraged to maximize their potential, and even if they wanted to pursue a degree that was unrelated to their position, the company paid for the classes. If they discovered something amiss in the production process, they were rewarded for bringing up the situation to their superiors. One associate was awarded $1,000 for an idea that increased efficiency and maintained quality of production. They were encouraged to be part of the process and to serve as resources to better the products produced.

José also had gone out into the field with sales representatives. He had talked directly with physicians, nurses, pharmacists, and hospital administrators about Stolltech's products and its vision. His sales representatives enjoyed his visits because he put them at ease, and he always bought them a nice lunch. José enjoyed the visits as well, for he got information directly from the health care professionals and could better understand what Stolltech was doing well and what it could improve on. José and his senior associates worked diligently to foster this climate and to encourage associates to believe in the company and its vision. It was one of his major concerns because he felt that if they worked together, they could create even better products and become a bigger company.

José also privately disclosed to Karen that because of its great promise, Stolltech was in a position where one of the larger pharmaceutical companies might want to buy it. Several companies had already expressed interest in a merger. He had to work hard to prevent a merger that would be more of a takeover.

José and Karen began to form a professional friendship that led to Karen being offered a chance to research Cyclofam's mortality profile. The product had been on the market for a couple of years, but whether it increased a person's lifespan was still unknown. Karen wanted to be part of the research. After much negotiation, José and his research department offered her the title of principal investigator of the clinical research on Cyclofam's mortality profile.

Since Stolltech could not afford a large research department with the necessary equipment for this type of research, the company contracted with universities that had staff and equipment necessary to accomplish such tasks. As principal investigator of the new clinical research, Karen was awarded one of the contracts. She worked with Carl Duncan, Ph.D., vice president of research at Stolltech, to develop a protocol for the research and begin recruiting patients. It was decided that she would report significant findings to both Dr. Duncan and José.

Research Gone Wrong

Karen and her other researchers were given the task of investigating the long-term effects of Cyclofam and determining if the drug increased lifespan, as well as quality of life, in cystic fibrosis patients. She and José were originally optimistic because of anecdotal evidence showing that many patients were living into their 40s instead of dying in their 30s or earlier.

After the first year of research, Karen investigated the data. Results were as hoped. The 300 patients on Cyclofam were feeling better than the 275 other patients taking different cystic fibrosis treatments. It was still too early to assess mortality, but all of the patients on Cyclofam were doing well. It was decided that, although over a million dollars had been invested in the research, additional resources should be employed and more careful following of the patients should occur.

When the second-year data were in, Karen was surprised by the results. She checked and rechecked her analyses. She knew that she had to call José right away with the news. When she reached José, she told him, "I hate to tell you this, but the one-year mortality statistics are in and they are not as we had hoped. Patients on Cyclofam had increased mortality rates. They were more likely to die on Cyclofam than on other traditional cystic fibrosis treatments."

"No! This can't be true!" José rarely lost his temper, but he suddenly felt very tense and frustrated. They had invested millions in Karen's research, and it might be the ruin of his company if it did not turn out well. Cyclofam was the product that kept the company running. It was often said that it "kept the lights on" at Stolltech's home office. Without Cyclofam, the company would certainly go under or be bought by a larger company, one that would take the company apart and keep only its products. The people of Stolltech could be fired, downsized, let go. José remembered other pharmaceutical products that he had seen taken off the market because of similar findings. It was a potential disaster. He quickly said, "Karen, please send me everything, OK? Let my staff take a look at what you have! I will get back to you right away."

Getting Others Involved

José called in Carl Duncan. He and his office staff monitored Stolltech-sponsored research projects at universities all over the world. Carl was a tall, intimidating man who always wore suits that showed off his broad shoulders and made him appear tall and severe. Because he did not seem like the type to work out, his office staff often joked that he wore shoulder pads. They swore that he worked 25-hour days because he was always in the office, breathing down their necks. "How are the clinical trials of Dryden going? Why are we not getting the results we want? Get the researcher on the phone!" he would demand of one staff person. To another he might yell, "I don't care how long the FDA says it is going to take for them to review our product, do something, call someone, get them to move faster!" His demands were impossible, but his frustrations with the slowness of the research process necessary to bring a product to market were often taken out on his office staff.

José did not like Dr. Duncan's methods, and they had had many disagreements about his treatment of his staff members. But José needed Duncan; he could not keep Stolltech afloat without Duncan's determination and ability to get pharmaceuticals to market. Now he grudgingly knew that he needed Duncan to give him good news but was afraid that it would not happen.

As Duncan entered José's office, José asked, "Have you been monitoring the progress of Dr. Karen Morgan's mortality research on Cyclofam?"

"Well, yes."

"And?"

"She is incompetent."

"Incompetent? That is not what I expected."

"She is not following the protocol that we initially established with her. We, my staff and I, asked her to select individuals who were close in age, weight, and other physical aspects. She is just choosing anyone she can find with cystic fibrosis. She has been ignoring our protocol agreement."

"I knew this. I thought we decided that it should not matter."

"Well, I have always had my reservations about her and, uh, your relationship with her. I think it has clouded the way you see this. I think that her violation of the protocol is a severe threat to the validity of the study. I don't think her results are viable. We should cut our losses and end our study with her before she does more damage."

After Duncan left, José sat down behind his desk and put his head in his hands. He had a heavy feeling in his chest because perhaps he had let a personal relationship influence his ability to understand the situation and handle it. He called Karen's office and left a message for her that they needed to speak immediately. She never returned his call.

Karen did not return the call because Duncan had left a message right before José. Duncan had rudely informed her that funding was probably going to be withdrawn from the project because she neglected to follow protocol and that, from now on, all her communication with Stolltech should go through him, not José. Deeply hurt by Duncan's message and by José's tone on the answering machine, she resigned herself to the inevitable: She had been wrong about José. Sales of Cyclofam were more important to him than the patients who could be hurt by it. Perhaps he was not the ethical person she thought he was. How could he just withdraw the funding without talking to her first? Why had he not told her this personally? They had developed what she had thought was a friendship over the last couple of years, and she was deeply disappointed. But she knew that her personal feelings were not the most important thing. She had to decide on the right thing to do to help Cyclofam patients. It was possible that the information would eventually get out, but people currently on the product had a right to know her results.

The Media Gets the Story

As José had eventually tired of trying to reach Karen, he turned the matter over to Duncan, asking him to handle the situation amicably. Duncan, of course, could not do so. He abruptly ended funding to the project and involved the legal department of Stolltech. He had them write a letter to Karen citing her lack of attention to protocol and, thus, her incompetent and inconclusive results. Consequently, the company saw no reason to continue funding her research.

Karen, angered and frustrated by the loss of funding, went to the press. She felt strongly that her results could save lives or at least give patients the ability to make an informed choice. They might feel better taking Cyclofam, but they also might live a shorter life. She thought of her mother and how she had lived a very hard life, but at least she was there for many years. Karen would have given anything to have taken away her mother's pain, but she could never have given up the time she had with her mother. People had to know.

She told a major newspaper about her preliminary findings and her belief regarding the company's motivations for the funding cut. She did not want to hurt Stolltech; she only wanted people to be able to make choices with all of the available information. Because Stolltech had recently gone public and their stock was growing in value quickly, this news article was important to all major investors. Stock prices fell drastically. Stolltech was now at risk for a takeover or potential bankruptcy.

Worst Case Scenario

To handle the problem, the director of public relations, Betty Fields, held a press conference and discussed the reasons for the funding cut. She believed that she well articulated the company's stance and their commitment to quality, but when she read the article in a major paper the next day, she was surprised at the coverage. Little of what she had discussed in the conference was included; the most important details were not mentioned in the article at all. Also, when the press had asked her for a comment on the ethics of the company, she had spoken emphatically: Stolltech was a company of high moral and ethical conduct. The article, however, claimed that she had "no comment" to the question. She was shocked and unsure how to proceed.

As this was occurring, the sales representatives were flooding the marketing department with questions regarding what they were to do. They were receiving calls from their customers (that is, physicians, pharmacies, and hospitals) which indicated that the major HMOs were thinking of removing Cyclofam from their formularies. If this happened, the company could not survive.

Betty asked John Goss, the head of the marketing department, to help her figure out how to proceed. John felt strongly that the information that the researcher released to the press should have remained private and wondered about the legality of Dr. Morgan's statements to the press. There were only two years of research, and the originally established protocol had been violated. At this point, John wondered if the company could sue Dr. Morgan for breach of contract or because she did not tell the press about her errors in the research. He argued that whether the research was valid or not was the major issue, and now the public believed in potentially inconclusive results.

Betty disagreed with John. She did not want it to become a legal issue because it could look worse for the company. They were discussing the appropriate actions that could be taken when they received a call from José: They were to come to his office for a meeting at 3 P.M.

At 3 P.M. on the day that the second negative article about Cyclofam came out, José sat in his office with all of his senior associates. Betty and John sat next to each other and looked across the table at the head of the legal department, Kyu Kim. Kyu looked prepared for the meeting with a large stack of papers in front of him. Betty looked at John and wondered if this should make them feel better or not.

José sat up straight in his chair and looked at his senior associates. He felt deep regret for his poor decisions and for turning over the situation to Duncan, who was noticeably absent. José had asked Duncan to go through the protocol violations and create a detailed report. The report was important, but José also used the task as a way of keeping Duncan too busy to attend the meeting. José believed that Duncan's inability to see the situation objectively had made it difficult for him to help make rational decisions.

José was also unable to be completely impartial. He felt a great responsibility for the current situation. Perhaps if he had worked harder to reach Karen himself, if he had thought to continue the research, if he had not panicked, the situation would not have occurred as it did. So many what-ifs. He thought of Jeremy Carr and what Jeremy might say or do. Did Jeremy ever deal with such a problem? He could not remember. José closed his eyes and pictured Jeremy. He then opened his eyes, looked at all of the individuals in the room, and started to speak. "Today we are faced with the most serious crisis that we have ever faced. There are many things that I want to say today, but I also want to hear from you. Let's start." ✦

*This case has been developed based on real organization(s) and real organizational experiences. Names, facts, and situations have been changed to protect the privacy of individuals and organizations.

Chapter 25

Bob's Dilemma

Erika L. Kirby

It was Monday morning, and after hitting the snooze button for the third and last time, 32-year-old Bob Anthony* awoke thinking of the issue that had plagued him for weeks.

"Lee is due in two months. I really should make my request for paternity leave by Friday if I want to stay at home with her once the girls are born. How much leave should I ask for? How should I bring it up? Should I just talk to the boss or should I tell the coworkers on my team as well?"

Until recently, Bob had never considered taking off the full six weeks at partial pay allowed for paternity leave at his workplace, Audits, Inc. In his mind, he was thinking something more like three days to a week. But last month in the obstetrician's office, looking at an ultrasound that showed twin girls, Lee somewhat nervously said to him, "Once they are born, I really think I would be more comfortable if you were home for an extended period, at least until we got situated as a family. I can't imagine nursing and caring for two children at once as a first-time mom!"

Bob rolled over and looked at Lee as she slept, wrapped around a body pillow to support her expanding belly. A few days after the ultrasound and news of the twins, Lee went to her supervisor at Clark Corporation, where she was a consultant. She asked for eight weeks of maternity leave instead of six, and her request was granted without question. But Bob had been putting off asking for his leave from Audits, Inc., where he was an accountant, since that day of the ultrasound.

"How are people going to react? For that matter, how would I react if another guy wanted six weeks off to stay home with newborn babies?" Bob continually wondered. Over the course of the past month, he had been thinking about prior conversations about work and family and seeking some opinions from people he respected about what they would do in his situation.

Assessing the Organizational and Societal Environment

Before he talked to his supervisor or the coworkers on his team about the issue, Bob wanted to find out exactly what his options were. He reviewed the employee handbook and read about the Family Medical Leave Act, a law instituted in 1993 mandating that, as a full-time employee, he be allowed to take up to 12 weeks of unpaid leave in a year. But the provisions at his company were more generous—the handbook actually outlined a paternity leave policy in which he could take up to six weeks *with* partial pay. It did make Bob more comfortable that both federal law and company policy were on his side. But still he wondered, "If it really is acceptable policy to take paternity leave at Audits, why doesn't anyone ever do it?"

In fact, from the limited research Bob had done since trying to decide how much leave to take, he discovered that most men rarely take advantage of the full amount of paternity leave afforded to them—not just at Audits, but at any organization. A recent article in the paper reported that only around 3% of fathers took more than a week off after the birth of a child, so his request was not a typical one. Accordingly, Bob was worried about the reactions he would get about taking six weeks of paternity leave from other people besides his coworkers. In particular, he was worried about his father's reaction. When he had asked him for advice about how much leave to request, Jim Anthony had replied, "I don't know why you are even considering staying home. Your job is to go out and earn money for the family so that Lee can stay home with the twins . . . who knows, maybe you can even convince Lee to stay at home until the girls are in school—home is where she belongs." Bob remembered being taught about men as breadwinners in a gender class in college, and he was surprised at how tempted he was to follow this traditional pattern.

Bob also felt deeply anxious about how his career success would be affected by taking six weeks of paternity leave. His job as an accountant at Audits required him to travel to different locations for the audits. He did this along with a group of colleagues—typically, in a team of five. Since their work was team-based, each person had a discrete part of the audit to cover, so if someone was sick or on leave, it affected the others, who had to increase their workload to make up for the absent person. In the past this had caused resentment. Bob recalled his own reaction when Mike was gone for three days while his son played in the state basketball tournament. "I was angry that I had to do his work, and that was for only a few days. I wondered why his family was more important than getting his work done. Now I am going to ask for six weeks? I just don't see how." Bob reflected how, when he was *not* an expectant father, he often found himself venting with other colleagues about work-family policies, complaining that "other people get benefits that we don't." Bob was now almost ashamed of his previous attitude. "My, how your views can change when the shoe is on the other foot," he thought to himself.

Some of the work-family benefits that Bob remembered complaining about included six weeks of paternity leave, 12 weeks of maternity leave, flexible scheduling, and part-time work. Because of these policies, Audits was touted as an award-winning family-friendly company. But the inner workings of Audits often told a different story. Bob remembered an especially ironic moment when he was reading the quarterly newsletter and saw an article about the importance of "making time for family and making time to play" on the same page as a list of deadlines by which audits must be completed. Now that Bob really thought about it, people he considered serious workers did not take advantage of these policies.

In fact, most of the people who were acknowledged as ideal workers at Audits were certainly not the type of person he expected would ever take advantage of paternity leave—or any other family-friendly policy, for that matter. In fact, many of these people worked more than 12 hours a day and almost had to be forced to take vacation. As word had it, the real "gunners" at Audits often worked weekends, occasionally sent emails at three in the morning, and stayed out at an audit (and thus away from their families) for as long as six weeks. Bob was not sure how convincing an example that set for making time for family.

The emphasis on dedication to the company reminded him of a long-circulating company story. Several times, Bob had heard that a well-respected vice president had told an expectant father (who wanted to make sure he was scheduled close to home around the birth of his child), "Audits, Inc., should not have to be concerned with people's family lives. If we meant for our employees to have children, we would issue them, just like the army." With all these mixed messages, Bob wondered, "What will happen to my career if I ask for six weeks of leave?"

Bob decided to talk to Beth, a 35-year-old married colleague who was one of his closest female friends. He felt safe talking to her because she was not on his auditing team, so she could keep his confidence, and she had taken 12 weeks of maternity leave the previous year, just recently returning on a part-time schedule.

"Beth, I wanted to ask you something. Lee really wants me to stay home for the full six weeks of paternity leave after the twins are born, but I'm not sure how people will react. Based on your experience with maternity leave, what do you think?"

Bob was not encouraged by the long pause Beth took. Then she responded. "Well, Bob, I think you may be in a rough position to get support for taking much paternity leave here at Audits. To be honest, I think my team resented my leave when I was home with Collin. Don't get me wrong, no one talked to me directly and said, 'Gee, I resent the fact that you were on maternity leave,' but I sensed that people felt that way. People don't understand that when I had those weeks off, I needed them. I didn't sit there and play cards or go shopping every day, you know what I mean? I'm afraid that you may face even more of that stigma, Bob, because there is *no* biological reason that you even need leave. You are not the one who is going to be nursing babies or recovering from childbirth, even though I am sure Lee will need and appreciate your help. Right or wrong, parental leave is still seen as very different for women than for men."

Since Beth had worked at Audits three years longer, Bob flat-out asked, "Why don't any fathers ever take the amount of paternity leave that is allowed here?"

Beth got a very serious look on her face and replied, "Through the grapevine I have heard of situations where men have communicated that they wanted to take paternity leave and have not gotten receptive feedback. Either not gotten it approved at all, or certainly not received what they had asked for." She added, "One of my former coworkers, Jake, wanted to take an extended paternity leave, and everybody laughed. They thought it was funny. Jake left for a place with a more family-friendly environment. I hate to be the bearer of bad news, but don't expect anyone to lay out a red carpet for you here."

Assessing Supervisor and Coworker Reactions

Bob appreciated Beth's perspective on how paternity leave was viewed in the organization as a whole. Yet he was most concerned with how his own supervisor and coworkers on his team would react, because those were the people he worked with every day. If there was resentment about his leave, that is where he would feel it. Anticipating their reaction, Bob reflected on conversations about work and family practices and policies he had heard over the years working at Audits.

Bob thought about Steve, his supervisor of five years, and what his response might be to a request for six weeks of paternity leave. Steve was 56 and married, with two adult children. Bob knew that Steve struggled with how to manage a staff that had varied work and family needs. He remembered having a discussion about scheduling travel around employees' differing marital and child-rearing responsibilities. Steve had said, "From my standpoint, it can be a problem. Married with young child. Single guy. Somebody has to travel. Who is it? The hardest thing for me has always been being fair because I can't necessarily be consistent." Steve had mentioned this philosophy several times—being fair if not consistent.

Although Steve had always kept Bob and his team informed of the family-friendly benefits that were available, he had never really encouraged their use. Instead, Steve was always pushing deadlines: "We've got to have this audit done by this date to get started on the next one." There was such an emphasis on time constraints and deadlines at Audits that people rarely took time off unless it was an emergency. Bob remembered his performance appraisal meeting nine months ago, where he was teasing Steve about all the long hours he was putting in. Steve got somewhat serious and replied, "Well, as you move up and get more years of service, you also get more leave as a benefit—but the irony is that you're less likely to be able to actually miss work and take the time to utilize your vacation hours."

Bob cringed as he remembered his comment at the time. "If that is what it takes, I'm ready to make sacrifices and put in all the necessary hours to keep moving up at Audits." Now he thought, "How hypocritical will I look in asking for this leave? What happened to my dedication? How would Steve react?"

Then Bob thought about his fellow accountants. Since they all worked as a team, Bob really felt a sense of peer pressure. If he took these weeks off, he would be putting everyone else in a bad spot. He was apprehensive that asking for this special treatment would require the other auditors to do more, and he wondered, "Why does my taking advantage of the paternity leave I deserve, and am allowed by company policy, have to be to their detriment? Isn't there something wrong with this system?" Bob knew that if his coworkers thought he was not pulling his weight, their consequent behaviors and attitudes could punish him.

Mike, 46, was married with three teenagers, and he would occasionally take time off—but only when important events, such as the state basketball tournament, warranted it. Bob remembered Mike being away from town on the birthdays of his children several times, and Mike always had the same calm reaction: "It's the structure of the job. If you want to move up, you keep quiet about family needs unless it is really important." When people would express resentment that work-family policies were unfair, Mike would always talk about the policies in terms of use versus abuse. He would say, "There is nothing wrong with these policies. The problem is when people try to take advantage of them and use them too much. When people are always gone because their kids are sick or whatever, then there is a problem."

Bob wondered, "Will Mike think I am using or abusing the policy by taking six weeks off?" He wasn't sure.

Judy, a 38-year-old single mother, was another coworker on Bob's team. Judy was outwardly supportive of the work-family programs and policies available at Audits. She always said, "I wish more people would take advantage of them, so this organization would truly practice being family-friendly rather than just having the policies on paper." Of those who denigrated the policies, Judy remarked, "All these people are going to have needs later on; whether they are married or not, whether they have kids or not, they are going to have needs eventually—isn't it nice that these policies exist to help balance those needs?"

Judy occasionally took time off to spend with her son, but since it was not typical to regularly use family-friendly benefits at Audits, even she did not do this very often. As she had commented once to Bob, "I am a single mother supporting a child. If I use the benefits, it might make me seem less dedicated, which could impact how my performance is appraised. I can't afford to lose this job, so in the long run, it probably is better for Josh for me not to take a lot of leave to spend more time with him. How ironic, huh?"

From these conversations, Bob felt that Judy would support his request 100%.

Manuel, a 29-year-old single male accountant, was Bob's closest friend on the team. About a year earlier, when both Mike and Judy were gone on the same day, Manuel had commented to Bob, "It isn't fair that they get more time off because their kids are sick or have special events. Why can't I get that same amount of time off? I think we are discriminated against because we don't have children."

Bob recalled replying, "Yeah, it has worked out very well for them. Unfortunately it has increased the workload for us."

Manuel joked that the two of them should become members of the Childfree Network, an organization he read about that believes many family-friendly policies are discriminatory and should be eliminated to provide equal treatment. Bob sensed that even though they were good friends, Manuel might be vocal about having to take on his work if Bob was granted an extended paternity leave. He could hear Manuel now: "You know, it just doesn't quite seem fair that just because you now have two babies, you get to take an extra 30 days off. It doesn't benefit the rest of us. What am I getting in return for that?" Although he hoped for the best, Bob was quite certain that he would get a negative reaction from Manuel.

The last accountant on his audit team was Jessica, a 24-year-old woman who had recently graduated from college, was engaged, and still had an ideal view of the world. Bob remembered Jessica saying, "What is all the fuss about these work-family policies anyway? If the company has them, you can use them—duh. No one will look at you differently because they are part of company policy." Although her communication indicated that Jessica would probably be supportive, Bob was not so sure how long her idealism would last once she started covering his work.

As Bob got out of bed, he continued to wrestle with his thoughts. "I love Lee and my baby girls with all my heart, but given the environment at Audits, I might be committing career suicide if I do what Lee wants and ask for six weeks of paternity leave. How much leave should I ask for, and when do I ask for it? Should I run it by my team first, since they are the ones affected, or should I start with Steve?"

Bob hoped a hot shower would bring him some clarity—he did not have much time left to decide. ✦

*This case has been developed based on real organization(s) and real organizational experiences. Names, facts, and situations have been changed to protect the privacy of individuals and organizations.

Chapter 26

Working Without Papers

Shawn D. Long

On Sunday, the *Daily News** reported the incident on its front page. It read, in part:

> Shouting "Go home!" at the brown-skinned drivers passing by, about 75 protesters gathered along Main Street in this Jackson County town on Saturday to blame immigrants for the area's high unemployment and crowded schools. The two-hour rally drew worried blue-collar workers, immigration opponents, and admitted white racists alarmed at the influx of Mexicans. Together, they stood near the town's Confederate monument and hoisted signs: "No Illegals. No Unemployment." "It's Our Borders, Stupid!" and "Now Swim Back."

The article acknowledged the existing tension between Latino immigrant workers and native-born Americans in this southern community. The picture above the article showed protesters, anxious and angry about the growing Latino population, carrying signs and yelling at vehicles with Latino drivers and passengers.

The article was especially troublesome to Javier, a Honduran construction supervisor, who was carpooling to work on Monday morning with Bob Jones, another line supervisor at Three Sources Construction, located in a neighboring town.

Javier and Bob

From all accounts, Javier and Bob were good friends. They lived in the same neighborhood, took their kids to the same park, and often carpooled back and forth to work. When Bob was laid off from his manufacturing job at Pales Manufacturing three years earlier, Javier had recommended that Bob apply at Three Sources Construction. There was an opening, and Javier knew Bob would be perfect for the job. Javier had even put in a good word with Jack Hart, the owner of Three Sources Construction. Bob applied and eventually got a job working on the line, with Javier's recommendation. Within a year, Bob was promoted to a line supervisor with Javier. Bob was primarily in charge of supervising the crew of American workers, whereas Javier was responsible for the crew of Latino workers.

The Tension

Although Javier had been pleased that he could help out his friend Bob, Javier was amazed at Bob's quick promotion. His amazement really reflected his disappointment in how Three Sources had treated him and other immigrant workers in regard to promotion and compensation. Javier was the first Latino worker to become a supervisor at Three Sources Construction, and it had taken him eight years to get the position. He had often applied for and asked about becoming a line supervisor, but he was repeatedly told he needed more experience and more time to build trust with the other line workers.

Although Javier had not been the first Latino to apply for a supervisory job, he was the first to land one. Many felt that his promotion was due in large part to the company's need for someone who could speak fluent Spanish, someone who could relate to the 70% of line workers who were Latino and who spoke very little or no English themselves. Nevertheless, Javier, his family, and the other Latino workers were thrilled when he finally got the nod.

The Company

Three Sources Construction, a small construction company in a county neighboring Jackson County, had a great reputation for producing quality work on schedule and below budget. Three Sources often served as a subcontractor for much larger construction companies, companies that appreciated the consistent effort and attention to detail that it provided.

However, among its immigrant workers, Three Sources had a less than favorable reputation. While it was always willing to hire workers without papers, it also consistently discriminated, harassed, and exploited Latino workers who were not legal. This side of Three Sources was hidden from the public view, including the prime contractors, but was well-known among immigrant workers. When Cortez and Roberto were in the process of showing John, a newly hired worker, how to put on a harness, Cortez warned John, "They treat you like a lower class. They take advantage of people who don't speak English."

Roberto piped up, "Maybe, maybe not. What happens is that the people don't speak English, so they get tossed to the side."

Cortez warned John especially about Joe, a Three Sources manager and the foreman on this site.

"Joe treats Latinos worse. There are a lot of things that we don't know, and he gets mad at us. He doesn't get mad at the Americans. Just us. Because we are not from this country."

Monday Morning at Three Sources

That day there was tension in the air at Three Sources. Many of the American workers had read the article in the *Daily News* before they arrived at work. Someone had placed the article on a workbench, in plain view of everyone, including the Latino workers, and several workers were uneasy about it.

Joe, the site foreman, walked toward Bob, his face scowling. "Bob, did you see the front page of the newspaper?"

"I did," Bob responded.

"What did you think about it?"

Bob replied in a rather disinterested tone, "It's a free country. Anybody can say what they want to." Then Bob quickly changed the subject. "Have our new drills arrived yet?"

"Not yet. I'll let you know when they arrive."

"Thanks a lot, Joe. I'll talk to you later." Bob quickly walked away from what could have been a very long and uncomfortable conversation with Joe.

The Latino workers were working steadily, with little conversation among themselves. It was clear that the workers were much more involved in their work than usual. They had been forewarned by Luis, an English-speaking Mexican, who had told them on their way from the worker pickup station in Jackson, "Everybody just work hard and stay to yourself. There are a lot of angry Americans around here, and we just need to stay low for a while."

Luis had worked in transportation for Three Sources for two years. One of his jobs was to pick up workers who did not have transportation at designated sites in the early morning hours. Luis was usually the first Three Sources contact many of the Latino workers had, and he was a valued and respected resource for the immigrant workers. He would often tell the workers what was going on at the site and what Joe's mood was for the day. Because he had been one of the drivers taunted at Saturday's protest, Luis was very tense this particular morning.

On the drive to work, one of the workers asked Luis why the Americans hate them so much. Luis explained, "Saturday's protest is part of a growing backlash against Latinos in the United States and in this state. My daughter is in fifth grade. She told me she learned in school last week that our Latino population has grown by 58% nationally and 394% in this state since 1990. We have 95,076 Latinos living here. Her teacher told her this huge increase in immigrants from Mexico and Central America was because people like us want to get jobs in construction and hotels and restaurants. In landscaping. And in manufacturing and agriculture."

"Pretty smart girl you got there, Luis," Ron replied.

"You better believe it." Luis grinned.

Luis went on to say, "Many employers have rewarded these workers for their strong work ethic. Others, like Three Sources, have taken advantage of this vulnerable workforce. They deny us the basic benefits of work guaranteed by state and federal labor laws. They abuse the basic right of workers to be paid for work they perform."

Luis and the immigrant workers were particularly familiar with these abuses because, over the last couple of weeks, they had not received their pay.

Issues at Three Source

Indeed, a common complaint among the immigrant workers at Three Sources was the company's failure to pay them for work performed. Jack Webster, Three Sources' owner, and Joe, the site foreman, would often ask Javier to tell the workers that the construction company had yet to be paid by the general contractor, so they were unable to pay their employees; they promised to pay them when Three Sources got paid. At the same time, many of the American workers under Bob's supervision never appeared to complain about not being compensated on time.

As Cortez explained to John, "We are illegal. We don't have papers. We came here to work, but the work that we do here does not benefit us much. It benefits Jack more than us workers." Cortez warned John about another problem. "John, I want you to know that those who have papers around here are paid more than the ones who don't have papers. Documented workers earn a little more money."

This kind of conversation was common among the Latino workers. It appeared to be part of their training process.

Conflicted Javier

Javier suspected the American workers were being paid while his Latino workers were not. Occasionally, Javier would ask Bob about this issue.

"Bob, how are your men handling Jack's news about not being paid again this week?"

Bob would always quickly change the subject to something else to avoid Javier's question, so most times Javier would just drop the topic and move on.

Javier's Tension at Work

Because most of the Latino workers could not speak English, Javier was a great resource for Three Sources, the workers, and the owner. Many of the Latino employees looked up to Javier because he treated them with respect and would often hire their family members and friends who needed a job but had no papers. The workers appreciated that Javier would hire immigrants without papers, but some also felt he did not stand up to Jack and Joe about issues affecting the Latino workers. José, a line worker, often said, "Javier is a racist because he thinks the workers should do everything. He wants to show off to the bosses. The Latinos who have papers, especially Javier, treat those who don't have papers very badly. Sometimes they don't even pay you."

José's work partner, Rocky, always mumbled, "Javier treats us worse than the gringos do. For good or bad, we came here to work, we have to work, whatever it is."

Javier felt this characterization was unfair, and he would often speak to Bob about this dilemma.

"It is a no-win situation for me. I work hard to get my people jobs because I know how hard it is to support a family, and then it seems as though they all turn on me at once. Sometimes people, even your own people, are just ungrateful and can be your worst enemies. I'm just trying to do my job."

On the other hand, Javier was genuinely concerned about Three Sources' treatment of workers and the off-colored comments and jokes made about the Latino workers by the Americans in managerial positions, especially Joe. Although Javier was often tempted to say something about the offensive comments, he felt that if he spoke up, he would alienate himself from everyone. Even worse, he would possibly be replaced for not being a team player or one of the boys. He knew how hard he had worked to get where he was. Making waves was not an option!

Monday Afternoon at Three Sources

José and several other men on Javier's crew met with Javier after lunch to discuss their lack of payment over the last couple of weeks.

"Javier, you told us on Friday that we would get our money on Monday. We have worked hard for you and the gringos have been paid. Where is our money?"

"Look, José, I understand your concern, but Jack told me he has not been paid from the general contractor. My hands are tied," Javier replied.

"You are a racist sellout, Javier," José retorted. "You and your gringo buddy Bob make sure his men are paid, while we work for free! You are no better than the Americans who treat us bad."

Javier quickly replied, "José, I am going to walk away now and let you and the boys cool off before you say anything else that will hurt you and your family."

"Javier, we need our money by tomorrow!" yelled José as Javier left.

Javier was angry and upset at José, and more so at Jack for putting him in this position. Javier's mind was racing. "Where was Jack? How come Joe could not provide any answers? Why weren't the Americans complaining as well?"

Construction resumed as usual, but there were obvious tensions in the air. Javier's men were not speaking to him. They only mumbled things when he walked by. The American workers were disturbed by the tension the article had brought to Three Sources and kept to themselves. When Javier walked by the American workers, they would suddenly stop talking and turn their backs to him.

Quitting Time

At 4:45 P.M., it was time for everyone to get off. Javier hated to leave the pay situation the way it was, but he had no more answers to provide his crew. Jack still had not shown up at the site.

"Joe, will Jack be in tomorrow?"

"Your guess is as good as mine, Javier."

"Is there anything that you can do for me?" asked Javier.

Joe's only response was, "Check with Jack!"

The End of the Day

After work, Javier and Bob were on their way home. Javier was outwardly frustrated. The first few minutes of the drive were deafeningly silent. Then Javier broke the silence.

"Where the hell was Jack today?" complained Javier.

"I think he was at the other site today," replied Bob, adding, "Today was sure one hell of a day."

Javier was silent. Glancing at Bob's hand, he saw a copy of the newspaper. This made Javier even angrier.

"Why the hell are you holding on to that piece of shit? I am getting it from all sides—my own people, your crew, and even you!"

Bob quickly cut Javier off. "Look, Javier, I was taking this paper off-site. I was going to throw it away before any of the wise guys at work decided to hang it up somewhere. Why are you busting my chops, man? You need a drink, my friend. My treat! Let's go to Blues Tavern."

The Blues Tavern Revelation

Once inside Blues Tavern, a favorite watering hole of Javier and Bob and other construction workers in the area, Javier quickly apologized.

"Bob, I'm so sorry for blowing up at you. You know that I didn't mean what I said. You and I are friends, and a lot has happened over the last few days. You know our men are pissed at Jack and everyone else about not being paid two weeks in a row. On top of that, Jack is nowhere to be found. José and his buddies are ganging up on me about their money. And then at work all I hear from your crew is mumbling about that damn article. You can cut the tension with a knife, and I feel like I'm going to be the one stabbed with it. I am stuck in the middle. My own people hate me and are losing respect for me, and the gringos, I mean the Americans, in this damn community hate me because I am just trying to support my family like anyone else. I am sick and tired of this."

Javier paused for a minute and then asked, "Bob, how are your men handling not being paid?"

Bob cautiously took a drink of his beer and began to stare deep into his glass. "Javier, I have something to tell you. Please don't be angry at me or my men, but my crew received their pay on time!"

Bob took another drink as silence fell upon both men. Then Bob continued, "Joe told me and my guys not to tell you. He felt as long as you got your money, things would be okay. You know, Javier, Joe and Jack really like you. They are thinking about promoting you to the foreman's position at the other site next summer."

Sitting silently, Javier showed no emotion.

"Javier, I'm sorry, man. Please don't say anything, man. Jack would probably fire me if they found out I told you. I'm not like those rednecks protesting in Jackson." Bob paused briefly. "Do you want another beer?"

Javier shook his head no and said, "I need to get home for dinner."

"Are you okay, Javier?"

"I'm fine. Maria is making her delicious enchilada casserole tonight," Javier said with a slight grin.

Inside Javier

Neither friend mentioned the Blues Tavern conversation in the car. "What else is Maria cooking tonight?" asked Bob.

"I think she may be baking a pie. She was rolling out dough last night. At least that's what I am hoping for."

Javier and Bob both laughed at Javier's dinner prospects as Javier pulled into Bob's driveway to drop him off. "Javier, see if Maria would put a slice of that pie in your lunch for me tomorrow."

"I sure will . . . maybe a little casserole, too?" asked Javier.

"You are the man, Javier. I'll see you in the morning. I'll bring the coffee."

Javier drove off and continued to reflect on his and Bob's conversation. His thoughts about Three Sources were confirmed. He knew he was in a vulnerable position. He loved his job and the opportunity that Three Sources gave him, and he felt an obligation to the company for giving him a chance, regardless of how long the company had taken to promote him. But he also felt a responsibility to the Latino workers and community to expose the blatant exploitation. Javier was struggling with the question "What should I do now?"

Javier knew most of the workers lacked knowledge about their rights as employees and they depended on him to see that they were treated fairly, even though other immigrant workers, like José, mistrusted Javier, considering him "Jack's Latino puppet." They often called Javier a racist to his own people because he didn't complain about them not being paid or their being put in dangerous work assignments. Javier did not want their criticisms to come true.

Javier recognized the serious implications involved in trying to improve the situation for his crew. If he became a whistle-blower, his opportunity to work again in construction and possibly in this area was in jeopardy. If he kept quiet, he would be promoted and eventually be able to make changes at Three Sources from a more powerful position, possibly this new foreman's position.

At Home

Javier pulled into his driveway and walked into the house. Maria greeted her husband with a big smile and a kiss.

"Good evening, honey. The casserole is almost done, and I am getting ready to put your favorite peach pie in the oven."

Javier did not respond.

Noticing Javier's apparent depressed state, Maria turned to him. "What's wrong, honey?"

Javier started to explain . . . ✦

*This case has been developed based on real organization(s) and real organizational experiences. Names, facts, and situations have been changed to protect the privacy of individuals and organizations.

Chapter 27

Corporate Counseling

Steven K. May

Elaine Jenkins* had just left another one-hour counseling session with her therapist, Marta, with a greater sense of well-being, satisfaction, and security. To her surprise, counseling seemed to help her, if only as a way to express some of her work- and family-related frustrations. In particular, counseling helped her cope with her anxieties about her job security as well as frustration with a new management team at her company, GeneSel, a large U.S. pharmaceutical firm. The new management team was the result of a merger between Genetair and Techsel, her original employer. The organizational change had taken its toll, both on employee morale overall and on her own sense of job security specifically. Her original employer, Techsel, producer of technical solutions for drug development and delivery, had been acquired nine months ago in a hostile takeover by Genetair, a British pharmaceutical company. The new CEO, however, dismissed claims that it was an acquisition. Instead, he called it a merger of equals, describing it as an "opportunity for GeneSel to develop integrative solutions that will provide greater economies of scale through reductions in force." In the end, though, Elaine felt that a new CEO, a new management team, and downsizing nearly 25% of Techsel's employees were clear indications that this was an acquisition, not a merger. Her most recent discussion with Marta had clarified how much the downsizing of many of her coworkers and friends at Techsel had affected her.

She was so comforted by her most recent session, though, that she let out an audible sigh of relief as she left Marta's dimly lit yet cozy office, looking around to make sure that nobody had noticed. Elaine never really expected to have such a favorable response to counseling sessions, particularly since it was only her third meeting with Marta. It would certainly have embarrassed her if the two other patients in the waiting room had noticed such a public show of emotion from her. She tried to keep such feelings to herself, if at all possible. Although she didn't recognize either of the patients, she still wondered whether they knew her. Deep down, she questioned whether going to a corporate counselor to discuss her feelings about the downsizing was such a good idea. GeneSel's Employee Assistance Program (EAP) touted the company-sponsored counseling program as an effective means of "integrating the needs of employer and employee to produce happier, more productive workers." Yet, even with the progress she made in the sessions, she still had her doubts.

Counseling Reservations

Thirty years old, college-educated, and very successful as a research associate at GeneSel, Elaine never thought that she would ever see a therapist for any problems. Even when her husband, Alan, suggested that they go to marital counseling because of stress-producing conflicts six months ago, she suggested that it would be a last resort, a sign of failure, to her.

"I just don't see the use of counseling. We should be able to work through our own problems without the help of anyone else."

Although he did not press the issue too far, for fear of increasing her resistance to the idea, Alan still tried to convince her. "But if it helps, why would you not want to try it?"

"Because to me it would mean that we had a bad marriage. That we had failed. That we had made a mistake and couldn't handle things on our own."

"So many people benefit from it, though, and I think that we do need the help. We're both struggling. The downsizing has taken a toll. We're not alone in that."

"Yes, Alan, but I still feel uneasy about it. In my head, I know it might help, but deep down I worry about trusting some stranger with my innermost fears and concerns."

Raised in a small rural town in the Midwest, Elaine had learned over the years that airing one's dirty laundry in public was not a good idea. It wasn't necessarily productive and, at worst, it could lead to gossip that was hard to dispel. At the time, she certainly didn't feel like talking about the downsizing, as Alan had frequently suggested to her. She thought it was more of a work-related topic than a personal one. So when she emerged from Marta's office, she still retained some mixed feelings about going to a counselor. She had a lingering feeling, an intuition, that it wasn't necessarily a smart thing to do, even if Marta's office was off-site, away from GeneSel. Part of Elaine's feeling came from the fact that she had been asked to meet with a counselor by her supervisor, Jackson Sunderlund. Although she trusted and respected Jackson, counseling still had not been her idea. She felt pushed, maybe even coerced, into going. Yet, it seemed to be helping.

Elaine had first considered counseling, somewhat reluctantly, at the suggestion of a coworker, Kathryn. Kathryn had praised her own therapist, to whom she was referred by the EAP at GeneSel. She had also reassured Elaine that it was safe to go to a company-sponsored counselor.

"It's not that bad. You don't have to worry about it. They are required to keep their sessions confidential. Plus, the cost is much more reasonable. Because you'll be going through the company, you'll get a group rate discount."

Elaine, however, was not convinced. "It's not the money that worries me. We can afford it, if necessary. It's more about the fact that it is company-sponsored. It feels a bit like Big Brother to me."

"No, it's not like that at all. They walk you through all the conditions and legal issues involved in going. The EAP counselors follow a strict professional code of ethics, just like any other therapists."

Although Kathryn's comments were somewhat reassuring, Elaine still had questions.

"But it doesn't seem exactly the same to me."

"Why?"

"Well, for one thing, it's unclear to me who the counselor is working for. Who is the client—me or the company?"

Kathryn had not necessarily thought of the EAP in these terms but responded confidently. "Elaine, I think you're being a bit paranoid about this. So many people I know have been helped by our EAP. It seems that the EAP works for both."

"Yes, maybe. But, in the end, as long as GeneSel is paying the bills, the counselor is ultimately working for them, not me."

"Elaine, loosen up. It's just like going to any other therapist. Just cheaper."

Learning About the EAP

Elaine's concerns had not been resolved even as the company began to further publicize its EAP. Maybe she had just never noticed it before, but now that she was considering counseling, the company's EAP seemed to be publicized everywhere. It was touted in the company newsletter, in company-wide emails, in brochures, and even in an occasional poster. To her, it seemed that the EAP was a way for GeneSel to address some of its rising health care costs, particularly since some of its workforce was aging.

As a part of the health care industry, employees at her company were all too aware of issues related to cost and access to health care. It was Elaine's job, in fact, to work on a project team to bring a new AIDS drug from research and development to delivery to the public. It was an expensive proposition and one that would take years—possibly without success. As a research associate on the AIDS drug development team, Elaine was responsible for analyzing and evaluating physicians' willingness to use the drug during development by including their patients in clinical trials sponsored by the company. Her three years as a pharmaceutical sales representative had prepared her well for her role as a research associate, a position she had held for the last four years. So GeneSel's effort to be more proactive about the physical and psychological well-being of employees seemed like a laudable goal to her. It fit with her own mind-set, as well as the company's core values.

In fact, one of the EAP brochures she had picked up in the HR office, out of curiosity, described it as a "win-win" situation for both GeneSel and its employees. According to the brochure, the EAP offered "affordable, accessible, and excellent professional services to employees, with the opportunity to be both more productive and satisfied at GeneSel."

Intrigued yet still skeptical, Elaine had read further. The brochure described the many services available to employees. These included counseling services for stress and anxiety, drug and alcohol problems, relational problems, debt, death and grieving, sexual dysfunction, and depression, among others. They even offered conflict resolution sessions for coworkers who needed on-the-job disputes settled. In addition to these services, the EAP also offered an array of medical services. The brochure explained how EAP professionals would be available to conduct a variety of tests and screenings for high blood pressure, body fat, high cholesterol, breast cancer, and migraines. Apparently, the weight loss workshops presented by the EAP had been particularly popular—and successful—at many other companies around the country. They also offered weekly specials which, according to the brochure, included services like free eye and hearing exams.

While reading the brochure, Elaine remembered how the new CEO had touted the company's new Wellness First program the last few months. He readily admitted that it would help the company reduce some of its health care costs, but he also explained how the program was the first step in a longer process for GeneSel to be included among *Fortune* magazine's 100 Best Places to Work. His plans included an expanded, modernized gym facility, an on-site day care center, and eventually the purchase of land surrounding GeneSel's offices to create a parklike campus with a lake, hiking trails, and bike paths. It all seemed a bit idealistic to Elaine, but it did give her hope about the future of the company. If this was his vision of the future, she liked it.

A 'Suggestion' From Jackson

Several days after reading the EAP brochure, Elaine was called in to her supervisor's office. Jackson Sunderlund, the project manager for her AIDS drug development team, was one of the few employees within Elaine's division that she knew well from her earlier employer, Techsel. He was known as a savvy yet supportive manager who had high aspirations. Only 36, Jackson seemed to be on the fast track to division manager, according to most of Elaine's former coworkers at Techsel. He was direct and demanding, but he also stood by his employees and listened to their input. As a result, he was known for leading highly motivated, cohesive teams.

Elaine trusted Jackson and had begun to view him as a mentor in the months following the acquisition. He had offered to help her find another job, but he had also encouraged her to stay. He told Elaine she had great potential in the company, but that it would take some time for former Techsel employees to be noticed and rewarded with the transition to a new management team. Jackson was a veteran of several mergers and acquisitions. As a result, he expected that the next few months would be difficult but that, eventually, things would get better.

The meeting began simply enough, as Jackson explained that he viewed the future direction of the company as very encouraging.

"Things look very good right now. We're on track with several new drugs that will go to market in the next two years, with FDA approval, and the stock has rebounded."

"That's very reassuring, Jackson. I'm glad to hear that."

"What we really need to talk about now, though, is your performance in the last few months."

Elaine had not expected the meeting to take this turn. Her performance appraisal was not scheduled for another three months. Jackson was always very meticulous about describing the process and preparing her for the appraisal meeting. This was not his typical manner. It was too sudden.

"So, why now? Can't this wait until our regularly scheduled appraisal meeting?"

"Well, Elaine, things are changing rapidly right now. I've been asked to do immediate evaluations of all members of my teams and submit a summary report of our expected progress for the upcoming quarter."

Elaine had been around long enough to know this wasn't good news. Jackson's more reserved, serious tone didn't help, either.

"The management team is interested in an across-the-board assessment of all personnel, myself included. Nobody is exempt."

"So, what does this mean?"

Jackson explained with some very unexpected news, that GeneSel's recent progress had been noticed by a number of larger pharmaceutical companies looking to expand their market shares. Elaine knew that the industry was increasingly competitive and was prone to consolidations, but she thought she had survived the worst when Genetair had acquired Techsel. Another acquisition? That seemed too disruptive. The even more disturbing news, though, came toward the end of their meeting, as Jackson explained how Elaine should proceed during the period of uncertainty about the merger. She listened intently.

"Elaine, you've done excellent work for me. There is no doubt about that. You have consistently met your specs and standards. Your past sales work with physicians gives you a great rapport with them that you have developed even further since you've been with us. However, since the acquisition, things have begun to slide a bit."

"I don't disagree that I have been stressed about the transition. I lost a lot of good friends. Isn't that natural, though, to have some downtime, when your work dips a bit? I hope that you can trust that things will improve, based on your experience with me."

"I can, but my superiors can't necessarily."

"What's that supposed to mean, Jackson?"

"It means that, right now, there is much greater scrutiny of everyone's performance. What's more, the management team is concerned about any employees who may struggle with possible changes or, worse, resist them."

"But you know that's not me."

"I do, Elaine, but they don't."

"So, what do I do?"

Choosing his words slowly and carefully, Jackson suggested that Elaine meet with one of GeneSel's EAP counselors. He told her that, according to the new management team, Elaine had been identified as a "troubled worker." Jackson told her not to be alarmed by the label, that it merely meant she was having some difficulty with the transition that was affecting her performance. Elaine admitted to herself that this was true. But she was reluctant to see a counselor.

"I don't see what going to a counselor will have to do with my work performance. It's true that I feel hurt and betrayed by the downsizing, but that's my personal business."

"Well, not exactly. It's my responsibility to ensure the positive performance of my teams and, if I feel that personal problems are affecting performance, it is my obligation to the company to consider counseling as an alternative."

"Jackson, you're serious?"

"I am."

"Is this you speaking or the new company?"

"Both."

"So, are you saying that I am required to go to the company's EAP counselor?"

"Elaine, I am saying that as your supervisor—and your friend—I strongly suggest that you make an appointment as soon as possible."

As she left the room, shaken and stunned, Jackson told her, "Be sure to let me know when you've made the appointment and I'll make a note of it."

In the next week, Elaine's work suffered even more. It was hard to focus on the work at hand, knowing that rumors of another merger—

and another downsizing–might be near. Worse, she felt like her personal connection with Jackson was gone. Their interactions during the next week were brief and awkward. Although she was not fully against the idea of counseling anymore, she wanted to go on her own terms, on her own time.

Elaine thought it might be time to do some additional digging about EAPs. By looking at several websites–some sponsored by the EAP profession and some sponsored by unions–she learned some interesting things. First, she learned that apparently EAP professionals took their code of ethics very seriously. For example, most websites spoke specifically about the need for patient confidentiality. On the other hand, she also found several legal cases in which employee information from counseling sessions had been used to fire or reassign employees. It was relatively rare and it was done in more extreme situations. But it did seem to happen. She even learned that some companies were beginning to fine employees who did not meet certain health standards. The EAP profession reasoned that this was appropriate, since the employees who incur greater health care costs should shoulder a greater portion of that financial burden.

Elaine became even more ambivalent about EAP counseling and so she made a quick call to one of her neighbors, who was a lawyer. He reminded her that the U.S. Constitution does not, in fact, guarantee an employee's privacy rights from intrusion by one's employer. Those rights are usually dependent on state statutes and he wasn't sure about their state, North Carolina. However, he was aware of several high-profile cases in which email messages and website use by employees had been subpoenaed. The standard was based on whether the employees' communication or Web use was in the business interest of the company–or if it occurred with or on company facilities.

Counseling Progress

Finally, after a week of soul-searching and uneasiness on her job, Elaine decided to schedule an appointment with one of GeneSel's EAP counselors, Marta Melendez. She called Jackson, as requested, and he thanked her, as if she had done him a favor. Given her ambivalence about going to Marta in the first place, Elaine was somewhat surprised by how comfortable she felt with her, even from their first meeting. It was a straightforward, easy meeting. Marta acknowledged that she understood Elaine's hesitation to meet with her. She also reassured Elaine that she was there to help her talk about whatever concerned her, whether work- or family-related. Marta also explained that their sessions were voluntary and that all conversations would be kept confidential, although she needed to tape-record the sessions to best assist her.

At the end of the first weekly meeting, Marta informed Elaine that she would need to stop by the HR department and complete a few items. The first was a legal disclosure statement. It stated that if the counselor were to notice problems that might put the company at risk, they could be notified. HR explained to Elaine that this was common practice, particularly since many companies were increasingly concerned about employee violence. It was a means to protect themselves and other employees. At the HR department, they also asked Elaine to take a couple of personality tests, the Myers-Briggs® and the MMPI, the Minnesota Multiphasic Personality Inventory.® Elaine knew this was now a common practice for new employees of Gene-Sel, but she had never been required to take one at Techsel. The request seemed harmless enough, though, and she was even a bit curious about her Myers-Briggs type, since some of her coworkers seemed to refer to the types in work-related conversations.

The second session was also fairly easy. Marta just asked her a series of basic questions about her background and, eventually, about her feelings at work. These were deemed background questions to provide Marta with a frame of reference for their work together. Slowly, but still somewhat reluctantly, Elaine was coming around. Marta seemed to be on her side and she felt comfortable talking to her. The nicest part was that, unlike her husband, Alan, Marta did not seem to evaluate her in any way. Elaine was free to say what she pleased, to confess any anxieties and insecurities, without fear that Marta would judge her.

By the third session, Elaine was beginning to feel like she was gaining new insights about herself. For the first time since the acquisition and subsequent downsizing, she was able to talk freely and openly about how it had affected her. She had been holding in so much anger, hurt, and frustration about how it had been handled. Elaine became aware of how very alone and betrayed she felt at work, and she began to realize how much it was affecting her marriage, too. It was a very emotional session, with Elaine breaking down in tears several times during the hour.

She left Marta's office that day feeling drained but with a greater sense of comfort. The counseling session was definitely cathartic. She wondered how the rest would go.

Her only reservation was related to Marta's last-minute reminder that she would be providing Jackson with an update on her progress on a monthly basis. She had forgotten that Jackson had mentioned this fact, if only briefly, in their initial meeting. Because of the initial shock of that meeting with Jackson, she couldn't remember exactly what he had said to her.

Aside from that minor concern, though, the next four sessions with Marta went quite well. Elaine was able to be more assertive about some of her frustrations with the new company, its management team, and some of its policies. She even felt like the sessions gave her some insights into how her work was affecting her marriage. That felt like real progress.

Organizational Redundancy

On the morning of her eighth counseling session with Marta, Jackson called Elaine into his office once more. It was only 9 A.M., still early by Jackson's standards. He rarely met with anyone until after he had his coffee and checked his overnight voice mail messages, so his request to meet with her first thing in the morning seemed unusual. In fact, it was. As she entered his all-too-familiar office, she immediately noticed a striking difference. Standing behind Jackson was an unfamiliar man, whom Jackson did not introduce. The man's stiff stance gave him an eerily ominous appearance.

"Elaine, sit down."

"What's up. What's going on? Who is this?"

"I'll explain in a minute. But first, I have to give you some bad news. I am very, very sorry to tell you that you have been let go. We are, in fact, being bought out and we need to streamline our operations. An assessment team has determined that your job is redundant."

"Redundant?"

"Yes, that is the word they used."

"This is absurd."

"Elaine, I know that it may feel that way, but it is true. You have no idea how difficult this is for me. Maybe the hardest thing I've ever done."

"Well, how do you think I feel?"

"Later, maybe we can talk about this further, but right now I have to ask you to leave with this man now. This is Jermaine. He will escort you to the outplacement office that the company has set up to process your transition."

"Process my transition?"

Jackson looked away and averted his eyes as Jermaine gently offered to help Elaine out of her seat and out the door. Before she left, though, Elaine turned and glanced at Jackson one more time. He stared blankly out his office window and it dawned on Elaine how old, how ragged, how tired he looked.

Transitioning Out

Jermaine slowly led Elaine out of Jackson's office, down the elevator, and through the glass doors that were dwarfed by the building's atrium. He led her across the lawn and into the company's small, antiquated gym. Once inside, the scope of the situation at GeneSel came into clearer focus. There in the gym were at least 10 cubicles that had been set up on the basketball floor. She could see inside them just enough to realize that they were nearly all full, with pairs of people. Jermaine led her to the nearest cubicle, asked her to sit, and provided a fuller explanation.

"My name is Jermaine and I will be working with you this morning on your transition. I understand that this is a stressful time for you, but I have some important items to discuss with you and some documents for you to sign."

Elaine met with Jermaine only for about 15 or 20 minutes, but it seemed so much longer, like she was in a slow-motion replay. Much of the conversation was a blur. Jermaine told her that the company would provide a severance package, and would offer her outplacement services to find another job, if she wished. In order to receive the package, he told her to sign a couple of documents. He also asked her to confirm her signature on a noncompete agreement that she had first signed as a new employee at Techsel. It seemed so long ago now. She told him that it was, in fact, her signature.

Jermaine said, "Elaine, you know this means that you cannot accept a job with a competitor in the industry within a 500-mile radius for the next two years?"

Elaine nodded her head.

"And I also need to inform you that, after this morning, it is unlawful for you to enter the GeneSel grounds or building again. You can have an hour to pack up your office. I'd discourage you from talking to any of your coworkers. It's usually easier that way for everyone."

Suddenly, she now understood why her coworkers at Techsel had left so abruptly without much conversation or, in some cases, even good-byes.

In their short meeting, Jermaine gave only a few details about the downsizing and, at the time, she didn't even feel like asking. She just wanted to get out of there as fast as possible, call Alan, and meet him at home. She strode back to GeneSel's main building, took the stairs instead of the elevator, and entered her small office packed with books, binders, and personal keepsakes. She sat down for a moment, took a deep breath, gathered herself a bit, and glanced at her calendar. It read: "3 P.M.—Marta two-month anniversary of counseling."

A Lingering Question

At that moment, it struck her. She vaguely remembered a brief segment of her conversation with Jermaine. In the midst of some of the legalistic chatter about noncompete clauses and placement services he had said, "I understand you've expressed some serious reservations about the management team." Where would he get that information? She had disclosed those concerns to only a couple of people. With a bolt of energy, she quickly rose from her chair, left her office, and began her way down the hallway. Where should she go first, she thought to herself. To Marta? Jackson? The HR office? ✦

*This case has been developed based on real organization(s) and real organizational experiences. Names, facts, and situations have been changed to protect the privacy of individuals and organizations.

Chapter 28

Managing Multiple Roles

Caryn E. Medved and Julie Apker

My coworkers told me I was crazy to request an alternative work schedule at the same time my employer, Mount Adams Hospital of Cleveland,* announced a merger with crosstown rival St. Mary's Hospital. The merger was promoted to employees as a marriage of equals—a joining of forces that naturally played upon the strengths of both health care facilities. As manager of internal communications for Mount Adams Hospital, I was well aware of the organization's growing economic woes and its need to solve its financial problems in order to remain competitive in the cutthroat health care marketplace.

Many Mount Adams employees had their doubts. They wondered how the consolidation would affect their job security, supervisory relationships, job tasks, and work autonomy. Officials from both organizations assured workers that the transition to the new "Consolidated Care Hospital" would be seamless and smooth. In fact, I was the one who wrote the new CEO's speech promising employees that their work lives would not be disrupted and urging them to conduct business as usual. Back then, I believed what I wrote. Today, I say to myself, "Marcus Hernandez, things have certainly changed in the past few months. What will the future bring?"

While issues related to the merger were beginning to be sorted out, a lot was also happening in my personal life that prompted me to request a change in my work schedule. I had been divorced from my wife for about three months, and although the visitation agreement for our 8-year-old twin daughters, Kate and Maggie, seemed okay initially, I quickly realized that seeing them every other weekend was not much time together. So with the approval of Tameka Anderson, the director of organizational development and my immediate supervisor, I changed my traditional 9 A.M.–5 P.M. work hours to 7 A.M.–3 P.M. on Mondays and Wednesdays. Sure, I had to skip lunch on those days, but my new schedule also allowed me to pick up my girls after school and spend time with them two afternoons a week. I could also squeeze in my responsibilities as vice president of the local Public Relations Society of American (PRSA) chapter and as chair of the hospital's United Way campaign. It seemed like the perfect solution to managing my hectic life.

Now, four months later, I don't question my decision to spend more time with my daughters, but I do wonder about my commitment to Consolidated Care Hospital. It's almost 10 A.M. and I have already been at work for three hours. I have drunk more cups of coffee than I care to remember and I'm still tired. In a few minutes, I have a follow-up meeting with Tameka to review how my new schedule is working and discuss future plans for internal communications in the newly merged organization. What I haven't told her is that there is one additional item for the meeting's agenda: my doubts about remaining here as an employee.

While waiting to meet with Tameka, I reflect on the events of the past four months, wondering how things could change so much in such a short time. How did I get from being employee of the month to dreading going to work each day? I still love many aspects of my job, but why do I feel so emotionally exhausted? When did I start to resent coworkers with less-demanding jobs or no children? Why do I often feel that I haven't accomplished anything at work, even though I work on weekends and longer hours on Tuesdays, Thursdays, and Fridays? How can I recapture my old enthusiasm for work? Or do I even want to? At least I can pinpoint when my quality of work life began to diminish—it happened shortly after my first meeting with Tameka to propose changing my work schedule and, at the same time, learn about my new job duties at Consolidated Care.

A New, More Challenging Role

Four months ago, on the day before my initial meeting with Tameka, Mount Adams CEO Helen Wilder had just announced to employees that the proposed merger with St. Mary's Hospital was a *go.* Members of the organizational development staff had quickly assembled to discuss implications and changes in internal communication resulting from the merger. Tameka led the staff meeting with her usual efficient and no-nonsense style. At age 35, Tameka had assumed leadership of the department after serving in a similar position at a major health insurance company. She knew the marketplace and was well connected with its key players. I'll be the first to admit I wasn't thrilled that someone from the *enemy* (insurance people) was joining our organization, but I will also be the first to say that Tameka is an outstanding boss. She's a straight talker, not the kind of person to hold back her opinions. In our relationship, I have always known where I stand with her and that my work is supported 100%.

Tameka concluded the meeting by briefly addressing the new roles to be assumed by various members of the department. I was surprised to hear my name mentioned and see my coworkers' heads whip around the small, crowded conference room to watch my reaction to Tameka's final comment.

"I will be visiting with each one of you this week to talk about your new roles. Marcus, I'd like you to codirect the merger transition team from the standpoint of internal communications. You'll work with Lorie Lockart, the public relations director from St. Mary's. We can iron out the details of your new assignment later, but I know that you will direct the dissemination of all merger-related information to both hospitals via their respective intranets. You will also oversee plans to integrate the two intranets as we finalize the merger. Are you up for the challenge?"

"Sure, ummm . . . okay," I responded. I tried to appear confident, but inside my stomach churned with uncertainty. Would I be able to balance these new job duties along with my existing work responsibilities? I was still determined to spend more time with my kids, even though my job appeared to be changing.

The next day I met with Tameka to learn about my new work responsibilities and pitch my idea for a new work schedule. I thought about the various internal communication challenges that lay ahead for the transition team as I walked down the hallway toward her office for our appointment. Cautiously knocking on her door, I also wondered how receptive she would be to my proposal to work a more family-friendly schedule during this time of transition.

"Please come in and have a seat, Marcus," said Tameka. "You seemed a little hesitant yesterday when I asked you to codirect the transition team. What's on your mind? Be honest. We've always had a good working relationship, and I am confident that you will do a great job codirecting the transition team."

I took a deep breath and said, "Tameka, I'm so glad you feel comfortable putting me in that position. I'm very excited about it! Of course, I have many questions about how this role will be defined. First, though, there is one issue that I'd like to talk to you about.

"As you know, it has been an adjustment for me to be a part-time father now that Sophie and I are divorced. Tameka, I miss seeing my daughters. I need to find a way to be with them more during the week. So I guess, as we move through this transition, I'd like to talk to you about ways that I can manage my schedule so I can spend some time with them without jeopardizing my work commitments. I have an idea to discuss with you, but maybe this isn't the time."

As always, Tameka got right to the point. She responded, "Marcus, you know we have a lot to talk about with the folks at St. Mary's, and I'm going to need you 110% for the next few months. The quality of your work in the past makes me believe that you are the best staff member to codirect the transition team. I wouldn't assign this job to anybody else in the department. What are you proposing?"

"Can we do some sort of an alternative work schedule? I've heard that Jan in accounts payable is doing something like this. She works four 10-hour days and takes Fridays off," I said. "In my case, I'd like to leave work at 3 P.M. on Mondays and Wednesdays so I can pick up my daughters from school. I would start work at 7 A.M. on those days and work through my lunch hour. I am happy to work longer on Tuesdays, Thursdays, and Fridays and come in on weekends when Kate and Maggie aren't visiting me."

"So you would still work at least 40 hours per week and be flexible to put in extra time when needed?" asked Tameka. "I'm counting on you not only to develop and maintain our new intranet site, but also to assess employee communication needs about the merger. We need to raise worker awareness of the benefits of the merger and reduce their fears about downsizing, job restructuring, and pay cuts. It will also give us an opportunity to get a pulse on overall employee quality of work life."

I answered quickly. "I am committed to making this schedule work and not reducing my productivity. I think that my plans will allow me to balance my job and family responsibilities more successfully. We may even be sending a positive message to other employees who are wondering how this merger will affect their quality of work life."

"I trust your ability to make this work, Marcus, so I will agree to these arrangements on a trial basis," said Tameka. "Let's try it out for four months and we will meet again to evaluate your performance. You can start the new hours next week, but make sure to contact Lorie Lockart, your partner at St. Mary's, about your new schedule."

The Road to Burnout

I was pleased that my meeting with Tameka had gone so smoothly. It was great to know that I was a valued employee. As I walked back to my desk, I thought, "It looks like having it all—successful career, being an involved father, United Way campaign chairperson, and PRSA officer—is within reach!" I was feeling so good that I decided to email Lorie Lockart and get the ball rolling on the transition team.

To: Lorie Lockart
From: Marcus Hernandez
cc: Tameka Anderson
Subject: Transition Team

Lorie: Tameka Anderson asked me to contact you to coordinate our codirector responsibilities for the Consolidated Care Hospital transition team. Tameka said that you would supervise information dissemination about the merger via company publications and all external communications with the public. For now, I am assigned to manage communications to employees via our respective organizational intranets. Eventually, I will also direct the creation and ongoing development of our joint intranet site. Tameka has also requested that we survey employees about the merger and quality of work life issues as we begin our communication efforts.

Before I propose a meeting, I need to mention that beginning next Monday, my hours will be 7 A.M. to 3 P.M. on Mondays and Wednesdays and 9 A.M. to 5 P.M. on Tuesdays, Thursdays, and Fridays. Tameka and I have agreed to implement this schedule on a four-month trial basis. While these changes will not affect my work responsibilities, I wanted to make you aware of them for future reference as we schedule our joint activities.

Would you be able to meet next Wednesday at 9 A.M. to begin discussions about the transition team and our assessment of employees' quality of work life? I can meet you at St. Mary's if that is most convenient for you. Please email me as soon as possible. I look forward to meeting with you to discuss our plans.

Thank you. Marcus

To: Marcus Hernandez
From: Lorie Lockart
cc: Tameka Anderson
Subject: Transition Team

Marcus: A meeting next week at 9 A.M. in my office works for me. I spoke with Tameka last week about the division of labor that you discussed in your email. I think the duties are clearly assigned, but we will need to work closely together to make sure that our internal and external organizational messages are consistent.

Tameka reinforced the importance of conducting a survey immediately to assess employees' perceptions and attitudes about their work lives, particularly in regard to the merger. St. Mary's employees completed a quality of work life (QWL) survey about five years ago that we can modify and update by adding items about the merger. In addition, I know our human resources staff is interested in learning more about employees' stress and burnout as well as how workers balance their job and family responsibilities. The HR director just mentioned to me the need to create schedules for employees (as in your case) that are more flexible for them to meet personal and professional obligations. Particularly with the shortage of nurses, we need a competitive edge for recruiting RNs.

Your new hours don't pose a problem for me, and I don't see any complications with them regarding the transition team. I am a part-time graduate student at City University, and my night courses this term require that I leave work at 4:30 P.M. on Tuesdays and Thursdays. Still, there are many hours that we can both meet face-to-face, and emails and telephone calls can help us communicate.

I'll see you next week. Lorie

Lorie and I met as planned to talk about the size, scope, and structure of the transition team. Our personalities clicked immediately, and soon we were discussing the team's first major responsibility—developing, distributing, and analyzing the QWL survey.

"This first project is really critical to the credibility of the transition team," I said. "It seems to me that we should divide up the assignments as equally as possible and enlist some help from our support staff."

"I couldn't agree more," Lorie replied. "I'm happy to be the contact person for the human resources departments at Mount Adams and St. Mary's. I have a good relationship with the St. Mary's HR unit already, and this project will help me establish a similar one with the Mount Adams HR staff. I know that they will want a lot of input in refining existing survey items and developing new questions that assess employees' opinions about stress, burnout, and work and family balance."

"That's fine with me. For my part, I will write survey items that specifically address workers' perceptions of their quality of work life as it relates to the merger and pilot test those items with employees. What do you think of each of us individually coordinating the distribution and collection of the surveys at our respective hospitals?"

"It makes good sense to me," said Lorie. "We know the key players in both of our organizations and it will be easier to manage the survey distribution system as a result. Soon we are going to be busier than before the merger, with our new transition tasks, regular job duties, and respective work schedules. We need to take every opportunity we have to streamline survey operations."

I left that first meeting with Lorie believing that I could handle the increased workload successfully, and at first I was able to easily manage my new transition team duties with my existing work responsibilities. It helped that Lorie and I had similar collaborative communication styles and we were able to work interdependently on our assigned tasks. Despite our multiple work and family obligations, telephone calls and emails allowed us to update each other on our progress, troubleshoot problems, and plan the next steps of the QWL survey process. Over time, our roles evolved and we both took on survey-related duties that we hadn't anticipated earlier. For example, Lorie began to be the main contact person to answer questions about the survey from other departments and coordinate the transition team's creation. I supervised personnel assisting with the survey and planned for survey data analysis. Even with these additional tasks, I felt that I was handling my work and family roles fairly well. I also enjoyed spending more time with Kate and Maggie as a result of my new work schedule. Sure, I had to work longer hours and come in on weekends, but now I was able to watch their after-school soccer games and help them with their homework. Admittedly, I hadn't spent much time on my PRSA responsibilities in the last few months and our company donations to the annual United Way campaign were down somewhat from the amount we contributed last year, but overall I felt that I was doing well.

Job Pressure Escalates

However, about six weeks into the QWL survey project, things at work heated up significantly. Countless technical problems arose as we integrated the two hospitals' intranet sites. It also became my job to put out the daily fires that occurred because of personality clashes between internal communications' staff members in both organizations. In addition, fears about job security in the merged hospital led frontline employees working at the patient bedside to leave in droves for jobs with other health care facilities. Thus, our department scrambled to develop messages to attract new employees to fill vacant openings and encourage current workers to remain. Morale kept dropping as new crises emerged. About this same time, I began to suffer from anxiety attacks not unlike the ones I experienced during stressful times in graduate school.

Just two months after the merger was announced, I felt that I was always behind in my work and hadn't accomplished anything. My new job duties forced me to come in early and work late most Tuesdays, Thursdays, and Fridays. I also worked every weekend that Kate and Maggie stayed with their mom. Even on the weekends the kids visited me, I had work assignments to complete after they went to bed. I stopped going to the gym and routinely canceled or avoided social events. I was angry with my coworkers, who had less work to do and fewer family obligations. One day, as I was walking down the hall, I overhead Emily and Jack, two colleagues whom I considered to be close friends, discussing my recent meltdown at our staff meeting, when I had discovered that the launch date for the Consolidated Care Hospital intranet needed to be delayed again.

"I couldn't believe Marcus' behavior yesterday at the meeting," remarked Emily in hushed tones. "All that yelling and finger-pointing at people who had nothing to do with our technical problems. All of us–including Marcus–knew that the launch date would have to be postponed. I was surprised at his lack of professionalism. What's wrong with him lately?"

"That incident was just the tip of the iceberg for me," said Jack. "I'm sick and tired of being snapped at by him when I walk into his office to ask a simple question or remind him to do something that is supposed to be *his* job. Marcus used to have an open-door policy, but now his door is shut most of the time. He doesn't even treat me like a colleague anymore, much less a friend. He told me the other day to stop whining about the merger like all of his other employees! I'm ready to start looking for another job."

I stormed into their conversation and announced, "Well, I wouldn't mind looking for another job myself because I'm sick and tired of you two complaining all of the time! You try having my job!"

Mad and embarrassed by my outburst, I turned around and quickly left. I went to the cafeteria, got a cup of coffee, and tried to calm down. Managing others used to be one of my greatest strengths, but now, after hearing Emily and Jack's comments, I realized I wasn't even getting *that* part of my job right. I shouldn't have yelled at them. I knew that I had to get back to being my old self somehow. I hoped that could happen once the QWL project was completed, but I also feared that my workload would only increase as the merger moved forward.

The QWL project was a bright spot in my job even though it increased my workload substantially. Three months after our first planning meeting, Lorie and I arranged to visit face-to-face to proofread the survey one last time and review its distribution and collection procedures. We had promised Tameka the survey would be mailed no later than the following week, even though I was scheduled to be at an out-of-town conference during this time period. Tameka was anxious to get its results and plan the next stage of internal communications. The survey findings were critical to what merger information would be communicated to employees and how this information would be disseminated, along with what training interventions would be designed to facilitate the transition.

A Work-Family Role Conflict Arises

Lorie and I deliberately set the meeting to finalize the survey for Friday at 3 P.M. Neither of us needed to leave work early for family or school obligations that afternoon. We planned to work until the job was done. We were both looking forward to finishing up the survey and getting on with our other job duties. Then, just after lunch, my former wife unexpectedly called on her cell phone from the Chicago airport.

"Marcus, this is Sophie. I have a huge favor to ask you. I missed my flight and now I'm stranded at the airport in Chicago. I won't be able to pick up Kate and Maggie. The next flight I can get won't get me home until late tonight. Could you meet the girls at school and bring them to your place until I get home?"

"Sophie, I have an important meeting this afternoon that I scheduled weeks ago. Can't you try another airline?"

"I've already tried that and all of the flights are booked solid. Why can't you reschedule your meeting? You always tell me that your daughters are the most important parts of your life."

"Being a father to Kate and Maggie is the most important thing in my life! But I can't reschedule the meeting because I'll be in San Diego next week for the PRSA annual conference. You know that. Can't you find someone else? How about your mother?"

"Mom is out of town with her boyfriend. I've called several other people, but no one can help me on such short notice. Marcus, it's up to you."

"Okay, Sophie, okay. I'll do it. I'll be at the girls' school at 3:30 P.M., but this is not the best time for you to have missed your flight. Why can't you ever be on time?"

After hanging up with Sophie, I dialed Lorie's office telephone number and left the following voice mail:

> Lorie, this is Marcus. I have to cancel our meeting about the QWL survey because Sophie had an emergency and can't pick up Kate and Maggie from school. I know we had been planning on finishing things up for the survey, but there is no one else to drive the girls home and stay with them until Sophie returns late tonight. I fly out in the morning, but I hate to leave you with the final details. Let me know what I can do via email from San Diego. I'm so sorry for the inconvenience.

When Lorie checked her voice mail, she was irritated that I had canceled our meeting on such short notice and left her with the responsibility of finalizing the survey. "Surely," Lorie thought, "Marcus could have made arrangements for another person to get his children from school. Or he could have brought them to the meeting. Now I have to deal with the last-minute details of the survey in order to meet Tameka's deadline."

As Lorie tackled fine-tuning the survey on her own, I brought my daughters home from school, made them dinner, and packed for my trip until Sophie arrived. I tried calling Lorie at home after doing some last-minute errands late that night, but she didn't answer the phone. I finally fell into bed at midnight. As I was drifting off to sleep, I promised myself I'd call Lorie first thing on Monday to check in on the survey. To be honest, I was so tired from rushing between my work and home responsibilities that I didn't even want to go to this conference anymore. I just wanted to sleep for a week with no interruptions. No coworkers. No kids. No ex-wife. Nobody.

Thankfully, Lorie and I were able to iron out the survey details over the phone while I was at the conference. Lorie gained the necessary approval from administrators, and her assistant made the final corrections to the survey. Despite the extra help, Lorie still was forced to skip class the week that I was away to ensure that the survey was completed and distributed by Tameka's target date. I felt so guilty that Lorie had to take on the extra stress that when I returned from my trip, I plunged directly into the QWL project. Even though my flight arrived at 9 P.M., I went directly to the office from the airport to begin analyzing the survey data.

About a week after my return from the conference, I felt completely burned out and used up by my job. My resentment toward my coworkers increased and I refused to socialize with most of them. My daily interactions with others became even more defensive than in the past. I knew things were at a crisis point when I called in sick one Monday simply because I couldn't face going in to the office. Suddenly, changing jobs and even switching careers were attractive alternatives. I had to talk to Tameka about my future at the hospital, but I didn't know what to say or do.

Strategizing Internal Communications

All these thoughts were going through my mind when Lorie and I sat down with Tameka the next month to review a few key findings from the quality of work life survey. The results were particularly interesting to me because it appeared that, as in my own experience, other employees were also struggling with stress due to work and family role conflict.

"The survey yielded a number of interesting findings that will help us develop communication strategies to enhance employees' quality of work life and ease the merger's transition period," Lorie said to Tameka. "I will highlight a few key results, and Marcus will outline our recommendations for internal communication strategies."

Lorie continued, "First, employees appear to understand why the merger was needed, but not necessarily if and how their jobs have

Consolidated Care Quality of Work Life Survey
Executive Summary

Consolidated Care employees were recently surveyed to better understand their attitudes and opinions on issues related to the recent organizational merger, job stress and burnout, and work/family balance. This summary reflects responses from all full-time personnel.

Perceptions of the Organizational Merger

The merger was necessary to maintain our financial stability.

Response	%
Strongly Agree	55%
Agree	5%
Neutral	10%
Disagree	25%
Strongly Disagree	5%

Since the merger, I clearly understand any changes in my job duties.

Response	%
Strongly Agree	10%
Agree	5%
Neutral	20%
Disagree	35%
Strongly Disagree	30%

Job Stress and Burnout

I often feel emotionally exhausted at the end of the workday.

Response	%
Strongly Agree	65%
Agree	20%
Neutral	5%
Disagree	5%
Strongly Disagree	5%

I often feel overwhelmed by the amount of work I need to accomplish each day.

Response	%
Strongly Agree	45%
Agree	35%
Neutral	10%
Disagree	5%
Strongly Disagree	5%

Work and Family Management

My supervisor is supportive when family emergencies arise.

Response	%
Strongly Agree	20%
Agree	45%
Neutral	15%
Disagree	10%
Strongly Disagree	10%

The stress from my job often negatively spills over into my personal life.

Response	%
Strongly Agree	45%
Agree	30%
Neutral	15%
Disagree	5%
Strongly Disagree	5%

been changed by the merger. This finding suggests that workers are experiencing uncertainty about their roles during this time of change. Second, the majority of employees reported experiencing job stress and burnout, particularly in the areas of work overload and emotional exhaustion. Finally, although employees believed that supervisors supported balancing work and family issues, the negative spillover from work-related stressors into workers' personal lives was high. Marcus?"

"Huh, what?" I asked. Rats! I had been caught daydreaming. "Sorry, Lorie and I had to work late last night finalizing our report for you, Tameka. I'm a little tired. Anyway, based on these findings, we propose several strategies to increase and enhance employee communication about the merger and managing stress and burnout."

I handed Tameka our recommendations.

Consolidated Care Quality of Work Life Survey
Employee Assessment Recommendations

1. Design a managerial training program on counseling employees about the merger's effects on their job responsibilities. Invite managers to bring along a key employee from their department to these sessions.
2. Include ongoing sections in the employee newsletter and on the Intranet that discuss merger-related issues. Topics would include job security, role restructuring, and answering general questions about the merger. The newsletter would also encourage employees to seek out their supervisors to discuss the effects of the merger.
3. Design a special component of the intranet that provides employees with information about job burnout—particularly as it relates to work and family stressors—as well as resources to help employees cope with these issues (e.g., related websites, practical tips and strategies, informal brown bag lunches to share information, etc.).
4. Create and disseminate an internal memo to supervisors that summarizes information about the hospital's work and family policies and strategies. This document would provide managers with organizational resources to which they could refer employees who need counseling, social support, job restructuring, etc.
5. Develop a task force made up of employees at all organizational levels to investigate and address QWL issues.

Tameka reviewed our recommendations and asked a few probing questions. At the end of her queries, she smiled and remarked, "I am really pleased with your work. Let's move forward with these suggestions. I've got to get to another meeting, so I'm going to let you two figure out how to get this done. Thanks for your hard work. Keep me updated on your progress."

Just as she was leaving the conference room, Tameka turned to me and added, "Marcus, we need to schedule that follow-up meeting to discuss how your schedule's been working out lately and a few other things. Call my office this week and set up an appointment." With that, she left us to figure out the details.

Lorie and I just sat at the small conference table for a minute, not talking, exhausted.

Then Lorie said wearily to me, "I'm glad she liked all of the recommendations, but now we need to actually do them!"

Although we laughed and relaxed for a minute, I couldn't stop the feeling of dread as I anticipated more long hours and weekends at work. Summer was coming up soon, and my girls would be out of school. How would I balance my workload and parenting responsibilities now? My stomach was in knots and I could feel a migraine coming on.

"I'm beginning to think we're crazy!" I told Lorie.

"Come on. Come on. Look at the bright side," Lorie replied encouragingly. "Tameka supported our ideas and we have complete autonomy to get our recommendations implemented. We just need to divide and conquer like before."

I still had my doubts, but after another hour of discussion, Lorie and I developed and delegated our assignments. The training program was assigned to one of the training specialists in the human resources department. Lorie agreed to work on recommendations two and four, and I took on implementing the intranet recommendation and facilitating the quality of work life committee. However, despite my close relationship with Lorie, I didn't tell her how uncertain I was about my future at the hospital. Would I let her down by leaving?

Later that day, I set up a meeting with Tameka for Friday at 10 A.M. to review my work schedule. I knew that I was at the end of my rope and it was time to make a choice to stay or leave. I just was so confused about what the right decision would be.

A Difficult Decision

The next week was busy, and Friday came fast. I spent much of my time designing the job stress and burnout section of the intranet. I asked a number of employees to write weekly columns about how they managed work and family roles to post on the site. I also added hyperlinks to a number of useful websites.

Suddenly, I stopped reflecting on the troubles and triumphs of the last four months and looked at the clock. Now we were back to where we started this story! It was 9:55 A.M. and I needed to get to my meeting with Tameka. I remembered my optimism of just a few months ago about balancing the two most important things in my life—my kids and my career. I still loved many aspects of my job: the autonomy, creativity, work relationships like the ones with Lorie and Tameka. But now, I also felt like a burned-out mess who couldn't do anything right. I had already written my resignation letter to give to Tameka during our meeting if necessary. As I knocked on Tameka's door and heard her say, "Come on in, Marcus," I checked inside my jacket pocket to make sure the letter was still there. It still was. ✦

*This case has been developed based on real organization(s) and real organizational experiences. Names, facts, and situations have been changed to protect the privacy of individuals and organizations.

Section 6

Diversity in Organizational Communication

Briefing Paper

Diversity in Organizational Communication

Diversity is commonly linked to race and ethnicity, but diversity can also occur in other dimensions, such as gender, age, geographic locale, sexual orientation, religion, political orientation, organizational tenure, and profession. Working in an organization will put you in contact with, and require you to interact with, people who are different from you. Diversity has potential benefits as well as challenges. Diverse organizations and work teams can be more creative, flexible, and better at problem solving than homogeneous organizations. However, diverse organizations may also experience greater conflict and less cohesiveness because individuals from diverse groups have different styles of communicating. These differences can create difficulties in creating shared meaning. Differences in styles can exacerbate problems, and they work to the advantage of members who have power and to the disadvantage of members of groups who do not have power.

Organizations are seldom gender neutral. The concepts of masculine and feminine values that exist in organizations do not emerge from men's and women's biological orientations. Rather they have been historically, socially, and economically constructed in patriarchy, a system that for centuries has privileged men and marginalized women. Patriarchy and its assignment of gendered values are reproduced and perpetuated in organizations. As a result, organizational practices routinely privilege masculine meanings, judgments, and actions over feminine. Women remain marginalized, as is manifest in lower pay, lower positions, and less power. This combination of masculine values as dominant and the discounting of feminine values may well establish an environment that normalizes discrimination and sexual harassment.

A feminist approach to organizational communication would suggest that many organizational cultures reflect masculine values and norms that are not inclusive of women. Because organizations have been historically designed by and for men, they include language and behaviors that are comfortable for men but not for women. Moreover, masculine cultures often privilege men's experiences and interests while devaluing those of women. Muted group theory and feminist standpoint theory are two frameworks that may help guide your analysis of diversity issues in organizations. Muted group theory suggests that social hierarchies privilege certain groups over others. Within organizations, the dominant group's interest becomes reflected in the communication structures and practices that guide work. This process essentially mutes some groups because marginalized voices and needs go largely unnoticed. Standpoint theory suggests that we consider organizational life from the lived experience of marginalized group members. People who come from nondominant groups often see new organizations in their positions as outsiders and may have insights into the workings of the organization that are not obvious to those who come from dominant groups. There are multiple perspectives (or standpoints) from which to observe any organization or interaction, not simply the dominant perspective and a single minority perspective.

Burnout may occur when an employee experiences role conflict, role ambiguity, and work overload, and these effects can be enhanced if diversity issues are not well managed at work. Symptoms of burnout include (a) emotional exhaustion—a condition in which an employee feels unable to go on because of fatigue or frustration; (b) decreased personal accomplishment—a condition in which an employee sees himself or herself as a failure; or (c) depersonalization—a condition in which an employee expects the worst from others, even actively disliking or mistrusting them. When individuals experience burnout, their communication is often altered and is often characterized by the use of derogatory language, emotional callousness and cynicism toward others, and a tendency to evaluate oneself negatively.

Today's organizations are in a state of flux due to ongoing information, technology, and economic changes. As a result, some of the traditional organizational practices, such as encouraging long employee tenure, have changed. Some employers prefer a new employment contract that rewards flexible workers who have a short-term mentality over a traditional contract system based on hierarchical position, tenure, and loyalty. These organizations and environmental changes contribute to workplace stress and abuse of power.

Potential abuses are particularly problematic when an employee's job requires emotion labor, or when the organization mandates commodification and control of employee emotional display. When employees are paid to churn out a smile, extend a stoic voice tone, or portray a polite demeanor, they are no longer engaging in simple emotion management but rather are entering the realm of emotion labor, something that can be processed, standardized, and subject to hierarchical control. Maintaining an organizationally prescribed mask can be difficult because, in many emotion-labor–laden jobs, the control of employees is multifaceted and unobtrusive and therefore difficult to resist. In some organizations, this control is unobtrusive or concertive, meaning that organizational values are so inculcated in employees that they make decisions in line with organizational priorities even when they believe that they are acting in their own interest.

Central to all of these issues is power—who has what type of power and how that power is communicated. More important, is power being abused to oppress others? Generally power is characterized by (a) reward power—power that leads people to act in order to be rewarded, (b) coercive power—power that is based on the threat of punishment for lack of cooperation or noncompliance, (c) referent power—power of a person who is likable or charismatic; people act because they admire and want to be like him or her, (d) expert power—power that a person with great knowledge or expertise has, and (e) legitimate power—power a person has based on his or her official position in the hierarchy. Power can be overt or covert. That which is covert is beneath the surface, harder to recognize, and, for that reason, dangerous in its veiled presence.

Organizations need to address diversity on a structural level in terms of policies and procedures. Simultaneously, they also need to provide assistance for organizational members developing interpersonal skills that will help them interact with people from a variety of backgrounds and develop constructive workplace relationships. By increasing awareness of differing standpoints and communication styles, organizations can foster a positive and productive climate that will result in greater productivity and employee satisfaction.

Suggested Readings

Allen, B. J. (1998). Black womanhood and feminist standpoints. *Management Communication Quarterly, 11,* 575–586.

Clair, R. P. (1993). The use of framing devices to sequester organizational narratives: Hegemony and harassment. *Communication Monographs, 60,* 133–136.

Dougherty, D. S. (1999). Dialogue through standpoint: Understanding women's and men's standpoints of sexual harassment. *Management Communication Quarterly, 12,* 436–468.

Fineman, S. (Ed.). (2000). *Emotion in organizations* (2nd ed.). London: Sage.

French, R., & Raven, B. (1968). The bases of social power. In D. Cartwright & A. Zander (Eds.), *Group dynamics* (pp. 601–623). New York: Harper and Row.

Johannesen, R. L. (2001). Communication ethics: Centrality, trends, and controversies. In W. B. Gudykunst (Ed.), *Communication yearbook* 24 (pp. 201–235). Thousand Oaks, CA: Sage.

Keyton, J., & Rhodes, S. C. (1999). Organizational sexual harassment: Translating research into application. *Journal of Applied Communication Research, 27,* 158–173.

Orbe, M. P. (1998). An outsider within perspective to organizational communication: Explicating the communicative practices of co-cultural group members. *Management Communication Quarterly, 12,* 230–279.

Ray, E. B., & Miller, K. I. (1991). The influence of communication structure and social support on job stress and burnout. *Management Communication Quarterly, 4,* 240–268.

Townsely, N. C., and Geist, P. (2000). The discursive enactment of hegemony: Sexual harassment and academic organizing. *Western Journal of Communication, 64,* 190–217.

Tracy, S. J. (2000). Becoming a character for commerce: Emotion labor, self subordination and discursive construction of identity in a total institution. *Management Communication Quarterly, 14,* 90–128. ✦

Chapter 29

Where Does It Hurt?

Cynthia A. Irizarry

"She said I was incompetent and if I couldn't schedule patients correctly you would fire me!"

"She said *what*?" Dr. Jason Mortensen* asked incredulously.

Sabrina Ramos, the office manager, stood shaking in Dr. Mortensen's office. "Dr. Swenson yelled at me in front of the entire office staff this morning! She said that I was scheduling too many patients for her to see. She asked me a couple of weeks ago to not schedule patients past four o'clock on the weekdays. I tried my best to accommodate her, but I can't turn patients away! The other doctors never seem to mind. You don't mind! Are you going to fire me?"

Dr. Jason Mortensen intently regarded the woman who had been his office manager for the past 15 years. "Of course I'm not going to fire you, Sabrina. I'll speak with Dr. Swenson about this."

As she turned to leave, she put in her final words. "You know, I thought it would be great to work with a female doctor. Now, I don't know what to think."

My thoughts exactly, thought Jason. Ever since Beth Swenson had her baby it's been one conflict after another. At this rate, she'll never become a partner, even if she was the first and only female physician in his practice.

Dr. Mortensen's Perspective

Jason Mortensen was the senior partner of Advanced Women's Health Care Associates, a thriving practice that specialized in obstetrics and gynecological care. The practice was located in a town just outside of Charlotte, North Carolina, one of the fastest growing cities in the nation. Jason had seen the population of his town grow from 5,000 to 50,000 in the past decade, as it slowly became a suburb of Charlotte. As a result, the practice began thriving with the attendant increase of women in the area requiring obstetrical and gynecological care. Jason often described his practice as one of the premier OB/GYN groups in the Piedmont area. Business was so good that they were set to open a separate clinic that would offer routine gynecological care. Advanced Women's Health Care Associates could then concentrate solely on surgery and obstetrics.

The influx of new patients also increased the hiring of new personnel. To date, the practice employed four doctors and was looking to hire a fifth. As senior partner and founder, Jason Mortensen was responsible for all final decisions made in the practice. The next senior partner was Dr. Dwight Solomon, who had been with the practice for 25 years. The most recent partner was Dr. Richard Worthy, who had joined seven years ago. The latest hire and potential partner was Dr. Beth Swenson, who started working at the practice one year ago.

It Seemed Like a Good Idea

Jason was reluctant to hire a woman. The issue had nothing to do with competency. He thought that women physicians were just as skilled as their male colleagues. However, Jason had always felt that women didn't make for good partners in a profitable practice. If a woman physician wanted to have a family, she would request more time off and other changes to her work schedule. Jason also figured once he bent the rules for one physician, he would have to bend the rules for all the physicians in the practice.

Yet, Jason also realized that many patients these days prefer to have a woman as a physician. Moreover, he didn't want their competitors to be the first to hire a woman. To Jason, it was simply a matter of good business sense to hire a highly competent woman physician. As he thought back, he remembered that Beth had seemed an excellent choice. She was fresh out of medical residency, and she came highly recommended. Her mentors at the medical school praised her work ethic and her ability to relate to patients. She consistently scored in the top 10% of her national board exams. She also was a winner of the Golden Stethoscope, for excellence in intern training. She wasn't perfect, of course. She still needed more surgical experience. But that was common for most new physicians straight out of residency programs. Jason was confident that she would learn from his guidance and instruction.

Beth also seemed committed to working in this town. Her father-in-law had founded one of the most established and lucrative dental practices in the community. Her mother-in-law owned a public relations agency. Moreover, Beth's husband would soon be joining the pediatric clinic down the street when he finished his medical residency. Because of her family connections, Beth would bring in good business, Jason surmised.

But Jason's worst fears were realized when Beth volunteered in her interview that she looked forward to having children and raising a family. Beth assured them that pregnancy wouldn't pose a problem with her work schedule. Besides, wouldn't a female physician who was also a mother understand obstetrical patients better?

Hiring Beth was one of the toughest decisions the partners ever made concerning the practice. While Jason would make the final decision about any hire, Richard and Dwight's opinions were still instrumental in the hiring process. Both Richard and Dwight seemed to concur that Beth was the best candidate they had interviewed. If they didn't hire her now, she would most certainly join one of their competitors. Yet, it was Richard's comment that ultimately swayed Jason's opinion about hiring Beth.

"After considering all of our criteria for a new hire, we would want a skilled surgeon and physician who is also a woman who does not want to get married and have children and is also willing to relocate to a suburb in the South," Richard stated.

"Gentlemen, I think we're going to be waiting a long time to find that person—even if she would be the ideal candidate. Beth is the best person we have interviewed. Besides, she is committed to living in town because of her family situation. If we don't make her a good offer and soon, she's going to join one of our competitors, guaranteed. If she joins us, we put a noncompete clause in her contract that prohibits her from joining a rival practice in the region for at least two years. I think she will be more motivated than most to conform to our partnership requirements."

Jason agreed with Richard's logic. Besides, it wasn't like they had a large pool of female candidates to choose from, Jason thought. With these issues in mind, Jason offered an annually renewable contract to Beth, which she accepted. She would start with the practice in three months. This time would allow her to finish the last few weeks of her residency and settle in her new community. Jason and the partners anxiously awaited Beth's start date. It would help the practice schedule to have another physician on board. Jason also actively promoted his new hire by placing advertisements in local newspapers announcing Beth's position at the practice. He even had one of the local papers run a biographical article introducing Beth to the community.

Although Jason and the partners knew that Beth would to want have children one day, they were completely caught off guard when she announced to them that she was pregnant two weeks after starting at the practice.

Jason was prepared to expect the worst. He thought that Beth would approach him soon to request a lighter work schedule. But contrary to his expectation, Beth seemed to work extraordinarily hard. In fact, Beth was tremendous, Jason thought.

Each physician in the practice was responsible for meeting patient appointments, making hospital rounds, assisting partners in surgery, and updating patient charts during the weekdays from 7:00 A.M. to 6:00 P.M. Each doctor was also scheduled to be on 24-hour call for labor and delivery at least twice a week. The practice work schedule was very tight. If a physician's on-call duties in labor and delivery fell on a weekend, that physician received no time off during the week. In order to receive a day off during the week, the physician would have to make a request weeks in advance to Sabrina, who was responsible for managing the physicians' work schedules.

Jason was pleased that Beth seemed to effortlessly adapt to her new work environment. She volunteered to see extra patients during the week. She often stayed as late as 10:00 P.M. to complete patient charts. She also volunteered to fill in on the call schedule for partners needing vacation or leave time. Jason recalled a conversation he had with Richard Worthy in the hospital cafeteria six weeks after Beth joined the practice.

As they sat down for a late dinner in a quiet corner of the room, Jason inquired, "So, Richard, what do you think of our new hire?"

"Beth? At the rate she's going, she'll make partner in a shorter time than I did," Richard laughed as he dove into his salad. "Makes me want to spend less time with my 3-iron."

"Yeah, I was a little concerned about hiring her," Jason confided. "But she seems like a very dedicated doctor. The office staff tell me she's also great with patients."

"Speaking of new hires, have you thought much about our fifth hire?" Richard hesitated a little before he added, "I was thinking since we started diversifying the practice we might want to consider hiring a minority physician."

"Whoa. Slow down a little, partner." Jason chuckled, nearly spilling his coffee. "I'm just getting comfortable with our first diversity experiment. Besides, Beth's working as hard as two doctors. Do we really need a fifth since we've hired her?"

"Yeah, but . . ." Richard started.

"Don't worry," Jason cut in. "I will handle it when the time comes. Speaking of 3-irons, the office is closed for the holiday. Want to hit the links?"

"Sounds like a plan," Richard said, relieved to change the subject. "I'll give Dwight a call to see if he wants to join us."

"Speaking of golf," Jason said, "I ran into Donald Mack at the country club last week. You should've seen his face when I told him we just hired a woman! You could see the envy in his face. His practice has been trying to snag a woman physician for the past six months."

Richard rose to leave. "Yeah, well, let's just keep our fingers crossed. Remember, she's pregnant."

"I guess we'll cross that bridge when we come to it," Jason said.

The Trouble Begins

Seven months into her pregnancy, Beth developed preterm labor and was confined to bed rest for the next two months. Everyone at the practice was relieved when she gave birth to a healthy baby girl. But most of all, they were all anxiously looking forward to Beth's return after maternity leave. It was tough on all the partners to take over Beth's patient schedule and labor and delivery call while she was out for 12 weeks.

But those problems weren't as bad as those that arose when she returned. Beth seemed irritable and distant with the partners and office support staff.

Jason wondered, with concern, how she was interacting with patients. While pondering the problem, Jason thought back to a conversation he had had just last month with Sabrina. According to Sabrina, Beth had yelled at one of the receptionists for sending home a patient who was 30 minutes late for an appointment. "Office policy clearly states that late patients lose their assigned time," Sabrina said in defense of her assistant. "She was just following our policy."

Jason had met with Beth in his office to ask her to explain her behavior. After a brief exchange of pleasantries, Jason inquired, "I understand you had some words with a receptionist about a late patient appointment." Pausing for effect, he continued, "Beth, what's going on?"

"I took the time on one of my rare days off that I scheduled weeks ago just to come in to the office and see that patient," Beth snapped. "This woman had a very long drive and had to bring along her 92-year-old mother, whom she supports. The receptionist sent her home when she was only 20 minutes late. She didn't even bother to tell me that the patient was here!"

"That may be the case, but you can't treat the office staff this way. It's not professional. You'll have to apologize," Jason said sternly.

"You're right," Beth conceded. "I'll apologize for my behavior, but what happened inconvenienced both me *and* the patient. I understand the need for a policy, but had the reception staff told me the patient was here, all of this could have been avoided." Beth was getting worked up again.

Pausing to control her emotions, Beth said, "It's just . . . I haven't been myself lately. Jason, my schedule is killing me. The baby has colic, and I haven't gotten a good night's sleep since she was born."

"Beth, I'm sorry to hear that you're having adjustment problems, but that isn't an excuse for the way you treated my office staff," Jason said disapprovingly. "Don't you have family to help you out?"

"Doug's family is here, but they're all working," Beth explained. "Things might get a little easier when Doug is out of his residency program in Atlanta, but that's still six months away."

"You know, my wife raised our four boys. If you need some parenting advice, I'm sure she would be willing to help you out."

"That's very *kind* of you," Beth said with an edge to her voice. "But I really think the problem is with the work schedule. Jason, my schedule has to change. Right now."

Exasperated, Jason said, "I'll arrange a meeting with Richard and Dwight. Any request to change the work schedule will have an effect on them too," Jason explained. "Beth, a good doctor keeps her problems at home. Do you understand me?"

A week later, a meeting was called during the lunch hour with all of the physicians in the practice to discuss Beth's request. Jason remembered what high hopes he had had that the scheduling problem could be solved and things would get back to normal.

At an oval table, with himself at the head, Jason tried reasoning with Beth. "Look, I know things are tough being a first-time mother, but there's no way we can give you two days off in the middle of the week. The practice is far too busy for such a luxury."

Beth pleaded, "Gentlemen, if you want to hire women doctors you need to know how to work with them. And you probably should have realized that women, indeed, have babies. How could you of all people not be sensitive to this! The reality of my situation is that I am alone in this town with an infant daughter. My contract states that I work Monday through Friday from 7:00 A.M. until 6:00 P.M., in addition to the call schedule. Right now I'm working weekdays until 8:00 P.M. If I'm lucky I get a Saturday or Sunday off. But if my two on-call days fall on Saturday and Sunday, I get no time off during the entire week. I never see my daughter, and she's only six months old! I need a little extra time. It doesn't have to be long term. This is important to me!"

"Beth, most of us here have children," Jason countered. "At the same time, we've made a professional commitment to the practice. We are only asking that you do the same. The *reality* of the situation is that this is a growing practice that requires dedicated doctors." He stopped and looked around at all the partners before he began. "We all know you're under emotional strain. Have you thought about counseling? You know, just to help you get over the rough spots?"

They had debated for over an hour, but in the end they conceded to giving Beth an additional half day off on Thursdays. Jason thought it was a generous offer and he, as well as the rest of the partners, had looked forward to things going back to normal.

Later in his office, as he reflected on the meeting, Jason was pleased with himself to have resolved the issue but a bit annoyed that Beth had talked them into an extra half day off. Still, he thought, maybe this is the best solution for now.

Then Sabrina had walked through his door again.

What to Do?

Is she ever going to get with the program, Jason thought, staring bleakly out of his office window. I can't lose loyal staff members just because she has a temper tantrum, he thought. But I also don't want to lose our only female doctor. We would be a laughingstock. The only practice to hire a woman, fires a woman. Even though her contract prohibited her from joining a rival practice, it was in force only for two years. Beth's lawyer could also challenge that arrangement. She could conceivably join one of our competitors within the year, he lamented. Donald Mack would love that!

Dr. Swenson's Perspective

"You're baby looks just fine, Mrs. Gandy. If you go to the front desk, they'll schedule you for your next appointment." Beth smiled at her patient, but it masked the turmoil she was feeling inside. She held her stomach, which always seemed to be upset these days.

She had seen Sabrina Ramos enter Jason Mortensen's office and close the door. I really did it this time, she thought, as she rubbed her bloodshot eyes. Another long night on call in the labor and delivery ward last night had nearly sapped her strength. It's only 10:00 A.M., she thought. How many patients were scheduled this morning? At least 20, she remembered. I never should have yelled at Sabrina this morning, she considered as she removed her latex gloves and started to wash her hands. I'm a nice person, she told herself. So why am I yelling at everyone?

When Beth joined private practice, she thought the long hours typical of her residency program were over. She recalled times when she would be on call in labor and delivery for 72 consecutive hours and worked 90 hours per week. The position at Advanced Women's Health Care Associates seemed ideal. The practice had a strong reputation, and it served some of the town's most prominent women. Advanced Women's Heath Care Associates had also offered the highest salary. But the most important reason for her accepting the offer was that the position was ideal for her husband, too. She knew Doug was excited to come back home. Anxious to start living a normal life, she and Doug had managed to juggle their residency schedules and get a few days off to go house hunting. They had bought their first house a month after signing her contract.

She remembered Jason's warning about the practice growing at a fast pace. The town of her husband's youth had changed from a sleepy southern hamlet to a major suburb dominated by office buildings, strip malls, and car dealerships. At first, the busy schedule was not a problem. Beth thought back to how she tried to show her commitment to the practice by working extra office hours and taking additional on-call duties. Since her husband was away, she enjoyed the extra work. Moreover, she didn't enjoy going home to an empty house. Unfortunately, she worked so hard it sent her into preterm labor.

The Problem Begins

When she returned to work after the birth of her daughter, it seemed that her workload only increased. On average she was delivering three to five babies a week. Just two weeks ago she had delivered 13 babies in three days. It was not uncommon for her to work the entire day and then return to the hospital for a delivery that lasted until midnight. She hardly had any time to spend with her daughter.

There have been too many times of going 36 hours without sleep, she told herself. It was after one of those long stretches that she first snapped and yelled at the office receptionist for sending a late patient away. Don't they see how that hurts our reputation with patients? She cringed when she thought that the worst part was never seeing her baby, who was being raised by a nanny and a procession of baby-sitters. I wonder what she's doing now, Beth thought sadly. Is she smiling, cooing, wondering who her mommy is?

Beth moved quickly to scan the chart of her next patient waiting in another examination room for at least 30 minutes. As she rushed down the hallway to meet her next appointment, she thought part of the problem was that she was the only woman physician in this practice.

Here I am, fresh out of residency, and women are lining up to make appointments with me instead of the other partners. While this development was flattering, it was also making her life hectic. Some of the problem could be alleviated if they would just hire a fifth doctor, preferably another woman. But they kept dragging their feet. She wondered, are they reluctant to hire a woman or are they reluctant to have to pay a fifth person? The physicians, including Beth, made very good money. She knew that a fifth doctor's pay would cut into profits; she wasn't naive. Jason also seemed reluctant to make any scheduling changes. He doesn't really want to hear my problems, she concluded before she stepped in to greet her next patient. He's just interested in the problem going away, she thought glumly as she opened the door to the examination room.

"Good morning Mrs. Halley," Beth said brightly, trying to mask her fatigue. "I'm sorry you had to wait so long. How have you been?" Beth hurried through the exam as she chatted with her patient about the weather. She noticed that Betty, the nurse attendant who assisted in the exam, remained strangely quiet through the entire appointment.

From Bad to Worse

Another problem being the only woman in this practice is the way the office staff treats me, she thought. She often saw the nurse attendants joking back and forth with her partners during examinations. It had a way of making patients feel at ease. But they never joke around with me, she recollected. Even worse, the front office staff ignored her.

How many times have I told Sabrina not to schedule patients past four o'clock? Sabrina's answer was always the same. "The other doctors don't mind seeing extra patients." Beth also wanted to retort, "But the other doctors have stay-at-home wives to raise their children, do the shopping, fix the dinners, and clean the house." Of course, she never said this to Sabrina. Rather, she just thought it and held her anger in.

Once she approached Dwight about the issue privately. He might have some sway over Jason, she surmised. Moreover, since she and Dwight attended the same church, she felt that he would be sympathetic to her dilemma. One day after service she approached him.

"Dwight, I really need your advice about work," Beth implored. She explained to him the problem with Sabrina ignoring her scheduling requests.

"Beth, as a family man and friend, I'm telling you this," said Dwight. "When you look back on your life, the most important thing you should remember is your family. Your child should be your first priority. Have you considered other work options?"

"Like what?" Beth inquired curiously.

"We need someone on staff at our new clinic," Dwight said. "Of course, you wouldn't be able to do surgery or obstetrics, but you wouldn't have to worry about being on call or working late hours," Dwight reasoned.

Beth felt deflated. "You mean I would be doing the work of a nurse practitioner. Would I be paid as one as well?"

"Well, yes. It would be a significant reduction in pay from what you receive now. On the other hand, it would solve your scheduling problems. Do you want me to mention it to Jason?" Dwight asked.

The implied demotion angered Beth. But instead she said, "I appreciate the thought, Dwight. But I went to medical school to learn how to be a surgeon. I'd also lose money, my partnership, and my surgical skill. My family really can't afford for me to take that kind of cut in pay. Doug is only making about $30,000 in his residency. We just bought a house that has a large mortgage." She shook her head sadly. "I just don't see it happening. Please don't mention our conversation to Jason."

"Just remember the offer is there if you change you mind," Dwight said as he turned to leave.

But Beth never took him up on his offer. Instead, she fought with the rest of the partners and managed to keep one lousy, half day off on Thursday on a permanent basis. Even that isn't helping me, she thought despairingly. That half day is filled with me taking patient charts home to complete because there's no other time to do it during the week. And Dwight, the man who told me children were the first priority, wouldn't even look at me during that entire meeting when I practically begged for a more humane work schedule! I just don't get it, she thought. They knew when they interviewed me that I wanted to start a family.

What to Do?

As Beth rushed to get the chart for her next patient, she noticed a Post-it® note on her office door. With hesitation she read it; "I need to see you tomorrow morning at 6:00 A.M. Jason." Beth knew what this meeting was about. She had better think long and hard about her job here. Could she afford to take the job at the new clinic? Could she afford not to? Getting her lawyer to challenge the noncompete clause in her contract would be expensive. She could leave the region, but how could she tell her husband? He was looking forward to being back home. Even if I do manage to get out of the noncompete clause, the other practices in town will wonder why I'm leaving, Beth thought. Potential employers would inevitably ask Jason for a reference. I can just imagine what he would tell them, Beth thought. "She's a skilled physician who doesn't want to work and has a hard time getting along with people," she envisioned Jason saying. Jason won't let me go easily, Beth lamented. He's just way too competitive.

These thoughts plagued Beth as she realized that the next patient had been waiting for over 40 minutes. ✦

*This case has been developed based on real organization(s) and real organizational experiences. Names, facts, and situations have been changed to protect the privacy of individuals and organizations.

Chapter 30

Not a Typical Friday

Marifran Mattson

It seemed like a typical Friday at the corporate offices of KJVM AM/FM Radio* when regional sales director Jim Dawson was asked to attend a meeting at 4:45 P.M. with the "agenda to be announced." Not sure what to expect, Dawson arrived at the conference room to find that only the sales manager, Mike Perrot, and the station manager, Eric Wilks, were there. Without any explanation, Perrot said, "Dawson, sign this employment termination agreement, give us all your building keys, clean out your desk, and be out of here by 5:30 P.M."

Stunned, Dawson did not sign the document but asked, "May I take it with me to read more carefully and think it over?"

Wilks and Perrot exchanged a glance and then nodded, indicating that Dawson could take the document. But Wilks quickly added, "Remember, you only have 24 hours before the offer will expire."

Dawson was shocked by what occurred at this meeting, and it wasn't until he was home that he realized that he had been fired after almost 30 years with the station. All he could ask was "Why me? First I was demoted, now they want to get rid of me entirely."

Both Wilks and Perrot believed this was the best way to handle a difficult situation. From their point of view, Dawson was not cooperating with them. Moreover, they did not consider him an integral part of KJVM's future plans. A few months after his termination, Dawson sued the company for age discrimination.

Management's Standpoint: Time for Change

KJVM is a small family-owned radio station operating in a medium-sized market in the Midwest. Ben LaDaire, the patriarch of the family, founded the radio station in the late 1940s. As the station's president, LaDaire was a friendly, open, visionary leader and a relatively hands-off manager. LaDaire handpicked his employees and he had high expectations of them, but he also rewarded them handsomely when they performed to his satisfaction.

For example, when employees were promoted or had employment anniversaries, they were always honored with celebration dinners and gifts. Unusual for stations of its size, KJVM implemented a profit-sharing and pension plan for all employees so that "each employee can one day afford to buy a house." He intended to take care of his employees, believing that his management style would ensure loyalty.

LaDaire knew Dawson before he invited him to join KJVM. LaDaire was on the board of directors of a semiprofessional hockey team and Dawson was the team's goalie. One day after hockey practice, LaDaire approached Dawson and asked, "How would you like to work for me during the day, and you can still play hockey at night and on the weekends?"

Dawson enthusiastically replied, "Sure, but I don't know much about the radio business." LaDaire chuckled. "Don't worry about that, I'll teach you everything you need to know. I just need a competitive person to sell advertising and you are definitely a competitor." LaDaire hired Dawson as an advertising sales representative and within six years Dawson was promoted to sales manager. Throughout their 25 years as colleagues, LaDaire and Dawson enjoyed a collegial and successful business relationship and regarded each other as friends.

When LaDaire died suddenly, his son, Junior, inherited the presidency of KJVM. Slowly but decisively the management philosophy changed. When Dawson began working for the senior LaDaire, Junior was in his early teens. So the two men knew one another, but only casually.

Soon after becoming president, Junior asked the station's general manager, whom his father had hired years earlier, to resign. Junior wanted Eric Wilks to be his new general manager. This pattern seemed to repeat itself two years later, when Junior gave Wilks the power to remove Dawson as sales manager. The strategy this time was to replace Dawson with Mike Perrot, a new employee. Perrot was in his late 30s and a personal friend and former coworker of Wilks at a local television station.

Wilks tried to lessen the blow of Dawson's demotion by creating and offering him the title of regional sales director. Wilks explained the change to Dawson by saying, "You can keep your account list and work on special projects with me. In addition, you must report to Perrot every morning." Essentially, Dawson once again became a sales representative—the position at which he started at the station more than 25 years ago. Adding insult to injury, he was reporting to Perrot, who had no managerial experience.

But Dawson continued on. He had a family to support. And, with his substantial account list, he believed that he could still make decent money selling radio time. Masking the hurt, Dawson made sales calls and reported, as instructed, to Perrot every morning.

Dawson reflected on the changes that had occurred since Junior replaced his father. Confused, angry, and hurt, once again Dawson approached Junior and asked about the changes.

Junior replied without looking up from his work, "New, fresh blood is needed!" Dawson left Junior's office when Junior continued to work on the reports in front of him.

What Junior didn't tell Dawson was that Wilks and Perrot contended that Dawson was practicing outdated sales techniques. When they explained to Junior that they wanted to terminate Dawson, Wilks and Perrot cited as examples that Dawson didn't meet with all of his accounts in person, and that he was not keeping up with the other salespeople in terms of his annual percentage of billing increase. In addition, the station manager and the sales manager characterized Dawson's conduct at sales meetings as difficult and inappropriate, saying that Dawson not only introduced items that lengthened the meetings unnecessarily but that he also refused to tell the sales manager in advance about the topics he wished to discuss.

In a recent performance evaluation, which Perrot put in the form of a warning letter, Perrot criticized Dawson for decisions concerning his accounts. Perrot gave him a list of "specific ways you must improve your performance to meet station standards." Perrot notified Dawson that he had "90 days to accomplish these stipulations or your employment will end."

Several months after Dawson's performance evaluation, Wilks and Perrot decided to dismiss Dawson because of "his defiant attitude toward authority and his unwillingness or inability to take direction from his superiors." Wilks also cited "personality conflicts" between Dawson and himself as part of the reason for his termination. After repeated complaining by Wilks and Perrot, Junior agreed that it was time for a change and gave Wilks his approval to fire Dawson. Prior to dismissing Dawson, the KJVM management consulted with its attorneys and was told that firing Dawson was within its rights and was consistent with its legal obligations and the current mission of the station.

Dawson's Standpoint: Sinister Plot

For the first 25 years of his employment, Dawson thrived in the friendly, open, and hands-off management style of KJVM. Dawson considered station members to be his family, and he respected LaDaire. Like other employees at the station, Dawson saw LaDaire as a father figure. LaDaire fostered this attitude when he told Dawson on more than one occasion, "Dawson, you are like one of my family." And it did seem like that to Dawson. After all, LaDaire regularly invited Dawson to socialize with him outside of work.

Dawson's career with KJVM quickly progressed, and six years after being hired by the company founder as an advertising sales representative, Dawson was promoted to sales manager. The president and general manager often consulted Dawson before making changes in KJVM sales department policy or procedures. If Dawson needed assistance with one of his advertising accounts, he felt free to discuss the matter with them. Dawson was always the top income-generating salesperson and was well respected and rewarded for his work and loyalty. Other radio stations in larger markets tried to recruit him, but he turned down the lucrative offers to remain with KJVM because he enjoyed his job, respected the management, especially LaDaire, and felt a sense of loyalty to the company. LaDaire often told him, "Dawson, you are Mr. KJVM!"

Around the twenty-fifth year of Dawson's tenure, the climate at KJVM changed when the president of KJVM died suddenly and his son, Junior, became president. Although Junior was only in his 30s, he seemed well versed in the technical aspects of music programming.

Junior also had specialized knowledge that helped KJVM make production more efficient by using computers and digital technology.

Initially, Dawson and Junior worked together in ways that were similar to the friendly style that Dawson enjoyed with Junior's father. For example, Junior and Dawson often took a morning and afternoon coffee break together at a local doughnut shop, during which they discussed many work-related and personal issues. Dawson believed that Junior appreciated his dedication, sales expertise, management style, and ability to generate income for the company. Junior often told Dawson, "You are doing a great job, and you can work for KJVM as long as you want."

Dawson considered these statements to be offers of lifetime employment and always replied, "I plan to work here forever!" He was proud to be thought of so highly by his employer.

However, little by little these interactions changed and the camaraderie between Junior and Dawson wore off. When Dawson asked Junior, as he often had in the past, "Want to join me for a coffee and doughnut break?" Junior replied, "I'm not going to have coffee and doughnuts with you anymore, I'm too busy." Dawson was surprised by the bluntness of Junior's response but believed that Junior was becoming so involved as president of the radio station that he no longer had time to take breaks.

The climate at KJVM changed even more when Perrot joined as sales manager. Wilks told Dawson that he was being promoted to the newly created position of regional sales director. Dawson was promised that he would be "working on special sales projects" with the station manager in addition to performing his duties as a sales representative. With these assurances, Dawson accepted the offer and new title. But the promise of working on special sales projects with Wilks never materialized. Dawson approached Wilks several times about this, saying, "What special projects will you and I be working on?"

Wilks responded, "There are no special projects for us to work on at this time." Eventually, Dawson stopped asking.

In spite of these troublesome developments, Dawson continued to increase his sales volume. Oddly, Junior, Wilks, and Perrrot did not seem pleased. For the first time in his tenure at KJVM, the management reduced Dawson's account list by redistributing some of his accounts to other sales representatives. Dawson was told that he was expected to acquire several new, active accounts per quarter. And he would have to in order to meet his sales goals and retain his commission level. Besides these changes in his sales responsibilities, Wilks required Dawson to have daily meetings with Perrot to report his progress. Dawson wondered why he had to have these meetings because, after asking other sales representatives, he realized that no one else was required to do this.

Wilks and Perrot also restrained Dawson's communication activities in the office. His telephone calls, incoming and outgoing correspondence, interoffice memos, and meeting input were monitored and restricted. Perrot often took telephone and other interoffice memos that contained leads on new accounts out of Dawson's mailbox and either gave these leads to other sales representatives or checked them out himself. Dawson questioned the receptionist: "What has happened to my incoming phone calls?"

She responded, "Perrot told me to give them to him."

Dawson wondered out loud, "Is he doing this to all sales reps?"

The receptionist replied empathically, "No, only you."

At routine sales meetings, Dawson was no longer allowed to offer input without prior consent from Wilks and Perrot. Dawson was required by Perrot to "present a list of potential agenda items prior to the meeting." However, when he did, the sales manager never mentioned those items during the meeting. Realizing this, Dawson discontinued suggesting meeting topics. As a result, Perrot began to criticize him for "not contributing to the meeting."

Other happenings around the office seemed odd to Dawson. For instance, at the sales meetings, the sales staff often requested and shared updated information on the activity of their accounts. Because Dawson kept his own computer files, he offered to, and made, copies of his spreadsheets available to all sales personnel. Perrot reprimanded him for doing this, saying, "It is not necessary for you to give all the information about your accounts to the other sales reps." Then, at another meeting, Perrot verbally chastised Dawson for not sharing account data. But the most egregious slap was when Perrot chastised Dawson for not "keeping us up to date on Hoover's."

Dawson could only explain, "I no longer have the data because the Hoover account has been given to another sales rep."

Perrot replied abruptly and loudly, "Dawson, you are not being a team player!"

Apparently Perrot kept a running list of these incidents. In a warning letter that followed a performance evaluation, Perrot criticized

Dawson for his handling of accounts. Perrot gave Dawson a list of "specific ways you must improve your performance to meet station standards." During the evaluation interview, Perrot warned Dawson that he had "90 days to accomplish these stipulations or your employment will end."

Dawson believed that management's accusations were fabrications, but he was not allowed the opportunity to respond to the allegations. Dawson thought that he had no other choice but to sign the document and comply with the demands—which he did. This was the first time in Dawson's 28-year career with KJVM that his sales strategies were formally questioned or criticized.

According to the document, Dawson's performance was supposed to be reviewed again in six months. But before the six months were up, he was asked to sign a termination agreement waiving any future claims of discrimination, and told to clear out his desk and permanently leave the building. As he packed his belongings, he was interrupted several times by Wilks and Perrot, who asked him, "Are you sure you are not taking company property?"

Dawson assured them, saying, "No, I am only taking what belongs to me." On his way out of the building that night, Dawson approached Junior and said, "You told me I would have a job here as long as I wanted."

Junior flatly replied, "I'm not going to discuss this with you! Please leave the building."

Dawson was shocked that, at 58 years of age and after almost 30 years with the company, he was fired. His feelings of shock and disbelief lasted for several days. These feelings changed to anger when he received numerous phone calls from current and former KJVM employees expressing surprise and sadness at his dismissal. He learned from his former coworkers that Wilks and Perrot had told some employees that they had "a plan to get rid of you because you have been with the company too long, are too old, have too much control over accounts, are making too much money, and are costing the company too much money in company contributions to profit-sharing."

Former colleagues also told Dawson, "Wilks and Perrot put restrictions on your work activities to decrease your production and create reasons to fire you." This talk of a conspiracy to fire him caused Dawson extreme emotional turmoil. His initial feeling that he had done something wrong to deserve the dismissal changed to a sense of betrayal by Junior, Wilks, and Perrot. In light of the conversations with some of his former coworkers, Dawson consulted the Equal Employment Opportunity Commission and an attorney, and later decided to file a lawsuit against KJVM for age discrimination.

Coworkers' Standpoint: Mixed Messages

Soon after his termination from KJVM, many of Dawson's coworkers expressed concern and fear. Current and former KJVM employees called Dawson to tell him that "Junior, Wilks, and Perrot had a plan to fire you because you are too old, and it costs the company too much to keep you in the profit-sharing plan." Salespeople told Dawson, "We were never required to perform any of the extra duties required of you." Some of his coworkers also feared for their own jobs because "if they can do it to you after all these years, they can do it to any of us at any time."

However, a few employees thought that Dawson deserved to be fired. They believed that he controlled too many of the best accounts and that he was servicing those accounts using outdated sales practices. In fact, some employees called Dawson "old fashioned." They also thought that Dawson, like any other employee, could be dismissed at any time and he should have seen it coming.

One coworker specifically expressed these mixed feelings about Dawson's termination situation. On the evening of Dawson's dismissal, a prominent sales staff member, Sinclair, called Dawson and offered, "I wanted you to know that Junior, Wilks, and Perrot made me aware that there was a plan to fire you long before you were officially dismissed." Further, Sinclair told Dawson, "I saw Wilks going through your desk today when you were out on a call. I figured management wanted to see what you had in your desk, and they did not want you to take any information that belonged to the station or could later be used as evidence against them. When I was hired, Perrot and Wilks told me that they were going to let you go eventually to make room for new salespeople. They planned to do this by setting your mandatory sales goals so high that you could not possibly reach them—then you would be fired due to flat sales." Sinclair went on to explain to Dawson, "Initially I agreed with their strategy because I believed it would give more salespeople a better chance for success, but over time I came to realize that it was not fair to you." Although

Sinclair knew for some time that Dawson was not in the future plans of KJVM management, like many others at the radio station she still was very surprised and dismayed when Dawson was terminated.

Dawson's Dilemma

While the attorney was pursuing his case, Dawson couldn't help but wonder . . . was he wrong for filing a discrimination suit? How would doing so affect his possibility of being employed by another radio station? After all, he had been a radio sales rep for nearly 30 years—all of his working life—and there weren't many job openings for retired hockey players. ✦

*This case has been developed based on real organization(s) and real organizational experiences. Names, facts, and situations have been changed to protect the privacy of individuals and organizations.

Chapter 31

A Case of Mistreatment at Work?

Mary M. Meares and John G. Oetzel

Jessica Martinez* stopped at the stoplight and tried to blink back her tears. What was she going to do? This job had started out as her ideal dream job.

A few months ago Jessica had just graduated from a well-respected, local university with a degree in communication. She had several job offers, but the most exciting and lucrative, not to mention the one closest to home, was with TechnoloComm. TechnoloComm was a research organization that created a variety of new communication technologies. The location had been one of the best things about the job offer. Jessica was very close to her family, and the thought of moving far away was not attractive. If she worked at TechnoloComm, she could continue to live at home, save money, and have her parents' support as she made the transition from being a student to working full time.

Jessica was hired in the human resources office to work on internal newsletters and publicity. She even knew a few people who worked at TechnoloComm, including her mother's aunt, who'd been there for 17 years. Auntie Maria warned her that the organization was not the ideal one that she imagined. Over dinner at her grandmother's one Sunday her great aunt had said, "Don't be too naive, Jessica. TechnoloComm's got some good things and some bad. For example, there are a lot of times I've been treated badly there by the higher-ups."

Jessica remembered now that she had discounted this vague warning, thinking every workplace had some people who were not great, but surely it would be only a few. She told her great-aunt, "Oh, I'm sure that I won't have any problems like that—Tom, my new boss, is really nice." Now Auntie Maria's comments seemed more realistic. "I should have paid more attention to what she said," Jessica thought.

Everything had started out fine, even though Jessica quickly noted that she was one of few employees in this part of the organization who was not European American. Jessica had a cubicle in an office with Peter, Alex, and Susan. As the communication team, they were responsible for creating newsletters, press releases, communication training, and maintaining the website. The team was one of several within the HR department, and their office was part of a suite of offices in the building that housed many of TechnoloComm's administrative functions. Jessica liked the fact that she got to see lots of people from different offices, and since her work included writing the newsletter, she had a chance to talk to people about their jobs.

Everything went fine for the first week or two, and then something happened that made her question her job and the organization. She was getting a cup of coffee one Monday morning and joined a conversation between two of her teammates, Peter and Alex. She had not had much of a chance to get to know them because she spent most of her time the first few weeks learning her job and going to mandatory organizational training. In the few instances when Jessica actually did the work her job required, she tended to work more with Susan. Peter and Alex were working together on other projects. So, when she saw them in the break room, she thought this was a great time to talk with them.

"Hi, Jessica," said Peter. "We were just talking about the big street party last weekend."

"Yeah," said Alex. "I was really frustrated because I couldn't get into my neighborhood. Did you experience the same problem?" After pausing, he added, "I guess not, since you probably don't live on the north side of town."

"Yeah, you must live in the el barrio, right?" questioned Peter, making sure to try to give a Latin twist to "el barrio."

Jessica nodded, felt her face flush, and faked a laugh. She lived with her family in a traditionally Hispanic area of town and would never want to live anywhere else. Her neighborhood was *home.* It was where she had grown up and where she knew everyone.

Before she could think of a good response, the men headed back to their desks, chatting about the day's work, seemingly oblivious to her embarrassment and anger. Jessica sat down at her desk and thought, "Why do they assume I live in the barrio? I *could* live anywhere, I just don't want to. And I certainly wouldn't want to live in their neighborhood with people like that!" After thinking about it for a while, though, she decided to try to forget it, thinking, "It might be a misunderstanding and they probably didn't mean anything by it."

Later that afternoon, while Jessica was participating in a seminar to learn about TechnoloComm's retirement package options, Susan, Alex, and Peter used their break to discuss the new addition to their office.

"What do you think of Jessica?" Susan said.

"She seems nice enough and she does great work," Alex replied.

"Yeah. She's a little too serious though," added Peter. "But that's probably because she's new and worried about making a good impression. We'll just have to loosen her up a bit so that she can relax and fit in."

The next week, the four of them were working in the office and Jessica decided to try again to get to know Peter and Alex better. The two of them were talking to Susan when Jessica walked over to join them.

"Hey, guys. How was your weekend?"

Alex replied, "Great! Peter and I got together with our families and had a huge barbecue."

"Oh, sounds good. What did you have?"

Alex said, "We had surf and turf—you know, steak and seafood. It was delicious. Peter really knows how to 'cue it up."

"Sounds good. I love barbecue."

Peter responded, "I'm surprised to hear that."

"Why's that?" Jessica asked, surprised and innocently.

"Well, you know I always heard that Hispanics don't like to barbecue."

She asked somewhat disgustedly, "And why not?"

"Well, the beans fall through the grill."

Alex and Peter started laughing as Susan grinned and shook her head. "You guys are terrible."

Jessica turned around and walked back to her desk feeling very annoyed. She was really starting to get angry and thought that maybe the exchange last week wasn't a misunderstanding after all. She needed to talk to someone. Luckily, she had already planned to get together with her friend Jennifer over lunch. Jennifer worked in another part of HR. They had been peers at school, graduating the same semester, and they were hired at about the same time. Jennifer was a great listener and Jessica felt really comfortable with her. Over their salads, she told Jennifer about Alex and Peter's comments.

"Wow! I can't believe that they would say something like that. What jerks! You should do something about this."

"What?"

"I don't know, Jess. I hope I've never said anything to offend you. I don't know how to tell you to deal with this kind of problem. I guess maybe you should just confront Alex and Peter and tell them to not say things like that."

"What if I don't feel comfortable doing that? I'm not sure I could say that to them directly. Plus there are two of them and only one of me—and they've both been here a long time and have Susan on their side. She thought their stupid joke was funny."

"Well, then maybe you should talk to Tom. Since he's your boss, maybe he can help you figure out what to do. Maybe he can talk to them for you."

"I'd hate to get Peter and Alex in trouble," Jessica replied cautiously. "And I don't want to be labeled a troublemaker. But on the other hand, they made me feel really bad." With renewed confidence in her voice, Jessica concluded, "They had no respect for me. Tom does seem really supportive. I don't want him to fight my battles for me, but maybe he can help me figure out what to do. Thanks, Jen."

"Good luck, Jess."

That afternoon, Jessica tentatively approached Tom's office.

"Um, Tom, do you have a minute?"

"Sure, Jessica. Come on in and have a seat. How's everything going with that newsletter?"

"Well, the newsletter's fine, but there's something else I want to talk to you about."

"What's that?" Tom asked as he motioned for Jessica to sit down.

"Well, I've had a couple of difficult things happen in the office." Jessica explained the conversations over the past week as well as she could without getting too defensive or angry. Then she waited to see his reaction.

"Oh, Jessica. I'm sure they didn't mean anything. Alex and Peter are both great guys. I'm sure they were just joking around. That's their way of including people. You've only been here a short time, so don't take it so personally. They do it to everyone."

"But—"

"No," Tom implored. "Don't worry about it. They're both great guys. When you get to know them better you'll understand. Now, are there any other problems?"

"No."

"Well, you'd better get back to work then. That newsletter has to be out by tomorrow."

As Jessica walked back to her desk, she felt frustrated, angry, and discouraged. How could he minimize everything she felt and let those guys totally off the hook? She was even angrier than before she talked to Tom. "Why did I even go to Tom? Now I know that I can't count on him for support," she thought. Jessica sat down at her desk. She had a newsletter to get done. Looking at the pictures of her family that decorated her cubicle, she decided that she would show them—her work would be excellent!

Over the next two months, Jessica received compliments from Tom, Alex, and Peter on the work that she did with the newsletter and the website. However, the compliments did not make her feel better. Although she smiled in response to the praise, internally she kept evaluating the comments for hidden meanings or any sense of their surprise that she, a Hispanic, could do a good job. Jessica found it hard to concentrate and relax. She felt jumpy and anxious, especially when she had to work with Peter and Alex without Susan being present.

As the weeks wore on, Alex and Peter continued to tease her about a lot of things. Many of these were not cultural references, but they still made fun of the barrio and also some of the foods she ate. They worked hard and knew their jobs, but personally she just did not like to be around them.

One day at lunch in the cafeteria, Susan, Peter, and Alex sat together, joking and giving each other a hard time. When there was a lull in the conversation, Susan asked Peter how things were going with Jessica.

"Ah, I get along fine with Jessica. We give her a bit of a hard time, but she really needs to loosen up. She just needs to learn to tease us back."

"I don't know, guys. Your jokes don't bother me, but I get the impression that your teasing may be making things worse," Susan replied. "She really looks offended by a lot of your comments. I don't know, but maybe you guys should actually *talk* to her, rather than just tease her."

Peter stated, "I think you're crazy, Susan, but we'll talk to her."

Except for Susan, who was working on a deadline, Alex, Peter, and Jessica left the office that afternoon at about the same time. As they were heading to their cars, the guys took the opportunity to confront Jessica.

Peter said, "Hey, Jess, Alex and I have been talking and it seems like you're upset with us. Do you have a problem with us?"

Startled, Jessica replied, "I don't have any problem."

Alex added, "Susan thinks you're upset with us."

Jessica felt a little uneasy about confronting them and simply said, "No, not really."

Peter asked, "So, we're cool then?"

"Um, yeah, I guess."

"OK then, we'll see you tomorrow."

As Jessica drove away, Peter said to Alex, "I told you nothing was wrong."

Alex nodded. "I guess you're right."

As Jessica was driving home her heart was pounding. She wanted to tell them what was wrong, but she was scared and hadn't prepared anything to say. She felt cornered and didn't feel safe, especially knowing that she was still in her probationary period at work. Even if she wasn't afraid, how could she say exactly what she felt so they would understand? Tom hadn't understood or even really listened. Why could she expect Alex and Peter to understand?

The next afternoon after work, the team—minus Jessica, who didn't want to spend any more time than necessary with them—went to work out in the TechnoloComm gym. Alex and Peter were lifting weights and Susan was riding the bike when Tom walked in to work out. Seeing Susan alone, Tom thought, "Great, Jessica's three-month probationary evaluation is coming up next week, and here's a chance to find out how things are *really* working out with her in the communication team." He went over to the stationary bike next to Susan's and climbed on. "Hey, Susan. How's everything going down in your office? Is everyone getting along okay?"

"Well, things are interesting," she replied with a smile.

"I'm not sure I like the sound of that. Interesting in what way?"

"Well, there's a lot of tension, to be honest. I really like Jessica and think she's doing great work, but there's some kind of problem between her and the guys. I can't figure out exactly what it is. She hasn't talked to me about it, but it's clear that there's tension between them. I told the guys that maybe they shouldn't tease her so much . . . you know how they are," Susan continued. "But they said they talked to her and she said that there's no problem."

"Hmm . . . with Alex and Peter, teasing is their way of making people feel comfortable. Usually they don't tease people they don't like. Maybe I need to encourage Jessica to be more a part of the group. Well, I appreciate your input, Susan. How many miles are you riding this afternoon?"

The next Friday morning, Jessica had her evaluation meeting with Tom. She was especially anxious as she sat down in the chair across from him and tried to take a deep breath.

"Well, Jessica. I'm not sure what to make of your performance. Your newsletters and websites are great, and I'm ready to give you additional responsibilities. But before we discuss task issues, I want to talk about some relationship issues that have surfaced." Without giving Jessica a chance to respond, he continued, "You don't seem to be part of our team here in human resources. When I talked with your coworkers, a couple of them mentioned that you aren't as much of a team player as we'd like. I'm going to recommend a second three-month probationary period. As you know, six months is standard, so no need to get worried. I'm going to mark your evaluation to indicate that you are making satisfactory progress. For me to change it to excellent at the end of six months, well, I'll need you to work on your teamwork skills. Let's talk about those."

But instead of letting Jessica explain her perspective or provide a response, Tom continued to talk. First he talked about the importance of the team concept at TechnoloComm, and then he addressed the communication team specifically . . . how well everyone has always gotten along, and how he expects everyone to be a team player.

Jessica just partially listened to Tom as she thought, "I don't get this. I'm doing excellent work, and that is what should matter for my evaluation. He just doesn't understand how hard it is to work with Peter and Alex. I bet they're the ones that told him I wasn't a team player. If I was on a different team, I wouldn't have this problem. I've always prided myself on my teamwork skills. I like this job and I don't want to leave it. But I can't live with the current situation, so I've got to do something. But what?"

At the end of the meeting, Tom asked for Jessica's agreement that she would work on getting along better with her team. Not knowing how else to respond, Jessica agreed by shaking her head up and down . . . but she couldn't look Tom in the eye. She left Tom's office dejected.

After mulling her evaluation over for a few days, she decided to talk to a few of the other employees whom she thought might share her perspective. She wanted to know about their experiences. First she approached Jamal, who worked in HR. He had spoken to Jessica only once before, but Jessica believed it important to gain insight from someone who had been with TechnoloComm so long.

As she told her story, Jamal said, "You're not crazy for feeling angry. This organization is rotten, but then so are most organizations." Then, pausing for effect, Jamal's voice became more dramatic. "We people of color are never going to be treated with respect. It's the system, and the people in power are never going to give up their power and position. They say everyone should be treated fairly and not mistreated, but they don't really mean it. Damn the people and damn the system."

Getting more of a response than she expected, Jessica waited a moment before asking, "So, how do you deal with it?"

"Oh, I'm just waiting to retire. I go up to my cabin and chop firewood. That gets some of it out of my system. I don't talk to anyone about it though—it wouldn't be fair to my family to complain to them. I just deal with it on my own. If you go to your boss or to anyone else in the organization, you get labeled a troublemaker."

"Then why do you stay?"

"The truth? I have a family to support. I can't just quit my job because I don't like the people here. It would be hard to find another job that pays as well as this one, and I have two children who're in college. When I started things were pretty much okay, but in the last few years . . . well, it's really deteriorated. I'm just not in a position to make a change, though. I'll stay here until I can retire. Until then, I just keep to myself as much as possible."

Jessica thought of Auntie Maria's comments about the problems at TechnoloComm. That afternoon she stopped by her office and brought up the topic of mistreatment and what had been going on in HR.

"Oh, honey," Auntie Maria said after closing the door to her boss' office so she and Jessica could talk more privately. "People have been disrespectful to me, too. I try to educate them, teach them some manners, but sometimes it doesn't make a difference. You have to realize that when someone has a lot of power, it doesn't matter what they say—powerful people are not going to be fired or disciplined, or even reprimanded. I've seen some of these people really mistreat their support staff, but TechnoloComm—for some reason—believes they can't be replaced very easily so they're not going to get fired."

"Is it hopeless then? Should I start looking for another job if I don't want to put up with this?" replied Jessica.

"Well, I don't think it's always hopeless. One time a group of us were able to get together to deal with it. A few of the women in my office were singled out for a problem that was really an overall office problem. We talked about it and we got mad that the men weren't held responsible. We went as a group to the supervisor's manager . . . because we acted together, they listened to us and took us seriously. If I hadn't had those other women to back me up, I doubt that I would have had the courage . . . but that time it worked out all right. You've got to pick your battles. Why don't you talk with my friend Rosa in accounting? I think you met her once before. She has worked with the diversity office on some of these issues."

Jessica met with Rosa and described the situation to her.

"You know, we have a policy against mistreatment," Rosa said. "I think this qualifies."

"Is this the diversity policy they talked about in our training?" Without waiting for an answer from Rosa, Jessica continued, "What should I do?"

"Well, that's a really good question—both of them. We don't really have any procedures to go along with the policy. I was talking to one of the women in procurement, and she said she thinks it's ambiguous on purpose, so TechnoloComm looks good but no one can really do much. She thinks it's management's strategy to make people happy, but really it masks the problems and keeps people from having a place to report them to."

"Then what should I do?" groaned Jessica.

"Well, maybe you should go to the diversity office and file a grievance claiming that this is a case of mistreatment. Who knows, maybe that would *encourage* their efforts to provide some procedures and some action to go along with the policy."

Jessica couldn't help but notice the way Rosa's voice changed on the word "encourage." She thanked Rosa for her time . . . but she was still uncertain about what to do. She thought to herself, "This is terrible. Surely I can do something to improve my situation. After all, they hired me to work in the HR office to deal with people. There must be something I can do to convince them to listen to me and everybody else who feels like this. I wonder if I should go to the diversity office?"

As Jessica was pondering her next move on the drive home, Tom, Alex, and Peter were meeting for happy hour. The guys often hung out together after work, and today Tom decided to bring up his concerns about Jessica. "Hey, you guys," he said as he sat down to join them. "What's going on with Jessica?"

Shaking his head, Peter said, "I think she's just too uptight."

Alex added, "We asked her if anything is wrong and she said no."

"Well, you can cut the tension with a knife whenever the three of you are together. I talked with Susan, and she thinks you guys are teasing her too much. Jessica came to me when she first started and said something to the same effect. I dismissed it then . . . I don't know . . . something needs to be done. She *is* pretty uptight, but she is a great worker and I don't want to lose her."

Alex explained, "We don't want her to leave either, but don't blame this on us. We've put a lot of effort into trying to help her fit in with our team. We've treated her like everyone else."

Peter added, "Yeah, and when we did try to talk to her about it, she said everything was okay. What else can we do?"

"I don't know exactly," Tom admitted, "but you need to think of something. Well, I gotta go. See you boys tomorrow."

"Later, boss." Peter turned to Alex and said, "What's going on here? We try to be nice and we just get in trouble. Man, I'm pissed."

"Calm down. Maybe we should talk to her again. She is definitely upset. Maybe we have teased her too much and should back off."

"Maybe you're right, but she needs to meet us halfway and talk to us about what's bothering her rather than just running to the boss."

"Yeah, in a perfect world, I agree. But what should we do?" ✦

*This case has been developed based on real organization(s) and real organizational experiences. Names, facts, and situations have been changed to protect the privacy of individuals and organizations.

Chapter 32

The Penis People

Diane K. Sloan

It was not her first consulting job or even the largest firm for which she'd worked. Her résumé as an independent consultant and trainer was solid and filled with successes, including, among many, her work with two of the largest insurance companies in the country. But this was the biggest and most lucrative job Emma* had taken on. The fee from it would help support her family in some comfort for two years and give them some much-needed breathing room.

Emma had entered into a contract with a plumbing manufacturer that had plants located throughout the United States. The agreement called for her to develop and deliver leadership training to the organization's 300 or so managers. It was a plum assignment, and Emma was grateful for it.

Because of the size of the project, Emma had asked Sheila, another independent consultant, to work with her. Over the years, Emma was pleased to have discovered a network of independent consultants who called upon each other when projects were too large to handle alone and who were willing to travel to where the work was. These consultant-to-consultant relationships were loose and flexible, and they served Emma well, allowing her to remain her own boss while drawing on the expertise of others when the job was complex, long-term, or particularly demanding.

For this job, Bruce, the CEO of the plumbing fixtures corporation, had decided to bring his managers in groups of 50 to the home office rather than send the consultants to them. It was his hope that the mangers would benefit from spending time with each other as well as from the time in the classroom. He also hoped that managers would build a sense of camaraderie from working together and from working together with home office management.

So Emma had agreed to a year contract requiring her to be a half continent away from her family for six to eight months of that time, a condition that caused her great loneliness and more than a little guilt. She, her husband, and their 17-year-old daughter had, as a family, talked through the pros and cons of this lucrative offer. And they had all agreed she should proceed.

Yet Emma realized the preciousness of lost time together, that each day family history was being written without her participation. It was, as she knew it would be, incredibly hard, a hardship barely softened by the occasional trips home and the luxury corporate hotel suite that was her temporary home, even though it had a sweeping view of the city lights. Tonight, looking down at those lights, Emma knew that she had never been more miserable in her work and she had never doubted herself more.

Nevertheless, it was time for her evening meeting and debriefing with her partner. Tonight she and Sheila had arranged to meet for drinks in the hotel bar. Entering and squinting to adjust to the darkness, she saw Sheila sitting at the far end, in the darkest corner, her head in her hands.

"Let me guess," said Emma, sliding into her chair. "Bad session?" While the two often team-taught, they had also built into the schedule sessions for which only one consultant was needed. And this afternoon had been Sheila's turn at the solo session. Emma bit back any further small talk when she saw Sheila's tears as her partner raised her head.

"I think I'm going to have to kill them all," said Sheila, her words slow and measured. "They aren't men, they aren't human, they are bloody monsters."

"Tell me what happened," said Emma softly.

"It was a really good class. At least I thought it was. They were attentive, did their group work well. I thought maybe we had passed some sort of test and that things would be all right. So right before the class ended, I asked if there were any questions. One guy raises his hand and I see him waving something pink in it. 'Yeah,' he says, 'I have a question, Sheila, baby. Did you forget something when you left my room last night?'

"Emma, he's waving panties, women's underwear, at me. And then another guy raises his hand and he's doing the same thing. All of a sudden there's a whole room full of men waving women's panties and saying vile things about me in their rooms. And they're laughing and thinking this is a great."

"Ohmigod. What did you do?"

"The truth, Emma? I don't remember. I don't even remember leaving the room. I just sort of went blank, you know? And it's just so humiliating. Here I am thinking what a good job I'm doing and that we're finally getting somewhere, while they're just waiting to pounce. Oh, geez, where do you suppose they got them? The panties, I mean. I don't even want to think about that."

"Don't," suggested Emma. "Listen, I need to tell you about something that happened to me two days ago. I didn't talk about it earlier because . . . well, because I didn't want it to spook you like it did me. And I guess I just wanted it all to go away."

She paused and took a deep breath. "I went down to get the room ready for my session, early like I usually do, around 7:00. So I go into the empty room, get my overheads in order, and turn on the machine. The glass base is covered with a piece of cardboard, you know, like the back of a yellow pad. I move it aside and . . ." Emma had to pause to take a breath. "There's a transparency under it, and showing up on the screen is a large erect penis with the written message 'Suck my d—.'"

"Oh, no, and if you hadn't come in early—" said Sheila.

"I guess everyone would have had a good ol' boy laugh and I would have been mortified—totally thrown off, probably for the rest of the morning. It's so sick."

"So what did you do when the class started?"

"First, I washed the porno picture off the overhead and then when they all came in, I just acted as if nothing had happened, ignored the whispers and looks, started talking, and didn't stop until noon. Four hours, no questions, no breakouts, no breaks, and I was out of there."

Neither said anything for a while, each fiddling with her drink.

"We have to do something, don't we?" asked Sheila thoughtfully.

"Yep, we do," said Emma. "I've thought about taking it all to Bruce. But then I try to imagine what I'd say. 'Hey, Bruce, I know you are putting out a great deal of money to have two highly trained and respected consultants do their magic in these dog and pony shows. But, golly gee, the guys are talking dirty and we wondered if you could just come in and tell them to knock it off.'"

"Right, and 'While you're at it, could you slay a couple of dragons for us too?' "

"Exactly," said Emma. "You know, I don't even know why they're doing this kind of crap. I don't know if it's completely hostile or if they just think this is all a bunch of fun. Or do you think the guys believe it's cute?"

"I think my brain just shut down. I'm exhausted," said Sheila.

"Me too. Tomorrow?"

"Tomorrow," agreed Sheila. Since the managers would be touring a local plant the next day, they agreed to meet for breakfast to see if they could come up with some ways to resolve this.

Later, in her room, Emma fixed a cup of tea, positioned herself on the sofa facing the lights, and thought hard about the four weeks or so she and Sheila had worked with this first group of managers. It started slowly, the sexual humor as a part of their class discussion, and seemed harmless at first. Sheila and Emma had talked about it but decided that making an issue might just inspire more and worse.

The fact that all 50 of the managers in this group were males could be an indication of the gendered nature of the company, Emma considered. It was also possible that this kind of talk had developed as a norm—one that developed just among this group. Emma continued her reflections. "We took the safe route, didn't we? For the most part, we ignored the sexual comments. When we did acknowledge them, I had hoped that our facial expressions would convey an 'Okay, back to business, guys.'"

But Emma knew one thing for sure. They had been careful not to join in, although at times Emma found it especially difficult not to verbally respond to the demeaning references to women with terms such as bimbos, broads, and worse.

"Do all sexist names for women start with the letter B?" she remembered Sheila whispering to her when the class was doing individual work.

"Let's hope so," Emma had answered.

But it hadn't slowed down. Emma and Sheila took some comfort in the fact that the daily evaluations from the class members were quite good and seemed sincere. But their time with the group became more and more difficult as the talk became raunchier and more obscene. The men focused, almost obsessively, on the male genitalia. In one morning session, she and Sheila had counted the number of times the word "penis" or their preferred term "d–," was said. They stopped counting at 25. Jokes were about penises, and casual talk filled with references. She remembered one guy saying to another, "If your d– is as short as your memory, no wonder your wife keeps calling me."

There was one incident that Emma still had trouble believing. She had organized breakout groups and sent them out of the room to do some work. When they came back, she asked how they had done on their assignment. The highest-ranking guy in the group, a vice president in the organization, said, "Great, we learned a lot." He then proceeded to tell the whole class that they had learned all about how one of their group members liked to "do it" in a variety of positions, some of which could be considered, uh, unusual. A vice president, no less.

In one class, while Sheila was teaching and Emma observing, Emma remembered how her anger filled her, and she started writing notes to herself. She wrote, "These guys are pigs. They look like pigs. They eat like pigs. They drink like pigs. They're the Pig People." And then she wrote, "No, they're not pig people. They're the Penis People. They're like some primitive tribe that worships the almighty penis. Everything is about their penis, their d–!" That's why, when she discovered the porno picture on her overhead, the first thing she thought was, "They've struck. The Penis People have struck again."

Okay, enough, she thought. Time for sleep. One thing was certain, though. She and Sheila would have to think of something fast. This was only the first group and if things got out of control, word would spread fast to those managers scheduled to attend in later sessions and this job, with all it meant to them, would crash and burn. ✦

*This case has been developed based on real organization(s) and real organizational experiences. Names, facts, and situations have been changed to protect the privacy of individuals and organizations.

Chapter 33

Navigating the Limits of a Smile

Sarah J. Tracy

Setting the (Back) Stage

With a weathered emery board, Cassie Donners* smoothed a jagged edge of one red fingernail before grabbing a new pair of nylon thigh highs and carefully tugging them up her long tanned legs. As she had done every Monday evening for the last three weeks, 24-year-old Cassie was prepping for the Welcome Cocktail Party, the first formal night of the trans-Panama Canal cruise on the *Radiant Spirit,* one of the largest ships of the Spirit Cruise Line. Her roommate and fellow junior assistant cruise director, Sally, was currently occupying the tiny bathroom in their cabin, so Cassie made do with the closet mirror to fluff her highlighted, shoulder-length blonde hair and apply mascara to the long lashes lining her amber eyes.

As Cassie donned her starched "creams"—fitted ivory-colored polyester suits issued by Spirit—she thought about the whirlwind world upon which she had embarked just three weeks ago. Cassie had interviewed for the cruise staff position a month after graduating from a small college in Oklahoma. She was hoping to improve her communication skills, acquire international experience, and visit exotic locales before settling down into a *real* job.

During her land-based one-day training with Spirit, Cassie was introduced to the central responsibilities of the position. As a junior assistant cruise director, Cassie would be part of the ship's five-person cruise staff team—the smallest but perhaps most visible departmental team on the ship. Cruise staff, whose job it was to keep the ship's 1,600 passengers entertained at sea, were required to wear uniforms and name badges whenever they were in passenger areas and thus could be on duty for up to 15 hours a day. A typical day at sea included refereeing table tennis and shuffleboard tournaments, calling bingo, creating and orchestrating trivia quiz games, running swimming pool Olympics, teaching line-dance classes, leading karaoke sing-alongs and other theme nights, performing on the main stage, and, most important, interacting with passengers. Cassie really looked forward to this last activity. She had always considered herself to be a people person and had especially enjoyed college classes that included small group activities.

Besides these basic duties, land-based management also provided Cassie with a training manual that outlined ship policies and procedures. Among other things, the training manual admonished, "Do everything you can to meet a passenger's request." Indeed, the manual warned that "discourteous work performance and/or service to passengers" warranted an official warning to the crew member, and three warnings constituted grounds for dismissal. And if crew members had any troubles fulfilling their service requirements? The Spirit complaints procedure indicated that a staff member who felt he or she had a "genuine grievance" should report it to his or her direct supervisor.

Indeed, the land-based director of passenger programs advised Cassie that the ship management was run military style, saying, "If you have any questions or complaints, talk to the cruise director, and then he'll contact us at headquarters if necessary. We just have too many employees on too many ships for you all to be calling us directly." Cassie nodded her head in eager concurrence. She could not imagine that she would have anything to complain about on a cruise ship! The director also warned Cassie, "Remember, you're never off-duty, especially when you're in a passenger area. On a cruise ship, you're basically public property."

Cassie shook off the warning, smiled warmly, and reassured the director, drawling sweetly, "I can take it. In fact, I'll love it." At the time, Cassie never could have imagined the extent this *public property* mentality would take on the ship.

Cassie's tour of duty began in Vancouver, British Columbia, Canada, a turnaround port for many Alaskan itineraries. Now into her third week, the ship had just begun to make its way down the west coast and into the Mexican Riviera. During her six-month contract, the ship would take Cassie from Alaska, to several Mexican ports of call, to parts of Central and South America, through the Panama Canal and throughout the Caribbean. She was assigned to the *Radiant Spirit,* a 70,000-ton floating paradise. At 14 stories, it would be the largest high-rise she had ever lived in, or upon. The job environment was also different from her past experience. She was one of only five Americans working on the ship, and most of the employees were men. Cassie estimated a 6-to-1 ratio of males to females. As a blonde American female, Cassie felt different and special.

Cassie pondered her uniqueness as she ran a brush through the tangles of her sea breeze-tousled hair. Her eyes drifted from her own reflection in the closet mirror to the alarm clock, and upon seeing the time, Cassie suddenly realized she needed to hurry up. She was surprised Sally was still in the bathroom. Sally, also a junior assistant director, was taking a break from graduate school. And it was Sally who was usually the more responsible one. The two had become quite close over the last three weeks. In fact, because they looked so much alike, fellow crew members had begun to call them the "little blonde American twins." Cassie checked the clock again. They were going to be the late and yelled-at little twins if Sally didn't hurry up. Cassie yelled through the bathroom door, "Hey, Sally, we only have five minutes before the Welcome Cocktail Party. Get your butt in gear!"

Sally emerged from the tiny bathroom with hair dripping wet. "Get your own butt in gear," she said with a smirk.

Cassie paused for a second, seriously considering Sally's comment. Peering at her backside in the closet mirror, Cassie conceded, "You know, you're right. I should get my butt in gear. It's just gotten bigger and bigger since I've been on this ship." It was one of the many self-deprecating comments Cassie would make about herself every day.

Sally shook her head and said, "Shut up, shut up. If you're fat, what does that make me, a beached whale?" Both weighed less than 120 pounds. Cassie was curvier, Sally a bit more athletic.

Cassie rolled the waistband of her skirt up a couple of times, a maneuver that loosened the skirt around her hips and thus masked the curviness of her supposedly big butt. Rolling the waistband also raised the skirt's hem several inches—something most of the female cruise staff agreed made the uniform appear more modern. She smiled at her reflection in the mirror; "Ahh, much better."

Meanwhile, Sally frantically turned over dirty clothes littering the 10- by 12-foot windowless cabin and muttered under her breath, "Where is my rhinestone hair comb? I just need to put my hair up and I'll be ready."

Ignoring her, Cassie said, "Listen, I'm assigned to trail Blake tonight to supposedly learn more about swanning, so I'll just go on ahead." *Swanning* was cruise staff speak for floating around and making conversation. As assistant cruise director Blake had informed Cassie upon her maiden voyage, "Our job is our personality." That was just fine with her.

Rushing around with rhinestone comb in hand, Sally said, "That's cool, go on. Blake will make some sarcastic comment if you aren't exactly on time, so I'll just meet you there." Cassie began to leave, but just before the door shut, Sally yelled out, "Wait, Cassie! Where's your service pin?" Cassie caught the door with one cream-colored two-inch-heeled pump.

"Shoot! I always forget that darn thing." Cassie was still getting used to the cruise ship's dress standards, which, among other things, required all crew members to wear a small lapel pin etched with the ship's customer service credo. Supervisors could write up a crew member who was caught in a passenger area without the pin.

Also as part of the program, two copies of Spirit's service credo were affixed to the inside of crew members' cabin doors and bathroom doors. The credo included mandates such as "We never say no," "We smile, we are onstage," "Never express negative opinions, argue, or be discourteous with passengers," and "We are ambassadors of our cruise ship when at work and at play." In addition, backstage crew areas of the ship were plastered with posters reading "Always greet passengers; say 'Hello, ma'am,' 'Good morning, sir,'" and "We always are cheerful and say 'Please' and 'Thank you.'" Crew members largely echoed these mandates in their own talk; one staff member warned Sally on her first day of work, "When you wake up in the morning, turn your smile on. Don't turn it back off again until you go to sleep."

As cruise staff understood it, management basically wanted crew members to be at the beck and call of passengers for their every request. Most staff complied without complaint. As Blake liked to remind the staff, "Passengers pay our salaries." Indeed, cruise staff's main evaluation technique was through passenger comment cards:

Cruise director Tim kept a detailed record of the number of passenger comments each employee received, subtracting negative ones from positive ones, and used this as a basis for cruise staff evaluation and promotion. As such, staff engaged in a number of activities to ensure they received good comments. Paul, the deputy cruise director, performed cartwheels—literally—at all his activities in the hope that passengers would remember to name him in the comment cards. Sally eventually cut her hair to distinguish herself from Cassie and thus potentially be named more often in the comment cards.

Cassie frantically poked the service pin through her cream blazer. "Ta-ta, I'm off to the party. See you at dinner if not before!"

Facing the Audience

Cassie pushed open the swinging doors that separated the crew area from the onstage passenger area, and on cue a smile spread across her face. She walked up the stairs to the ship's grand atrium, the open showcase area of the ship, spanning decks five through seven. Scanning the chandelier-lit space, she spotted Blake, the Donny Osmond look-alike assistant cruise director she was assigned to trail. He stood surrounded by female passengers, flashing a smile, his helmet of brown hair slick with mousse. Blake was a 30-year-old high school dropout, ex-car salesman, and chess wiz. He had worked more than two years for Spirit and seemed to gain pleasure in telling Cassie what to do.

Seabreeze Jazz, one of the ship's six bands, accompanied the evening with piano and guitar. Passengers dressed in evening gowns and tuxedos stood huddled in groups, furiously sucking down cocktails provided free of charge during the half-hour party. Cassie sidled up to Blake and the group, trying to decide whether the women were a group of divorcées, widows, or wives with tardy husbands. In his singsong voice, Blake announced, "Ladies, ladies, let me introduce you to *Radiant Spirit*'s newest employee. And this," he motioned grandly, "is Cassie." Cassie smiled.

A woman wearing lots of sparkly eye makeup turned to Cassie and said, "So, where are you from . . . England, I bet."

Cassie gently corrected her, saying, "Actually, I'm from the United States—Oklahoma." Cassie continued, "So how are you ladies enjoying the cruise so far?" Swanning was easier if you got the passengers to talk.

Another woman, this one wearing a large emerald choker that perfectly complemented her green-sequined dress, said, "Wow, I didn't think there were any American crew members on this ship." Cassie began to explain how the ship employed few Americans, largely because most Americans would not put up with working for six to eight months without a day off. Suddenly, Cassie felt Blake's disapproving stare, and she abruptly stopped.

He changed the subject with a flash of his teeth, querying, "So, did you all have a nice time in Cabo San Lucas today?"

Without hesitation, Sparkly Eye Shadow jumped in and said, "Actually, I've been there three times before, so instead I went to the bridge tournament here on the ship. Do you play bridge, honey?" She winked at Cassie.

"Uh, no . . . but my mom and grandmother do." Then she added with great enthusiasm, "I can play Go Fish!" Immediately she recoiled. Cassie thought she sounded as stupid as Blake, but no one else seemed to mind.

The ship suddenly lurched. The room lost balance en masse, and a gentleman from an adjoining group stumbled into the ladies' space, taking center stage. He adjusted his black satin cummerbund, appreciating the instant audience, and declared, "And I've only had one drink so far, ha, ha, ha. Maybe I'll be able to stand straight after I'm drunk!" The ladies and Cassie giggled. A pained expression broke through Blake's smiley mask. Cassie would soon learn that passengers continually made this same *original* joke, all seeming to believe they were the first to think it up.

At last, the dinner bell rang. Passengers quickly gulped the remainder of their drinks and scurried toward the elevators to go up the one flight to dinner. Blake and Cassie headed for the stairs, ready to meet other cruise staffers in the officers' mess for dinner of their own. On their way, a couple stopped and asked them which way it was to dinner. In unison they explained that the dining room was "up one deck and back to the aft of the ship," but the couple still seemed confused. The woman, with a gray beehive, pointed to the elevator and tentatively asked, "Does this elevator go to the *back* of the ship?" Cassie stopped, thought for a second, and realized she had no idea how to answer this question.

Blake obviously didn't care, and with another toothy grin said, "Yeah, honey, on the *Radiant* we have special high-tech diagonal elevators." Cassie laughed nervously, trying to cover up her embarrassment at Blake's sarcasm.

Feeling a little sorry for the woman, she began to explain away Blake's tone to Beehive by giving her more detailed directions. But before she could finish, Blake grabbed her arm and whispered in her ear, "They'll get it. We're out of here." Cassie consoled herself; he *was* the expert. Cassie was ready to turn off her smile and relax, and at this point the passengers had already wandered into the elevator.

Blake and Cassie made their way to the backstage crew galley, finally out of sight of passengers. As they walked through the long hallway to the aft of the ship, various male crew members whistled and made comments in Italian as the duo passed. Blake yelled back, "Hey, you never whistle at me when I'm alone."

One of them teased in accented English, "That is because we are not whistling at you." Then, directing his gaze on Cassie, he continued, "Ooh, la, la, look at those legs!"

Cassie was becoming increasingly aware that she served as a sex object for the male crew members and the male passengers. While she usually enjoyed being the center of attention, she was not used to blatant innuendo. She leaned over to Blake, saying, "I don't know whether to be flattered or insulted."

Blake replied, "Well, you don't have any control over it, so I'd just learn to live with it."

In the officers' mess, Blake and Cassie met up with the other cruise staff. Compared with the menu of macaroni and cheese that Cassie was used to at college, the meal was a delectable delight—escargot swimming in garlic butter, French onion soup with a thick gooey layer of mozzarella cheese, and hazelnut soufflé with hot amaretto cream sauce. As she spooned in the last of her dessert, Cassie declared, "I swear, I'm going to get sooo fat on this ship!" As usual, the others ignored her. Instead, they began one of their favorite backstage rituals—swapping stories of stupid passenger questions. Cassie was proud to have one of her own to share. "You know, a couple just asked us if our elevators go to the back of the ship. It's like, 'give me a break!'"

The Ups and Downs of Customer Service

Two months into her contract, Cassie had heard an uncountable number of stupid questions. She had become adept at dealing with them, and almost as good as Blake at ignoring or subtly deflecting passenger criticisms and complaints. However, her probationary review was quickly approaching, and she knew that she needed to keep a clean record, or better yet, receive a lot of positive passenger comments in order to receive a favorable review and be eligible for promotion at the end of her contract. It also made sense to make nicey-nice with the cruise director, Tim, someone with whom Cassie had not hit it off very well. Tim, a 45-year-old Los Angeleno, considered Cassie to be a dumb blonde, a part she herself admitted playing when it helped to get her way. As she explained to Sally, "Sometimes it's just easier to smile and laugh off stuff like you don't get it." Cassie continued, "*But,* that doesn't make me dumb. For goodness sake, I have a college degree—something Tim doesn't have. I may not be part of his little group of friends, but I don't want to have to be a brown-noser to get there."

Sally said, "Believe me, I don't like Tim much either. At the same time, though, keep in mind that it may be easier in the long run just to kiss up to him." Cassie sighed. Maybe she *would* suck it up for the next couple of weeks, at least until she got through her probationary review.

Three hours later, Cassie and the rest of the cruise staff raced around backstage preparing for Cruise Fun Night. Tim, already onstage, boomed over the show-lounge microphone, "Welcome to Cruise Fun Night, the show where *you* are the show!" The lounge was packed with nearly 800 passengers. Cassie and Sally were double-checking the prizes for the fun night games when Jean, the ship's exercise manager, limped over, having sprained her ankle earlier in the day while teaching aerobics. "Hey, guys, I'm not going to be able to do the balloon game tonight because of my ankle. Can one of you do it?"

A grimace spread across Sally's face. "Hey, I'm willing to be Naughty Nursie and stuff two balloons in my blouse for the cruise staff skit, but I'm not up to the balloon game."

Jean said, "You think I *like* getting jumped on by passengers week after week?"

Dan, a new assistant cruise director in training, approached the threesome and asked, "Hey, what's this about getting jumped on?"

Sally explained. "See these balloons here?" She pointed to two industrial-size paper bags, each stuffed with eight balloons, and continued, "They're for the balloon game. Earlier in the day, Cassie and I blew 'em up. And we blow them up in a special way—first as big as we can, and then we let out a lot of air. That makes them really stretchy and difficult to break. Well, during the show, we get eight female and eight male passengers to volunteer for the game. We line them up on opposite sides of the stage and give each of them a balloon. The passengers have to stick the balloon between their legs and kind of jump or skip over to either Blake or Jean—whoever is of the opposite sex—and break the balloon by sitting down and bouncing it between their butt and Blake or Jean's lap. Whichever team gets done first wins, and the thing is, it usually takes a while. Because the balloons are so stretchy, they usually have to bounce five or six times before the balloon pops!"

Dan grinned, beginning to understand as the mental picture formed in his mind.

Cassie added, "And what Sally failed to mention is that Tim tells the passengers that they have to sit forward, *straddling* you to break the balloon. It's *totally* disgusting."

Blake walked by and interrupted. "It's only disgusting if you get peed on, like I did two weeks ago. Now *that's* gross."

Cassie's face contorted in disgust. "I'm sorry, but I just don't want 60-year-old, dirty old men jumping up and down on me simulating sex."

Neither did Sally, and she was smart enough to convince Cassie to do the game. "Come on, Cassie, you'll be great at it. The passengers love you. Anyway, I have to hand out balloons and prizes to the contestants." It was a lame excuse, and both of them knew it. Sally added, "Anyway, you're going up for your probationary review soon . . . this could win you some points with the passengers and with Tim."

Cassie exclaimed, "I just wish they had put this in the job description!"

"Yeah, right, would you have signed up for this job if they had?" Sally muttered, "If only my feminist friends back at graduate school could see me now."

With a deep sigh, Cassie agreed to be bounced upon. When it came time for the balloon game, Cassie and Blake took their positions on opposite balloon game chairs and braced themselves for what was to come. The audience screamed with laughter as the lineup of male and female passengers ran across the stage and frantically bounced on their laps, trying to break the balloons. Cassie's face was crimson. Her hands gripped the seat, and with every bounce a slight wince leaked through her ear-to-ear smile. Finally she could stand it no longer. For the last four men in line, Cassie did not allow them to bounce up and down more than twice before she herself pricked and popped their balloon with her fingernail. The game, which usually lasted at least four minutes, continued for only two. Tim, emceeing the evening, grabbed the microphone and merrily announced that the male passengers were the winners in this *Battle of the Sexes.* When he turned from the audience toward Cassie, though, his eyes were narrow in anger. In her haste to rid her lap of bouncing men, Cassie had ruined the game. She knew it, and it was clear now that Tim knew it too.

The show continued without ado, and the passengers gave a standing ovation. The cruise staff, sweaty, tired, and satisfied with the show, trotted backstage.

Cassie and Sally were peeling off their costumes when Tim approached them. "What the hell were you thinking, Cassie?" he barked in her face.

"What are you talking about, Tim?" Cassie whipped her head around but tried to sound nonconfrontational.

"That balloon game was freakin' ruined. If you can't do it right, why the heck did you do it? Are you so stupid that you didn't see you were popping the balloons twice as quickly as Blake's? Are you blind? Stupid? Or both?"

Cassie's eyes began to blaze. Sally silently pleaded for her to just leave it all alone. "Let's go, Cassie," she whispered.

Negotiating the Dark Side

The next evening, Sally and Cassie prepared for the Fifties Sock Hop theme night, dressed in denim blue miniskirts and cheap white T-shirts with "Spirit Sock Hop" silk-screened across the front. Sally was "Bambi" for the night; Blake was "Rocco"; Cassie was "Trixie." Passengers were beginning to wander into the ship's disco, the home of this and various other theme nights the cruise staff held to keep passengers awake and buying revenue-producing drinks. Engineered entertainment. They came to watch. The cruise staff's job was to get 10% of the passengers involved, so that the other 90% would have something to watch. The disco's glitter globe cast shadowy illuminations upon about 30 passengers sitting at tables and a handful of couples who were dancing the swing on the sunken dance floor.

As the band finished, Blake took center stage. Unsuccessfully trying to appear fifties-ish in rolled-up jeans and a semitransparent Spirit tee, Blake grabbed the microphone and in a stupid tough-guy accent heralded the crowd into motion. "Good evening, ladies and gentlemen. My name is Rocco, and those are my girls down there, Bambi and Trixie." Blake gestured to Cassie and Sally, who twirled and bowed on the dance floor. Blake continued, "Now, this is a fifties sock hop, and a sock hop can't be complete without a twist contest, so if you're already on the dance floor, stay there, and if you're not, come on down." Couples who minutes before happily danced the swing made a beeline for the dance floor exits.

Sally blocked one of the exits, literally sitting on one exit post and kicking her feet up to the other, and told passengers in wide-eyed innocence, "There's an invisible laser barrier here, and if you pass it, you'll blow up into a billion pieces." Two of the couples smiled at Sally's attempt at humor and agreed to participate in the game. Another couple turned and left through another exit.

Blake continued to explain the contest. "Now, this isn't just any twist contest, it's the balloon twist. Just watch Trixie and Bambi demonstrate." Cassie and Sally sprang onto the small disco stage, placed a balloon between their chests, and began to wiggle. Sally whispered to Cassie, "I've done this so many times that I am actually kinda *proud* of my balloon twisting abilities." Cassie rolled her eyes but kept smiling.

Blake continued, "Now the goal is to keep the balloon pressed between you and your partner, and you can't use your hands. If it falls to the floor, you're out. Now come on down, ladies and gentlemen. There's nothing to be afraid of." The room was still, silent. "Did I mention that we'll give a bottle of champagne to the winners?" Three more couples straggled to the floor, likely unaware that the champagne prize cost Spirit about 50 cents.

The contest began. A couple won. The cruise staff delivered the champagne with a cheer and continued with a hula-hoop contest. Blake closed the theme night with a beach party line dance, providing an opportunity for all the single women to come to the floor. Sally and Cassie danced along with the passengers, egging them on to spice it up with turns and hip shakes. Blake finally turned over the evening to the disc jockey, and Sally and Cassie made their way up to the passenger bar, ready for a drink and a break.

A tall man who appeared to be in his mid-60s approached the bobby-socked duo. "Hi, gals. You sure were looking fine out there on the dance floor. Can I buy you a drink?"

After quickly examining the man with a long thin ponytail of gray hair, dressed in an expensive-looking black suit, Cassie and Sally responded in unison, "Sure." Passenger-bought drinks were one of the perks of the job, and staff were usually quick to take up offers. Drinking with passengers was a way to relax and swan at the same time. Cruise director Tim usually made the rounds of the various ship lounges throughout the evening to ensure that the cruise staff continued to "work" the passengers until at least 11 P.M. Sally glanced at the new watch she had bought in St. Thomas earlier that day. It was 10:30 P.M.—only a half hour to go.

The three of them gathered at a small table near the dance floor. Cassie and Sally quickly learned that the man's name was Fred. As he leaned in close to hear them over the beat of the music, they also learned that he had cigarette breath and sickeningly sweet cologne. After some small talk about his day in St. Thomas, Fred asked Cassie to dance. Female cruise staff were not technically required to dance with passengers. However, it usually made for positive comments in the comment cards, and quite simply it was sometimes less effortful to dance than to make conversation. Cassie agreed. The man, almost three times her age, triumphantly grabbed Cassie's hand. As he tugged her to the dance floor, Cassie looked back at Sally and mouthed the word "Gross."

In return, Sally mouthed "Yuck." Then she quickly looked around to make sure none of the passengers had noticed this interchange. No one had. Sally sank back into the chair, quietly sipping the $8 glass of wine Fred had just purchased for her. She was relieved that he had chosen Cassie rather than her—a perk of being the more athletic and less curvy of the little blonde American twins.

Once on the dance floor, Fred and Cassie began to move in rhythm with the beat of the disco music. Tired of feeling his sweaty grip, Cassie tried to break free of Fred's hand. She twirled out and away from him, but the moment she began dancing on her own, Fred somehow grabbed on again. Cassie resigned herself to being firmly anchored to Fred throughout the dance. As the song continued, Fred pulled Cassie closer and closer. Cassie pushed back and playfully quipped, "Aren't you a little devil? I'd actually like to dance further back, like this." She pointed to four inches of space she had managed to squeeze between their bodies.

Fred smiled slowly, saying, "I know girls like you. You're just a tease, like when you were wiggling with that balloon between you and that other girl."

Cassie began to feel uneasy. "That was a performance," she thought. "That's not me—the *real* Cassie."

Fred pulled her close again and, brushing his lips to her ear, said, "Come on now, tell me, would you ever consider me if you came over to the dark side?"

The dark side? Cassie's heart began to race. She did not know whether to laugh or to run. She decided to play dumb. "Huh? What do you mean?"

He persisted, "You know, the dark side. Would you consider being with me?"

Cassie again said "Huh?" and pretended not to hear him by holding her hand to her ear. But while she was able to ignore his words, it was more difficult to ignore his gyrating body pressed against hers. The smell of his sweat was beginning to leak through his heavy cologne. Pushing back the anger that stung her eyes, Cassie thought to herself, "Don't act offended, or he will win this game." She endured the last 20 seconds of the dance, disentangled herself from Fred's embrace, and ran back to the table where Sally was sitting.

"Come on. We are leaving *now*!" Cassie pulled Sally into the hallway and then through the swinging doors into the crew elevator area. She leaned against the hallway wall, slid down into a huddled figure, and looked like she was about to cry. Perplexed, Sally slid down and sat next to her. "Cassie, what? What is it? What's wrong? I know he was ugly, but . . ."

Taking a ragged breath, Cassie interrupted, "He kept rubbing up against me and actually asked me if I wanted to come to the 'dark side.' What the hell? I swear these passengers think when they buy the cruise, they also buy us—that we should be entertaining them in all areas. I feel like a freakin' call girl!"

Attempting to get Cassie out of her funk, Sally cracked, "Call girl, huh? Yeah, I wonder how the passengers ever get that impression, with us running around in short skirts and you letting men jump on top of you and all."

Sally's last comment perturbed Cassie; she did not find it funny. She protested, "Geez, Sally, you think this is my fault?"

"No, no, no, I didn't mean that. Gosh, I don't know," Sally responded.

Cassie reflected, "It's weird, because he wasn't saying anything blatant, like 'Come to bed with me,' but I just felt so violated, like I had no control. I was trying not to say anything mean to him, but . . ."

"You were being offended in making sure he wasn't offended," Sally finished Cassie's thought.

Cassie nodded vigorously. "Exactly!"

Sally paused and then continued. "So are you going to do anything about it?"

Cassie shrugged her shoulders, bit her lower lip, and thought about her options. She had accepted a drink from and agreed to dance with the guy. Did this make her a tease? Did this make her responsible? At the same time, she was angry. Her amber eyes narrowing, she said to Sally with more certainty, "You know we do *not* have to touch these guys, we do *not* have to dance with them, and I should *not* have to deal with this."

Sally said, "Well, you could just march up to him and tell him that."

"Yeah, right, and he would just march up to the comment card drop box and write something nasty about me," Cassie said. "I definitely don't need that right before next week's probationary review. Anyway, I don't feel like seeing that guy again, let alone confronting him."

Sally continued, "Well, maybe you should talk to Tim . . ."

Cassie exclaimed, "Yeah, I'm sure he's going to be real understanding after last night's balloon fiasco!"

"Well, maybe you could go above his head?" Sally questioned uncertainly and then quickly recouped, answering her own question. "Actually, no, that probably wouldn't be good considering the rumors of other staff who've gone over their supervisors' heads."

Cassie agreed, "Yeah, there's no way I'm going to do that. Remember, we're not supposed to contact headquarters directly, and anyway, Tim would make my life hell." She bowed and shook her head. "I don't know, Sally, I just don't know." ✦

*This case has been developed based on real organization(s) and real organizational experiences. Names, facts, and situations have been changed to protect the privacy of individuals and organizations.

About the Editors

Joann Keyton, is Professor of Communication Studies at the University of Kansas. Her research agenda has two distinct disciplinary focuses. In organizational communication, Keyton focuses on organizational culture and sexual harassment. In group communication, Keyton explores the relational behaviors organizational group members engage in while addressing task concerns. Her research appears in *Communication Studies, Communication Yearbook, Journal of Applied Communication Research, Management Communication Quarterly, Small Group Research, Southern Communication Journal,* and numerous edited collections, including the *Handbook of Group Communication Theory and Research.* She has published two textbooks: *Communication Research: Asking Questions, Finding Answers* and *Communicating in Groups: Building Relationships for Effective Decision Making* (2nd ed.). Both are published by McGraw-Hill. Keyton is also the editor of the *Journal of Applied Communication Research.*

Pamela Shockley-Zalabak is Chancellor and Professor of Communication at the University of Colorado at Colorado Springs. The author of five books and over 100 articles and productions on organizational communication, Dr. Shockley's research interests include organizational cultures as they relate to individual employee values and overall organizational effectiveness. Prior to assuming Chancellor responsibilities, Dr. Shockley was Vice Chancellor for Student Success and the founding chair of the University of Colorado at Colorado Springs Communication Department. Dr. Shockley is the recipient of the University of Colorado Thomas Jefferson Award, President's Award for Outstanding Service, Chancellor's Award for Distinguished Faculty, and the Colorado Speech Communication Association Distinguished Member Award. ✦

About the Editors

About the Contributors

Carolyn M. Anderson (Ph.D., Kent State University) is Professor at the School of Communication at the University of Akron.

Julie Apker (Ph.D., University of Kansas) is Assistant Professor of Communication at Western Michigan University.

Edward C. Brewer (Ph.D., Bowling Green State University) is Assistant Professor of Organizational Communication at Murray State University.

Patrice M. Buzzanell (Ph.D., Purdue University) is Associate Professor of Communication at Purdue University.

Jensen Chung (Ph.D., SUNY at Buffalo) is Professor of Speech and Communication Studies at San Francisco State University.

Edward J. Coyle (Ph.D., Princeton University) is Professor of Electrical and Computer Engineering and Assistant Vice President for Research in Computing and Communications at Purdue University.

Christine S. Davis (M.A., University of North Carolina at Greensboro) is a doctoral student in the Department of Communication at the University of South Florida and a Technical Analyst at the Louis de la Parte Florida Mental Health Institute at the University of South Florida.

Julie A. Davis (Ph.D., University of Kansas) is Assistant Professor of Communication at the College of Charleston.

Andrew J. Flanagin (Ph.D., University of Southern California) is Associate Professor of Communication at the University of California, Santa Barbara.

G. L. Forward (Ph.D., Ohio State University) is Professor of Communication at Point Loma Nazarene University.

Adelina Gomez (Ph.D., University of Colorado, Boulder) is Associate Professor of Communication at the University of Colorado, Colorado Springs.

Melissa Gibson Hancox (Ph.D., Ohio University) is Assistant Professor of Communication at Mercyhurst College.

Joy L. Hart (Ph.D., University of Kentucky) is Associate Professor of Communication at the University of Louisville.

Mary Hoffman (Ph.D., University of Kansas) is Assistant Professor of Communication Studies at Southwest Texas State University.

Marian L. Houser (Ph.D., University of Tennessee) is a faculty member in the Speech Communication Department at the University of Tennessee.

Anne P. Hubbell (Ph.D., Michigan State University) is Assistant Professor of Communication Studies at New Mexico State University.

Cynthia A. Irizarry (Ph.D., University of Nebraska) is Assistant Professor of Communication at Stetson University.

Leah H. Jamieson (Ph.D., Princeton University) is the Ransburg Professor of Electrical and Computer Engineering at Purdue University.

Erika L. Kirby (Ph.D., University of Nebraska) is Assistant Professor of Communication Studies at Creighton University.

Robert L. Krizek (Ph.D., Arizona State University) is Associate Professor of Communication at Saint Louis University.

Rajeev Kumar is a faculty member at Defense Services Staff College, India, and is working toward his Ph.D. in Organizational Communication.

Gregory S. Larson (Ph.D., University of Colorado at Boulder) is Assistant Professor of Communication at the University of Minnesota, Duluth.

Greg B. Leichty (Ph.D., University of Kentucky) is Associate Professor of Communication at the University of Louisville.

Shawn D. Long (Ph.D., University of Kentucky) is Assistant Professor of Communication Studies at the University of North Carolina at Charlotte.

Marifran Mattson (Ph.D., Arizona State University) is Associate Professor of Communication at Purdue University.

Steven K. May (Ph.D., University of Utah) is Associate Professor of Communication Studies at the University of North Carolina at Chapel Hill.

Mary M. Meares (Ph.D., University of New Mexico) is Assistant Professor of Communication at Washington State University.

Caryn E. Medved (Ph.D., University of Kansas) is Assistant Professor in the School of Interpersonal Communication at Ohio University.

Trudy A. Milburn (Ph.D., University of Massachusetts, Amherst) is Assistant Professor of Communication Studies at Baruch College, the City University of New York.

William C. Oakes (Ph.D., Purdue University) is Assistant Professor of Freshman Engineering at Purdue University.

John G. Oetzel (Ph.D., University of Iowa) is Associate Professor of Communication at the University of New Mexico.

Terri Toles Patkin (Ph.D., Cornell University) is Professor of Communication at Eastern Connecticut State University.

Gerald L. Pepper (Ph.D., University of Minnesota) is Associate Professor of Communication at the University of Minnesota, Duluth.

Philip Salem (Ph.D., University of Denver) is Professor of Communication Studies at Southwest Texas State University.

Nancy M. Schullery (Ph.D., Wayne State University) is Associate Professor of Business Information Systems at Western Michigan University.

Astrid Sheil is a doctoral student in the Speech Communication Department at the University of Tennessee and Executive Director of the Polaris Team, a consulting group specializing in management communication.

Diane K. Sloan (Ph.D., University of Nebraska, Lincoln) is Assistant Professor of Communication Studies at the University of Minnesota, Duluth.

Sarah J. Tracy (Ph.D., University of Colorado, Boulder) is Assistant Professor at the Hugh Downs School of Human Communication at Arizona State University.

Paaige K. Turner (Ph.D., Purdue University) is Assistant Professor of Communication at Saint Louis University.

Mary E. Vielhaber (Ph.D., University of Michigan) is Professor of Management at Eastern Michigan University.

Melinda M. Villagran (Ph.D., University of Oklahoma) is Assistant Professor of Communication Studies at Southwest Texas State University.

Heather L. Walter (Ph.D., State University of New York, Buffalo) is Assistant Professor at the School of Communication at the University of Akron.

Maryanne Wanca-Thibault (Ph.D., University of Colorado, Boulder) is the Director of the Oral Communication Center and an instructor in the Communication Department at the University of Colorado, Colorado Springs.

Niranjala D. Weerakkody (Ph.D., Rutgers University) is Lecturer in Communication Studies at Deakin University, Australia.

Shirley Willihnganz (Ph.D., University of Illinois at Urbana-Champaign) is Professor of Communication at the University of Louisville.

Theodore E. Zorn, Jr. (Ph.D., University of Kentucky) is Professor of Management Communication at the University of Waikato (Hamilton, New Zealand). ✦

Detailed Case Content Index

SUBJECT	CASES
Interpersonal context (continued)	11
	15
	23
	24
	25
	26
	28
	29
	30
	31
	33
J, K, L	
Job satisfaction	3
	28
Knowledge management	21
Layoffs	2
	4
	27
Leadership	2
	4
	5
	7
	13
	15
	16
	18
	23
	24
M, N, O	
Mergers and acquisitions	6
	27
	28
Motivation	3